INVISIBLE SEASONS

Sports and Entertainment
Steven A. Riess, *Series Editor*

INVISIBLE SEASONS

Title IX and the Fight
for Equity in College Sports

Kelly Belanger

Syracuse University Press

Syracuse University Press
Syracuse, New York 13244-5290

First Edition 2016

16 17 18 19 20   5 4 3 2 1

∞ The paper used in this publication meets the minimum requirements
of the American National Standard for Information Sciences—Permanence
of Paper for Printed Library Materials, ANSI Z39.48-1992.

For a listing of books published and distributed by Syracuse University Press,
visit www.SyracuseUniversityPress.syr.edu.

ISBN: 978-0-8156-3484-3 (hardcover)
      978-0-8156-3470-6 (paperback)
      978-0-8156-5382-0 (e-book)

Library of Congress Cataloging-in-Publication Data

Names: Belanger, Kelly.
Title: Invisible seasons : Title IX and the fight for equity in college sports / Kelly Belanger.
Description: First Edition. | Syracuse, New York : Syracuse University Press, [2016] |
    Series: Sports and Entertainment | Includes bibliographical references and index.
Identifiers: LCCN 2016040652 (print) | LCCN 2016045018 (ebook) | ISBN 9780815634843
    (hardcover : alk. paper) | ISBN 9780815634706 (paperback : alk. paper) |
    ISBN 9780815653820 (e-book)
Subjects: LCSH: Women athletes—Government policy—United States. | Sex discrimination
    in sports—Law and legislation—United States. | College sports for women—United
    States—History. | College sports—United States. | United States. Education Amendments
    of 1972. Title IX.
Classification: LCC GV709.18.U6 B45 2016 (print) | LCC GV709.18.U6 (ebook) |
    DDC 796.04/3—dc23
LC record available at https://lccn.loc.gov/2016040652

Manufactured in the United States of America

No person in the United States shall, on the basis of sex, be excluded from participation in, be denied the benefits of, or be subjected to discrimination under any education program or activity receiving Federal financial assistance.

—Title IX of the Education Amendments Act of 1972

Contents

Illustrations

Preface

No person in the United States shall, on the basis of sex, be excluded from participation in, be denied the benefits of, or be subjected to discrimination under any education program or activity receiving Federal financial assistance.
—Title IX of the Education Amendments
Act of 1972[1]

I have written *Invisible Seasons* to provide an up-close, inside look at Title IX and its relationship to college sports from a confluence of personal and professional standpoints: as a former high school and college athlete, as a faculty member who has worked at several different types of universities, and as a scholar of rhetoric. Athletes of my generation (now in their fifties) are situated "in the middle," sandwiched between the pioneers of Title IX–era athletics (women today in their sixties and seventies) and the younger women of a post-second-wave feminist generation (in their twenties, thirties, and forties). When I played basketball at Michigan State in the 1980s, and before that in high school and junior high, the WNBA did not exist, and for the few of us who were even looking, you couldn't find a basketball shoe in women's sizes in any sporting goods store. Buying the Converse high-tops so popular then required a translation for girls and women; I remember thinking, "Okay, a size 8½ men's equals about a women's size 10." Women's sports then were like a different dialect of a mainstream language. Unlike the mainstream male athletes, women athletes were seen as different, nonstandard, a subculture sometimes difficult for outsiders to understand.

Women in the younger generations sometimes know little of the struggles that created the radically transformed, though still not completely equal, sports culture they experience today. Despite coming from a sports-minded family with four athletic girls (three of whom played college sports), I don't recall either of my parents ever mentioning Title IX as I was growing up. When the law prohibiting sex discrimination in federally funded programs and activities was enacted in 1972, I was only eight years old, the oldest of four sisters. I first heard of Title IX in 1979 when a reporter for my hometown newspaper interviewed me and my high school softball and basketball coach for an article about all the new opportunities opening up for girls in sports. But as a fifteen-year-old student at East Kentwood High School near Grand Rapids, Michigan, I knew little of the larger factors affecting my athletic pursuits. The article correctly stated that I "just liked to compete."[2]

Actually, both of my parents encouraged me—even pressured me at times—to play sports and take them seriously. I remember crying when, in sixth grade, my mom took me to sign up for my first official team: little league softball in the Kentwood Baseball League. But once practices started and I began to develop some skills, I loved playing for the Forest Hills ShopRite Daisies. Whereas I had friends and teammates whose mothers could not understand, or even actively discouraged, their participation in athletics, my mom wanted me to experience the sporting opportunities that she wished had been available to her in the more limiting 1950s and 1960s. And my dad always had time to play "pickle" in the backyard or take my sisters and me over to the field for batting practice. Although I occasionally feel that my family emphasized sports too much, the result of my parents' support and enthusiasm for their daughters competing in athletics is that I truly love participating in sports and physical fitness: they remain integral to my everyday life and identity.

If someone had asked me as a ninth grader in 1979 whether I had an equal opportunity to pursue my interest in athletics as boys my age, I would have said that the basic—though not equal—opportunities were there. Even so, I knew that boys' sports were better covered by the media and that the school and community almost always considered their games more important than ours. Every boys' coach I knew brought more coaching and athletic experience to their teams, which I sometimes envied because I wanted to learn as much as I could about the sports I played. I set ambitious goals for my high school teams, in some cases even higher goals than my coaches did. But to focus on these differences seemed ungrateful and pointless considering how much better my opportunities were compared to those for girls of my mother's generation and how unlikely it seemed that anything would significantly change. For the most part, I compared my situation not to that of the boys but to what my mother told me she had experienced.

At the time, I had a clearer picture of how far girls and women had come than of how much further we might be able to go. Meanwhile, most of my teammates were fully satisfied with the status quo: even some incredibly talented, competitive girls had no interest in playing sports in college. For the girls I played with, and for many of our coaches, high school sports were truly just for fun. I have to admit that perspective sounds almost refreshing considering how kids today, especially those from middle- and high-income families, can be overscheduled and sometimes relentlessly pushed to earn athletic scholarships.

But as a girl who took sports seriously, the gender differences I experienced became increasingly apparent and frustrating. While I sometimes enjoyed being seen as an exceptional girl for my athletic skills, I hated being excluded from pick-up games unless the boys were desperate for another player. I also dreaded the visible discomfort of the boy assigned to (or "stuck") guarding me if I did get in a game. If I played too well, he would be ridiculed, but if he was strong enough a player to make me look bad, his friends would taunt him for picking on the girl. And while I mostly enjoyed any praise earned for my athletic accomplishments, I felt insulted by unearned or exaggerated praise seemingly offered because people held such low expectations for girls.

My vision broadened gradually, not in a series of eureka moments. Like most kids, I became aware of the hierarchies that exist within girls' sports, within boys' sports, and even between academics and athletics. (Increasingly for girls and boys alike, athletics is valued more than academics in some families.) By the time I was a high school junior, I knew that basketball was the best-supported sport for girls. Although I loved playing volleyball and would gladly have continued playing the sport in college, athletic scholarships available to girls in the 1980s were disproportionately allocated to basketball. Our basketball games received more press coverage, more fans attended our games, and I could practice my skills in the summer against boys who were also playing the same sport. Women's basketball most likely received more respect and resources because the public was familiar with boys' basketball. Also, because more people had seen the game or played it themselves, they knew the rules and something about strategy. They respected the skills it required and could appreciate finer points of the game. So when my high school basketball coach once observed to a news reporter that I "played like a boy," she meant it as a great compliment, and no one, including me at the time, thought otherwise.

Just as countless messages told us that some girls' sports were more important than others and that real athletes are male, kids in the United States learned and still learn early on that, among boys, superior athletes play football. Football is the gold standard for athletics in this country, and the ideology of football superiority is inculcated into young people, parents, and the public. A brochure I saw a few years ago for a youth football league in the rural town of Coopersville, Michigan, clearly communicates the sport's ethos, including its sense of entitlement: it warns parents that football participation must take precedence over all other school and religious activities, that coaches may be "assertive," and that "timid children should be discouraged from participating." Interestingly, the brochure uses the sex-neutral pronoun "s/he" throughout to suggest that both boys and girls can play as long as they are willing to "hit and be hit" and understand that football comes first.

Kids, especially boys, face some difficult choices in a football-centric sports world. Peer, social, and parental pressures may be even harder for those kids who go against the grain and prefer to focus on school and perhaps attend a summer foreign language, science, art, music, or technology camp rather than (or in addition to) joining a sports team. Although kids at the nation's elite academic high schools regularly participate in summer academic camps or other intellectual enrichment opportunities, the perception in many schools prevails that it's more important to be a successful athlete than a great student, especially among boys but increasingly among girls. In boys' sports, even players who mostly warm the bench enjoy status for being on the team. Critics of girls' and women's sports accurately observe that females are less likely to stick with it when they don't get to play. I suspect that girls who don't get to play sometimes drop out because, while the status of girls' and women's sports has increased since the 1970s, it still doesn't bring the social capital available to male team members regardless of their roles on their teams.

I mention these often-unexamined hierarchies not because I dislike football or other men's sports. After all, my dad played football in high school and college, where he focused on baseball before going on to compete professionally. I value highly what he taught me over the years from his participation in organized sports: lessons about competition, cooperation, fitness, discipline, fair play, hard work, persistence, and functioning effectively within a team. And I met my husband, a former high school and college football player, when we were both graduate students at Ohio State University and playing basketball at the Jesse Owens North Recreation Center when, by chance, he was the guy who "got stuck guarding the girl." On Saturday afternoons, we sometimes rode down the streets of Columbus, Ohio, atop a 1938 fire truck to tailgate at an OSU football game. (I admit to liking how enthusiastically he carried the Buckeye flag and explained the OSU tradition of dotting the "i" at halftime.) Years later, one of our nieces, an eighth grader at the time, played on her junior high football team for a season, perhaps caught up in the enthusiasm for the sport that she saw all around her at school and home. Or maybe she (also) played because, like many boys, she enjoyed the chance to be with her friends and to hit hard to release aggression within the sanctioned rules of a game.

I mention the persistent hierarchies in how sports are valued for just one reason: I am convinced that to have meaningful dialogue about equality in higher education athletics requires honestly assessing whether resource allocations dictated by such hierarchies are fair, affordable, necessary, and desirable. Certainly the way we currently value some sports more than others is not natural or inevitable, and we need to acknowledge that the status quo advantages some people while disadvantaging others. I contend—and this book aims to demonstrate—that even those who participate in the most valued, well-funded, and celebrated sports can benefit from thoughtful reconsiderations of fairness. For me, the 1979 news article that hung on my parents' kitchen bulletin board for months marked the beginning of a decades-long journey toward an ever-sharper vision of what gender equality could mean and what it would take to get there. Writing *Invisible Seasons* has been part of that journey.

The story of Michigan State University women's basketball is, to some extent, my personal story. I competed in that program as a scholarship athlete from 1982 to 1986, partly during the years just after a Supreme Court decision determined that Title IX no longer applied to athletics (the 1984 *Grove City College v. Bell* decision was overturned by Congress's Civil Rights Restoration Act of 1987).[3] Although I didn't fully realize it at the time, my teammates and I also played under the shadow of an ongoing, contentious lawsuit, which was not fully settled until the year I graduated. Soon after I signed a letter of intent to attend MSU, I received a letter informing me that the women's basketball team had filed a class action lawsuit. At the time, I hardly gave it a thought.

As I researched the story of the MSU Title IX controversy more than twenty years later, I learned to my surprise that just a few months before I was interviewed about Title IX as a high school student, the MSU women's basketball team was the subject of a caustic editorial by the sports editor of the area's major newspaper, the *Grand Rapids Press*. The editorial responded to the ruling of federal judge Noel Fox on the sex discrimination lawsuit filed by the women's team, and the editor chastised the women plaintiffs for wanting too much too soon. His primary argument was that "women had better walk before they can run" and that "instead of crying to the courts for a handout, they should be spending more time on the basketball court learning how the game is played, or better, how it's played well enough to get people to watch them." To emphasize his point, he explained, "I have a daughter who just found out the hard way that if you try to run too soon, you end up falling on your face."[4] Ironically, this same editor later became an ardent supporter of girls' and women's sports in Michigan, increasingly so after his own daughter was denied equal access to training facilities when she suffered a sports injury as a high school athlete.

Beyond my own experiences, while conducting research for this book, I have read many excellent books and articles that document the history of women's athletics, offer clear explanations of Title IX as it applies to athletics, and deploy insightful critiques of the "separate but equal" premise upon which Title IX's regulations for athletics were created. Linda Carpenter and Vivian Acosta's clear, authoritative, comprehensive text *Title IX* provides an especially helpful primer on details surrounding the law that are critical for understanding how it works and why it has been so controversial. Frequently in reading their book and in other historical, theoretical, and informational texts on women's sports, I noted tantalizing glimpses—sometimes amid historical timelines and explanations of legal regulations—of the compelling human drama surrounding Title IX's history. These patterns of struggle at schools, colleges, and universities across the United States will remain buried in the memories of students, coaches, and administrators unless someone tells their stories.

Yet to be told are tales of lawsuits not filed, complaints submitted but never addressed, and conflicts that garnered news coverage for a time but were soon forgotten as issues were settled, students graduated, or coaches and administrators were hushed, either leaving the institution or transferring internally to other jobs. As Bernice Sandler, an activist and strategist once described as the "Godmother of Title IX," wrote, "Many people have little idea of the kind of courage, strength, persistence and just plain hard work that happened in colleges throughout the nation to implement the changes required under Title IX. It is an important part of American social history—a story begging to be told."[5] *Invisible Seasons* tells one such story.

Acknowledgments

This book exists because generous family members, friends, colleagues, and research participants helped make it possible. I can name only some of them here but am grateful for the support so many people offered during a ten-year process of researching and writing.

At the University of Wyoming, Katy Brown helped with early research, and I was inspired by English Department colleagues who are also dear friends: April Heaney, Carolyn Young, Diane Panozzo, Michael Knievel, Joyce Stewart, and Beth Loffreda. In addition, my Virginia Tech writing group was invaluable, especially Kathleen Jones and Kathryn Albright. Colleagues in the field of rhetoric and writing gave essential feedback and encouragement, including Andrea Lunsford, Diana George, Carolyn Rude, Beverly Moss, Kerri Morris, and Julie Bokser. Two anonymous reviewers read the manuscript carefully and offered sound advice, for which I am grateful.

Research assistants and faculty in the Center for the Study of Rhetoric in Society (Virginia Tech Department of English) provided feedback and research help: Katie Fallon, Brian Gogan, Heidi Nobles, Ashley Patriarca, Megan O'Neill, Kara LeFleur, Amy Reed Patterson, Tana Schiewer, and Jennifer Mooney. Professional writing intern Jessica Abel edited the first and second drafts of the manuscript.

A grant from Virginia Tech's Institute for Society, Culture, and the Environment funded summer work on this project, including beginning a documentary film, and I thank Karen Roberto for her support. A National Endowment for the Arts grant allowed me to film interviews. The efforts of archivists Portia Vescio (MSU), Andrea Melvin (Grand Rapids Public Museum), and Judy Miller (Valparaiso University) made available key images; and Betty Reagan (NCAA) helped to identify archived articles. I thank Fred Wellner for the cover design, Suzanne Guiod for overseeing the publication process, Kelly Balenske for editorial work, Elizabeth Myers for copyediting, and Jessica L. Bax for proofreading. This book benefits too from keynote talks by Billie Jean King, Donna Lopiano, and Bernice Sandler, and groundbreaking work of Bonnie Parkhouse, Jackie Lapin, Patricia Ann Rosenbrock, Gail Maloney, Kim Golombisky, and Meredith Bagley.

Most recently, at Valparaiso University, I benefited from wise feedback by Sara Danger, advice and technology help from Betsy Burrow-Flak, and a caring community in the English Department and university. The College of Arts and Sciences provided writing time, and the provost's office gave funds for proofreading and the index. Lois Stuck provided careful editing, indexing, food, and friendship.

My heartfelt thanks go to each person I interviewed. Kathleen DeBoer and Mark Pittman provided core primary sources and unwavering commitment. Deb Traxinger helped in countless ways, making her an essential part of my book-writing team. I am grateful too for encouragement from Ronna Bordoley, Coleen Wilder, Philip Hess, Bonnie Sponberg, Jeffrey Emmons, Yun Xia, and the whole Fetter family.

Through the entire writing process, my mother, Jan Belanger, has been an anchor. She helped enormously with editing, honest critiques, and belief in the project's value. I am grateful also to my father, Larry Belanger, and to my sisters, Becky Sikkema and Jane Thomas, for conversations and feedback. My sister Tracy Hill offered useful suggestions on a complete manuscript draft. I appreciate all of their love and support when I needed it most.

Unexpected events, good and bad, interrupt every writing project, but I could never have foreseen a tragedy that made me wonder if I would even finish at all. My husband, Gary Fetter, who died suddenly in 2014 while playing racquetball, was my closest collaborator, advisor, and supporter from the moment the idea to write this book was conceived. I depended on his energy, honesty, enthusiasm, creativity, and technical abilities to keep going when difficulties arose. Gary loved sports as a participant and a fan, but he could also critique the injustices that are part of sporting experiences, including the unfairness of gender inequalities. He wanted to see this book completed as much as I did, and it's hard to believe he won't see the final product in hand. But he read every word of it—most pages more than just once—and it would not exist without the love and support he gave me every day.

INVISIBLE SEASONS

1 Introduction

In the brief period between 1974 and 1979 . . . the coupling of state
power and women's activism unleashed a chain reaction that caused
rapid change.

—Mary Jo Festle, *Playing Nice: Politics and Apologies
in Women's Sports*[1]

Almost immediately after Congress passed Title IX in 1972, this landmark law became nearly synonymous with women's sports. And precisely
because Title IX has been alternatively celebrated and demonized as a
"women's sports law," many people do not realize that this law prohibits
discrimination based on sex not only in sports but in *all parts* of federally
funded education in the United States. In fact, Title IX law covers everything from admissions and science research laboratories to school lunch
programs and vocational education. More recently, following an April
2011 policy letter from the US Department of Education, Title IX became
a significant legal tool for addressing discrimination against students in
the form of sexual harassment, sexual assault, stalking, and domestic or
dating violence in school districts, colleges, and universities.[2]

Despite its broad scope, Title IX's long-standing association with athletics remains a key to understanding its impact on American society and
culture—and to seeing why this law is still needed today. In 1972 when
Title IX was first enacted, college women athletes were virtually invisible
to the public and to other students. People thought of them, and many
viewed themselves, as "just the women."[3] Yet like their male peers, many
of these women were talented, dedicated athletes and strong leaders who,

in those days, played mostly for themselves. The situation was decidedly different for male athletes of the same era.

To understand Title IX deeply means entering a subculture of women's athletics. Early stories of women athletes highlight factors that constrain or discourage marginalized girls and women from pursuing their rights and working for social change under the law. Usually mere traces of sportswomen's stories appear in the work of sports historians and other Title IX scholars, who mention early activists in passing and offer few details. Who knows the story of Colleen Pavey, an athlete at the University of Alaska and plaintiff in one of the first Title IX sports-related cases? Her name is cited briefly in Welch Sugg's A *Place on the Team: The Triumph and Tragedy of Title IX*, but that is all. What motivated Rollin Haffer to file a groundbreaking Title IX and constitutional lawsuit at Temple University in 1980? Some details of the case can be found in legal journals and other publications, but neither the plaintiff nor her attorneys have spoken or written for the public about their experiences. These names of change-makers who challenged their institutions under Title IX are a mere sampling of those I encountered in researching this book.

Yet Eileen McDonagh and Laura Pappano argue in their 2008 book that women athletes have been largely complacent and ineffective as advocates on their own behalf. They contend that "women haven't argued about deserving better. . . . There are few Billie Jean Kings." And they observe that most women see things not "as a matter of equality" but a matter of "the distance traveled, the gains made."[4] They correctly note that few activists for college women's sports have the high profile of tennis star Billie Jean King in professional sports and that equality has not sustained support as a movement goal. They also rightly acknowledge that many advocates worked cautiously for change within a confining web of constraints. However, McDonagh's and Pappano's arguments overlook the contributions of hundreds of lesser-known individuals, many of whom sacrificed jobs and reputations to work for change.

By 1972, the long-standing differences between men's and women's separate and obviously unequal sports programs in higher education had become intolerable to some of the most motivated, highly skilled women athletes in US colleges and universities. These individuals wanted the same opportunities afforded to their male counterparts: they sought to develop their athletic potential to its fullest and represent their schools by competing in intercollegiate athletics at the highest possible level. *Invisible Seasons* invites you into the worlds of these women and their supporters in the years just after Title IX's enactment.

To help readers to enter fully into their stories, this book presumes that in history, as in sports, what happens "off the ball" matters greatly. That is, while eyes naturally gravitate to the player with the ball—or to well-known figures who make headlines—the important action that sets up everything else often occurs somewhere else, where few people think to look. This behind-the-scenes story introduces little-known but remarkable people who changed college sports and used the art of rhetoric to do it.[5]

Why Title IX Needs Rhetoric

I realize that in common parlance, the term rhetoric often connotes "just talk" without action. Even a 2010 "Dear Colleague" policy letter from the US Department of Education invokes the idea that rhetoric means only talk with no meaningful action. The first paragraph ends by proclaiming, "Title IX stands for the proposition that equality of opportunity in America is not rhetoric, but rather a guiding principle."[6] On the contrary, for those who study rhetoric as an academic discipline, "equality of opportunity" *is* a powerful example of rhetoric: it is a phrase, an ideograph, that can be invoked precisely to motivate action. Scholars of rhetoric recognize that from the metaphors we employ to the facts we provide or omit, language choices create, sustain, and change realities. In this book, then, I define rhetoric as the strategic use of language to influence action and perceptions, especially surrounding civic issues.

Although the media often associates rhetoric with negative ends such as manipulation or deception—and certainly language can be and is used to manipulate and deceive—the art of rhetoric is also a remedy for misunderstandings. It is integral to movements both for and against social change. Rhetorical analysis can be a means for achieving inclusive communication practices essential for decision making and problem solving in democratic groups or societies. As political theorist Iris Marion Young noted, "rhetoric is an important means by which people situated in particular social positions can adjust their claims to be heard by those in differing social situations."[7] This definition allows me to highlight the challenges that faced advocates for women's rights in colleges and universities in the 1970s, similar to challenges facing other marginalized groups struggling to be heard and respected. However, while Young's definition emphasizes "claims," rhetoric includes "the entire range of resources that human beings share for producing effects on one another," including "words, images, and bodies."[8]

In the chapters that follow, I illuminate the rhetorical strategies from Title IX's first decade that moved higher education athletics from pervasive sex discrimination in the 1970s to a compromised state of "gender equity" today. I show how the interplay of social movement and status quo rhetoric has led to vastly improved opportunities for women athletes, as well as to significantly compromised end goals. Undeniably, the growth in girls' and women's school-sponsored sports since 1972 has been staggering. Yet true equality, and even full compliance with the law, remains elusive.

Specifically, an up-close look at the struggle for equality in women's college sports reveals that the movement's initial goal of obtaining "sex *equality*" with male student athletes has been gradually replaced with a more ambiguous goal of "gender *equity*."[9] Focusing on Title IX rhetoric requires distinguishing between these two similar-sounding terms and noting the consequences that follow from how and when each is used. The terms "equity" and "equality" are pivotal to the discourse around Title IX, and which term is used when can shape expectations and influence material realities.

Whereas "equality" denotes having the same rights and an even proportion of opportunities and resources, the term "equity" denotes a fair, just, or earned proportion. And whereas "equality" can more easily be defined and quantified, "equity" is measured by a sliding scale. Fairness is determined by some (and someone's) standard of impartiality and reasonableness. That is, definitions of what constitutes "reasonable" and "fair" are matters of opinion. What is equal may not always seem fair; what is fair in one person's eyes might be unfair in another's. While equality appears to be a more straightforward concept, definitions of equity are more widely open to interpretation. To be sure, different and often hidden life circumstances and degrees of opportunity can make true equality itself an impossible goal. But even more than definitions of equality, perceptions of equity are influenced by subtle or unconscious biases—presumptions created by deeply ingrained social values and received wisdom. Complicating matters further, the two terms often are used interchangeably, whether by civil rights attorneys or the general public.

By this book's conclusion, I show how compromises reflected in the shift toward using the term "equity" instead of "equality" were needed to advance the women's sports movement in the 1970s. I argue further that the pioneering period of Title IX's first decade yielded rich rhetorical resources that women's sports advocates today must employ to continue moving toward equality.

The Case of Michigan State University Basketball

To explore how this rhetorical history can influence present-day actions, the core of this book focuses on an emblematic struggle in the 1970s against sex discrimination at Michigan State University (MSU), a story that offers a microhistory of rhetorical activity at the genesis of Title IX. As a microhistory, the MSU story, which focuses on the struggle of the women's basketball team, becomes "a search for answers to large questions in small places."[10] It provides a broadly contextualized example of how sports and the rhetorical activities of college athletes played a role in the grassroots persuasion of second-wave feminism (that is, the part of the feminist movement that took place between approximately 1960 and 1990). The MSU team's story illustrates how the law does not self-execute: the struggle for rights often continues long after a law has been passed. Through this account of a decade-long struggle that included the federal lawsuit *Hutchins v. Board of Trustees of Michigan State University*, I identify issues that women athletes faced, rhetorical practices they employed, and communication strategies used against them.

The MSU women's case played out against the backdrop of a legendary sports story revisited by sportswriters Fred Stabley Jr. and Tim Staudt in their 2003 book *Tales of the Magical Spartans*: how Earvin "Magic" Johnson and the MSU men's basketball team won the 1979 national championship against Larry Bird and Indiana State.[11] This game remains the most-watched NCAA tournament game in history. As television commentators pointed out on the thirtieth anniversary of the 1979 men's NCAA basketball championship, the Magic–Bird game not only marked the entry of Entertainment and Sports Programming Network (ESPN) into the sports entertainment marketplace but also ushered in the current era of commercialized men's college sports.

What Stabley, Staudt, and other experts on men's sports never mention is that during the same 1978–79 season when the men's team enjoyed national accolades, the women's basketball team was fighting for basic rights under Title IX and the Constitution's Fourteenth Amendment. When I picked up *Tales of the Magical Spartans* at the MSU bookstore, I was disappointed, but not entirely surprised, to find no mention of the women's struggle. Contrasted with the men's "magical season," these women competed in an invisible season that, more than thirty years later, remains completely unacknowledged by the state of Michigan's most prominent sportswriters.

While these writers and their readers continue to relive stories of a legendary men's championship, advocates for low-profile men's sports (including Olympic sports such as wrestling) charge that Title IX is destroying their opportunities, and expenditures for big-time college sports spiral out of control.[12] Those escalating costs are rooted in the pursuit of revenue, especially efforts to field teams that win and therefore attract the most lucrative television and corporate sponsorships. I believe, as critics of big-time college sports argue, that Division I college football is now a quasi-professional sport, even as it benefits from the nonprofit status of universities that house the teams. These universities incur increasing expenses required to maintain football's quasi-professional status, expenses that erode academic values as the university accepts the commercialization of college sports as inevitable and necessary to attract students, donations, and status. Rather than focusing on these unaffordable and unnecessary expenses, critics of Title IX argue instead that women athletes receive too many resources and opportunities. Meanwhile, the history of struggle that took place in the formative years of the women's program and the dangers of women following the same commercialized path as men remains largely ignored.

Brief Overview of the Book

Invisible Seasons is organized into four parts. In part 1 (chapters 2–5), I focus on roles and rhetorics of three groups—feminists, women's athletic administrators, and the men's sports establishment—to describe the context in which Title IX's implementing regulations were developed between 1972 and 1975. The rhetorical battle among these groups led to an interpretation of Title IX focused on equity rather than equality. In part 2 (chapters 6–8), I introduce key students, coaches, administrators, and activists and set the stage for the struggle to come. Parts 3 (chapters 9–11) and 4 (chapters 12–15) focus in detail on events at Michigan State University from September 1977 to August 1978 that show how a campaign seeking full equality was mobilized under the banner of Title IX. Chapter 15 moves more quickly through time to provide a telescopic view of how that campaign played out in the legal system between 1978 and 1986.

Throughout these parts, I also situate the MSU story within a national context of other early Title IX battles and within the institutional history of collegiate sports at MSU. I reconstruct events through original oral history interviews, archival research, observations from visits to locations where the events unfolded, news articles, legal documents, and secondary sources. The discourse documented through these sources also serves as data, or a rhetorical artifact, for the book's conclusions, which are presented in chapter 16.

Making Struggles Visible

The MSU story parallels thousands of yet-untold Title IX stories across the nation. In some cases, the Spartans' story intersects directly with those of other institutions. But even when other schools are not specifically mentioned, the problems confronted by the MSU women's basketball players are similar to those faced by women athletes on many other campuses at that same time. One longtime advocate for girls' and women's sports in Michigan, Elizabeth (Geise) Homer, has noted that "people have no idea how many complaints and lawsuits have been filed to open up Title IX because they've all been local, and people don't see how many valiant people across the nation have stood up with that law behind them and gotten their district to change. The districts did not change by just immediately supporting the law; it has been a long battle!"[13] As Bernice Sandler noted in a letter written to support a grant application for this project, the MSU story "illustrates more than a mere history of one institution."[14] It represents a series of larger narratives about Title IX and also calls into question some conventional understandings of the law's social history.

I offer this story in part because it makes a great sports history tale. Just as important, richly textured, local stories like this one particularize a history that is often painted in broad strokes or focuses on iconic stories. If we hear stories of only the prominent (or once prominent) programs, coaches, and players—Tennessee, Rutgers, Old Dominion, or Connecticut—our understanding of how change in college sports happened under Title IX remains incomplete, and our public narratives remain partial or even misleading. Often the most well-known stories involved widely publicized or strikingly dramatic events, such as the 1976 protest at Yale in which female crew members bared chests and backs with the words "Title IX" written across them. (This event inspired the 1999 documentary film *A Hero for Daisy*.) Or they involve highly charismatic individuals such as Pat Summit at Tennessee, who orchestrated change in her program while guiding her basketball teams to national prominence. The MSU story, by contrast, shows how more extended collective action can unfold through the words and actions of a complex cast of individuals whose roles shift during the course of a long struggle.

Indeed, even the stories of the best-known programs remain to be told in depth, brought to the attention of a wider public, and situated in the context of other lesser-known or forgotten narratives. As historian Karen Offen reminds us, "amnesia is feminism's worst enemy."[15] To reconstruct and incorporate into our public memory our nation's struggle for equality under Title IX has meant asking the individuals who took professional and personal risks to ensure its promises would be fulfilled in both the letter and spirit of the law to share publically some acutely painful experiences. Through their activism, people lost jobs, careers were derailed, and previously positive relationships with colleagues and institutions were altered or even destroyed. As subsequent chapters show, the principal actors in the story of the Michigan State Spartans' struggle for gender equality are no exception. Some individuals, both women and men, still fear the possible consequences of speaking out and have shared their memories and perspectives with me only as background information, choosing not to be identified in this book.

I hope that those who read this book come away with a better understanding of the tradition of struggle that has created today's increasingly remarkable opportunities for girls and women athletes. Students, along with their supporters and advocates, employed a full range of persuasive tools and strategies at the genesis of Title IX when there were no trails blazed or footsteps to follow. Ideally, the stories told here will inspire similar acts of courage and principle where they are needed most—whether in the movement for equality in sports, workplaces, families, neighborhoods, or civic life. Beyond inspiration, I want readers to see how what appear to be sports-specific debates about equity and equality have broader significance. The site of college athletics after Title IX can be viewed as a proxy for other settings in which conflicting ideas about limited resources, gender, power, status, and competition collide. I hope that thinking about issues of equality and economics in higher education athletics through the rhetorical lens will advance our understanding of how dialogues about limited resources in a variety of contexts can move beyond polarized points of disagreement to sustainable and just social change.

PART ONE

Do Women Want the Rose Bowl?

When enacted in 1972, Title IX made discrimination based on sex illegal in institutions with federally funded educational programs. But what did the law really mean in practice for athletics? Did women athletes, coaches, and administrators actually want the pressure, intensity, and competitiveness that accompany the visibility and glorified status of men's big-time college sports? In 1974, renowned University of Michigan football coach Bo Schembechler argued in a letter to President Gerald Ford (a Michigan football alum) that Title IX posed a serious threat to men's college sports because, he conjectured, most women athletes *would* be interested in a Rose Bowl–like experience for themselves. Like many of his peers, he feared that sharing resources with women athletes would threaten the viability of men's college sports.

But in the 1970s, the worlds of men's and women's college athletics were completely separate and just as completely unequal, making the idea of high-profile women's college sports hard for most people to imagine, and the potential demise of men's big-time sports unlikely (if not absurd). Women's programs were closely tied to academics and physical education departments, while men's programs, especially at large public universities, were becoming increasingly commercialized and disconnected from educational missions and values. Women athletes drove themselves to games in station wagons, while their male counterparts took buses or planes. Women's teams juggled minuscule budgets that allowed scant per diem allotments for food and lodging when they traveled to compete; no funds were available to publicize their events (the public was assumed to be uninterested); and female athletes struggled to reach their athletic potential while guided by inexperienced, poorly paid, often part-time coaches. The old notion of "ladies' portions" applied to nearly every aspect of intercollegiate athletics; women athletes were assumed to want and need less of almost everything simply because they were female. To complicate matters, many women's physical education leaders themselves accepted these assumptions in part because they valued maintaining a student-oriented separate sphere for women's athletics that emphasized "caring and fairness" over "winning and external rewards."[1] Their acquiescence to the status quo made little sense to the most competitive and aspiring women athletes, who saw hardly any value in maintaining a completely segregated space when resources and opportunities were so unevenly distributed.

These factors combined to set the stage for a highly charged debate over how Title IX should be interpreted and implemented when it came to college sports. In this part, I provide an extended backdrop for the central example of the book—the story of the MSU women's basketball team's struggle for equal treatment—by describing the context in which the regulations for implementing Title IX were developed. This context is critical for appreciating the communication options and constraints that confronted the central figures in the MSU story—from basketball players Kathleen DeBoer, Cookie Mankowski, Carol Hutchins, and Deb Traxinger to their teammates, coaches, athletics directors, supporters, and attorney. The players, for instance, started out as typical college students; they only gradually saw that they might be participating in a pivotal moment for the history of women's college sports. Some readers of this book may be eager to dive into their story and get the broader context afterward. If so, you might move ahead now to read parts 2 through 4 first; then return to read part 1 before or after you read the book's conclusion. Whichever pathway you choose, this first part will provide deeper insight into the communication choices made by key figures in the MSU story. The brief stories presented here provide snapshots that reveal how communication choices made in local situations reflect broader patterns, recurring rhetorical situations, and commonly played roles.

To provide those snapshots, I focus on how three groups—feminist activists (represented primarily by the example of attorney Jean Ledwith

King), the Association of Intercollegiate Athletics for Women (AIAW), and the National Collegiate Athletic Association (NCAA)—responded to Title IX between 1972 and 1975 as lawmakers developed its regulations for athletics. As a result of the push and pull among these groups, the law's regulations for athletics became a compromise designed to protect two competing interests: (1) the opportunity for girls and women to develop as athletes without having to compete directly with males, and (2) the special status of football (and, to a lesser extent, men's basketball). The compromising nature of the regulations made them both flexible and somewhat confusing, especially to opponents of sex equality, who were in no hurry to comply.[2] The 1975 regulations gave higher education institutions three years to phase in their compliance with Title IX. Most schools, however, viewed those years as a waiting period and did not take the necessary steps to comply by the July 21, 1978, deadline. Michigan State University was among those institutions.

Regulating Title IX

A federal statute's regulations matter greatly: they not only establish a foundation for how the law will be applied, interpreted, and enforced, they actually carry the force of law themselves. But, as Title IX scholars Linda Carpenter and R. Vivian Acosta remind us, "regulations are not created by one person sitting alone in an office with a pen and paper."[3] For Title IX, the task of writing regulations fell to policymakers at the US Department of Health, Education, and Welfare (HEW). HEW staffers began with the language of the brief Title IX statute: in just thirty-nine words, the law states that sex discrimination is prohibited in federally funded educational programs and activities. But how exactly was sex discrimination in athletics to be identified? Writers of the regulations faced complicated decisions about what equality—or at least the absence of discrimination—meant for the separate, different, and completely unequal athletic programs for college men and women in the 1970s.

Such complex decisions make the process of writing regulations for any law richly rhetorical, involving "debate, comment, interchange of ideas, and numerous hearings."[4] In the case of Title IX, stakeholders from lobbyists to attorneys, coaches, and parents attempted to influence the outcome through the media, face-to-face meetings, letters, lawsuits, and other means. Battles over how draft regulations interpreted the law and the possible consequences of those interpretations began even before the draft came before the public for comment. By 1974, the impending regulations had prompted streams of discourse from policy makers, women's and men's athletic administrators, feminist activists, politicians, and other members of the public. The typical six-month comment period was stretched to nine months, and President Ford was implored to veto the regulations by a flood of protests from administrators of the nation's higher education athletics programs.[5]

Both the intense debate over the Title IX regulations that occurred between 1972 and 1975 and the extended (and often ignored) compliance period (1975–78) set the stage for a wave of sex discrimination complaints filed between 1975 and 1980, including the federal complaint filed in 1978 by the women's basketball team at Michigan State. However, college students (and sometimes even their coaches) who filed complaints and protested inequalities during this time were largely unaware that the Title IX regulations had generated such controversy. Neither were they aware that, during its formative decades, as a new statute Title IX was little more than "a paper tiger with no bite."[6] They also did not know that to gain access for high school girls to baseball, football, and basketball, attorneys often relied on the Constitution's Fourteenth Amendment. This amendment, ratified in 1868 to protect the rights of freed slaves, guarantees all persons equal protection under law, and the precedent-setting cases won by Ruth Bader Ginsburg in the 1970s established that the amendment protects against discrimination based on sex as well as race.

Although the Fourteenth Amendment proved a powerful legal tool for girls and women, including athletes, as the Title IX regulations were being drafted, published, and interpreted, it was Title IX that struck fear into the men's athletic establishment and to which women athletes and coaches first turned. What women didn't initially realize is that enforcing Title IX (or the Fourteenth Amendment, for that matter) required struggle and risk on their part. As one college administrator for women's sports put it, "We were never reviewed by Title IX. I kept my fingers crossed, I kept hoping

Title IX would come here."[7] Her personification of the law communicates her unrealistic sense that, eventually, the law itself would step in to make things right. Women athletes' lack of awareness regarding conflicts over regulations and the relative weakness of a new, untested law might have contributed to their sense of clarity and purpose in seeking their rights. Meanwhile, when they moved slowly or not at all in responding to athletes' and coaches' assertions of rights under Title IX, administrators often cited these ongoing conflicts as justification for inaction.

Whether they fully realized it or not, both women athletes asserting their rights and administrators to whom they appealed were a small part of a larger constellation of groups and individuals who responded with speech and writing to rhetorical situations that emerged in response to the impending Title IX regulations. These rhetorical situations—that is, the circumstances under which discourses that aim to influence are produced—inherently involved constraints that limited what speakers or writers could feasibly or effectively communicate at any given time. These constraints related to occupations, access to power holders, individual rhetorical abilities, and other factors. Macro-level factors, such as the economic climate of the country and dominant attitudes toward feminism and female athleticism, also shaped the persuasive discourses potentially viable for different individuals and groups. Just before 1975, when the federal regulation for implementing Title IX was published, feminist groups, members of the NCAA, and AIAW leaders all navigated these constraints as they vied to exercise influence.

2 Teaming Up

Sports and Feminism

Still, one place that gives us a sense of bravery is the gym, and it was one of the only places that taught us to be strong, to speak out, to push our presence onto the world with a little more assurance than being "nice" allowed.

—Leslie Heywood and Shari L. Dworkin,
"Sport as Stealth Feminism of the Third Wave"[1]

The 1973 "Battle of the Sexes" between tennis star Billie Jean King and Bobby Riggs marked the first time that many 1970s feminists saw athletics as an arena for women's rights. Although she knew "things were not right" in her realm of tennis, it took a while for King herself to realize that feminists were protesting the same thing she was in sports: "lack of equal opportunity."[2] Certainly when King defeated Riggs in the 1973 match, the words "Title IX" had not entered public discourse. As historian Susan Ware noted in *Game, Set, Match: Billie Jean King and the Women's Sports Revolution*, it was still a relatively obscure education law not yet widely associated with athletics. But not long after King's historic match with Riggs, the controversy over Title IX's athletics regulations erupted.

In 1974, the tennis star, then ranked number one in the world for women's players, lobbied several US senators to support a strong Title IX. Through a form letter with her signature (written on paper with letterhead from her new magazine, *womenSports*), King played a role in reminding a small but powerful group of senators of "tremendous" inequities facing college women athletes, including the fact that spending for men's programs "sometimes outpace[d] that of women's by a ratio of 1,000 to

1."[3] Rhetorically, King's efforts to reach politically powerful individuals illustrate strategies that women's sports movement leader and strategist Donna Lopiano identified in 2007 as a key to the women's sports movement: "mountaintop politics" and "the power of the celebrity voice."[4]

In the 1970s, though, Billie Jean King was among a small minority of athletes who viewed sport through a feminist lens. She explained and defended women athletes' lack of involvement in the feminist movement by identifying sports participation itself as a form of physical rhetoric: "Tennis helps the women's movement just by *doing*. We're there, we're visual, like blacks in sports helped their movement. If people see us out there every day, that changes people's minds, not *talking* about it."[5] In fact, King's own contributions to, and relationship with, feminist rhetoric were sometimes conflicted and occasionally novel, as described by Ware in *Game, Set, Match*. While King appreciated the image of "Women on the Move" as a slogan for the 1977 National Women's Conference in Houston, the feminist symbolic act of bra-burning did not resonate with her. You need a bra to play sports, she reasoned.[6] Especially after the invention of the sports bra in 1977, the bra became not a constraining undergarment but instead a piece of athletic gear that could empower female athletes.

King's keen rhetorical sensibility extended to what social movement rhetoricians call *languaging strategies*. She suggested that the proposed Equal Rights Amendment (ERA) might have been more aptly termed the "Equal Opportunity Amendment" or the "Equal Chance Amendment."[7] With a rhetorician's eye, she questioned whether the terminological emphasis on rights instead of chances or opportunities emphasized force more than persuasion. Overall, her general approach to influencing others' viewpoints or actions was, whenever possible, to "persuade sweetly and privately."[8] She found her own efforts most effective when she started out by being nice, which might mean phrasing requests as gently posed questions. In a keynote talk for a 2007 conference on Title IX, she provided examples of phrasing she found effective. Phrases such as "Will you do me a favor?" or "You're going to include the women, aren't you?" drew upon expectations that women would be "nice" (a traditional feminine rhetorical tone) and upon the power of suggestion through a leading question. She added, "I only go front page when I'm desperate."[9]

In the same talk, King emphasized the value of welcoming and cultivating men as allies. If the situation were ever reversed and men experienced sex discrimination, she liked to think that she would support them as well. That sentiment reflects King's liberal feminist sensibility: she "wanted all people to be treated as individuals, regardless of sex."[10] King often "resisted the feminist mantle, wanting to be seen as an individual and athlete, not as the spokesperson for a cause."[11]

When King did embrace a vocal rhetorical role in the feminist movement, it redirected her energies away from a single-minded focus on her athletic goals, an inevitability that might explain the apolitical nature of many high-level athletes. Nor were athlete spokespeople always sought out or welcomed by the feminist movement. Just as athletes were reluctant to embrace feminism or activism, feminist groups were slow to seek alliances with sportswomen. Many feminists saw sports, especially men's sports culture, as connected with all they found abhorrent in a patriarchal society that glorified competition, winning at all costs, and norms for masculinity rooted in "misogyny, homophobia, and violence."[12]

On their campuses, women coaches and athletics administrators likewise distanced themselves from known feminists. As women already considered suspect because of their nontraditional careers in athletics, some of them found that if they spoke out strongly for equal opportunity "the label of man-hater or lesbian [was] used to silence them."[13] So whereas feminists in the 1960s and 1970s were associated with sometimes dramatic protests in which they symbolically discarded bras, cosmetics, high heels, and other symbols of femininity and limitations placed on women, women in athletics sought ways to emphasize their conventionality. Many practiced an apologetic rhetoric, striving to emphasize their femininity in order to maintain social acceptability while violating societal gender roles by competing in sports. Examples of apologetic practices included displaying "artifacts of femininity," such as hair ribbons or ruffles on uniforms; asserting traditionally feminine goals or interests, such as cooking or caring for children; focusing on sports, such as figure skating, that emphasize feminine beauty, grace, and fashion as well as athleticism; and pursuing sport primarily for socializing rather than achievement or competition.[14] Women sometimes bridged this divide among themselves, when feminists discovered sport as an avenue for advancing women's rights and when sportswomen sought out unapologetic feminist attorneys to help them confront intractable opposition within their institutions. One of these feminist attorneys was Jean Ledwith King.

Ledwith King (no relation to Billie Jean King) was active in the women's rights movement before deciding at age forty-one to attend law school. With a law degree, she hoped to garner the respect she saw men getting and to further causes she believed in. In her words, "I went to law school to do good."[15] Having secured the promise of her husband (an engineer) to help with domestic responsibilities, she was accepted into law school and enrolled in 1968 during a period when an unofficial quota system restricted women's admission to professional schools around the country. (This quota system motivated Patsy Mink, the Representative to Congress from Hawaii, to play a leading role in enacting Title IX; medical schools that were not accepting female students had excluded her.) On the political front, Ledwith King (hereafter referred to simply as "King") worked for change by helping give women equal representation in Michigan's delegation to the 1972 Democratic National Convention; she also cofounded a group dedicated to equal employment for women.[16]

When King opened her law practice in 1972, the challenges facing the women's movement were significant: although in 1970 more than 40 percent of wives worked for wages, by 1979 women's wages were still only 59 percent of men's.[17] She recalled, "There was discrimination everywhere, in every occupation, in every setting."[18] To help create social change for women, King led a study requested by the Governor of Michigan through the Michigan Women's Commission (Department of Civil Rights). Her group surveyed Michigan law as it pertained to the proposed ERA, which was then being voted on state by state. Describing King as a significant "player" in Michigan Democratic politics, a colleague who worked with her on the study while a law student called her "very esteemed as a woman activist lawyer, a real model for women like me."[19]

Even before completing her law degree, King used a little-known weapon available to women's rights attorneys and activists: Executive Order 11375, an order signed by President Lyndon B. Johnson in 1967 forbidding federal contractors from sex discrimination. Bernice Sandler (who served as deputy director of HEW's Women's Action Program in 1971) famously discovered this order in a footnote of a US Commission on Civil Rights report; she used it as the basis for complaints filed by the newly established Women's Equity Action League (WEAL) against more than 250 higher education institutions, asking for "an investigation of admission quotas, financial assistance, hiring practices, promotions, and salary differentials."[20]

In touch with national feminist networks, including WEAL, King used the executive order to advance the cause of academic women at her own institution. A self-described "bomb-thrower,"[21] she coauthored a landmark administrative complaint against the University of Michigan that resulted in the federal government withholding $15 million in funds from the institution. The complaint caused the university to double the salaries of one hundred women faculty by 1971 and pressured administrators to address "sex discrimination in admissions, financial aid, employment, and athletics."[22] Although these women surely appreciated their raises, some of them confided to advocates such as King that they were happy to be working at all. They felt the institution was doing them a favor simply by hiring them. It took a paradigm shift for the activists among them to initiate a process of change. Once the activists became upset, they had to find a way to mobilize everyone else.

Throughout this period, King mentored advocacy lawyers and women who initially feared confrontation because they had been punished when they stood up for themselves. She taught them a premise behind rhetorical strategies for confrontation: "You can't negotiate when you have nothing—no power and no respect." She reminded those who sought her counsel that "if a whole lot of people are mad at you, you must be doing something right."[23]

While King espoused the benefits of confrontation, she also understood the value of reading an audience. She could turn to her husband to help anticipate how a male judge might view a situation and what appeals might register with a man. And in her legal philosophy and strategy, especially the pragmatic "reductionist" approach of narrowing a case to its most basic winnable elements, she worked in the tradition of Ruth Bader

Ginsburg (who went on to become the second female US Supreme Court Justice). In a 2009 interview for the *New York Times,* Justice Ginsburg offered her own advice to members of marginalized groups trying to influence change and become welcomed, accepted, and respected in spaces from which they have been excluded: "Be with the people who hold the levers" but "use a gentle touch" and "have a sense of humor."[24]

In the tradition of Ginsburg's groundbreaking work, King was among the pioneers who employed creative legal and rhetorical strategies to advance the cause of women's rights during the nearly two decades that it took for Title IX to become a fully effective legal tool. Although she would later become an honored member of the Michigan Women's Historical Center and Hall of Fame, King never imagined early in her career that she would make a name for herself in part based on cases involving sports. As she put it, "Sports found me as an issue."[25]

In fact, one of the first issues surrounding Title IX that captured the attention of feminist activists, including King, had nothing to do with athletics. It was the question of whether the law applied to biased representations of males and females in school textbooks and curricula. Although feminist groups strongly objected, the federal government determined that Title IX regulations would not cover textbook bias, citing the right of publishers to free speech. Aware that the Title IX regulations would exclude textbooks, activist attorneys had a small window of opportunity to take action. King seized the moment. In 1974, she filed a Title IX textbook complaint against Houghton Mifflin of Boston, Massachusetts. Her clients, a group in Kalamazoo, Michigan, objected to gender bias in the publisher's textbooks. Her preemptive action persuaded the publisher to issue a revised version of textbooks and eliminate sexism in subsequent books, a move that influenced other publishers to do the same.

Controversy surrounding Title IX increasingly focused on sports, however, and King's legal and rhetorical strategies reflected a pragmatic thread of 1970s feminism that may have resonated particularly well with competitive athletes and their parents. Social or materialist feminists during that era feared that a less goal-oriented approach emphasizing consciousness-raising groups might be a "dead end" and consequently argued for a feminist rhetoric unabashedly focused on "winning." Although some

1970s feminists rejected competition as unsisterly in any form, a 1972 position paper published by the Chicago Women's Liberation Union outlined strategy guidelines for the women's movement that emphasized the need to compete. In a section of the paper entitled "Winning," the group contended that "if we want to speak to most women, we have to be serious about winning. Women have been losers too long. Women will only flock to women's liberation ideas when they know that it will help them and others become winners, gain something that they want for themselves and their daughters and others." The position paper also articulated criteria for prioritizing reforms for which to fight while focusing on "meeting our immediate needs."[26]

In this same spirit, attorney King emphasized priorities, expediency, winning, and the necessity of confronting power with power. The activists, clients, and attorneys whom King mentored recalled her repeated admonition, one paraphrased from the famous words of abolitionist and orator Frederick Douglass: "power yields only to power, and not without a struggle."[27]

Initially, colleagues say, King viewed athletics as a relatively unimportant area in which to empower women. Another Ann Arbor attorney, Lawrence Sperling, represented high school girls in one of the first sports discrimination cases in Michigan (and in the United States). Sperling argued his case before a prominent African American federal judge, Damon Keith, who both understood civil rights and had daughters. At first, feminist attorneys such as King were more likely to lecture colleagues like Keith on the importance of employment and education than to take on a sports case. Sports, by comparison, seemed frivolous.

But if King initially held that view, she subsequently changed her mind. As she and other feminists began to realize, sports could be important for girls' self-esteem. The experience with competing and confronting that King gained through activism and in law school could be available through sports to even more girls and women. Through competitive sports, girls and women could learn to deal with men in the home and workplace, showing strength when needed, striving to win (whether it be an argument, a contract, or a job), and knowing how to be a good sport when beaten.

King took her first athletics case in 1974, just before the Title IX regulations were published. She filed suit on behalf of Julie Alexander, an eighth-grade student who wanted to run track at Mona Shores High School, as her father had done, but was prevented from doing so by the track coach, who told her he was "leery" of having girls on the team.[28] Alexander was the only girl who became a plaintiff, but when the *Grand Rapids Press* and sports editor Bob Becker played up the filing of the lawsuit, the publicity led the school to settle out of court, and forty girls joined the team.[29] This lawsuit solidified a growing conviction for King that sports mattered. She remarked in a *Detroit Free Press* profile in 1999, "I was looking at education and politics, but it all fits together. Sports build character—you learn teamwork . . . if you can't follow a simple order, you'll fall on your face in a workplace."[30]

King's realization about the value of sports for females was slow in coming to many of her feminist colleagues as well. As recently as 2005, the editor for a prominent women's studies journal argued that "until men and women can learn to appreciate the activities of accomplished, athletic females (in the many sizes and shapes they attain for sports), women will never accomplish the task of their liberation."[31] This editor speculated about why "until recently there have been few feminists interested in or conversant with the very explosive debates that emanate from sports" by pointing to feminist ambivalence about the "nature of competition (and its inherent aggressions)."[32]

In the 1970s, however, the task of creating Title IX's regulations unexpectedly catapulted feminists into the world of college athletics. Early on, the National Organization for Women (NOW) took note that sports were "the most visible piece of discrimination in American education"; one of NOW's leaders highlighted inequalities in athletics in an October 1972 *Ms.* magazine article, likely after attending an informational session on the law offered by federal policymakers.[33] However, the US Department of Health, Education, and Welfare's secretary found that "the NOW staff in Washington knew practically nothing about sports."[34]

The focus on Title IX's impact on athletics surprised even the originators of Title IX. Like attorney King, they expected that the law would rectify the egregious inequalities in faculty employment and student admissions to law, medical, and other professional schools; protect the rights of pregnant students; assure access to vocational education courses regardless of sex; prohibit sexual harassment in schools; require school counseling materials and other curricula to be free of sex-role stereotypes; and more. The increasing focus on Title IX as a "sports law" came as a shock. According to Sandler, "Some of us thought, oh, it will be nice for girls to have more extensive field-day activities, or something like that."[35] Not being athletes themselves, they initially had no idea that long-standing different and segregated traditions in men's and women's sports—each with their own power structures, philosophies, and leaders—had created widespread and controversial differences in opportunities and resources. The originators of Title IX had no idea about the level of frustration girls and women faced across the country when pursuing a more equal chance to achieve their athletic aspirations.

Knowing relatively little of this context, a feminist project associate with the Association of American Colleges, Margaret Dunkle, was charged with gathering data to "show the world, with facts and figures, that women deserve more, deserve to be equal."[36] Having no previous association with athletics herself, Dunkle posed a question that became the title of a 1974 paper published with Sandler: "What Constitutes Equality for Women in Sport?" The paper examined a range of concerns (such as physiological differences between the sexes), issues (such as the question of single-sex versus mixed teams), and possible administrative structures (separate but equal programs for each sex versus merged structures).[37] The Carnegie, Danforth, and Exxon Foundations funded her efforts on behalf of women, but the opposition was formidable. Dunkle identified her opponents as not only the men's athletic establishment but also women themselves, including women athletes and coaches. She feared that she would have difficulty convincing women because, when faced with having "to fight for every inch of ground gained" against men, many of whom were seen as "national heroes" and "the great minds of big-time college athletics," they would be too willing to accept "crumbs."[38]

Seen in that light, the alternative of maintaining autonomy and control of women's programs—despite poor funding and a lack of respect from men or the public—held a certain appeal for many women's physical

educators. While feminist activists considered Title IX a much-to-be celebrated victory, for some women's college sports leaders, the law invited
intervention by outsiders into their previously segregated world; for many,
it posed an unexpected threat.

3 Identity Crisis

The Association for Intercollegiate Athletics for Women

> I grew up hearing my mom's stories of playing six-player, half-court basketball, the game that became so wildly popular in Iowa that public interest in girls' basketball eclipsed attention and support for the boys' five-player, full-court game. Although my mother resented the athletic restrictions that girls in the 1950s and 1960s faced, she loved every minute of whatever opportunities she had to compete even in the most circumscribed ways. Playing the "rover" position was the best, she would say, because she could move up and down, covering both sides of the court.
>
> —Kelly Belanger, MSU student athlete, 1982–86

Title IX resulted from the feminist movement, and it rocked the world of a group of women who did not consider themselves feminists: the physical education professors who oversaw athletic activities for American college women. Unlike the feminists behind Title IX, women's physical educators mostly accepted restrictions placed on women athletes—such as the rules in basketball limiting them to six-player, half-court games—and did not want to call attention to themselves. In part, these women feared that an emphasis on competition (associated with masculinity) would bring stigma and stereotyping that would lead to questioning of their sexual orientation. Thus, their cause was a quiet one: to develop opportunities for college women to enjoy the spirit of play while experiencing sport as a means of physical, intellectual, and emotional growth. The new law sparked collaboration between female athletes and feminists, exerting

27

unwelcome, unexpected pressure on the women's physical educators responsible for overseeing college women's athletic activities.

Even gaining greater visibility and resources posed a threat. If more were given, expectations would shift. If women's sports adopted the men's competitive philosophy, the close tie between college sports and physical education as an academic discipline would be severed for women, as it had been for men. Moreover, many women physical educators had internalized societal notions that devalued female athleticism and had "grown accustomed to meager resources for women's sports."[1] Whereas today's intercollegiate athletes, male and female, often experience sports as a full-time job taking up as much or more time than academic work, women physical educators emphasized a spirit of play rather than the importance of winning. In this tradition, Mikki Baile, the first women's basketball coach at Michigan State (1972–75), recalled that she considered herself a coach of "people" first and of athletes second. To underscore her point that it was acceptable for women athletes in that day to focus on more than just their sport, she recounted how a player called to say she'd be late getting to a game because she was in Washington, DC, protesting the Vietnam War. Baile couldn't recall the team's record that year (it was 6–3), but winning was not the team's first priority.[2]

For coaches like Baile and other women physical educators, Title IX and its impending regulations presented a point of redefinition. Would women's physical educators continue to pursue their own model of college sports (perhaps a different but equal model)? Or would they seek programs that mirrored those of the men? Women's sports leaders contemplated two seemingly opposing goals: (1) to preserve the "ideological purity" of a mostly separate "educational model" controlled by women, or (2) to seek equality with men through a more commercialized model. A few leaders, however, imagined a third way: to seek equality and a degree of integration with men but work for reforms to curtail corruption and commercialization.

These different perspectives were apparent in the Association for Intercollegiate Athletics for Women (AIAW), which was formed in 1971 to serve as a governing body for quickly changing programs in women's college athletics. It was a counterpart to the National Collegiate Athletics

Association (NCAA), which had governed men's college sports since 1906. From the standpoint of many AIAW leaders, the NCAA was formed primarily to clean up problems in men's college athletics, whereas the AIAW was formed with a more idealistic vision: to enact a completely different and radically student-centered model of intercollegiate sport.[3] Looking back on the AIAW (which governed women's college sports until 1982), members described its more tacit purpose as the "organizing, bonding, and empowering of women administrators" as they developed their programs in departments where "men in athletics did not want women in their system."[4] To AIAW members, it was a prized sorority that fostered gender solidarity.[5]

But not long after the AIAW was formed, Title IX fractured the unity among women's sports leaders. The law precipitated an identity crisis that became a rhetorical exigency: strong leaders asserted conflicting positions and ideologies, each one seeking to influence the direction of changes that were certain to come. Margaret Dunkle, who became a legislative assistant for the US Department of Health, Education, and Welfare in 1977, summed up the situation: "As the battle lines were drawn, it became clear that Title IX was stimulating new and unique coalitions. The various sides could not be identified by labels, party, geography, liberal/conservative, or even sex."[6] The unpredictable alliances and fractured relationships that emerged from these battle lines reflect the complicated development of women's sports, which contrasted with the relatively straightforward trajectory of men's programs.

Standpoint Rhetoric

Often torn between conflicting goals, women sports leaders of this period developed rhetorical strategies that can appear befuddling from a contemporary standpoint. Their everyday words and actions sometimes appeared timid, contradictory, and fearful. Alternatively, they sometimes boldly and eloquently evoked their vision for the future of women's sports. From a historical perspective, however, the rhetorical strategies employed by the rank-and-file of AIAW members make sense. Their contrasting strategies reflected their appreciation of the situations and positions from which they spoke and wrote. That is, they exerted influence through *standpoint rhetoric*. Some of them were tenured physical education professors, others more vulnerable program administrators working under yearly contracts. Some sought to build women's programs in schools with big-time men's sports programs; others worked in smaller institutions without aspirations to become athletic powerhouses.

AIAW women needed to negotiate across different athletic cultures. Often they mediated between the demands of student athletes seeking more resources and competitive opportunities, the policies and philosophy of their own governing organization, and their own ideologies regarding sport and gender. They regularly communicated with male administrators who were unfamiliar with—and sometimes confused by—the AIAW's culture, history, and philosophy, as well as by the fluid and much-contested interpretations of Title IX's regulations.

To appreciate fully the standpoint rhetorics of women's sports leaders, anyone unfamiliar with the history of college sports needs a deeper understanding of the different paths by which men's and women's sports developed. The sections that follow briefly trace those paths. These histories also reveal why the Title IX draft regulations published first in 1973 were received without immediate, completely unified, determined lobbying from the AIAW.

Common Roots, Different Paths

Today, intercollegiate sports on many campuses operate within a separate "family," one largely divorced from the academic institution in its budgets, salaries, values, and culture. For most intercollegiate student athletes, sports have become a full-time job rather than an extracurricular activity. At large, nonprofit public universities, salaries paid to athletics directors, coaches, assistants, administrative and promotional staff, and others associated with college sports signal that coaching undergraduates in sport is considered more important than the role played by even the most accomplished teachers and researchers. And the differences, on the whole, between salaries paid to coaches of young men and young women signals that providing the best possible coaching for male students who play sports is the most important institutional mission. Yet both men's and women's sports began with common roots in the idea that college sports existed to provide fun, leisure, recreation, and an outlet for the tensions or pressures of academic work for the general student body. Over the past century, both men's and women's sports shifted away from these common roots at different paces, in different ways, and for different reasons.

A key difference separated the development of men's and women's sports in college: faculty in physical education departments (typically segregated by sex) played a much stronger role in directing sports for women than they did for men. One strand of physical education philosophy emphasized sport as a means not only to physical development but also to moral and ethical growth. This philosophy, although developed by male professors, never gained significant traction in men's programs; however, it was compatible with a gendered socialization process that celebrated women's role as "moral uplifters of society." As such, it was ready-made for adoption by women's physical educators.[7] Thus, for women college students, the physical education philosophy their professors adopted complemented societal gender expectations and socialization. Initially, this philosophy resulted in constant limitations on the degree and type of participation deemed acceptable for women. Early on, emphases on modesty and decorum even meant prohibiting male spectators from watching women compete. Opportunities that emphasized competition for the most highly skilled athletes were especially limited.

In contrast with their female counterparts, male physical educators held far less influence over men's athletics. According to sport historians John Lucas and Ronald Smith, male students were not thought to need the physiological and psychological support of a physical educator to sustain them in coping with the strains of college life. Not so for women. Prior to 1850, when some US colleges first opened to women, females were assumed to need a professional physical educator to monitor their health and physical education needs. As a result, physical activities for female students remained closely tied to women physical education faculty, but male college students began organizing and running sports activities within their institutions completely separate from physical education departments.[8] By the turn of the twentieth century, men's programs increasingly emphasized intercollegiate competition, recruiting of players, and winning.[9] In 1929, the Carnegie Foundation for the Advancement of Teaching published a study of men's college athletics concluding that "recruiting had replaced amateurs, education was being neglected, and commercialism reigned."[10]

By contrast, during the 1920s, "playdays" provided circumscribed opportunities for women to compete with other schools, often with punch, cookies, tea, and socializing afterward. "The concern was a sport for every woman and for every woman a sport—that was the motto for years," recalled Phyllis Bailey, who led the women's sports programs at Ohio State University from 1957 to 1994, first as coordinator of intramurals and recreation and the women's sports program and then as assistant athletics director beginning in 1974.[11] However, Bailey also pointed out, the philosophy of "play for play's sake" meant that rules were modified for women to enable participation by all skill levels. Such modifications also deferred to the feared social and physiological consequences of overexertion for women; for example, muscles developed through sport were deemed unfeminine, and rigorous exercise was purported to adversely affect women's reproductive organs. "The result, of course," Bailey explained, "was that the most highly skilled [women] were not being satisfied and were totally frustrated by most of the rules they had to play by. In volleyball, for example, you had to set the ball to yourself before you could pass to anyone else; basketball was the half-floor game with six players."[12]

Even within these circumscribed rules, basketball held a strong appeal for girls and women wherever they had encouragement to compete, mainly in historically black colleges and in high schools, particularly in rural communities. By 1928, "girls' basketball had become an institution in communities across the nation" and "one of Iowa's most beloved institutions."[13] Yet female physical educators continually fought to abolish the popular Iowa state championships and promote less competitive play for females everywhere.[14]

These enforcers of Victorian-era feminine traits initially had less influence in African American communities, where women participated in a wider range of nontraditional activities to meet economic and social challenges posed by segregation and discrimination. In the 1930s and 1940s, the women of Alabama's Tuskegee Institute won a string of basketball titles and played full court by men's rules (many of the outstanding track athletes for which the school became known competed in both sports).[15] Thus, at the time, the strong traditions of highly competitive girls' and women's sports in rural high schools and historically black colleges contrasted sharply with the overall lack of mainstream support for female athleticism.

During the 1940s, though, a few change agents in the large midwestern public universities began to challenge the grip that women's physical educators had on their programs. At Ohio State, Phyllis Bailey's predecessor, a professor of physical education named Gladys Palmer, made up her mind to institute change. Although Palmer was acculturated into the traditional philosophy governing women's physical education, she was strongly influenced by meeting a student golf athlete at the University of Minnesota, Patty Berg, who later became a professional golfer, first president of the Ladies Professional Golf Association (LPGA), and member of the World Golf Hall of Fame. Berg served as student representative for a national meeting of women physical educators that Palmer attended, where Berg spoke of her desire to play with college students and her lack of opportunity to "play with anyone else other than middle-aged and older women who belonged to the Ladies Groups at all the country clubs around the country."[16]

Sparked by hearing about Berg's frustrating situation, Palmer instituted a policy at OSU that for the first time allowed female students, or "girls," to travel more than fifty miles from campus in order to access greater competition.[17] Even more boldly, when Ohio State opened its golf course in 1941, she initiated a national golf tournament for women. But she paid a price. She was shunned by her female physical education colleagues around the country, whose attitudes were, "What in the world are you doing? You're just destroying the whole intent of women's physical education."[18] When Palmer approached the NCAA about starting a women's division in the early 1940s, Bailey recalled, she received no better response: "They wanted nothing to do with it; they just were not going to do that at all."[19]

When World War II took men away from factories and professional playing fields in 1941, an unexpected professional opportunity for women emerged with the All-American Girls Baseball League, as portrayed in the 1992 movie *A League of Their Own*. The male sponsors of the league explicitly required players to adopt apologetic behaviors, honed by charm school attendance, as a marketing strategy that emphasized their femininity.[20] During the same period, women's contributions to factory and military work familiarized them with teamwork (individual, noncontact sports such as bowling, swimming, or ice skating were initially considered more ladylike and acceptable) and encouraged a new view of women as physically capable.[21]

Throughout the 1940s, Catholic schools in Philadelphia had basketball teams for girls and women, most notably the all-girls Immaculata College, which launched a varsity program in 1939 and won a string of national championships between 1973 and 1975. In *O God of Players: The Story of the Immaculata Mighty Macs*, Julie Byrne attributed the birth of this program to three primary factors: (1) the relatively inexpensive nature of the sport, (2) a "separate but equal" philosophy that brought similar facilities to Catholic all-girls and all-boys schools, and (3) support from an energetic superintendent of schools in the Philadelphia Archdiocese. This influential leader, Father John Bonner, had been an outstanding athlete himself, and his love of sports, along with his belief that athletics were integral to education, led him to encourage athletic programs for both boys and girls.[22] As a rule, though, sports opportunities for college women, including playdays, dwindled during the 1940s because travel resources were shifted to the war effort.[23]

The same wartime limitations that restricted women's participation in the early 1940s threatened the existence of big-time college football as major schools began dropping their programs.[24] In fact, before men's college sports allegedly needed to be "saved" from the threat of Title IX and women's sports, they faced extinction first as a result of World War II and later due to outrageous scandals and corruption. To combat the trend toward dropping football teams, men's athletic leaders argued that sports teamwork and competition inculcated the same skills needed for waging successful war. They even feared that men's college sports would turn back the clock and embrace a physical education perspective on college athletics, one akin to the ideology behind women's programs. Just as the commercial model enticed competitive and highly skilled women who were restricted to playdays, the specter of reverting to a physical education philosophy of sport haunted men's coaches and administrators, who had much to lose financially and professionally should a commercialized model of sport for men be abandoned. The tension between the two philosophies is apparent in these comments by Columbia University football coach Lou Little in 1943: "I'm convinced that the [college] physical education directors want to get rid of coaches in all [intercollegiate] sports, build themselves up and have their [recreational] programs accepted by all. What good is it to have muscles developed if a boy loses the desire for competition. *When I take part in a sport, I want to win and kick the brains out of the other fellow.* I'm not content to play with someone. I want to play *against* them."[25]

As physical educators feared, the pressures created by this win-at-all-costs mentality made men's college sports programs ripe for abuse. By the 1930s, in some regions men's college basketball rivaled college football as a premiere spectator sport, and both men's Division I football and basketball programs were developing into quasi-professional spectator sports marred by corruption and scandal. In *Onward to Victory: The Crises that Shaped College Sports*—by which he meant only *men's* sports—Murray Sperber cited a widely publicized academic cheating scandal exposed in 1951 at West Point as the culmination of decades of abuses that created a system out of control. He recounted an escalating gambling problem surrounding post-war NCAA basketball games and how, to protect their own careers, sports writers were complicit in maintaining the "open secret."[26] Sperber cited example after example of how games were fixed, with point shaving a common practice. Few incentives existed for players, coaches, administrators, and even a happily naïve public to resist corruption: "[Basketball] has developed a phenomenal following of millions. Giant arenas . . . have been built to house it. Schools have made money from it. Coaches have received better salaries because of it. Newspapers, radio, now television . . . benefited from it."[27]

Sperber contended that "late 1951 marked an exceptional moment in the history of college sports—the only time that meaningful change was possible."[28] He attributed the lack of much-needed reform at the time largely to two factors: the NCAA's propensity to loudly proclaim reform while doing little to enable it, and the appointment of a "Booster President," Michigan State University's Jack Hannah, to lead a reform movement organized by a group of ten prominent college presidents. Sperber's definition of the Booster President justifies many of the greatest fears of women physical educators: "the executive who believes that he can promote his school nationally and regionally through success in big-time college sports—only victory, in his view, attracts attention and an aura of accomplishment—and who averts his eyes when coaches, alumni, and admissions officers break the rules to build winning teams."[29] At MSU, beginning with his appointment to the presidency in 1941, Hannah facilitated the growth of commercialized men's sports. According to Sperber, "most Big Ten programs cut corners," but as Hannah employed "athletic bootstrapping" to move MSU from an agricultural college to a major university, cheating existed on a larger and more organized scale than at other schools."[30] Not surprisingly, Hannah was less than fully committed to reform, so under his leadership the reform movement was inconsequential.

Just as the unsuccessful reform effort for men's college sports got underway, the first college women's program that mirrored the men's commercialized model broke the mold (though not the apologetic imperative prescribed by physical educators). At Wayland Baptist College in Texas, women's basketball players in the 1950s experienced some of the attention, support, and resources to which big-time male athletes were accustomed. Businessman Claude Hutcherson, who owned a local air service, acted as their benefactor beginning in 1950. Between 1953 and 1958, the "Hutcherson Flying Queens" established what is still the longest winning streak for college women's basketball (their 131 straight wins, accumulated before either AIAW or NCAA governance of women's college sports, remains unsurpassed even by the 2010–11 University of Connecticut team that broke the UCLA men's NCAA record).[31]

The mostly working-class, rural women who attended the college and played on the team were, like African American students, less beholden to the prescriptions of white, middle-class physical educators. Still, when possible, Hutcherson encouraged the coach to select prettier players for the team and paid careful attention to the team's image.[32] They often played against Amateur Athletic Union (AAU) teams and semipro teams sponsored by businesses, which provided most of the pre–Title IX opportunities for women athletes. Hutcherson supported the women's college team in a style resembling today's treatment of big-time college athletes: he provided a private plane, flashy uniforms, scholarships, showy warm-up routines, and upscale hotels and meals. As one player put it, "It was reverse discrimination. The men's team had to travel in a bus."[33] However, the situation reversed again in 1961 when the school, citing a budget crunch, voted to end the women's basketball scholarship program but continue the men's (although the women's program received donations to continue the following year and the decision was reversed).[34]

During their heydays, colleges such as Wayland Baptist, the Tuskegee Institute, and Immaculata College were the exceptions, not the rule. Even if women's college sports leaders could have gained access to the resources, most did not desire for their own programs the marketing professionals, recruiters, media promoters, television exposure, and spectator interest that launched men's college sports into an entertainment industry. Despite the fears of women's physical educators, women's college athletics pre–Title IX had little opportunity to fall prey to the scourge of point shaving and rigged games that characterized the men's basketball gambling scandals of the late 1940s and early 1950s.[35]

Movement toward a more competitive model of sport inched along nonetheless. In the postwar 1950s, playdays became sportsdays, and winning was increasingly emphasized as "honors" teams began representing schools. By that time, the Division for Girls' and Women's Sports began to govern standards and playing rules, along with providing coaching and officiating clinics. In the 1960s, the women's movement began to make room for broader definitions of roles for females than those that existed in the restrictive 1950s, and college women's sports programs continued to move away from a playday and intramural focus to include a more competitive varsity intercollegiate experience. In 1966, a commission formed that organized championships, first in track and field, then gymnastics (1969), and, finally, swimming, badminton, and volleyball (1970).[36]

For men's college sports, the 1960s produced a mindset among fans that Sperber compared to George Orwellian "doublethink"; that is, fans "embrace[d] contradictory ideas simultaneously, acknowledging the systemic dysfunction of intercollegiate athletics while maintaining that their favorite athletic programs worked well and deserved their support."[37] An added element also came into play in this era when, between 1957 and 1971, major universities recruited the first black male athletes on scholarships, many of whom were encouraged to see sports as a passport out of poverty. For men's college sports programs, these athletes offered a pool of talent to fuel the revenue stream that institutions hoped would result from winning seasons, TV appearances, and Bowl games. In his book *The Student Athlete: Eligibility and Academic Integrity,* Clarence Underwood (who served as Michigan State's director of athletic academic support services and senior associate athletics director before being appointed athletics director in 1999) vividly described the plight of students promised "an active social life, an education, an environment free of racism, and a chance for a professional contract." Instead, Underwood wrote, "black athletes found a life of misery."[38]

In the 1960s, protests, boycotts, and walkouts sometimes became means by which black male athletes sought fair treatment, a decade before primarily white women athletes who sought more opportunities employed similar social change strategies. In predominately white schools with big-time men's sports programs and no scholarships for women, black women often simply chose not to participate in sports. At Ohio State, Bailey recalled that she was criticized for the scarcity of black women in OSU's programs, but her efforts to approach students in black sororities and dormitories and invite them to clinics had few results. "They just weren't going to do that," she recalled. She speculated that the lack of interest might have stemmed from black Americans who had migrated north for factory jobs and saw sports as activities they didn't associate with their middle-class aspirations but rather with their "friends [down South] who still weren't making money."[39] Certainly, in those pre–Title IX days, without scholarships, women who already faced race discrimination had little incentive, compared to their male counterparts, to subject themselves to the stigmatism faced by women athletes as well. Instead, it made sense to focus on work that could help pay for tuition, academics, and social activities that might cultivate middle-class networks.

This logic notwithstanding, a 1981 publication of the National Association for Girls and Women in Sport called *Black Women in Sport* records the academic and professional accomplishments of black sportswomen who did participate, persevere, and achieve despite barriers connected with sex, race, and social class. Often educated at historically black colleges or smaller teaching-oriented schools, many of these highly skilled athletic women became physical educators themselves. As such, despite their own strong competitive spirits, they espoused the idea of an alternative model of sport for women—one they thought should apply no less to men. This idea of a student-centered "educational model" became the core doctrine of the AIAW when it was formed in 1971. The AIAW philosophy is prominently featured in the response to a survey for the *Black Women in Sport* book provided by Dr. Nell Jackson, a 1951 graduate of Tuskegee Institute whose many accolades include coaching two US track and field Olympic teams and setting an American record herself in the 200 meters. Jackson stated:

> Athletics should be treated as one of the educational experiences a student encounters in school rather than treating it like a business that must make a profit for the institution. The athletic fields and basketball courts are merely classrooms without walls and chairs. The coaches should be educators who can teach as well as coach. They should also be skilled researchers because they have an excellent opportunity to conduct meaningful research with their student athletes. The results should be reinvested into their program to improve the sport.[40]

With the enactment of Title IX in 1972, just a year after the AIAW was established, this philosophy faced unexpected challenges that shook the foundations of the organization and frayed relationships among its members.

Persuading from the Middle

To some extent, the AIAW was a hybrid organization. Within the organization were members who bridled under the unequal treatment their programs and athletes endured. Many AIAW leaders and members, however, admired the strong, capable, highly educated women physical educators who had mentored them and who were deeply committed to a sex-separate philosophy of sport. Basketball coach Vivian Stringer, who led three different teams to the NCAA Final Four, recalled, "These women were so strong. They had doctorate degrees and stood up for their rights. My role models were women for once in my life."[41]

Whether or not most AIAW members truly shared the physical educators' philosophy of sport in its purest form, they seem to have shared Stringer's respect for the strong leaders among them. Like women before them in the Progressive Era who led new professions such as social work, these leaders in physical education effectively used the rhetorical strategy of recasting limitations as virtues. In response to stereotypes against "outspoken" or "aggressive" women (seen as abnormal and unfeminine), they quietly staked out a separate, nonthreatening territory for women's sports. Within a circumscribed, segregated sphere, they largely accepted the idea that women had more limited physical capabilities than men. They also assumed that emphasis on competition and winning led to the corruption seen in men's big-time college sports. Whether they realized it or not, like women of the first-wave feminist movement in the late nineteenth and early twentieth centuries, they employed the Victorian notion that women ought to be held to higher standards for virtuous conduct to justify their goal of self-determination. This ideology had the practical benefit of supporting women educators' dominion over women's college sports, including the AIAW as an incubator for women's leadership in a male-dominated sports world.[42]

However, in 1973, some women athletes on scholarships and their coaches, who included a former AIAW president, felt particularly stifled and discriminated against by the AIAW's policy prohibiting scholarship athletes from participating in association events. The AIAW considered scholarships and recruiting incompatible with an educational model of sport ("talent assessment" was allowed, as long as coaches did not talk with players). Efforts to prohibit scholarships based on athletic ability had supporters within men's intercollegiate athletics as well, including Bill Reed, who was the Big Ten commissioner in 1965 when he participated in a conference on competition for girls and women in sports. There, he advised the women against scholarships, which he had unsuccessfully tried to prohibit in the Big Ten. According to sports historian Ying Wushanley, Reed and the other men advisors at the conference were not true representatives of men's intercollegiate sports because they did not speak for the big-time sports perspective. Wushanley goes so far as to describe them as "men," using quotation marks that seem to imply that by not representing the mainstream, big-time sports ideology, they could not be considered real men![43]

Wushanley's rendering of this history reveals a permeation of the gendered hierarchies within men's sports into scholarly discourse, wherein participants in minor- or low-revenue men's sports are seen as less masculine and less equal within the men's sports economy. For men's sports leaders, to ally themselves with women sports leaders' emphasis on egalitarianism, and to join them in favoring broad sports participation over development and support for an elite few, was (and is) akin to emasculation. For women, according to Mary Jo Festle, "The scholarship issue illustrated one of the dilemmas of the modern feminist movement—how to pursue equal opportunity yet not unquestioningly accept sameness."[44]

In a case that shifted women's college sports toward "sameness," the AIAW scholarship policy was challenged almost immediately upon Title IX's enactment by a lawsuit filed under the Fourteenth Amendment's Equal Protection Clause, Title IX, and other statutes. One of the multiple plaintiffs, Fern "Peachy" Kellmeyer, was a women's athletics director and star tennis player who went on to become senior vice president of the professional World Tennis Tour. Their lawsuit targeted eight organizations, including the AIAW and the National Education Association (NEA), and it pressured the AIAW to change its scholarship policy.[45] AIAW leaders decided to tightly regulate practices surrounding scholarships rather than engage in a legal battle they would likely lose while also risking loss of AIAW memberships required for a viable organization.[46]

The Kellmeyer lawsuit publicly exposed a fissure between the longstanding philosophical stance of women's physical educators and the highly skilled athletes and coaches who sought equality with men. Within the ranks of the AIAW and within physical education departments, strong minority voices emerged. Among them were Linda Estes at the University of New Mexico and Ellen Gerber at the University of Massachusetts. Employing contrasting rhetorical styles, these individuals became catalysts for change and advocates for equality under Title IX.

Arguing "Sameness": Estes and Gerber

Within the AIAW, the rights-oriented discourse of the athletes and coaches responsible for the Kellmeyer lawsuit found expression in the voice of Linda Estes, director of women's athletics at the University of New Mexico. Estes adopted a strong liberal feminist stance and employed an assertive, uncompromising rhetorical style that contrasted strongly with that of the majority of her AIAW colleagues. She was frustrated by the initial resistance to Title IX within the AIAW and by talk of an "educational model" that she viewed as elitist and discriminatory against women, especially because some women athletes needed the financial support of a scholarship to attend college. She was prepared to join the Kellmeyer suit or participate in a comparable action if necessary. In a 2006 interview, she acknowledged that she lacked patience with AIAW leaders who embraced feminism cautiously.[47]

Unlike many of her colleagues, Estes expressed her pro-equality, pro–Title IX stance bluntly, even undiplomatically. She insistently charged the AIAW with actually encouraging discrimination against women and characterized one leader's suggestion that athletes and coaches sought increased resources out of envy as "an unforgivable blunder."[48] She accused the AIAW of sexism and of ignoring the law, freely using loaded language to make her points, describing policies as "archaic," "stupid," and "illegal," and alleging that AIAW stood for the "Association for Interfering with Athletics for Women."[49] Perhaps most controversial was her firm conviction that preserving women's self-determination was less important than women gaining the same resources as men.

Estes's personal background explains, in part, the roots of her nonconforming voice. A self-described "political junkie," Estes was influenced by her grandmother, who was active in Democratic politics. Like Jean

Ledwith King, Estes served on the board of the American Civil Liberties Union in the 1970s, and she "would go so far as to bet there wasn't another [AIAW] colleague nationwide that was even a member of the ACLU."[50] She learned about sex discrimination and equal protection law from a case involving golfer Nancy Lopez. As a high school student, the future LPGA star wanted to play on the boys' team. Estes followed the case and the arguments employed by Lopez's attorney, Roberta Ramul, who was the first woman president of the American Bar Association.[51]

Estes's strong will and sense of clarity allowed her to take unpopular stances. In one early vote at the AIAW convention regarding the organization's position on Title IX, she was outvoted 351 to 1 by colleagues supporting a purely separate women's model. At the University of New Mexico, when Estes announced that they would give scholarships to women the next fall, she recalled, "The women in PE sent a memo to the university president saying I should be fired." But she knew "the country was changing," and unlike most of her colleagues, she advocated for change at her institution from a protected position. As she put it, "I had very good political contacts," including the governor and legislators, and "I would have been out of there in a New York minute if I hadn't been protected. That's what I had and most of the other women didn't have." Years later, Estes's institution hailed her as a valuable pioneer. The "university thought I saved them," she recollected, by pushing them in the direction the country was moving in anyway. Even so, she pointed out, "It was never equality. But for a long time we were making more progress than most other schools."[52]

Because backing from power holders enabled her strong discourse, Estes's philosophy and rhetorical style resembled fellow ACLU member King's "fight power with power" approach. Perhaps because of her secure position, Estes gave little thought to strategizing how to influence the recipients of her discourse; she simply spoke her mind. By all accounts, when it came to influencing AIAW leaders, she was unpersuasive and downright unpopular. Nevertheless, she represents an important grassroots voice that highlights tensions within the AIAW that challenged the organization's sense of identity. Her discourse confronted AIAW leaders with a feminist lens that they could not completely reject much longer.

Estes's perspective on women's rights, but not her rhetorical style, was shared by another influential leader of the period: Ellen "Lennie" Gerber, a physical education professor. Gerber spent significant time with those who held different views and, as Estes herself acknowledged, probably better understood them. In 1974, Gerber coauthored a groundbreaking book, *American Women in Sport*, which filled a stunning gap in the literature on sports—the dearth of research focused on women. Gerber's bibliography alone hints at the wide net she cast in writing her history, with titles such as these in each decade telling the story:

- "Fainting of Females During Public Worship" (1831)
- "A Medical View of Cycling for Ladies" (1896)
- "Interest in Sport and Physical Education as a Phase of Women's Development" (1915)
- *A Study of the Physical Vigor of American Women* (1920)
- "The Case For and Against Intercollegiate Athletics for Women" (1931)
- "Basketball for the Employed Girl" (1941)
- *The Revolt of the American Woman* (1952)
- *The Feminine Mystique* (1963)
- "Who are All These Women and What Are They Doing on My Golf Course?" (1972)

When Gerber turned her attention to more overtly rhetorical discourse, she brought this rich historical and social context to her persuasive work. Surely her historical perspective helped her understand the mindset of her audience as she strategically crafted appeals to influence those who disagreed with her stance on equality for women in sport. Her philosophical, logical, historical, and sociological approach contrasted sharply with Estes's bluntness. Gerber, who eventually left the physical education profession to work as an attorney, practiced a logic-based, translational rhetoric. Through logical appeals, humor, and indirection, she sought to translate a liberal feminist perspective to two audiences that, for different reasons, resisted her message: physical educators who viewed Title IX and the women's movement as a threat to their sex-separate culture and university administrators who had the power to provide resources to women's programs.

Whereas Estes worked on the front lines as an athletic administrator, dealing daily with both men and women who opposed her, Gerber worked as a scholar within academe. In the early 1960s, she had firsthand experience with the sports program at Ithaca College, where she "begged for money" for women's volleyball and basketball when they were allotted a budget of just five hundred dollars for both. "I said to them," she recalled, "you spent $500 on jock straps for men."[53]

Unlike many women physical educators, she had not been an athlete herself and admitted that physical education was an "odd" career choice; her father had encouraged her to be an attorney. As with Estes, Gerber's upbringing established her feminist sensibilities. She originally wanted to be an English major, and later earned a master's in English, but Boston University's Sargent College, a prestigious program for physical education, offered her a full scholarship. The daughter of two public school teachers, she learned to appreciate history from her historian father, and her parents modeled equality in handling household tasks, which Gerber considered typical in middle-class Jewish families. Her parents' value system, which emphasized social justice and socialist politics, led to her awareness of gender equality. She was also exposed to the black civil rights movement as a young person: when she traveled to the South, segregation outraged her, although she later experienced anti-Semitism in the movement that "gave her a reason to focus on the women's movement." Still, she saw all these causes as connected, and she was drawn to them by a "passion for equality."[54]

Gerber's experience with activism and knowledge of history gave her a different perspective than many colleagues in the physical education discipline. She opposed the practice of separate departments for men's and women's physical education, though when she experienced a merged department at Wayne State in the 1960s she was dismayed to find that women lost all their power in the transition and men controlled everything. This experience helped her understand why women physical educators initially resisted Title IX: she had seen how quickly they could lose power and control of their programs when they had to negotiate with men. Also, she saw that because separate departments had existed for so long, women physical educators "didn't realize they were being discriminated against. They weren't comparing."[55]

Gerber, however, noticed differences. In 1968, men and women met for their separate but comparable conferences at the same location, but the university covered more of the men's expenses. Gerber noted, "It was just absurd. I was outspoken." For those individuals who did not notice such inequities, it took Title IX to reframe their worldview; the legislation forced them to think about things differently, to look around and ask, "What does this mean?" Gerber understood their fear—"everyone wants things to be better, but no one wants change," as she put it. She described the field of physical education as "a little schizophrenic" because the prominent philosophies of sport tended to contradict one another; varsity athletics and coaches represented a whole different area and often were seen as distinct from the rest of the faculty.[56]

In 1970, Gerber initiated what she termed "a signature event" that catalyzed her subsequent persuasive work on behalf of women's college sports. While attending a National Association for Physical Education conference, she realized that it was the fiftieth anniversary of women's suffrage. She proposed a resolution on equality of women in honor of the anniversary, only to be met with disparaging remarks such as, "What's the matter with you, Lennie? Are you some kind of bra burner?" Younger women especially resisted the idea, as they had just begun their careers and had not yet noticed discrimination. Gerber persisted. The result was a three-hour meeting in which "everything was fought over," ending with "a resolution with all kinds of 'whereas' in it" in which those present pledged to fight for women's equality. Two years later, when the organization put up a resolution to support the proposed ERA, she felt gratified that her work had made a difference. When Title IX passed, Gerber's colleagues often first turned to her when they needed someone to talk with about the new statute.[57]

As legislators drafted the Title IX regulations, Gerber took a year off from her academic position and traveled the country, meeting with physical educators and college administrators, giving speeches, and holding press conferences. She needed to overcome the dichotomous idea that "men's sports were bad and women's sports were good." To do so, she reminded people that men's sports included much more than just the high-profile, often corrupt programs. She pointed out that college men played tennis, swam, wrestled, and participated in a multitude of intercollegiate sports in ways that were not exploitative but ethical.[58]

Both women's and men's sports, she believed, could find a workable model without following the path charted by men's big-time sports. Her main message was that "men and women are 80 percent alike, and differences are at the extremes." She reasoned it unnecessary to determine the path of women's and men's athletic programs based on dichotomous thinking and extremes; instead, she contended that many differences between women and men result from "how we are raised." "Human characteristics," she emphasized, "exist in both sexes, both good and bad." She rejected the idea of women as morally superior and therefore more responsible than men for charting an ethical course for college sports, often at the expense of their own opportunities. Using syllogistic reasoning, she presented the premise that "good traits should be emphasized in both sexes and the bad discouraged in both." Assuming people would find that premise hard to contest, she followed up with "if competition is good for men, then it is good for everyone." She employed emotional appeals, too, that "emphasizing differences just hurts people": "focusing on differences just hurts strong women and gentle men."[59]

When Gerber met individually with administrators, she sometimes used more indirect arguments and pointed humor that allowed the person she spoke with to get her point by filling in the conclusion themselves (with the effect being similar to the enthymeme, a logical appeal in which the missing premise is filled in by the listener or reader, enhancing the effectiveness of the appeal). When she visited a small college where the per diem was two dollars a day for women and five dollars a day for men, she was taken to visit the president. She did not confront him with a direct argument about the injustice of unequal resources. But she wanted to establish common ground around her premise that males and females are more alike than different, with the logical conclusion being that they deserved to be treated the same in comparable situations. So she asked if they could go downtown to get a cup of coffee. Then she said, "I'm curious whether they would charge you less than me for a sandwich."

Gerber recalled that he laughed and got the point, though she was not sure whether anything changed as a result.

These campus visits filled her year as she travelled about every ten days to different institutions, speaking to groups at each one. On her visits, Gerber interacted mainly with physical educators and higher-level male administrators and less often with AIAW members such as coaches and directors of women's varsity sports. However, with social change happening all around them, AIAW leaders, including the organization's presidents whom Estes confronted with her arguments, eventually experienced an awakening of their own. It could not happen soon enough to satisfy the skilled athletes whose window of opportunity to experience high-level college competition was limited to the four-year span of their college years.

A Silent Feminist: Christine Grant

Former AIAW President Donna Lopiano once called Title IX "an accident of history" that "unexpectedly threw [women's college sports leaders] onto the court in the national championship" with the expectation that they would "win one for the good guys."[60] In a series of speeches to AIAW delegates in 1980, Christine Grant, one of the organization's most respected presidents, reflected on her somewhat late emerging awareness that the interests of women athletes were tied to the interests of the women's movement:

> For years I have struggled, like you, with the various problems related to women's intercollegiate athletics; first one problem, then another, and another, all somewhat related, but not clearly so. At the same time, perhaps as a respite from intercollegiate athletics problems, I have concerned myself, to a limited extent, with the problems surrounding women in general.
>
> What had never dawned on me was the idea that what women in intercollegiate athletics are fighting for, is in actuality no different to what women generally in our nation are fighting for. It struck me that the main issue we face in women's athletics has little to do with athletics; what *is* at issue is the redefinition and acceptance of a new role for women in our entire society. This simple thought was for me, the key

to the puzzle. Somehow, fighting for small gains in various aspects of athletics has caused me to miss the forest for the trees.[61]

Grant's reflections allude to the "click" experience often described as a defining moment of a feminist consciousness-raising process. She described an ideological shift in worldview when "a mental framework is created" and regret for times she remained a "silent feminist . . . neglecting to stress [her] feminist beliefs."[62] With these new realizations, she came to envision women athletes as well positioned to become "troops leading the charge," reasoning that "women in sport already have an advantage over other women in our society, for we have already gained, through competitive sport, experience dealing with both challenge and apprehension."[63]

In the early 1970s, as debates over Title IX regulations heated up, Grant and other women athletics administrators had just begun to move toward such an empowered stance. They began to believe that women deserved more than crumbs and even embraced limited commercial opportunities for women's college sports (such as televised championships in some sports). Although this shifting stance led historians Ying Wushanley and Ronald Smith to label these women as hypocrites who sold out,[64] Festle's more sympathetic, feminist standpoint analyzed them as social movement actors operating from marginalized positions, accustomed to assuming that directly demanding more from those in power only made things worse. Festle attributed their conservatism and previous lack of political action to psychological oppression, having "unconsciously internalized society's attitudes and expectations" while "accept[ing] and promulgat[ing] exaggerated notions of difference between the sexes and of proper feminine behavior."[65] Their shift in attitude, then, demonstrated not hypocrisy but the transformative power of a new rhetoric: "Furnished with a new lens through which to view their conditions, most physical educators became less satisfied with them. They saw their efforts to improve women's sports as a continuation of their historical role, but provided in turn with a new, critical language, they began to call some of their treatment unjust."[66]

Emboldened by the language of feminist rhetoric, AIAW women's new critical consciousness also found support in the federal government's backing through Title IX. But they still feared and philosophically opposed a highly commercialized, win-at-all-costs model of sport.

Only when the NCAA unexpectedly put on a full-court press against Title IX did the trajectory of the AIAW's identity crisis take a definitive shift toward "equality" over "difference." The NCAA's heated opposition unified the AIAW in ways feminist discourse alone could never have accomplished, spurring AIAW leaders to turn their considerable rhetorical skills toward lobbying politicians to support a strong interpretation of the law's athletics regulations.

4 Full-Court Press

The National Collegiate Athletic Association

The physical educators who controlled women's college sports in the 1970s have been characterized as everything from victims (of discrimination by men), to oppressors (of other women), to idealistic reformers (seeking a new model of sport). What's certain is that when Title IX was enacted, few of them had experience with political action or activism. Feminist attorney Margot Polivy described them as "the least likely women to be involved in a social movement."[1]

But the NCAA was lobbying insistently to put their stamp on the Title IX regulations, and when they couldn't get athletics exempted entirely from Title IX, their goal became to exempt the high-revenue men's sports of football and basketball. If the most expensive men's sports need not be considered when comparing men's and women's athletic resources and opportunities, the result would, of course, be an extremely watered-down definition of equality. As it was, women's athletic budgets in 1974 were miniscule compared with men's, which were on average a whopping 98 percent higher.[2] At the AIAW national delegate assembly in 1973, an invited speaker from the Women's Equity Action League warned the delegates that they must not let their concerns about Title IX, or even their focus on creating a new model of athletics, prevent them from influencing how it would be interpreted. The motivation she gave them to start lobbying was clear: "the men are already doing it."[3]

Also in 1973, physical educators heard a similar message in a speech from their colleague Jan Felshin at their national convention. "The 'full court press' is a contemporary female strategy in social and legal

51

frameworks as well as basketball," Felshin stated. Described as a "provocative new thinker" in physical education, Felshin urged her colleagues to partner with feminists in their communities and to apply pressure tactics when necessary, "even at the risk of using 'masculine' methods of aggressive and unyielding demand."[4] In fact, they faced a formidable opponent, the NCAA, and a formidable ideology: the capitalist idea that lucrative programs should keep the funds they have earned for themselves. AIAW leaders also faced a stubborn misconception that high revenues automatically meant high profits. Even today, observers who see thousands of fans pouring into a college football stadium can hardly conceive that an NCAA football program could be operating in the red.

Despite their advantages, the leaders of the NCAA felt threatened. NCAA executive director Walter Byers feared what would happen if women teamed up: "It's tough for a woman to do battle with the football coach at a Division I-A campus, but a collection of determined women at the national level—with political support and media attention—could take on the NCAA and look very good indeed."[5] So the NCAA went on the offense, launching an assertive campaign to shape how members perceived Title IX and its draft regulations. Between 1974 and 1975, articles and editorials in the *NCAA News*, the organization's bimonthly newsletter, reflected an intense agenda-building process that alerted members to protect the interests of men's sports from the "threat" of federally mandated equality for men's and women's sports. What was missing from these articles is any reflection on the merits of arguments for equality, or even equity, in light of the undeniable discrepancies between men's and women's college sports programs. These articles did not frame women and their needs or rights under the law as the main issue. Instead, the articles created a crisis narrative that portrayed men's college sports as an innocent protagonist struggling against the prying federal government, an antagonist interfering in matters that should not concern it, oblivious to economic considerations, and intentionally bent on destroying men's college sports.

As feminist leaders from WEAL, the AIAW, and other women's groups began to confront the powerful anti–Title IX lobby of the NCAA, they faced a unified NCAA membership arguing vociferously that high-revenue-generating sports should not be subject to Title IX at all. They also faced what historian Mary Jo Festle aptly described as a rhetorically "astute" campaign spearheaded by NCAA executive director Walter Byers. This "shrewdly" conceived effort focused on *"limiting the change that did occur"* while publicly declaring support for women's sports and rarely attacking women or the basic American value of equality.[6] The NCAA claimed to be concerned about protecting the interests of women's college sports even as they stepped up a colonizing effort to merge the AIAW with the wealthier and more powerful NCAA.

Context for the NCAA Opposing Title IX

The men's sports establishment did not initially perceive Title IX as a threat. Congresswoman Edith Green had strategically counseled women's groups to not raise the subject of athletics as Congress debated the statute, fearing that the subsequent discussion could open a can of worms and sidetrack the legislation. Not surprisingly, then, the *NCAA News* did not mention Title IX until March 1, 1974. Up until that point, the NCAA had other problems holding its attention—most important, it faced financial challenges tied to overspending and the heightening economic recession. The organization also faced another examination by the same group of American colleges that investigated corruption in college sports during the 1950s (the investigation led halfheartedly by MSU president Jack Hannah). These contextual factors compounded the urgency with which the NCAA responded once Title IX registered on its radar. Considering the times, sexism (and resulting intentional or unintentional discrimination) undoubtedly shaped attitudes and responses to Title IX, especially behind the scenes. Sexism aside, however, financial considerations alone would have restrained men's athletics administrators from responding to Title IX with rhetorics of abundance, generosity, and support.

Financial Pressures

Even before the issue of sex discrimination had to be addressed under Title IX, the men's college sports establishment experienced economic difficulties and sometimes responded by cutting teams such as swimming, wrestling, tennis, and gymnastics.[7] In his 2000 article "Good Sports? Historical Perspectives on the Political Economy of Intercollegiate Athletics in the Era of Title IX, 1972–1997," John R. Thelin documented evidence that in Division I athletics programs, "expenses had been outpacing revenues for years—often in such allegedly 'revenue producing sports' as football and men's basketball."[8] He cited "wasteful" practices, including "large numbers of grants-in-aid for 'major' sports and for newly added sports; rejection of financial aid based on financial need in the NCAA Division IA group; construction and expansion of elaborate athletics facilities; and expansion of highly paid administration and coaching staff for selected sports."[9]

In addition to the financial burden created by escalating expenses related to spectator-oriented sports, members of the NCAA experienced the 1970s economic recession along with the rest of Americans. In January and February 1974, the newsletters of the NCAA sounded an alarm about a deepening recession in which the national energy crisis was "[squeezing] athletics."[10] The United States was under an oil embargo, and Americans faced calls for gasoline rationing, long lines at gas stations, and a national advertising campaign admonishing all consumers, "Don't Be Fuelish."[11] NCAA members resolved to reduce athletics-related travel, and one newsletter column listed seventy-four different ways to cut unnecessary costs, such as reducing long-distance travel for nonconference competition, adopting divisional play within the conference to reduce travel costs, and eliminating in-person scouting of opponents and "duplicative" trips for recruiting.[12]

Ironically, these more energy-efficient travel policies resembled the approach that women's programs had already taken under the AIAW philosophy that focused on state rather than conference championships and prohibited recruiting athletes altogether. The relative frugality exercised by women's programs resulted not only from the constraints of their comparatively small budgets but also from their educational philosophy of sport. Even though the AIAW officially rejected a highly commercialized model of college sports focused on entertaining the public and generating revenue, temptations of the commercial model held allure for women athletes as well (for example: publicity, prestige, celebrity, higher pay for coaches, corporate contracts that supplemented coaches' pay and provided personal clothing and equipment funds, and scholarships for athletes).[13] With all of these benefits at stake for men's sports leaders, the talk of energy-saving practices belied a deep-seated resistance to cutting back their programs in meaningful ways. On one hand, an NCAA member quoted in the February 1, 1974, newsletter asserted, "We will do our patriotic duty . . . along with millions of other Americans"; on the other hand, he warned, "we should not over-react and possibly damage our great game of intercollegiate football."[14] Another member put it this way: "college athletics will cooperate with the federal government" but will "not dilute the quality of our programs."[15] These comments suggest that room for cost cutting existed; however, they also illustrate the sacred tone in which NCAA members spoke of college football.

Commercialization and Academic Fraud

As NCAA leaders confronted the difficult economy, they depended on commercialization to sustain and promote college football and, increasingly, men's basketball. Having ignored the reports from the 1950s that called for abolishing spring football practice and postseason Bowl games, the NCAA faced further critique from a 1974 study sponsored by the American Council of Education and the Ford Foundation. The partial list of abuses showed that nothing had improved since the 1950s; if anything, problems had worsened. They included problematic public behavior of coaches and "altering transcripts, tampering with admissions tests; offering jobs to relatives of recruits; bait and switch financial aid offers; retaliatory tactics against athletes and families who refused recruitment; paying athletes with cash, cars, [and] housing; getting athletes grades for courses they never attended; using federal work study money to pay athletes for nonexistent jobs; kicking back work study monies to athletic departments; and forcing injured players to play."[16]

This outrageous list, however, caused far less of a public uproar than did Title IX itself. If college sports fans heard of the abuses that underwrote their college sports entertainment experience, they registered no public response. Instead, they seemed to turn a blind eye, flip on the TV, and enjoy the growing number of televised games. By the mid-1970s, television audiences had raised the commercial stakes for colleges: television revenues for football and men's basketball exceeded $25 million a year.[17]

Rhetorical Strategies

Remarkably, considering the publicly aired list of their abuses, writers in the March 1974 *NCAA News* complained that Title IX would impose "unrealistic administrative and operating requirements." They justified these complaints with statements noting that "impressive progress is being made in the development of women's intramural and intercollegiate programs on most, if not all college campuses."[18] They reminded their readers that the NCAA welcomed such progress and at its 1973 convention had even adopted its own policy against sex discrimination. Further positioning the NCAA as a supporter of women's sports, one writer claimed that having removed the restrictions placed on women by women themselves (that is, the AIAW scholarship policy), there was no need for a federal anti-sex-discrimination law to cover athletics. They contrasted their own "reasonable, practical manner" of addressing women's programs with the government's approach that would "seek to damage by design the revenue-producing sports programs and increase the $49.5 million annual deficit of NCAA members in conducting intercollegiate athletic programs."[19]

The writers seemed unaware of the contradiction inherent in their argument: if intercollegiate sports were managing their own affairs just fine without federal involvement, why were athletic departments running huge deficits even before Title IX came into the picture (not to mention being investigated for corruption and abuse of academic integrity)?

The NCAA's rhetorical strategy initially involved setting forth a series of reasoned arguments. A primary argument opposing the Title IX regulations emerged early on—namely, that Title IX should not apply to athletics because athletics are not specifically mentioned in the words of the statute enacted by Congress.[20] In addition, a member of the NCCA's legislative committee articulated another argument—one that has proven to have great traction with the public over the years—by asserting that income from men's sports, and from any revenue-producing sports, should be assigned to the administrators of those sports to allocate at their own discretion. This argument assumed a business model of sports and asserted an American capitalistic value; that is, those who earn capital should be rewarded with the profits of that capital. What often went unstated was the importance of all the "extras" in creating sports programs with the potential to generate revenue (clearly, investment in promoting particular teams and recruiting star players, then as now, creates increased opportunities to draw fans and bring in revenue). This argument also failed to acknowledge the reality that even revenue-producing men's sports rarely proved profitable after expenses were taken into consideration. Nor did these early debates reference the considerable benefits and resources enjoyed by college sports programs because of their status as part of nonprofit academic institutions—institutions that happen to also be subject to federal civil rights laws.

On March 15, 1974, the *NCAA News* summarized the agenda that its legislative committee was urging upon the US Department of Health, Education, and Welfare as its lobbying intensified. In this list of agenda items, the origins of several key criteria that became part of the final Title IX regulations and policy interpretations are strikingly apparent. The NCAA lobbied for *progress* in developing programs to count as *compliance*. This idea complemented an argument made in other civil rights discourse: that gradual progress toward equity was the most reasonable and practical approach. For instance, in *Brown v. Board of Education*, the Supreme Court determined that public schools need not be racially desegregated immediately but that change must proceed "with all deliberate speed." The NCAA similarly argued for the practicality of gradual change because women's competitive college sports programs started so much later than men's. The association also contended that *interest* expressed by students should be considered in determining what equity under Title IX would mean. This idea was likely comforting to men's sports leaders who felt certain that women were, and would continue to be, less interested in sports than men. NCAA leaders argued that the *ratio of male to female enrollment* should determine the athletic opportunities provided for each sex. Although men's athletic interest groups later attacked this idea as an unfair "quota system," the concept originated with the NCAA's lobbying efforts at the genesis of Title IX. During that time, the NCAA must have been well aware that men were attending college in higher numbers than women—only 42 percent of college juniors and seniors were women, according to the June 1, 1974, *NCAA News*. Finally, NCAA leaders writing in the newsletter also insisted the special needs of "revenue sports" must be considered, including allowance for donors to provide supplementary funds for men's sports presumed to be high moneymakers.

A month after the NCAA newsletter published its legislative committee's agenda concerning Title IX, writers in the next *NCAA News* objected that HEW's very early draft regulations in 1973 employed a definition of "nondiscrimination" that had too much "reach," extending to equal opportunity and even equal expenditures. NCAA writers objected strenuously to the idea of "instant equality" when boys' programs "have developed over a century."[21] An August 15 article claimed bluntly that "going to the extreme of complete equality is just ridiculous."[22] The organization's leaders seem to have recognized that, historically, women physical educators agreed with them on this point, in part because of what they viewed as ridiculous corruption in men's college sports.

Seizing a possible point of identification, the NCAA's discourse appealed to the traditional values promulgated by women's physical educators. A column entitled "Federal Money Can Haunt You in Unexpected Ways" warned that equal funding under Title IX would "produce an overmuscled women's sports program that even most women's athletic administrators don't want." This reference to "overmuscled" women clearly evoked the apologetic idea that women athletes don't want to build big muscles and look unfeminine. It also supported the NCAA's continuing contention that HEW simply did not understand college sports (men's or women's) and lacked the expertise to create compliance regulations.

A May 15, 1974, NCAA resolution further articulated the organization's hope for an alliance with women physical educators, whose stance toward restrictions on women athletes had suited the NCAA fine for decades. The NCAA called for "encouraging and promoting the orderly growth of competitive athletics for women," working closely and supportively "with leaders of the women's sports movement."[23] However, by this time, the women's sports movement leaders had begun to mobilize—and to view their own interests differently.

The AIAW on Defense

In 1974, the AIAW took a bold step to push back against the NCAA's challenges by hiring feminist attorney Margot Polivy, who put the AIAW in touch with women's groups such as NOW, WEAL, and the American Association of University Women.[24] The AIAW's leaders had noted the intense opposition to Title IX from the men's sports establishment, and they had already capitulated to the desires of highly skilled athletes seeking scholarships through the Kellmeyer suit. They knew they wanted a voice in the struggle to influence how HEW interpreted Title IX, so in the face of the NCAA's full-court offensive they implemented their own "press breaker."

With Polivy's guidance in navigating Washington politics, the AIAW organized a campaign to oppose an amendment to Title IX that would exempt revenue-producing sports from the law, proposed by Senator John Tower of Texas on May 20, 1974.[25] Among those who spoke before a congressional committee to oppose the amendment was N. Peggy Burke. A colleague of Christine Grant's at the University of Iowa, Burke was a professor of physical education and future AIAW president (1976–77). Her strong rhetorical skills, as well as her views on the relationship between language and power, are illustrated in her speech "Power and Power Plays: Women as Leaders," which was published in *Vital Speeches of the Day*.[26]

Although delivered in 1979, some years after her congressional testimony, that speech provided a window into an informal feminist rhetorical theory tailored specifically to athletic women. Burke urged the women physical educators and students in her audience: "First you must learn to recognize power plays and then you must formulate your own power plays. And don't allow yourself to be caught in a position of reacting to someone else's moves." She pointedly used the NCAA as an example of an organization capable of "brazen and obvious" power plays, as well as more subtle ones. In her list of steps to take if an individual chooses to engage in a power struggle, she recommended beginning with "the power of persuasion between reasonable people."[27] For women in particular (who have been socialized to project a "tentative and confined" physical presence), she emphasized the importance of projecting power through body language, something she noted may come readily to athletic women. However, she also acknowledged women athletes' socialization into apologetic postures and attacked that mode head on: "And you, my fellow movers, should have an advantage in this area because you have learned to have confidence in your body. But you were uniquely crippled in another way. Because society had defined weakness and softness as desirable characteristics for women and because you chose to be strong and skilled, you had to be dealt with. And so you were labeled abnormal and probably made to pay a terrible price for choosing to be physically competent."[28]

Burke urged women to embrace their strength and "feel comfortable striding into a room instead of mincing." She simultaneously emphasized the importance of critical thinking and the ability to "articulate your ideas in verbal and written form."[29]

In her testimony before Congress in 1975, Burke put her own rhetorical advice into practice. She pointedly critiqued the ambiguity of the Tower Amendment's language, especially interrogating the term "revenue-producing." She questioned how the amendment could prohibit something it had not even clearly defined. In fact, she claimed, all sports that charge admission bring in revenue, so the use of the word in the amendment was virtually meaningless. By the time Burke and others finished their testimony, the Tower Amendment had died in committee.[30]

In June 1974, a month after Tower proposed his amendment, a draft of the Title IX athletics regulations were completed and open for public comment until October 1974. The June 1974 draft sparked controversy—hearings across the nation resulted in 9,700 comments.[31] The response was large enough to prompt Secretary of Education Caspar Weinberger to observe sarcastically that he had no idea "that the most important issue in the United States today is intercollegiate athletics."[32] What Weinberger did not say, or perhaps failed to see, was that the controversy over Title IX and intercollegiate athletics represented a larger class of anxieties in American culture that were fueled by yet another challenge to traditional gender roles—in this case, Title IX's challenge to sports-related entitlements long associated with masculinity.

In response to the vigorous debate, Weinberger gave a June 18 press conference, a transcript of which is printed in the August 1, 1974, *NCAA News*. The secretary of education attempted both to placate and persuade the men's sports community. He emphasized that HEW was seeking to provide opportunity for women, not disruption for the NCAA. He sought to communicate an "attitude of cooperation, not coercion" and wanted institutions to comply voluntarily.[33] In language that echoed N. Peggy's Burke's arguments (and which could have been influenced by her discourse), he explained that revenue-producing was not a fixed category given that sports are not guaranteed to generate the same amount of money in any given year. Thus, he pointed out, the concept of "revenue sports" did not offer a useful distinction.[34]

In an editorial published in the same newsletter issue, the NCAA called Weinberger's commentary "tragic." The head of the NCAA's legislative committee continued to insist that not protecting the revenue sports (code for football and men's basketball) would damage "women as well as men."[35] The men even took a page from the women's playbook, pleading men's rights to "self-determination," a core argument of the AIAW women who wanted to develop their own model of sport.[36] In the next newsletter, an NCAA editorial entitled "Logic Lacking in Title IX Guidelines" predicted that "all of athletics seems destined to suffer under the Federal boot."[37]

The NCAA leaders' reasoning can be summed up in this simple logic: starve the breadwinner and you starve the whole family. Of course, 1970s feminists critiqued the gendered paradigm that assumes a male breadwinner. Furthermore, the men's sports establishment never acknowledged that a history of discrimination, not to mention corruption, contributed to the opportunities men's football and basketball had access to in order to become, or at least appear to be, "breadwinning" sports.

A Time Out

In October 1974, the NCAA and AIAW leaders met face to face, in part so that the NCAA could test the waters on its backup plan if it failed in efforts to restrict the reach of Title IX. The women assumed that they met to discuss differences between the rules of the NCAA and AIAW; however, the men hoped to persuade the AIAW to allow the NCAA to absorb women's programs. Afterward, the women felt the meeting brought them no closer to a common understanding,[38] while the NCAA more optimistically cited "fruitful and worthwhile discussions."[39] The different perceptions reflected their very different goals for the meeting. The lack of common ground was apparently interpreted by the NCAA as a signal to go ahead and move toward establishing its own women's championships, which would in effect allow the organization to control women's programs and their soon-to-be more equitable budgets under Title IX.[40] This move was the action that Burke later singled out as an example of a brazen power play.

On the Attack

As the NCAA proceeded with behind-the-scenes maneuvering, its newsletter used increasingly hyperbolic language on the topic of Title IX. The NCAA focused its attacks on HEW, calling HEW attorney Gwen Gregory ill qualified "to dictate to schools what is best for their students." They also deemed Title IX "superfluous" and "dangerous"[41] and characterized both Gregory and Weinberger as "people not knowledgeable in our field."[42] Gregory herself concluded that "the NCAA is determined to sabotage Title IX."[43]

The NCAA went so far as to decry HEW's involvement in the business of college sports, and the editor of the NCAA News denounced the United States as a "bureaucratic dictatorship" rather than a true democracy.[44] The president of Iowa State University wrote an article on the possible impacts of Title IX entitled "Assassination or Assimilation," in which he articulated fears that the law would require women's programs to receive the "extras" to which men's programs had grown accustomed: funds for "recruitment, financial aid, audiovisual equipment, and promotion."[45] The chair of the NCAA's legislative committee pleaded in the organization's newsletter that HEW acknowledge athletic departments' "rights to self-determination."[46] Here, the NCAA again mimicked an appeal to self-determination that they often heard from women physical educators as the women resisted being subsumed under the NCAA.

Networking

After the proposed regulations were published in June 1974, both women's groups and the NCAA cultivated their networks in Washington. During this time, President Nixon resigned over the Watergate scandal, which meant that Gerald Ford, the incoming president, would sign the Title IX regulations. The lobbying brought victories for both the NCAA and women's sports advocates.

Most notably, the Javits Amendment was passed, providing "reasonable provisions" for differences in sports. In a blow to women's sports advocates who sought full equality, the amendment stipulated that equal *per capita* expenditures for men's and women's programs sought by women's sports advocates were not required; in fact, certain sports could even increase expenditures. Seen as a loophole in Title IX by women's sports advocates, the amendment seemed designed to tacitly protect spending on one certain sport in particular: football. Its language opened the door for a status quo argument often repeated in years to come—that differences based on the *type of sport*, including its ability to generate revenue, could not be construed as *sex* discrimination.[47] The notion of what constitutes "reasonable provisions" continues to be open to wide, yet rarely questioned, interpretation.

The struggle over the regulations did not end even after President Ford signed them into law in May 1975. Congress was permitted forty-five days to approve the regulations, leaving more room for debate. This part of the ongoing controversy played out during Ford's administration, and Congressman O'Hara (from Ford's home state of Michigan) took up a campaign to exempt football from the law's regulations, while the University of Michigan's athletics director Donald Canham became an outspoken advocate for exempting football from any regulations governing Title IX. Director of athletics at Michigan from 1968 to 1988, Canham was respected by his peers around the country as an innovative and highly successful promoter of college football. Remembered today for transforming "glorified intramural games into big-time, big-money athletics, one of the country's most enduring traditions," he strongly opposed any regulations for Title IX that treated football the same as other sports.[48]

Canham's position found an advocate in Senator John Tower, who introduced a second amendment (Tower II) that again proposed exempting athletics from Title IX. Six other senators also worked together to submit resolutions that would prohibit Title IX's application to athletics. However, strong advocates for women's rights in the House and Senate, including Senator Birch Bayh, pushed back and successfully blocked these early efforts to exclude athletics from the law's provisions. Undeterred, leaders of men's athletics and their supporters in Washington continued to push for regulations that exempted, or at least somehow protected, football's resources and special place in college sports.

To understand better the behind-the-scenes forces that sought to shape Title IX athletics regulations, it is helpful to consider the importance of football in President Ford's life and career, as it relates to the power of gendered sports networks to influence policy at the highest levels of government. After Ford graduated from Michigan, a football coaching job at Yale got his foot in the door for admittance to Yale Law School, which positioned him for a career in politics. Later Nixon's Watergate crimes and his trust in Ford's abilities opened the door to the White House, but the Michigan alum's participation in big-time college athletics was also part of his trajectory. His life story supports the feminist argument that sports opportunities—including networks created and experience gained performing under huge amounts of pressure and scrutiny—are as important for women as for men.

In the 1970s, though, women did have a strong advocate in the White House in First Lady Betty Ford, who pushed for the ultimately failed Equal Rights Amendment and thereby created difficulties for her husband with some of his more conservative supporters. The Ford Presidential Museum in Grand Rapids, Michigan, includes an ERA display with an excerpt from a *Seventeen* magazine article in which the Fords' daughter, Susan, described her love for "all sports." However, amid exhibits displaying 1970s memorabilia, the story of Watergate, and plenty about University of Michigan football, nothing in the museum mentions Title IX.

By contrast, in the Ford Presidential Library in Ann Arbor, Michigan, archival materials document how Ford administration attorneys dealt with the Title IX regulations for college athletics. Among the materials is a letter from head University of Michigan football coach Bo Schembechler to President Ford. His letter reflects the unique access that coaches of big-time men's college sports had to the president as they sought his support for their campaign to repeal the very regulations he had just signed. While feminist groups had the ear of a First Lady committed to equal rights for women, football coaches and men's athletics directors had the ear of the president and his advisors.

The tone of the letter is striking: Schembechler addressed Ford with familiarity, as "My dear Mr. President."[49] The letter's heading features a picture of the football stadium at the University of Michigan, and the letterhead reads "Michigan Football Department," rather than "Athletics Department." This language choice communicated a football-centric view of college athletics that made frequent proposals to exempt football from Title IX seem entirely reasonable. Proponents of this interpretation of Title IX contended that football should be considered a "third sex" and not included in any contrasts between opportunities provided for males and for females.

Dated July 14, 1975, the letter would have reached Ford just days before the Title IX regulations were due for release on July 21. The first sentence references a recent personal meeting with Ford and expresses gratitude for the president's "interest and concern in the major problems and damages which HEW's sex-discrimination rules threaten to impose on college athletics." It summarizes the NCAA attorneys' understanding of the regulations and expresses concern "that some remedial action be taken soon" to protect the interests of college athletics.[50] Schembechler equated college athletics with men's athletics and especially with football. His language shows that he did not consider women's athletics as a legitimate part of college athletics, an interpretation verified by his actions; for example, he famously opposed University of Michigan women athletes being awarded a varsity letter that was the same size as the traditional "M" awarded to the men.

The renowned football coach's concerns both echo and undermine some of the primary arguments that still today continue to be marshaled in opposition to Title IX's regulations and their interpretations. The regulations Ford was preparing to sign in 1975 required that males and females be offered athletic scholarships in proportion to their participation in sports. Schembechler, however, implied that he preferred a common measure of skill and accomplishment be applied regardless of the athlete's sex. It is not clear whether he really believed such a "gender blind" approach would be more fair or only that it would better prevent "injury to intercollegiate athletics." He did, though, clearly address the issue of whether women are as interested as men are in athletics, an ongoing point of contention in debates over gender equity. Schembechler pointed out the regulations' stipulation that "facilities, coaching, scheduling, travel, etc. provided for female student athletes need to be equal to what is provided for male athletes if females are just as interested in athletic programs that are suited to their abilities and interests."[51]

Schembechler's grounds for objecting to this policy appear in a parenthetical statement: he could not imagine how an institution "can possibly prove that female students would not be interested in, for example, a counterpart to the football team's participation in the Rose Bowl."[52] Here, Schembechler implicitly acknowledged that women are just as interested as men in events that celebrate, acknowledge, and advertise their accomplishments in athletics. Schembechler's comment inadvertently underlined the injustice of making participation in high-profile events, such as the Rose Bowl, available to only male students at the University of Michigan and other federally funded institutions. It seems that he intended to point out the impossibility of schools financially supporting such opportunities for both males and females, even though conventional wisdom asserts that Bowl competitions make money to support whole athletics departments. While they do generate considerable revenue, the hidden, often recurring costs of these events—including extraordinary investments in stadiums, recruiting, coaches' salaries, special practice fields, and promotions—are seldom emphasized or calculated.

Finally, in a blatant appeal to the power of sports celebrity, the letter reminded Ford that Schembechler was speaking on behalf of other well-known football coaches when he requested that the president take action to support men's intercollegiate athletics in the face of Title IX. The coach cited two names: Darrell Royal of the University of Texas and Barry Switzer at the University of Oklahoma.[53]

Ford took action. On July 21, 1975, as the Title IX regulations took effect, he wrote letters to the chairs of the House and Senate subcommittees with jurisdiction over Title IX. These subcommittees were already hearing testimony concerning a resolution by Congressman O'Hara of Michigan that would exempt "certain intercollegiate activities from Title IX."[54] Ford informed them that he welcomed congressional hearings on the O'Hara bill.

No evidence exists that suggests President Ford personally intervened in the congressional deliberations. However, the fact that these coaches could take their case to the president of the United States speaks to the power of men's sports networks and to the political and professional price women pay when excluded from them. The NCAA itself had made a point of reminding President Ford that he belonged to a brotherhood of football athletes when they honored him with their Theodore Roosevelt Award in 1975, just months before the president was asked to sign the controversial Title IX regulations. Perhaps not coincidently, the NCAA News reported in its January 1, 1975, issue that the award is named for a former president who "prevented the abolishment of intercollegiate football by calling together college administrators to formulate a regulation of rules in 1905. The NCAA was formed in 1906."[55] Could the implied message have been that, once again, a president was called upon to save college football?

The article, entitled "Ford Recipient of 1975 'Teddy' Award," appeared on the front page above an article entitled "Sen. Tower Comments on Title IX Regulations," which continued a few pages later with a nearly full-page discussion under the headline "Tower Comments Reveal Serious Flaws in Title IX." In the same issue, the News quoted Representative Edith Green (the sponsor of Title IX in the House of Representatives) claiming that if Title IX ended up requiring sex-integrated physical education classes (it does) and sex-integrated contact sport teams (it makes exceptions for contact sports), then she would view such interpretations of the law as "nonsense" and "overboard." Even though Green never disputed that Title IX should apply to athletic programs in some fashion, the headline stated the point that the NCAA wanted to communicate: "HEW 'Overboard' on Title IX—Green." The NCAA's message was clear: even Title IX's greatest supporters thought the law was going too far.[56]

AIAW Guerrilla Tactics

While the NCAA worked with members of Congress to limit the impact of Title IX, at their 1975 national conference, its members also began to pursue seriously the idea of offering women's championships. If they couldn't limit or eliminate Title IX, they wanted to profit from the growth of women's college sports or at least control their future. When the AIAW leaders got wind of this effort the day before the 1975 NCAA convention, they used "guerilla tactics"[57] to prevent the NCAA from (secretly) voting to adopt women's championships. Women attending the AIAW's 1975 national convention, held at the same venue as the NCAA meeting, coordinated an effort to confront their own schools' NCAA delegates simultaneously. As the NCAA delegates gathered together in the hotel lobby, the AIAW women lobbied delegates from their own institutions to oppose the efforts of NCAA leaders who sought to control both men's and women's sports. These tactics proved successful: the women forestalled the move by the NCAA, at least for the moment. The AIAW leaders and members had worked together to defend their right to determine their own future.[58]

O'Hara Resolution Hearing

Statements and testimony submitted for a July 14, 1975, congressional hearing on the O'Hara Resolution before the Subcommittee on Equal Opportunities of the Committee on Education and Labor exhibit further examples of the persuasive appeals marshaled by athletic leaders who opposed Title IX's athletics regulations and by education and women's groups who supported them. Statements by Louisiana Tech athletics director Maxie T. Lambright and WEAL director Norma Raffel represent themes of the discourse each side employed.

Lambright's testimony invoked a language of crisis and completely avoided the term "discrimination." Although he had claimed that he was "not against women's athletics" and noted that Louisiana Tech "provides intercollegiate athletic teams for these young ladies," he contended that concerns for women's opportunities paled when compared with the importance of preserving the history and tradition of men's intercollegiate sports.[59] College sports for men, he testified, "have played an important part in the history of our nation and [are] today part of our American heritage."[60] He feared for the "survival" of athletic departments if they were subject to HEW's regulations, which he termed a "death knell" that would "destroy college athletics as we now know them."[61] In addition to using apocalyptic language to describe the consequences of reducing resources for men's sports, he ignored the obvious risks for women in his alternative proposal: that change in women's programs take place at a pace and to an extent deemed reasonable by leaders of men's athletics.

Specifically, Lambright called for Americans to trust the nation's male sports leaders to do the right thing, in their own time, "on their own volition."[62] But he also pointed out that comparable funding for men's and women's athletic programs would be impossible. So why should leaders of men's athletics be trusted? To address this anticipated question, Lambright cited a recent meeting of the NCAA at which its leaders discussed cost containment measures under consideration for men's athletics such as "fewer scholarships, limited numbers of coaches, less scouting, devaluation of scholarships, limiting the size of traveling squads, and many other things." The NCAA's challenge, he explained, was to identify ways to cut costs and "still keep a program which is attractive to the paying public."[63] He failed to mention that these cost-cutting measures were presented in other forums as a patriotic response to the adverse economic conditions of the 1970s. Nor did he go so far as to suggest that downsizing men's athletics to allow for growth in women's programs was likewise a patriotic duty. And he did not address whether women's programs might appeal to a paying public or question whether public entertainment and revenue generation ought to be the focus of college sports at all.

Assurances of trustworthiness from men's athletic leaders and promises that they could impartially guide a process of change must have sounded like the fox watching the henhouse to feminist leaders who also submitted statements to Congress. The term "sex discrimination" hardly seemed part of the men's sports leaders' vocabulary. Norma Raffel, the head of WEAL, who was not herself involved with girls' or women's athletics, submitted to the congressional Subcommittee on Equal Opportunities a detailed, four-page statement in which she used the word "discrimination" twenty-five times.[64] In contrast, the only time the term "sex discrimination" appeared in statements submitted for the hearing by members of the men's sports establishment is when the president of the National Association of Basketball Coaches, Bill Foster (Duke University), referred to the Title IX regulations as having been written "under the pretense of eliminating sex discrimination."[65] This reference underscored the reluctance of men's athletics directors to label differences in funding as discriminatory, a word that to them may have implied intentionally disparate treatment. Differences in athletic funding and opportunity, in their view, simply resulted from different traditions for males and females that reflected long-standing societal traditions rather than purposeful discrimination. They implicitly argued that unintentional discrimination was not actually discrimination at all.

Raffel devoted the second half of her lengthy statement to athletics in particular (after focusing for two pages on the scope of Title IX's coverage). She began by citing studies of high school and college sports programs that show evidence of gross underfunding of girls' and women's sports. Midway through her statement, she pointed to the value Americans place on healthy minds and bodies as the basis for her arguments: "The American public has supported athletic programs because it is convinced that such activities help develop sound minds and bodies. Yet half of the students—girls and women—are largely excluded. They are deprived of the benefits of active sports participation including the opportunity to establish life-time habits of exercise which promote an increased level of good health in adult life."[66]

Raffel then refuted arguments employed by the NCAA, especially those concerning money. She admitted that sharing limited resources would be "something of a shock," but she contended that doing so would be necessary to go from "preferential treatment to equal treatment."[67] However, she also yielded to the power of the status quo by emphasizing that under Title IX, women were not expecting full equality and equal expenditures but rather equal opportunity appropriate for female's interests and abilities. She pointed out that only one in ten athletic departments made a profit and argued (as Thelin did again twenty-five years later) that the NCAA's own deficits were more likely than Title IX to "end intercollegiate athletics as we have known it."[68] She attacked the NCAA for arguing to exempt profit-making sports from Title IX, characterizing the attitude as mercenary: "when dollars come in, principle goes out!"[69] She contrasted the pursuit of profit with the pursuit of healthy minds and bodies, while acknowledging that more needs to be learned about physiological differences between males and females and how those differences should affect our understanding of equal opportunity in athletics.

Raffel's acknowledgment of a need to consider the significance of physical differences between the sexes with regard to sports complicated a standard 1970s liberal feminist call for equality as "sameness." At the same time, like sportswomen themselves, she stopped short of allying herself completely with the most radical "difference feminists" who advocated for separatism and celebration of women's differences. These groups rarely participated in conversations about sports, which they saw as a thoroughly male-dominated, male-created preserve that would need to be completely reinvented to be suitable for women.

To conclude her statement, Raffel tied her appeal specifically to the liberal feminist tradition. She noted that "more than 100 years ago at a conference in Pennsylvania, women called for more educational opportunities for their daughters—a goal not yet achieved."[70] In this appeal, she also firmly subsumed athletics under the umbrella of education. By contrast, the NCAA and men's athletic leaders rarely emphasized the connection between the two. In debates over sex discrimination or equal opportunity, the NCAA usually considered it more advantageous to argue that athletic programs operated separately from the educational activities of schools and universities. They used this argument despite assertions by Raffel and subsequently by numerous women's sports advocates that men's athletics programs often depend on "student activity fees or the educational dollar."[71]

The statements at the hearing suggest the extent to which men's college sports leaders benefited from the unified backing of the NCAA. The NCAA's rhetorical strategy depended on repetition of arguments based on income and profit, separation of athletics from academics, and the special place of college men's sports in the hearts of American sports fans. The men who spoke for the NCAA's interests adeptly implemented the strategy of repeating key points frequently and with confidence, a practice that works well when arguments connect with already-established values and beliefs. Quite simply, the prospect of being required to spend equal amounts on men's and women's athletics was unacceptable to them.

Even aside from financial considerations, which were undoubtedly paramount, these leaders appeared ideologically and sociologically unprepared to share power and control. Based on appeals to tradition and the special status of football in American culture, they argued to preserve a patriarchal structure that retained autonomy, control, and decision-making power for men's sports leaders. They implored women's groups to trust that they would adequately provide for the needs of female athletes if they were assimilated into male-directed athletics departments and participated in NCAA-sponsored competitions. Despite these well-articulated arguments, they never promised complete equality among all teams, citing economic constraints. They assumed women would naturally take their place on the second rung of their sports hierarchy, among the lower-revenue-generating men's teams. If the NCAA realized its integrated vision, women's athletics would never become more than a pale image of the most privileged men's sports.

5 Transition to Equality

The 1975 Title IX Athletics Regulations

When Congress finally approved the 1975 Title IX regulations, the US Department of Health, Education, and Welfare had mandated what is often described as a "separate but equal" approach to college athletics. The phrase "separate but equitable," however, is more accurate. Consider former AIAW President Christine Grant's reflections on the meanings and connotations of the terms "equality" and "equity" in her 1977 essay, "What Does Equality Mean?" She pondered what she called "the problem of words," suggesting that the 1975 regulations placed intercollegiate athletics in a transitional phase. As Grant put it, the regulations put guidelines in place for women's college sports to "accelerate the *move toward* equality." However, she believed that the law could not possibly "merge two unequal parts and create a whole which demonstrates equality." Based on her reading of the regulations, Grant conceded that "while equality might be the immediate objective, perhaps equity should be the immediate objective." Turning to a dictionary definition, Grant defined equity as that which is "just" or "fair." By contrast, she pointed out that "equality" or "equal opportunity" could be defined as involving either *no differences* in opportunities and benefits or *comparable* opportunities and benefits.[1]

Grant accurately characterized Title IX's regulations as a guide through a transitional stage. They did not mandate equality, but they gave agents of change a basis from which to argue for ongoing movement toward it. They also protected big-time men's college sports from having to immediately share resources with women's intercollegiate athletics. In short, they affirmed and protected the interests of both the status quo and of those seeking change.

In general, the regulations require that schools designate a responsible employee to coordinate efforts to comply with Title IX and adopt grievance procedures (a Title IX coordinator). The regulations require "reasonable opportunity"[2] for female athletes to earn athletic scholarships; they allow for (but don't require) separate teams segregated by sex (with special stipulations related to contact sports and situations in which no team is offered for members of the historically excluded sex); and they require equal opportunities to be available for males and females based on ten factors. These factors, sometimes called the Title IX "Laundry List," include the following:

1. Whether the selection of sports and levels of competition effectively accommodate the interests and abilities of members of both sexes
2. The provision of equipment and supplies
3. Scheduling of games and practice times
4. Travel and per diem allowance
5. Opportunity to receive coaching and academic tutoring
5. Assignment and compensation of coaches and tutors
7. Provision of locker rooms as well as practice and competitive facilities
8. Provision of medical and training facilities
9. Provision of housing and dining facilities and services
10. Publicity[3]

A key statement appears at the end of the list: "Unequal aggregate expenditures for members of each sex or unequal expenditures for male and female teams if a recipient operates or sponsors separate teams will not constitute noncompliance with this section, but the Assistant Secretary may consider the failure to provide necessary funds for teams for one sex in assessing equality of opportunity for members of each sex."[4]

Based on this statement, the regulations do not require equal expenditures for each individual athlete, nor do they require the same amount of money to be spent on women's teams as is spent on men's teams. Instead, the regulations take into account the fact that if males and females participate in different sports, costs for necessary equipment and other expenditures may vary from sport to sport. Football was, and continues to be, the most expensive sport because of its equipment costs and large team sizes.[5]

Overall, the 1975 athletics regulations exact a compromise that simultaneously protects two competing interests often articulated by lobbyists: (1) the opportunity for girls and women to develop as athletes without having to compete directly with males, and (2) the special status of football. The regulations' statement that equal aggregate expenditures for men's and women's programs were not required was a clear concession to the men's athletic establishment. In particular, it protects football—as long as that sport requires more equipment, includes as many as eighty-five scholarship players on a roster (which was more than any other sport in 1975), and continues to draw more spectators than other sports (which bring with them associated event-management costs). In short, institutions are free to spend what they deem necessary on men's football as long as they provide "necessary" funds for women's teams in each of the areas listed. The term "necessary," of course, is open to interpretation.

Women athletes, in turn, obtained their own sought-after protections in the 1975 Title IX regulations, which allow for single-sex teams, a guarantee women's athletic administrators argued was necessary to ensure equal opportunity. With sex-segregated teams, women need not compete for playing opportunities directly against male athletes, whose skills as a group had developed through decades of expert coaching, highly competitive playing opportunities, and social support. Advocates for women's sports also cited physiological sex differences in strength, height, and weight that would exclude large numbers of interested and skilled women in most sports if they were required to compete with men. Both at the time and in recent years, some feminists have argued that such sex-segregation amounts to discrimination because separate teams can never be truly equal; likewise, some legal experts have charged that the regulations' allowance for separate teams is unconstitutional because separate teams are inherently unequal. In 1975, though, most women's sports advocates welcomed a sex-separate model. Some of them simply objected to the regulations' prohibition against girls and women joining men's teams in contact sports when all-female teams were unavailable in sports such as football, basketball, or ice hockey. They contended that, along with purporting to protect women, the prohibition also and conveniently protected the most masculine sports from "invasion" by women.

Summing up the situation in June 1975, the *New York Times* reported that while the nation's athletics directors and football coaches labeled the Title IX regulations as "destructive," women's groups described them as "ineffective."[6] Certainly, they were open to an ongoing process of contestation and interpretation. Because the regulations rely on defining terms such as "reasonable," "fair," "comparable," and "necessary," gray areas abound, leaving room for legal contests, debate within institutions, and federal auditors' mediation in response to complaints. Thus a decades-long rhetorical battle began. Groups representing competing interests sought to convince lawmakers and the public at large to hear their stories and support their favored interpretations of "equity." These persuasive efforts ultimately determine the real impact of any law, with a host of factors coming into play: "the intensity of opponents' resistance, the capacity of beneficiaries of Court decisions to capitalize on them, the ease with which particular rulings are evaded, the availability of sanctions against those who violate rights, the relative attractiveness of rights-holders, and the availability of lawyers to press claims."[7]

To implement the goals set forth in the Title IX athletics regulations, the federal government eventually provided further guidance, beginning with an official 1979 policy interpretation. In subsequent years, other statements issued by the US Department of Education's Office for Civil Rights provided additional direction, most notably a highly influential letter of clarification in 1996 (the letter established three options for complying with Title IX's requirements for participation opportunities, options known as the "three-part test").[8] In the meantime, colleges and universities had a generous three-year period, until July 1978, in which to begin a federally mandated transition toward equality. During this extended period of time, administrators, athletes, coaches, attorneys, and members of the general public wrestled with interpretations, resisted the law's regulations, or fought for their rights under the law.

By 1975, hundreds of Title IX complaints concerning high school and college athletics had already been filed with HEW, and a growing number of lawsuits were filed in the courts. Overwhelmed by the flood of complaints, HEW announced that it "was trying to get away from a 'mailbag' approach of having to investigate every complaint within 90 days" and would instead wait until "a pattern developed." WEAL objected, "It's kind of like having a police department saying it won't respond to complaints because they are too busy." Bernice Sandler predicted that HEW's new approach would "push women . . . into the courts."[9]

Sandler's prediction proved true. By 1978, college athletics cases were making their way into courts across the country. At the time, it remained unclear whether individuals even had the right to sue under Title IX. If they did, it was unclear whether universities receiving state funds were immune from monetary damages in Title IX lawsuits. During that uncertain time, the Michigan State University women's basketball team filed internal and federal Title IX complaints. In 1979, they were among the first college athletes to file suit in federal court. Their institutional and legal struggles demonstrate which appeals for equality were available, viable, and effective in Title IX's first decade.

PART TWO

Grassroots of Change

In 2005, the MSU women's basketball program began annually inviting former players to campus to share a brunch, see a game, tour the facilities, meet current players, and reconnect with teammates and coaches. In 2007, I attended this event, called "A Day of Gratitude," and invited attorney Jean Ledwith King to join me as a guest. I had just met King and had begun researching her role in the 1979 lawsuit filed by the MSU women's basketball team, *Hutchins v. Board of Trustees of Michigan State University*. I wanted her to see what three decades of change and struggle had brought to the MSU women's basketball program. And I wanted to learn more about the program's past by bringing the past and present together.

Just two years earlier, under coach JoAnne McCallie, the MSU women's basketball team had experienced a spectacular season, making it to the NCAA Final Four and defeating Pat Summit's University of Tennessee team before losing to Baylor University in the national championship game. The team's success afforded their coach other opportunities. After McCallie left the Spartans to coach at Duke, MSU's new coach, Suzy Merchant, was charged with continuing to build the program.

On a cold December day, my husband and I drove north from Virginia to meet a few former MSU players in Detroit before picking up Jean Ledwith King in Ann Arbor and continuing on to East Lansing. MSU faced Ohio State that day, and we looked forward to a competitive, closely matched contest. But when we walked into Breslin Center, a state-of-the-art facility filled with thousands of serious, excited fans, we saw a whole new world of women's basketball, one that players from past eras feel both part of and separate from. The contrast with sparsely attended games in the 1970s and 1980s was unmistakable and poignant.

"Shock and awe" were the first words that came to mind for my teammate Ronna Greenberg Bordoley (1983–86) when she saw the $7.5 million Alfred Berkowitz Basketball Complex. Her second thought was that "with all this, they better win." The 2008–9 media guide described MSU's facilities as "one of the finest in the nation," including a spa-like locker room, portraits of each player above her locker, and high tech features such as a "mini theatre" for videos, press conferences, team meetings, or coaching sessions. "A serious upgrade" was Lorraine (Lori) Hyman's wry observation as she contrasted the present-day coach's office with the "hole in the wall" that her coach, Karen Langeland, once inhabited.

Just across the hall, separated by a grand rotunda, the men's facilities are nearly identical, though with even more video equipment and production staff, reflecting the still significantly larger role of the men's program as a national sports entertainment provider. Directly or indirectly, MSU's facilities have become a model for the nation's aspiring and established big-time basketball programs. Virginia Tech, for example, completed its own $21-million facility in 2009, including "every imaginable feature needed to build a program," according to the 2012–13 media guides. Such facilities, the argument goes, are needed to attract top players and achieve the often-articulated goal of intercollegiate athletics: to compete at the highest level. Looking at these facilities, and still grander ones for top football programs, it's hard to believe that men's athletic leaders ever feared that Title IX would destroy men's college sports.

Not only have participation opportunities in college sports for men survived, but the growth of women's sports has not deterred the "arms race" for increasingly opulent facilities and spectacular events in men's basketball and football programs. In a nod to gender equality, some institutions now ensure that women's basketball programs receive comparable facilities, but their programs are still considered a distant third priority to men's football and basketball. Within athletic departments—and unabashedly to the tax-paying public—sports administrators and even many women's coaches accept this hierarchy of priorities as "natural." Some of these same coaches would be hard pressed to explain exactly what Title IX's regulations require, with many of them under the mistaken impression that Title IX simply requires similar teams to be treated equally but leaves football out of the equation. These assumptions remain largely unquestioned even after forty years under Title IX. One big-time college sports administrator who asked not to be identified told me, "In our administrative meetings, we never talk about Title IX. It's irrelevant. All that matters is money."

At MSU in the mid-2000s, women's basketball teams started attracting crowds comparable to those the Spartan men's teams drew in the 1970s, including a record-breaking fifteen thousand fans at one home game. Meanwhile, the men's team had upped the ante. Their celebrity coach, Tom Izzo, was now paid millions per year, and the athletic department staged creative events designed to draw national and worldwide attention, such as playing on an aircraft carrier for US military troops. Aspirations for making men's intercollegiate athletics visible and profitable seemed unbounded. This dynamic of upping the ante is summed up in the memorable title of former Stanford University and professional basketball player Mariah Burton Nelson's 1994 book, *The Stronger Women Get, the More Men Love Football.*[1]

In the decades after this book's publication, much has changed for women athletes, yet much remains the same. Many—if not most—intercollegiate female athletes are well provided for, but gender equality remains elusive. Specific knowledge of how to evaluate equality under Title IX—and the will to struggle further to change an intractable sports hierarchy—is in short supply. Meanwhile, even in bleak economic times, athletic departments continue to boast of the royal treatment they provide for athletes, coaches, and administrators. And the sports-loving public, despite high unemployment rates and cities struggling to make ends meet, continues to cheer them on.

On a brighter note, many women athletes now enjoy the appreciation and applause once reserved for men. The spirit of genuine celebration and support that pervades MSU's Breslin Center during Sunday afternoon women's basketball games represents a giant step forward for the women's sports movement. As sports history shows, athletics have long been a vehicle for the devaluation as well as the empowerment of girls and women.

Empowered by their sporting experiences, many of the individuals you will meet in the pages that follow are still involved with education and athletics, now with decades of first-hand experience in roles ranging from player to coach, teacher, and senior athletic administrator. In the story of Spartan women's basketball, we see how a group of determined individuals used the power of student activist rhetoric to reject the lower social value placed on them as female athletes.

6 Spartans

In 1975, the same year President Ford signed the new federal regulations for implementing Title IX, Michigan State University sought two new basketball coaches—one for the men's team and one for the women's. While the budgets for men's teams (other than football) in 1975 would have been considered skeletal by today's standards, women's varsity teams in *every* sport were starving. With change in the air, the new coaches hired for men's and women's basketball at MSU would each help usher in a new era for their sport.

Two seemingly parallel movements shaped the new era in college athletics: one toward gender equality fueled by the proposed national Equal Rights Amendment and Title IX, the other toward commercialization. But the two movements were intertwined. To increase resources for women athletes required raising additional revenue, reducing expenditures for men's sports, or combining the two approaches. Raising more revenue held an obvious appeal at schools with highly competitive athletics programs, especially because men's college sports had already long ago separated from their roots in academic physical education programs. Commercialization promised more money, status, and celebrity for universities as a whole and sports programs specifically. For many taxpayers who support public higher education, these sports and associated "tailgating rituals, painted faces and screaming fans" offered a highly visible point of connection more accessible than "physics labs and seminars on Milton."[1] And, rationally or not, as college athletes imagine their possible futures, they often look ahead to professional sports, just as many high school kids are motivated by dreams of a college scholarship.

In the mid-1970s world of sports, men's professional athletics was becoming increasingly commercialized, with players receiving product endorsement contracts and the first million-dollar salaries. College players began to see dollar signs as they fantasized about professional careers. By the end of the decade, women's basketball would launch a professional league, the Women's Basketball League (WBL). This enterprise also relied upon corporate sponsorships and media contracts to stay afloat. Although salaries in that new league would be too low to provide even a year's living wage, the league gave women who played college basketball just a hint of the hoop dreams that motivated so many young men.

Meanwhile, the launch of twenty-four-hour sports programming fueled the commercialization of men's college athletics. In 1979, the new ESPN network quickly negotiated the rights to broadcast early rounds of a men's NCAA basketball tournament that had recently expanded to include forty teams. ESPN's extended broadcasting helped create a record-breaking audience for the much-celebrated 1979 national championship match-up between Larry Bird and Earvin "Magic" Johnson, igniting the cultural phenomenon known as March Madness. But along with increasing commercialization and pressure to win came problems. A growing number of football programs around the country faced NCAA sanctions for recruiting violations and questions about athletes' academic preparedness. These problems reflected long-standing critiques of values and practices in the tradition of men's sports.

Women's college sports also changed. Because of athletic financial aid and other benefits secured by Title IX, the era in women's sports when a small school with few monetary resources, such as Immaculata College, could dominate women's college basketball was ending. Women's teams increasingly sought to compete nationally as well as against traditional in-state rivals. To do so, they needed increased resources.

The push for more college sports resources began as the country faced a growing battle over the proposed national ERA, the students' rights movement, racial tensions, and economic anxieties created by a national recession and fuel crisis. These factors converged to shape people's attitudes toward women, students, college sports, and federal government regulation. As a result, public and private discourses about race, economics, and gender roles became a backdrop for events that unfolded at MSU and across the nation.

Tensions Involving Race, Resources, and Commercialization at MSU

In the mid-1970s, the MSU men's basketball program was struggling. The Spartan men had not played in the NCAA tournament since 1959, and they barely filled five thousand seats for their home games at Jenison Fieldhouse, an aging, unconventional facility that men's basketball coaches felt ashamed to show recruits. Jenison undoubtedly lacked the luster of new facilities in the Big Ten, but the women's team would have loved to play there. Instead, except for occasional games in Jenison, they were relegated to play and practice in different campus intramural buildings, with no permanent locker room or court to call their home. The men, however, compared themselves with their Big Ten peers, not with their female counterparts at MSU. Like men's basketball teams across the country, the Spartan men competed not with women athletes but with college football for scholarships, recruiting budgets, university vehicles for coaches' use, and other resources. With Jenison Fieldhouse as their home court, the Spartan men's basketball team faced the additional challenge of contending with track athletes, both men and women, who competed with them for practice times in the field house. They had to deal with the aggravatingly loud sound of the starting pistol for the track team interrupting their practices.[2]

To address the problem, the athletics director offered the men's basketball team a small upstairs gym in the field house near where the gymnastics team practiced, but their coach considered that facility unsafe because of chalk dust from the gymnastics team. While the men's team considered this facility unacceptable, the women's basketball team practiced in that same gym across from the gymnasts into the mid-1980s, and they considered the space an upgrade from the intramurals buildings that they had previously used.[3] While the women appreciated at least moving into the upstairs of Jenison Fieldhouse, the men's basketball team was not prepared to settle for second best. With MSU's football team on lengthy probation for NCAA violations, they saw an opportunity to develop a higher profile at MSU. To do so, conventional wisdom said they needed more publicity and a winning team. That combination would translate into increased revenue from ticket sales, more corporate sponsorships, and other potentially lucrative benefits of quasi-professional, commercially oriented college sports. In the discourse of athletic administrators and university trustees, pursuing commercial interests in those ways was often described as creating "cash cows" or protecting a "golden goose" (the metaphors varied). For college athletic departments focused on supporting a golden goose, addressing problems with gender inequalities—regardless of Title IX's requirements—was simply not urgent.

In the mid-1970s, commercialization was not the only item on college sports agendas that took precedence over serious attention to Title IX compliance. As is frequently the case in civil rights movements, some issues got addressed before others. At MSU and elsewhere, men's basketball programs faced disturbing racial tensions. The previous MSU men's basketball coach, Gus Ganakas, lost his coaching job following a 1975 walkout of ten black players who accused the basketball program of racism. To address the situation, the university transferred Ganakas to an administrative position in athletics and arranged interviews with each of the aggrieved players.[4] The black players had undoubtedly experienced racism in their careers as athletes, and the frequently unfair treatment of black male athletes in many athletic programs up to and during that time period has been well documented.[5] Coaches often instituted quotas for the number of black players who could play starting positions. "Stacking" meant that black players had to wait in line to play limited kinds of positions while white players had the opportunity to play any position, including leadership roles such as point guard or quarterback (positions to which black players lacked access due to racial stereotypes). Likewise, minority female athletes faced a range of discriminatory practices, including exclusion from prestigious competitions.[6] This context of decades-long discrimination suffered by black athletes helps explain why a decision by the MSU men's basketball coach to start a white player instead of a regular starter precipitated the walkout. However, in addition to racism, the players identified an additional source of anger: the comparatively royal treatment received by football players.

Men's basketball players who had spoken with football players recognized inequities in the privileges afforded to football players under the social class hierarchy of intercollegiate sports, a class system in which football is king. According to a former MSU administrator, men's basketball players had buddies on the football team who told them about "all the great treatment they were getting that [the basketball players] weren't getting." Football players received per diem and lodging for two players per room, while men's basketball players slept four to a room, two per bed. Football players flew to their games, while the men's basketball team took buses. The football team ate at training tables with specially prepared meals, but men's basketball players did not have that. Although the men's basketball team had some real complaints about the coach and racial issues, "all these other things were grinding on them." Contrasts between men's basketball and football became "the stimulus that ignited the bomb to go off."[7]

A Search for New Basketball Coaches

With the walkout and subsequent player complaints as a backdrop, the MSU administration put together a high-level selection committee for a new MSU men's basketball coach. The committee included MSU president, Dr. Clifton Wharton; faculty representative to the Big Ten Conference, Dr. Gwen Norrell; assistant athletics director, Dr. Clarence Underwood; and several others, including a few students. This group was notably diverse for the time: Wharton was the first black president of a Big Ten school and Norrell was a female faculty member in counseling who served on MSU's Athletics Council. Underwood, a black man with experience counseling minority athletes, was also responsible for the institution's compliance with NCAA and AIAW policies.

One key person not included on the hiring committee was Dr. Nell Jackson, who had joined MSU in 1973 as assistant director of women's athletics responsible for administering the women's sports program. As was common for women sports administrators at the time, she held a coaching position as well, serving as MSU women's track and field coach. In addition, Jackson held a tenured faculty position in physical education and on occasion taught courses at MSU. Presumably, Jackson, a black woman, could have brought to the table important experiences as a both a coach and athlete that would have made her an asset to the men's basketball search committee. An Olympian and American record holder in the 200 meters, Jackson had coached Olympic teams in 1956 and 1972 and served as coach/manager of ten national touring teams.[8] She cited competing in the 1951 Pan American Games as a track athlete as one of her most significant accomplishments, yet she was almost barred from participating.[9] Although she and the other US track and field athletes had clearly qualified athletically, their qualification sparked a debate over whether the black athletes would be permitted to participate and represent the United States during that period of legalized racial segregation.

In hiring Jackson, MSU had signaled a measure of support both for diversity and for women's programs. She was placed in charge of a program that was ahead of the times when it came to opportunities for women athletes. The institution offered a broad-based athletics program with a wider range of teams for male and female students than many of its peers. MSU's budget for women's athletics was about 8 percent of the men's, but higher than other schools in the Big Ten Conference (the MSU women's budget, including salaries, was $94,843 for nine sports; whereas, the men's budget, including salaries, was $1,181,525 for fourteen sports).[10] Jackson's administrative title as a "director"—albeit an "assistant" director—reflected yet another shift in the quickly changing world of women's college sports. Her title marked a move that the men had made much earlier—out of physical education and intramurals and into intercollegiate athletics. And her hiring obviously broke ground. A *Detroit News* article highlighted how unexpected it was for a major university to hire a woman as an assistant athletics director: the headline read, "Lady Gets the MSU Job."[11] Another article mistakenly reported her name as "Dr. Neil" Jackson, apparently presuming an athletics director—or someone holding the title "Dr."—must be male.[12]

Although not involved in the search for a new men's basketball coach, that same year Jackson had at least one women's coaching position to fill. In a much lower-profile search, she sought a new *women's* basketball coach. For this search, Jackson *was* the search committee. The person she hired would face rapid, unpredictable change for women's intercollegiate sports, but the MSU women's basketball position was not deemed important enough for a presidential-level, national search committee. In the 1970s, some of the most outstanding women's coaches in the game were hired almost by happenstance with barely an interview. Governed by the AIAW with its educational model of athletics, women's sports often deliberately maintained a lower profile than men's. However, after initial resistance, women's college national championships, first in golf and later in basketball, gained popularity and support from AIAW members.

To her position at MSU, and her search for a new women's basketball coach, Jackson brought experiences as a devoted AIAW member, world-class track athlete, coach, and tenured physical education faculty member. Her conflicting identities added up to a complex viewpoint on women's athletics. As a highly skilled athlete with significant international experience, she supported AIAW philosophies, but the discrimination that women faced in "facilities, budget, opportunity, and awards" frustrated her.[13] She also thought comments made by her colleagues in women's sports signaled rejection of *competitive* sports for women. When she spoke at a national conference on the topic of "Sex Differences and Public Attitudes in Sports," she cited a long list of colleagues' concerns that she viewed as "rejecting"; they ranged from "time will be lost from academic work" to "girls are too high-strung emotionally to participate in competitive activities" to participation "on varsity teams would curtail a girl's freedom to pursue normal things of student life."[14] Based on her own experience, Jackson contended that physically and psychologically serious male and female athletes are more alike than different, and she cited as proof high achievement needs and the fact that "athletic training does have the same basic physiological effects on the female organs as it has on the male organs" such as the heart, lungs, blood, and muscles. However, Jackson herself was concerned when male coaches used "boys' standards on girls." When a male coach at the conference suggested that women could train in track at the same distances and intensity as men, she disagreed—or at least explained that none of her athletes could do that.[15]

Overall, Jackson straddled different standpoints on women's higher education athletics. More than some of her colleagues and friends, such as MSU physical education professor and Spartan volleyball coach Annelies Knoppers, she sometimes used language that characterized athletes as prospects. But she also joined many of her physical education colleagues in resisting a fully commercial model in which the primary goal of attending college was not a degree but a chance at a first-round draft pick and a hefty paycheck (or whatever comparable dreams women might have had at a time when women's professional sports opportunities were even more limited than today). Like her AIAW peers, Jackson wanted women athletes to reach their highest potential but did not want to see women exploited for their entertainment value.

Langeland Hired

In 1975, Jackson selected a head coach for MSU women's basketball who also straddled several eras and philosophies of women's sports. Karen Langeland, age twenty-seven, had graduated from Calvin College five years earlier, having studied physical education and played Division III college sports during the late 1960s, a period when schools restricted women players in many areas of the United States to a six-player, half-court version of basketball. Although the private, Christian junior high that she attended had offered sports for girls, Langeland recalled that her public high school offered no programs. As an athletically inclined girl, she experienced this time as "kind of a blank period" until her senior year when the school organized a basketball team. After college graduation, Langeland accepted a physical education teaching position in the Kentwood, Michigan, school system, where she also coached track, soccer, softball, volleyball, basketball, and tennis. To earn a permanent teaching certificate, she enrolled in graduate courses in Grand Rapids, where she took courses from MSU faculty, including studying physical education with Jackson, who sometimes taught extension courses.[16]

Langeland remembered when she received an unexpected call from Jackson, and their conversation changed the course of her life and career: "One August, I got a call from Dr. Jackson. She said she needed a basketball coach and wondered if I'd be interested, and I said 'absolutely.' I had already applied to grad school [for an MSU master's program in athletic training] and had been accepted. So I came."[17]

The job paid six thousand dollars. According to Langeland, Jackson wanted to hire a female coach, and Langeland came recommended by Knoppers, who was not only Jackson's colleague but had coached Langeland in volleyball at Calvin. In her first years at MSU, Langeland made ends meet by working as a graduate assistant and teaching additional physical education activity classes on the side.[18] In those days, women's coaches could be hired with no experience coaching college players; many of these coaches had not experienced high-level competition themselves. Most of these pioneers were accustomed to the idea that under the AIAW at that time, women's college sports did not include recruiting and full-ride scholarships. They simply coached the players who came to their programs and institutions. These early coaches faced the double challenge of developing their own coaching skills as they developed the game of women's basketball.

The MSU program needed development. When the first Spartan women's intercollegiate basketball coach (1972–75), Mikki Baile, stepped down after a few seasons, a graduate student manager of the men's team was hired mainly because he was "around all the time." According to an MSU athletics administrator at the time, "He was a gopher. He said he had coached in high school or some junior college in Pennsylvania, so they gave him the job." By all accounts, the young man was a nice guy, a familiar face, and "a complete failure" as a coach—an evaluation supported by his one-year tenure, losing record, and zero victories in home games.[19]

With this brief and largely unsuccessful history to build on, along with her own limited experience, Langeland could not have fully anticipated the challenges ahead. Like other pioneering coaches of the time, she would need to develop a nationally focused team capable of succeeding in Big Ten Conference play out of a fledgling program centered on regionally focused, in-state competition.

Even before Langeland was hired, MSU women's basketball had changed dramatically over the years. As early as 1900, the MSU yearbooks allotted the women's basketball team equal space with the men's team. College teams for both men and women at that time functioned essentially as sports clubs, and by the 1920s, MSU sponsored a variety of such clubs for women including fencing, rifle, tennis, swimming, synchronized swimming, archery, soccer, field hockey, and softball. A Women's Athletic Association, organized in 1925 by Helen Grimes (director of MSU's Department of Physical Education for Women) involved one hundred students by 1926.[20] During this growth period, athletic opportunities for women remained almost entirely intramural, emphasizing mildly competitive play. Meanwhile, men's teams developed to follow the competitive, increasingly commercialized model we know today.

In 1962, MSU took a significant step by hiring Carol Harding as the first full-time director of women's intramural athletics in the Big Ten. Under her direction, women's teams participated in quasi-varsity intercollegiate experiences, raising their own funds for state and national competitions.[21] Women's basketball players of the 1960s, along with other women athletes, prized these playing opportunities. Many traveled to MSU in 2002 for a ceremony in which they were awarded varsity letters, along with other MSU women athletes from the years prior to 1980 when letters were first awarded to women.[22]

Despite this commitment in the 1960s to a fledgling competitive program, by 1972, when MSU created official intercollegiate varsity sports for women, the women's basketball team had funds for only five uniforms. This inadequate supply actually forced players to share and quickly change into uniforms when subbing into a game. The program lacked recordkeeping as well. As Langeland explained, "When I took the job [at MSU] there were no records of anything. . . . I couldn't even find rosters from previous years." She recalled that typical conversations about women athletes focused on research that examined whether women could run long distances without harming themselves physically. During her own playing days, the rules for women's basketball changed yearly, becoming less and less restrictive.

As MSU's new women's basketball coach, Langeland had a remarkable opportunity to embrace new possibilities for women athletes. Even without Title IX as a catalyst (although in some places it was), opportunities for women in sports were opening up as girls and women sought out athletic opportunities and bridled against what many saw as outdated restrictions. In 1976, Langeland did not need a federal law to help her envision moving sports for women toward a more gender-equal future. As a teacher at heart, she wanted to see continued change without compromising educational values.

Heathcote Hired

With a women's basketball coach secured, Jackson still faced an ongoing rhetorical challenge: to persuade the head athletics director, university president, board of trustees, and community to continue investing new resources in building MSU women's athletics to the next level, one step at a time. Meanwhile, the new men's program—in particular the new basketball coach—had a once-in-a-lifetime opportunity to catapult the Spartan men's team to national prominence. To make that leap, they needed to persuade just one young man to become a Spartan.

For Spartan sports fans, the well-chronicled story of MSU and Earvin Johnson hardly needs repeating. An incredible fifteen-year-old high school basketball player nicknamed "Magic" had shown serious interest in playing basketball at MSU, his hometown university. The incoming MSU men's basketball coach would need only to convince him to choose Michigan State over in-state rival University of Michigan. To select a new coach, the search committee interviewed head coaches from Virginia Tech, University of North Carolina-Charlotte, Ohio University, and Miami (Ohio) before selecting George "Jud" Heathcote, then head coach at the University of Montana. MSU athletics director Joe Kearney had known Heathcote from a network he developed as athletics director at the University of Washington. Heathcote had played college basketball and coached at Washington State as "a kind of graduate assistant" before moving on to teach and coach at the high school level for fourteen years and then taking the Montana job.[23] Described as "extremely honest" as well as "tough, demanding, and intimidating" by former player Greg Kelser, Heathcote fit the university's needs.[24]

Like Langeland, Heathcote faced a few surprises when he arrived in East Lansing. Early on, he confronted what he termed an "interrogation" over lunch with minority East Lansing businessmen.[25] In the wake of the players' walkout in 1975, the businessmen expressed concern about Heathcote's ability as a white man to coach, recruit, and generally treat black players fairly. Heathcote also faced a practical obstacle to recruiting Earvin Johnson. At the time, "special admits" were reserved primarily for football players (these waivers of the regular admissions requirements gave college and intercollegiate sports access to socioeconomically disadvantaged kids, often minorities, who had struggled academically in frequently under-resourced high schools). In his memoir, Heathcote described how he and football coach Darryl Rogers negotiated more special admits for basketball and football, pressuring President Wharton with the argument that while other Big Ten teams had no limits on special admits, MSU allowed only ten, and they could not compete in the conference with this disadvantage.[26] Wharton initially resisted by reminding them that excellence in athletics and academics "go hand in hand" and that the institution needed to maintain its image, but he eventually gave in. The imminent importance of these waivers for men's basketball was clear: they would need one for their top recruit.[27]

Meanwhile, the MSU men's basketball program could not afford more negative fallout from the walkout by the black players. As Heathcote noted, "The black walkout in '75 really hurt us. A lot of kids were afraid."[28] So, in effect, the players' walkout opened up the coaching position for Heathcote, led to improved treatment for the men's basketball players on closer par with what football athletes received, and kept pressure on Heathcote to run a disciplined, racially sensitive basketball program. Under these circumstances, when Magic Johnson decided to sign with Michigan State, the men's basketball program and the institution at large were highly motivated to provide Heathcote with as much tangible and intangible support as they could. They well understood that maximizing Johnson's athletic potential also meant maximizing his potential value to MSU.

Under these circumstances—the dawning of the Magic years at MSU and March Madness nationwide—the women's basketball team and their new coach seemed more invisible than ever.

The "Invisible" Players

When Magic Johnson became a Spartan in the fall of 1977, the women's basketball team had talented players with equally high hopes of reaching their full potential as athletes, including (for some) hopes of playing professionally. Kathleen (Kathy) DeBoer, for example, who transferred to MSU from Langeland's alma mater, Calvin College, had led the 1976 team in scoring, rebounding, and free throw percentages. She was a gifted athlete who also starred on the Spartan volleyball team and would go on to play in the Women's Basketball League (the WBL, a precursor to the WNBA). She later became a successful coach, senior university athletic administrator, city manager, and executive director of the National Volleyball Coaches Association. A teammate on the 1979 squad, Deb Traxinger, who earned Academic All-American honors in basketball at MSU and later became a high school biology teacher, teachers' union president, coach, and basketball referee, recalled her awe of DeBoer's athleticism: "I kind of idolized Kathy when I was a youngster. . . . I'd never seen anybody be able to spike a volleyball inside the ten foot line. I mean she was [an even] better volleyball player than she was a basketball player, just a phenomenal athlete."[29]

DeBoer's teammate Mary Kay Itnyre, at six feet tall, led their team in scoring for the next three years and played just as memorably. As a college freshman, Traxinger had an unforgettable first impression of Itnyre: "We were scrimmaging, and a shot goes up and I'm getting ready to get this rebound. MK [Itnyre], she took it off the rim with ONE HAND. And she always thought she was a guard, so she took off down the court. And I thought, wow, I'm playing with the big dogs now. She was a PHENOMENAL basketball player, had such skill." Remembering her teammate's dominating play, Traxinger could only ask emphatically, "Do you know how good Mary Kay Itnyre was?"[30] But Spartan fans have only statistics and a few black-and-white photos to help envision the feats of players like

Itnyre on the court. Game films from the 1970s and early 1980s were not preserved, and coaches working with minimal budgets recall filming over the top of game footage.

Backing up Itnyre at center was Mariann "Cookie" Mankowski. The 1977 women's basketball team media guide touted her—in rhetoric of sports promotion rife with gender stereotypes—as "a bubbly performer with an invaluable sense of humor . . . who adds sparkle to the Spartan team whether on the floor or seated next to Coach Langeland." On the court, the media guide attested, "her aggressive play frequently draws the attention of the officials, a situation which causes her to lead the team in foul disqualifications."

Rounding out the roster were other women who, like DeBoer, competed in several different sports—a practice discouraged by a commercial model of sport in which athletes on full scholarships typically devote their energies year-round to a single sport. Diane Spoelstra, another transfer from Calvin and graduate of East Kentwood High School (where Langeland taught and coached), played volleyball, softball, and basketball for the Spartans. Karen Santoni joined the basketball team late each year, an accommodation that allowed her to compete with the field hockey team in the fall.

Carol Hutchins ("Hutch") played shortstop for the 1976 AIAW National Championship Spartan softball team, a team whose exploits inspired Traxinger to attend MSU. She recalled their bold confidence, marching onto the field playing their own trumpets, literally tooting their own horns in the absence of actual fans or pep bands. That national championship team inspired young women who watched them to identify with MSU, as surely as the magic of the Earvin Johnson years would later compel athletes—both male and female—to want to play for the Green and White. The women's basketball team, however, projected a low-key ethos. The team's 1977 media guide described the sophomore Hutchins as a versatile, consistent, and even-tempered player "who contributes quietly to the Spartan cause." The guide noted that "although she cannot be described as a flashy player, she came off the bench last season to stun the opposition with her effective shooting."

Hutchins served as co-captain the following season, 1978–79, with Lori Hyman, who was described in the 1977 media guide as "the one Spartan who can 'do it all'" and "one of the best one-on-one players on the team." After graduation, Hyman coached high school basketball and became athletics director at Livonia Stevenson High School near Detroit, Michigan. Each of these players, and many of their teammates, went on to hold highly visible positions and continued to pursue their love of sports through their chosen professions. But in the 1970s, they competed in a marginalized subculture of intercollegiate athletics. Hutchins recalled, "We played mostly for ourselves."[31]

After a 6–16 record during Langeland's first season as head coach (1976–77), Langeland's 1977–78 team bounced back to finish 23–6 and take second place at the "Big Ten Tournament" (that is, a tournament for women's teams in the then male-only Big Ten Conference). The next year, the team looked forward to the Queen's College Holiday Tournament in Flushing, New York, where they would compete against top teams and had scheduled three double-headers with the men's varsity games. They increasingly set their sights on national-level competition.

To some extent, though, those treasured years of college sports competition became overshadowed by an impending off-the-court struggle that would garner more attention than the team's winning seasons or basketball skills. As in most situations, a broader context came into play.

In 1977, the men's team played their most visible season ever. The previous year, Heathcote's first with the Spartans, future NBA player and MSU Academic All-American Gregory Kelser led the men's team with 21.7 points per game, but they finished 12–15 overall and took only fifth place in the Big Ten. Heathcote and his staff struggled to develop student interest in the team. They "went to the dorms and did anything [they] could to generate interest," a task made more difficult because "there were not TV games to speak of in those days."[32] The coaches' difficulty in garnering student interest changed quickly when the news came that Magic Johnson would play as a Spartan.

Johnson's arrival catalyzed the local media. Sports journalist Tim Staudt, who understood the media's critical role in creating spectator interest, convinced the TV station he worked for (WJIM-TV) to cover MSU men's basketball for the first time ever. He recalled, "My station was a hero to the community because we provided them free access to these marvelous Michigan State players. And I've always believed that because more people got to watch them play on local television, more fans were created and thus the frenzy for Earvin [Johnson], Jay [Vincent], and Special K [Greg Kelser] continued to grow."[33]

Palpable new life breathed into the Spartan men's program as they poised for the excitement and visibility certain to come. Meanwhile, a perfect storm of factors more quietly converged to bring change to the women's program. Nell Jackson, along with other leaders of women's athletics, contemplated what the new law, Title IX, meant for their programs as they attended national AIAW meetings. In October 1977, MSU women's basketball team leader Kathy DeBoer sold car decals to raise money for her team to drive to their holiday tournament in New York, but she had yet to hear of Title IX. She would not remain in the dark for long.

The federal government's July 1978 deadline for universities to conduct self-evaluations and comply with Title IX's regulations for athletics was quickly approaching, and each institution receiving federal funds had been required by law to hire a designated Title IX coordinator. Several MSU employees had already held that position, but none of them had much influence with key decision makers. In August 1977, a catalyst for real change came to East Lansing: thirty-three-year-old Mary Pollock joined MSU as the director of women's programs and Title IX coordinator.

7   An Activist's Story

At age thirty-three, Mary Pollock was starting a new life: her mother had recently died, and she had just left her first professional job, which she had held for eight years at the University of Illinois, Champaign-Urbana. Her mother, a stay-at-home mom, had counseled her daughter early on to "never be financially dependent on a man," so she always assumed that she would work to earn a living.[1] A graduate of Penn State with a bachelor of arts degree in English, she also held a master's degree from the University of Florida in Counseling and Guidance/Higher Education Administration. Since 1969, she had worked at the University of Illinois as an assistant dean of students and then a part-time residence hall director while she pursued graduate studies in higher education administration. From 1973 to 1977 she served on the Champaign City Council. Pollock's experiences at Illinois proved a formative backdrop for the role she subsequently played in the MSU women's basketball team's struggle for equality. Her time at Illinois also provides a glimpse into how the enactment of Title IX mobilized students, faculty, and administrators at another large, midwestern public university.

Papers in the institutional archives at Illinois document Pollock's leadership in the National Organization for Women's gender equality work and her integral role in a campus group called Concerned Women Athletes (CWA). When she left Illinois to take the position as director of women's programs at MSU, she donated to the Illinois library hundreds of papers related to her job and activism (e.g., memos, letters, reports, handwritten brainstorming notes, news articles). Taken together, these documents show how Title IX's first decade unfolded at Illinois. The papers reveal how local factors from personalities to politics influenced responses to Title IX at Illinois, just as they did everywhere. The papers also show how Pollock developed the expertise, passion, and experience she later brought to her position at MSU. When Pollock mentioned casually in an interview that she had "done gender equity in athletics work" at Illinois, she was being modest. Her collected papers document a carefully orchestrated change movement.[2]

While at Illinois, the intellectually curious Pollock took courses in political science and labor relations as part of doctoral studies in higher education administration. She became increasingly active in local politics and the women's movement. She worked with a group of ministers doing referrals for illegal abortions before *Rowe v. Wade*, fully realizing that by doing so she could have been fired from her job, fined, or arrested. Looking back, Pollock recalled, "the situation I ran into at MSU was not the first risk I had ever taken on behalf of women." She remembered being ready to picket for a cause at a moment's notice, with "picket sticks and poster boards and magic markers and a staple gun and masking tape ready to put up signs."[3]

Pollock had been the first student and youngest person ever elected to the Champaign City Council, where she learned the literacies needed to participate in civic dialogue and activism. She also ardently supported students' voting rights in university communities and lobbied for the Equal Rights Amendment. During her years on the city council, she advocated for women's rights in the workplace, pushing for changes to height and weight requirements that prevented women from working as firefighters and police officers. She was exposed to discourses concerning workplace equality and affirmative action, including logical, research-based appeals that referenced statistics, budgets, and revenue sources.[4] By the 1970s, two paperback books became bibles for her circle of activists: Robin Morgan's anthology *Sisterhood Is Powerful*[5] and Vivian Gornick and Barbara K. Moran's *Women in a Sexist Society: Studies in Power and Powerlessness*.[6] As Pollock put it, "We were very serious about changing the world."[7]

Pollock maintained a uniquely broad vision for change influenced by her education abroad. Unlike many feminists at that time, she appreciated athletics. As a high school girl, her father's work brought the family to India, where she attended a Christian mission-supported private boarding school and competed in four different school-sponsored sports, an experience she would not likely have had at that time in the United States. These opportunities convinced her that girls and women needed access to organized athletics.[8]

As the type of person who put her beliefs into action, in the early 1970s Pollock helped found the Urbana-Champaign chapter of NOW and volunteered to cosponsor its Sports Task Force.[9] Perhaps because of her interest in athletics, while at Illinois, Pollock became loosely acquainted with her future MSU colleague Nell Jackson. From 1970 to 1973, Jackson was an associate professor of physical education at Illinois, where she also coached women's track and field and mentored athletes who sought out her expertise as an Olympic coach and athlete.[10] Although the two women did not know each other well, in 1973 Jackson gave a talk on "Women in Sport" to the NOW group to which Pollock belonged. Later that year, Jackson left Illinois to become assistant director of women's athletics and track and cross-country coach at MSU, attracted by an administrative position with a sixty-thousand-dollar budget for women's athletics that, for the time period, signaled an impressive investment in women's sports. As Pollock would soon learn, universities across the country increasingly needed to fill administrative positions for directing women's athletics (almost always as an "assistant" to the primary—and always male—athletics director). However, administrators at Illinois did not initially envision a need for one.

Just before Jackson left Illinois for MSU in 1973, Pollock became involved in a movement on the University of Illinois campus to improve the status of women's athletics. Before long, she acted as the key strategist and primary spokesperson for a group of athletes representing every sport for women at Illinois. The athletes, Pollock, and others, including sociology assistant professor Joan Huber, mobilized after the university's shocking response to Title IX's enactment: Illinois cut, rather than expanded, athletic teams for women. University leaders reasoned that by cutting softball, gymnastics, and swimming, the meager budget provided by the state for women's athletics, $4,500, could better support the remaining women's teams. Cutting these sports may have been a strategic move designed to create a crisis and thereby call attention to the long-neglected situation of women's poorly funded athletics at the university. Whether or not the university intended the move in this way, it gave women athletes an exigency to act.[11]

Illinois's yearly budget for women's athletics ranked lowest among the state's colleges and universities and second lowest in the Big Ten. Only the University of Michigan allocated less to women's athletics, with a budget of zero.[12] At more than $60,000, Michigan State's budget for women's intercollegiate athletics put them at the top of the conference. Conversely, men's sports at Illinois, like their peers throughout the conference, operated on considerably more: they had a $2.5 million budget administered by an Athletic Association (AA) with a little-understood relationship to the university. Football, especially when the team had a winning record, brought in significant revenue but did not always make a profit. The AA budget also covered numerous men's teams that generated low or no revenue, such as tennis, swimming, golf, and wrestling. According to a report in the Illinois student newspaper, in 1973 the AA operated at $1.6 million in the red.[13] The last thing that the association director and its board wanted was to take on responsibility for additional sports—much less the entire women's program—unless new varsity sports were guaranteed to bring in money without a significant investment. The university already continuously offered the NCAA maximum of 120 football scholarships and planned to invest more than half a million dollars in new artificial turf to further upgrade an already expensive football program.[14]

Meanwhile, as a graduate student, assistant dean of students, and then in 1973 "housemother" (the 1970s term for today's residence hall directors) for Scott Residence Hall, Pollock heard horror stories from women athletes.[15] One student asked that her remarks about coaching remain anonymous. She explained to Pollock, "The talent exists at this university but doesn't even get developed to its full extent because the coaches are pretty ignorant in basketball and swimming and to a degree in tennis . . . with the exception of volleyball. Ms. Kahrs is a good volleyball coach." This student, a swimmer, added that "the general consensus of the team is that we could do as good or better without our present coach. She doesn't even take our splits (individual length times) during meets. She claimed that she got too excited by watching the meet to operate a stop watch."[16]

A tennis player wrote that her coach "takes 8 players (1 station wagon) to meets and leaves six that do not play every meet," a situation that led her to wonder why there was not enough money for two cars. She described "ancient, dead practice balls" and "courts with huge cracks and lumps, creating an uneven surface that balls go crazy on," while she observed that "the boys get new shoes every week, new balls every day, a ball machine, plus indoor practice time in the Armory." For emphasis, she added a note in the margin: "I wouldn't make my worst enemy play on Freer Courts."[17]

Pollock acted as the chief advisor to the group of undergraduates led by Kathy Murphy, a University of Illinois student and former softball and field hockey athlete. They initially planned to research the status of women's athletics on other campuses, create a group identity under the name Concerned Women Athletes, hold regular meetings, contact the university attorney, write to state representatives, and issue a press release to garner public support. Pollock's exposure to the activist strategies of the women's movement undoubtedly served the group well. For example, in 1972, she had acquired a copy of a speech delivered at the New American Movement Conference on Feminism and Socialism that emphasized strategies developed by the Chicago Women's Liberation Union for developing effective action plans. The speech focused on working for reforms that both "meet real needs of women" and gain recognition for the movement's victories. Organizing for change, speakers at the conference asserted, requires "audacity" and risk taking; women gain "a sense of their own power" by working together through organizations in order to "alter the relations of power."[18]

Pollock certainly saw her experience in team sports as an important training ground for learning what can be accomplished in groups. In a sense, members of the 1970s women's movement served as coaches and cheerleaders for activists like Pollock, guiding them in translating big-picture questions of principle into grassroots tactics. Even though many in the movement rejected an ideology of competition, leaders in the Chicago Women's Liberation Union nonetheless evoked the metaphor of a competitive game as an "intermediate strategy." They asserted that "fighting in an arena where we will win or lose" was a necessary means toward a greater good—a societal revolution in which nonhierarchical cooperation would trump the need to perpetually compete and assert power.[19] These rallying cries by movement leaders meshed well with, and perhaps influenced, Pollock's style as an activist. A brief report in the July 1973 NOW newsletter reveals a glimpse of the straightforward approach she applied just a few months later to sport equality activism:

> Mary Pollock had a copy of the recent Supreme Court decision on sex-segregated want ads (*Pittsburg[h] Press*). She prepared a letter to the *Courier* and the *News-Gazette* asking that they voluntarily de-sex their want ads and let us know their decision by July 4. She also stated in the letter that if they will not comply, NOW will take the matter to both city councils to pass ordnances [*sic*] prohibiting this sex discrimination (as did *Pittsburg[h]*). Mary's letter and press release were approved by the Chapter and distributed.[20]

Pollock's approach, as reported here, demonstrates that she could take action assertively, even audaciously, when she believed the occasion warranted it. However, her collected papers also include more philosophical, reflective documents, in which she addressed the root questions that guided effective activism according to the Chicago Women's Liberation Union:
- "What kind of organization are you trying to create?"
- "Whose problem is it?"
- "What are the various self-interests among women interested in the issue?"
- "What are the sources of the problem?"
- "Who has the power to change the situation?"

These questions led to more pragmatic considerations:
- "What specifically can be demanded?"
- "What are points where pressure can be used at the state, local and private sector levels?"
- "How can the problem be divided into more manageable parts that can be fought for and won?"[21]

Pollock's first inquiries regarding gender equality in sport acquainted her with the ways in which advocates for change at other institutions were thinking about many of these questions. She learned that students at the University of Wisconsin and at the University of Michigan had filed two of the first federal complaints under Title IX. Not to be confused with lawsuits, administrative complaints were followed up with an investigation by the Department of Health, Education, and Welfare, which was responsible for investigating Title IX complaints. Pollock received a copy of the fifty-eight-page University of Michigan complaint filed on August 15, 1973, by a group calling themselves "Committee to Bring about Equal Opportunity in Athletics for Women and Men at the University of Michigan." In a handwritten note addressed "Dear Mary," the group's coordinator, Marcia Federbush, told Pollock that HEW, led at the time by Caspar Weinberger, "won't do anything until guidelines are formulated—who knows when?"[22] Typically, what Federbush called guidelines, actually regulations, can take up to two years to be developed when a new law is passed. In the case of the Title IX regulations, the process was slower and more contentious than usual.

The Michigan complaint posed the question of what equality in school-sponsored athletics meant in practice, as well as raising other fundamental questions. Should males and females compete together on the same teams? Due to biological differences between males and females, should schools adopt a *separate but equal* approach to equality? Would it make sense for the same federal agency working on racial integration after the 1954 *Brown v. Board of Education* decision to become responsible for regulating a *separate but equal* system in response to sex discrimination? If so, should athletic funds be split exactly down the middle, with half going to women's programs and the other half to men's? Where would additional funding come from, unless men's athletics were to be drastically reduced in every way? The complaint posed the very same questions that staff members at HEW wrestled with as they drafted the regulations for complying with Title IX.

As federal government staff debated these issues and prepared regulations for Title IX, Pollock and the newly formed advocacy group at Illinois faced a decision that confronted other activists, women's athletic administrators, athletes, and coaches: how urgently should they push within their institutions for immediate action? In July, the chancellor appointed a committee "to look into the matter" and issue a report by April 1, 1974.[23] Rather than simply wait for the committee to report back, the CWA continued researching the intricacies of the Athletic Association's funding for men's athletics. They tackled the task like a class group writing assignment: students interviewed administrators, took notes, and brought back diagrams to other CWA members. One handwritten diagram illustrated how funds to support men's athletics flowed from donors (who received tax write-offs) to a fundraising organization called "Grants-in-Aid" (a subdivision of the University of Illinois Foundation), then through the university administration, then into the Athletic Association, which provided athletic scholarships for eleven men's sports.[24] This diagram served as an effective piece of visual rhetoric: it illustrated how money was funneled in such a way as to allow the men's Athletic Association to legitimately claim to be separate from the university yet still benefit from tax-payer-supported donations that funded athletic aid to male, but not female, athletes. Other notes included telling facts that belied claims of separateness, such as "Cecil Coleman is AA athletic director and also athletic department director."[25] This sort of discovery must have motivated the group to keep digging for more information.

By the fall of 1973, Pollock and the Concerned Women Athletes group felt that efforts to gain support from university administrators had failed. As athlete Susan Shade reflected a year later, "It seemed like everywhere we went [to raise funds last year] we were given a lot of encouragement, a lot of sympathy, but no funds."[26]

In a series of handwritten notes and lists, a behind-the-scenes action plan created by the CWA unfolded. The group initially distributed a flyer to inform the university community of the budget inequities for men's and women's intercollegiate athletics. On September 3, 1973, they filed a complaint with HEW. A copy of the complaint in the University of Illinois Archives shows that it included seventy-six students' signatures and phone numbers, along with attachments, including Athletic Association budgets. The complaint pointed out that the university awarded three hundred thousand dollars in scholarships for men and zero dollars for women. Meanwhile, the women's program's budget of forty-five hundred dollars approximately equaled the amount that the men's program paid just for their yearly NCAA fees. One sentence struck an especially plaintive note: "It seems everyone has the spirit and commitment but no one can bear to make the men's program smaller to bring a little equity for women." The document stressed the funding structure for athletics as the key issue.[27] The Athletic Association frequently argued that the men's athletic program and the university were two separate entities and that men's athletics therefore should not be subject to Title IX. This argument endlessly blocked women athletes' efforts to improve their opportunities and resources. The ultimate point was always that even if the association *wanted* to support women's sports (because legally they don't *have* to), they could not *afford* to because they already struggled to make ends meet financially.

The Concerned Women Athletes group followed their Title IX complaint with an appeal for public support that they published as an advertisement in the *Chicago Tribune*. Claiming that women's sports were dying at the University of Illinois, they listed the efforts they had made to plead their case within the institution: "We've been to the Chancellor, the head of the Athletic Association, the college of Physical Education Dean, the U of I Foundation, the Campus Programs Office, the Affirmative Action Officer and . . . we've gotten nowhere." Their appeal concluded by asking members of the public to contact the chancellor "and tell him that you think women's sports are important and should be fully funded."[28]

At the end of October, Pollock's group finally got some support when *Tribune* columnist John Husar picked up the story. In an editorial on October 30, 1973, Husar pointed to "the traditional separation of men's and women's programs and facilities" as a factor that "helps maintain the women's historic back seat status." He alluded to a conundrum for those working on the Title IX regulations: complete segregation allowed inequities to perpetuate, and complete integration would mean even fewer opportunities for women who lacked the skill, training, and physical attributes to compete with men in sports oriented toward physical strength and speed, especially contact sports. Husar's editorial described the "humiliations" and "often ignorant mishandling by employees who do not think women 'belong'" that women athletes suffered in Illinois's sex-segregated track and field program.[29]

Incidents involving the women's track team at Illinois verified Husar's claims. During the men's track season, the men's track coach allowed the women's team to train in the stadium, but they experienced "harassment" by stadium workers. A 1972 Olympic hopeful in the pentathlon, Donna Schulenberg, described how university crews covered up the jumping pits after the boys' season ended, and she and her coach had to "sneak in" and take off the heavy lids to practice. Finally, Schulenberg said, "they built a 6-foot fence around the long jump pit—just to keep me out. No one else was using it." A javelin thrower had to borrow a javelin from the junior high, and a shot putter recalls team members being locked in the stadium if they weren't out by four o'clock each day. The list of outrages culminated with Jackson actually being "threatened with arrest by a grounds crew member after she and one of her athletes climbed into the Stadium for a workout."[30] Considering the indignities Jackson suffered growing up in the racially segregated South, this story, which does not identify her by race, could have delivered an additional rhetorical impact if it had done so.

But Illinois's Concerned Women Athletes had nevertheless gained attention for their cause. In November 1973, *Daily Illini* sports writer Fred Eisenhammer responded with a probing three-part series that examined the relationship of the (men's) University Athletic Association to the university. He pinpointed a series of key questions similar to those the women athletes group was investigating:

- How is the University Athletic Association (AA) related to the university itself?
- Does the AA receive financial assistance from the university?
- Who determines the AA's policies, and who makes decisions on matters affecting the AA's budget?
- Why does the AA currently pay for 120 football scholarships, compared to 18 for basketball and only 17 for the remaining sports?

As Eisenhammer explained, to even begin to understand how the AA worked required "mastery of such concepts as 'tradeout' agreements, allied agencies and private corporations . . . and familiarity with positions and agencies outside the AA, such as the University Board of Trustees, the

University Foundation and Chancellor J. W. Peltason."[31] Without these legal and financial literacies, it was no wonder that the general taxpaying public found it difficult or impossible to engage knowledgably in debates about gender equality in higher education sports.

Although few people questioned or understood the inner workings of public university athletics budgets, the struggle for equality in women's athletics was heating up around the country. In May 1973, the women's sports movement had gotten a boost from a series in *Sports Illustrated* entitled "Sport Is Unfair to Women."[32] The authors anticipated HEW's Title IX regulations being completed in July, but the summer passed and they were not. In November 1973, the nation's college sports community was still waiting. That month, AIAW leader Marjorie Blaufarb spoke to an increasingly divided group of women's college sports administrators, all of whom anxiously awaited word on the details of the impending Title IX regulations. Blaufarb offered a preview of the impending regulations, urging women to work for "orderly integration" with men's programs. She suggested that women take the time to "go to the men and talk things over" since it would be "the better part of wisdom to look for constructive ways to achieve what we all want." And she reminded women to consider the perspective of their male audience: "After all, they [men] are going to lose a lot they have taken for granted, both financially and in privilege. But true equality will preclude the men just taking over."[33] At Illinois, Pollock took note and filed away both the groundbreaking *Sports Illustrated* article and Blaufarb's speech.

Few women's sports administrators, however, harbored illusions about the power of federal mandates to produce true equality—or even to prevent men from taking over. Anticipating a struggle, they shared persuasive strategies through publications, conferences, letters, phone calls, and word of mouth. In early November 1973, Dr. Huber, the primary faculty supporter of Illinois's Concerned Women Athletes, wrote to Bernice Sandler in Washington, DC, seeking advice. Huber asked Sandler for "the inside dope about the publication of the guidelines for Title IX," the names of other universities planning to take action, suggestions for attorneys, and advice about a public relations campaign. Huber noted her group's lack of funds for a lawsuit, adding that "not a single woman attorney practices in this county, and the few sympathetic males are already in firms doing business with the Athletic Association, so finding an attorney will be a problem, but no doubt we shall be able to do so." Huber's memo emphasized the group's goal was not to file suit but to convince the university attorney and chancellor they were serious. She wrote, "So far, this group has been put off and put down, but I shall not repeat the usual details." Elaborating on the group's rhetorical strategy, she explained, "We will emphasize that we do not want to destroy men's sports, nor do we expect equal financing." A hurried note on top of the page suggests she was not able to reach Sandler that day by phone, but they likely spoke eventually.[34]

One strategy that circulated in such conversations was using analogies to racial discrimination to make a point. In a speech to the Association of Health, Physical Education, and Recreation, Margaret Dunkle suggested,

> When in doubt, a good rule of thumb is to substitute the word "BLACK" for "GIRL." For example, when "I wouldn't want to compete against a girl" becomes "I wouldn't want to compete against a black," the discrimination becomes obvious. Similarly, "Women don't have what it takes to compete;" "Blacks don't have what it takes to compete." "Nothing is more humiliating than to be beaten by a girl;" "Nothing is more humiliating than to be beaten by a black." "No one will take a woman coach seriously;" "No one will take a black coach seriously." "Women coaches need less pay;" "Black coaches need less pay." When these changes are made, the discrimination sticks out like a sore thumb.[35]

Other suggested rhetorical strategies included threatening (but ideally not actually filing) a lawsuit, showing reasonableness by not demanding too much (such as dollar-for-dollar matching funds for men's and women's sports), and having a sense of humor.

The Concerned Women Athletes group used all of these approaches. Pollock held a press conference to state that the students were considering filing a class action lawsuit. Part of the threat's credibility rested in the specific listing of laws under which the group could sue, including the Illinois Constitution's equal rights clause, Title IX, and the Fourteenth Amendment of the US Constitution. With great effect, Pollock also introduced a populist argument that caught on with the media: she objected to the Athletic Association prioritizing purchasing artificial turf—which, pointedly, she called "plastic grass"—for the football field over funding for women's athletics. Pollock claimed, "It's outrageous that the UI Foundation can begin a multi-million dollar fundraising project to buy plastic grass for the football field when women have to go through what they've gone through."[36] The term proved tractable enough to frame the ensuing media coverage of the controversy. The following day, a *Daily Illini* editorial writer, Jeff Metcalfe, quoted Pollock so extensively that it almost sounds like she wrote the editorial. The term "plastic grass" interjected a lighter (yet still audacious) note into a serious matter as the student editorial writer responded with his own tongue-in-cheek tone, noting that he now no longer believed that "nothing in the world would be better for University sports than artificial turf in Memorial Stadium."[37]

Metcalfe's editorial detailed Pollock's activist rhetorical strategies, including her displays of what social movement theorist Charles Tilly calls WUNCs: "public representations of worthiness, unity, numbers, and commitment."[38] She led the group in passing out handouts at the Ohio State–Illinois football game and considered other ways for the CWA organization to "dramatize its position." In one news article, Pollock suggested that the group "may go as far as chaining ourselves to the stadium," but she stopped short when asked about the possibility of initiating a student boycott of the upcoming Minnesota football game.[39]

Having also made public the threat of a lawsuit, representatives of CWA secured a meeting with the university attorney. The group asked him whether "grounds for a suit [would] . . . have existed under the Civil Rights Act" if "the association [had] denied financial support to black athletes." Although the attorney confidently rebutted their assertions that the Athletic Association was not completely separate from the university (albeit not to their satisfaction), when posed their questions about race, "he did not answer," according to a faculty member who was present. The attorney's response may be implied in his subsequent inquiry as to "what the women would define as a reasonable settlement."[40]

Mary Pollock's multifaceted efforts eventually achieved some success. Along with getting the press on her side, the publicity generated a series of hearings on gender equity in college sports by the Illinois state legislative representatives. Pollock communicated regularly with the state politicians who set up the hearings, providing them with information.[41] Before the state task force held its final hearing, the university's task force issued its recommendations for administering and funding women's athletics. In the end, the university agreed to increase the women's budget to eighty-two thousand dollars, a significant increase but still miniscule in comparison with the men's multimillion-dollar budget. Two of the cut sports—softball and field hockey—were not reinstated under the new plan. However, women's sports—for better or worse—were to be organized under the Athletic Association, and a new administrator for women's athletics was appointed.[42]

In May, Pollock presented to the Illinois chancellor a list of six "Problem Areas with the Task Force on Women's Athletics Report." She critiqued the task force for short sightedness. Their one-year plan failed to envision how women would achieve equity in training, travel expenses, coaching, equipment, and scholarships. She stated bluntly, "Under Title IX of the Educational Amendments of 1972, providing scholarships for men only will be illegal." As for the new women's athletics director, Pollock cautioned that the position not be auxiliary to men's activities, even if it meant a "reorganization of the Athletic Association upper echelon staff." She warned that "there is a feeling of great protectionism toward the AA and its budget which overshadows most people's sense of equity, fair play, or protectionism for women. This could become a serious problem."[43] These words, more or less, became Pollock's parting message to the University of Illinois.

In 1976, as Illinois's new assistant director of women's athletics took on the still considerable challenges of building the Illinois program, Pollock decided it was time to move on. In a nationwide job search, Pollock applied for administrative jobs both in university student affairs and the new field of affirmative action. By that time, she had learned quite a lot about the politics of gender equity and intercollegiate athletics. She also felt "over exposed as a resident radical." When she applied for jobs, she assumed quite reasonably that the schools would carefully check the references she provided. Through that process, she expected that her strong activist commitments as well as her experience with women's programming would be disclosed. Later, though, she wondered whether anyone ever made the calls.[44]

Pollock applied lipstick and dressed in a pink suit for her interviews. She described accomplishments such as starting a Women's Week at Illinois, and two universities offered her appealing jobs relatively quickly. Although Pollock was elated to accept the offer from Michigan State, campus women's groups worried that their school might not have made the best choice. They felt under siege and believed that they needed strong new leaders and funds. The directorship had previously operated as a revolving door, with three different leaders between 1973 and 1977, including a nine-month period with no director at all. When the university hired Pollock, women's groups feared that university administrators had intentionally chosen a weak advocate for women on campus.[45] These groups had built an activist coalition to combat sex discrimination on campus for several years and knew the resistance the new director of women's programs would face. They assumed that a relatively young woman without the protection of tenure could not make an impact, but Mary Pollock would soon prove them wrong.

8 Catalysts

I was a hardcore tomboy; if not exactly a girl who wanted to be a boy,
then certainly a girl who wanted to do the things boys did—wrestle,
roughhouse, lead the neighborhood gang, and urinate standing up. I
hated dresses, playing with dolls, and coloring inside the lines.
—Kathleen DeBoer, *Gender and Competition*[1]

In retrospect, it seems inevitable that Mary Pollock, MSU's new director of women's programs, would eventually meet student athlete Kathy
DeBoer, a young woman who wrestled with the same constraints facing the student athletes for whom Pollock had advocated so strongly at
Illinois. Though in very different roles, they each brought to MSU a
common character trait that often motivated their speech and writing:
an unwavering sense of principle. Both young women also possessed the
courage required to speak out and defend unpopular ideas. While different life experiences shaped their capacities as speakers and writers, they
had each been female athletes at a time when girls and women received
little encouragement in that role.

Athletics, as Christine Grant contended in a speech to AIAW members, can be a powerful rhetorical training ground for social change agents:
"I think women in sport have an advantage over other women in society,
for we have already gained, through competitive sport, experience dealing
with both the challenge [to become more than we are] and the apprehension [of testing oneself]."[2]

By Grant's reasoning, DeBoer's early experiences with sports help
explain how she came to play a catalyzing role in the Title IX controversy
soon to erupt at MSU. In 1976, when DeBoer transferred to Michigan
State from a small, private college in her hometown of Grand Rapids,

Michigan, she sought greater opportunities for herself, especially in athletics. As a student in high school and later at Calvin College, both private religious institutions, she played tennis, volleyball, basketball, and softball. Her high school voted her Female Athlete of the Year at a time when many public schools had no programs at all for girls. At Calvin College, Annelies Knoppers coached DeBoer in volleyball during her freshman year, and when Knoppers took a job at MSU, DeBoer thought about following her. She considered Knoppers "the best coach at a four-year college around" and knew "there would be much more traveling opportunities at MSU."[3] Focusing on volleyball also made sense to her because she had found through playing tennis that she "really wasn't an individual sport person." In an interview conducted when she transferred to MSU at age 21, she said, "I'm fiercely competitive and I guess I don't hide it very well—I used to throw my racket when I lost a match. I lost because of my own temper . . . hopefully, I'm growing out of that . . . it's been a personal problem that I'll have to overcome if I really want to excel."[4]

DeBoer had never been a person to accept the place in life that was assigned to her by accident of birth or circumstances. Her elementary school teacher had laughed at her when she said she wanted to be a minister like her dad when she grew up. When her teacher said that girls couldn't be ministers, DeBoer refused to make another choice. Years later, she recalled the incident vividly: "She clucked her tongue and shook her head slowly from side to side. Her twenty years of teaching had exposed her to more than one child who would suffer for irascibly refusing to accept his or her place in life. Wheeling around as if she were the one who had been affronted, she moved to a more cooperative child."[5]

When DeBoer arrived at MSU, she had no scholarship money until her last year of volleyball and basketball. By the time the university began to offer women athletes some funding, DeBoer had encountered tenets of the women's movement through courses she took for a minor in women's studies. Based on the basic principle of equality, she found it difficult to feel grateful as she slowly realized how much more male athletes received. "Instead of being excited about what I was given, I was angry about what wasn't given," she recalled. "We get this cheesy 250 bucks. Look at what they get" was her feeling at the time.[6]

Strangely enough, if DeBoer had played women's basketball at MSU in 1900 rather than in 1976, she would have found her (albeit limited) athletic opportunities more similar to those available to her male peers. In 1900, it was just eight years since James Naismith had invented basketball and a year since physical education teachers had formed a national Women's Basketball Committee to govern the women's game and prevent the sport from overemphasizing winning when played by females.[7] In 1901, the yearbook at Michigan State (then called Michigan Agricultural College, or MAC) reported, "Basket ball is one of the new sports with us, but the boys won from Ypsi's 'crack' team with a score of 25 to 8 and the girls from the L.H.S. team with a score of 16 to 14." By 1904, however, evidence of women's sports disappeared from the yearbooks, and by 1920, two different models of athletics were emerging. An administrator of the college described his sex-separate vision for athletics at MAC this way: "In my mind's eye, I see our girls skating, canoeing, hiking, playing games— thereby learning and receiving that splendid social training that comes from competition. I see all the men of the institution 'in the game,' insuring unlimited material and unlimited competition for Varsity teams."[8]

In the 1920s, the university hired Helen Grimes to develop women's athletics in the anticompetition model that the nation's physical educators had adopted as the standard philosophy. Cultural stereotypes and misinformation about women and athleticism heavily influenced this philosophy. Grimes's program for women emphasized "good health created through the study of physical education."[9]

By the time DeBoer and her peers came to MSU, the women's program had only recently entered a realm of varsity intercollegiate competition that had been developing on the men's side since 1900. For seventy-four years, MSU (and many other institutions) had a men's varsity basketball team but no varsity team for the women. Then, when the inaugural varsity women's hoops team was established in 1973 (along with a junior varsity squad), local reporters referred to the women's team members with a diminutive version of the school's nickname, dubbing pioneering players Linda Stoik, Jo Spano, and their teammates "Spartanettes."[10] Vast differences in how the university and community perceived the Spartans and

Spartanettes ensured that neither Title IX nor its 1975 regulations could create instant equality, despite the athletic establishment's fears.

For decades, administrators had invested in developing their men's athletic programs, especially football and basketball, which they considered potentially significant revenue generators. Meanwhile, athletic female students who accepted their different status and opportunities as the norm did so in part because they saw no other possibilities. They also likely subscribed, in some measure, to the dominant ideologies against which the women's liberation movement was struggling. The idea that for men, sports were an entitlement and a key to developing and demonstrating their masculinity was communicated to both males and females in multiple ways, directly and indirectly, from an early age. No one could fail to see the strikingly different sporting opportunities available for girls and boys, women and men, at every stage of their socialization. Not surprisingly, many college women accepted the idea of athletics as an "extra" to be pursued as long as it was fun and did not interfere with their feminine and/or heterosexual image, education, or plans to marry and have children. However, there were always highly skilled and competitive women who felt unduly constrained by the invisibility and lack of high-level coaching, competition, and resources available to them. It was only a matter of time before these women gained access to information about their rights under Title IX.

It was Mary Pollock's job to educate MSU about women's rights under the new law, and she took that responsibility seriously.

Coaches and Athletes Learn of Title IX

A few months after her start date of August 1, 1977, Pollock attended a meeting for coaches of MSU women's intercollegiate athletics. Her goal was simple: to inform them about Title IX. With her MSU budget, she had sufficient resources to keep up to date on interpretations of the law, including attendance at a conference sponsored by the federal government. As she put it, "I got the people who had passed this law and were implementing this law and loved this law to teach me the whole nine yards." Always "a joiner and a networker," she had affiliated herself with a national group of Title IX coordinators and was highly motivated to bring her knowledge back to MSU. Armed with her customary "boatload of booklets," she addressed the coaches gathered in a classroom in the MSU women's intramural building. To illustrate what she perceived to be illegal practices, she gave examples from a complaint involving MSU's all-male Varsity Alumni Club. Pollock explained that the university's founding male donors had long enjoyed privileges such as fifty-yard-line seats, characterizing the club's board as a "lion's den." Her goal became to persuade the club's leaders that they needed to include women members. Instead of simply citing chapter and verse of the law, however, Pollock tried a different logic. By focusing on the economic benefits of more members, she quickly persuaded the club's leader that sex integration made sense. She described the potential growth in membership and donations, and he "saw dollar signs."[11]

Looking back at this period of her career, Pollock saw her job at MSU as "a kind of extension of what [she'd] been doing [at Illinois]—only [with] a budget."[12] She contrasted her director of women's programs work at MSU, however, with her activism at Illinois, calling herself "a management-side investigator." But in both roles, she saw herself as a problem-solver. In 2010, she summed up how she viewed her mission as Title IX coordinator: "You see discrimination, you identify it, you name it, you describe who the culprits are, you design a remedy, you go after it—bing, bang, you get it done! I mean, you know, just cure it!"[13]

At MSU, Pollock also brought her problem-solving skills and eye for injustice to realms beyond athletics—for example, to the veterinary school, which provided shower facilities and lockers for men only and subjected women applicants to "stress interviews" to weed them out before they even started (men were not required to participate in an interview at all). Wherever she looked, she "just saw segregation of opportunity and segregation of facilities" that seemed invisible to many others on campus.[14] Her investigations were intended to send a strong message that campus leaders could not dismiss or minimize the accumulating complaints. But as the young, newly hired director of women's programs, Pollock was hardly a power broker.

Among the women's coaches who attended Pollock's talk in the fall quarter of 1977, at least one person took her very seriously. Thirty-two-year-old Mark Pittman coached the women's cross-country team and was assistant coach of women's track and field. Prompted by Pollock's meeting, he began recording—first in his head and a few months later on paper—a detailed, annotated chronology of events concerning Title IX that unfolded on campus. For nearly two years, Pittman maintained this document, which he labeled "Title IX: Chronology and Comments and Complaints," anticipating that he might write a book on the politics of women's athletics. His account—typewritten on now-yellowed paper that Pittman kept in his possession for decades—would eventually grow to nearly sixty single-spaced pages.

As MSU volleyball and track athlete, friend, and (eventually) fellow activist Mary Jo Hardy recalled, "Mark always had his typewriter there and was constantly writing things down. He'd add things on and change them and correct them and try to get it all documented." Another friend, Bruce Alexander, explained that "a number of us contributed at various times. Once [Mark] started putting the notes together, it was a matter of getting several people to look at them and review."[15] Looking back at his typed notes nearly forty years later, Pittman himself marveled at their level of detail: "Holy cow, that is amazing. I don't want to look at this. This is ridiculous—I can't believe all this material. OCD . . . Holy Cow. I spent time and time and time on this instead of writing my dissertation!"[16] His "Chronology," stored in a cardboard box for more than thirty years in Pittman's basement, provides a remarkably detailed account of local events at MSU in relation to the national movement for equality in college sports. What the "Chronology"—along with associated news clippings and documents—only partly explains is how Pittman came to play a central yet behind-the-scenes role in the struggle for Title IX rights at MSU.

Pittman, DeBoer, and Alexander

Pittman began coaching the MSU women's track and cross-country team in 1974, shortly after the university hired Nell Jackson from Illinois to direct women's intercollegiate athletics and coach women's track and field.

Because of her significant administrative responsibilities overseeing nine sports, Jackson needed to hire a cross-country coach who could also assist with track and field coaching duties. A colleague of Jackson's, MSU's assistant men's track and cross-country coach Jim Bibbs, recommended Pittman. (Bibbs later became a highly regarded, longtime head coach and, like Jackson, a member of the MSU Athletics Hall of Fame.)

Bibbs and Pittman had often talked together during Saturday competitions held by the Mid-Michigan Track Club on the MSU track, where Bibbs trained MSU men's sprinters. Pittman competed with the club and designed training programs for the more serious club members. He recalled talking with Bibbs "now and then about training, recruiting, and [Bibbs's] dreams for his career." A sociology graduate student on the GI Bill, Pittman "had been around national and international elite middle and long distance runners" as a college cross-country athlete and as a member of the US Marine Corp's track team. In 1970, he had also served as an artillery officer and aerial observer in Vietnam. When Jackson offered Pittman the unexpected opportunity to coach college-level athletes, he accepted it, hoping to earn a bit of extra income.[17] The informality of his hiring speaks to the less-than-professional recruitment and status of women's college coaches at the time.

Pittman soon learned that the world of women's track and field resembled his experience with men's intercollegiate nonrevenue sports in some ways but not others. At the time, the women came from undeveloped high school programs, making many of them less prepared than men for college-level competition and therefore sometimes more challenging to coach. But both women's sports and men's nonrevenue teams shared the challenges that came with relatively meager budgets. Pittman had grown accustomed to fundraisers for men's track and cross-country—sports also historically underfunded compared with football and men's basketball. Similarly, while professional university fundraisers solicited donors for the big-time sports, women's coaches and players often raised their own funds to support travel to out-of-state competitions.

In October 1976, Pittman met Kathy DeBoer through one such fundraiser. That year, DeBoer competed on the MSU women's basketball and volleyball teams. The volleyball team—fresh from having competed at an

AIAW national championship tournament that established the Spartans as a top team in the Midwest—wanted to test their skills against the West Coast competition. "We want to go to UCLA and play the best," a teammate told a reporter from the *Grand Rapids Press*, DeBoer's hometown newspaper. DeBoer herself had already gained national experience when she took her "blistering spikes" on tour with the Adidas Junior National Team, a team that scrimmaged with Olympic contenders for a month in Montreal and also competed in Hawaii, California, and New Mexico.[18] To earn funds to help pay for a West Coast trip, the team's coach had organized a "Jump-a-thon." As DeBoer recalled, they solicited pledges to pay players a certain amount for each inch they jumped on a given "testing" day. In the team's quest for donors, they "ranged around campus seeking out any 'soft touch' for women's athletics." DeBoer's coach, Annelies Knoppers, suggested she talk with Mark Pittman.[19]

DeBoer found Pittman "working in some cage handing out towels or equipment or something," and he immediately pledged two dollars an inch, twice as much as any previous pledge (her parents had generously pledged one dollar, and others typically pledged five to twenty-five cents per inch). At the time, DeBoer "fancied [herself] an elite jumper" because she could touch the rim of a basketball hoop using a volleyball approach jump. Yet as she noted years later, "a jump approach of ten feet is [now] just the starting point for outside hitters seeking major college scholarships and the 'elite' women players are touching ten feet four inches and above."[20]

DeBoer's initial reaction to Pittman's pledge reflected what she later described as typical of her "angry feminist" phase (now she considers herself just a feminist, no longer seeing herself as a victim, no longer angry): "I immediately thought, 'this guy is an idiot and obviously doesn't think that women can jump a lick.'" She elaborated, "I don't remember if I informed him that day that his sexist opinion was going to cost him over fifty dollars or whether I waited until it was time to collect, but, in either case, he never flinched and gave me fifty-four dollars toward our trip."[21] Pittman recalled that he simply wanted to support the team.

Pittman's participation in the Jump-a-thon prompted him to attend a few of MSU's home volleyball matches, and he admired the team's athleticism and DeBoer's skills. He even asked DeBoer for a date that fall, though she declined, explaining that she needed to stay focused during volleyball season. Later that term, though, DeBoer and Pittman did join a few of his friends on the men's track team at a local pub for "a little to eat, lots of beer, and a four-way discussion about a variety of topics, mostly related to athletics."[22] They had a lot in common: both children of pastors, both athletic, each of them inclined to take action to support their ideals. This like-mindedness would be a catalytic element that unified the two of them as key individuals in a core group of students who came together to take collective rhetorical action.

By the fall of 1977, Pittman had coached MSU cross-country and track for nearly three years and had learned more about the differences between coaching men's and women's teams. Even though budgets were relatively small for all the lower revenue sports (both men's and women's), Pittman's experience made him aware of larger differences in coaches' salaries. He noted in his "Chronology" that he called the state civil rights offices that semester "to see if there were procedures to file a complaint against the university concerning salary discrepancies between coaches" (of women's teams compared to men's teams). He found "no procedures available according to those contacted," and he told his supervisor, Nell Jackson, about his conversations.[23] Looking back, he admitted that his interest in, and acute awareness of, the material differences between resources stemmed in part from self-interest—he could have used the increased salary that greater equality between men's and women's programs would have brought him as a women's coach. But he also brought to his experiences at MSU a commitment to social justice that emerged from his parents' work with civil rights as ordained ministers in the Disciples of Christ Church and with the National Association for the Advancement of Colored People (NAACP). "That background of civil rights and the idea that fundamental rights for people shouldn't be denied based on—well, race and religion— was something that was in my upbringing," he observed in an interview.[24] Pittman also brought the interpretive lens of his doctoral studies in sociology to how he viewed MSU's athletic programs. On papers filed away in the box containing his "Chronology," he jotted phrases by Karl Marx and other social theorists juxtaposed with notes about athletic budgets.

Helping relatively powerless individuals take on a large institution appealed to Pittman's antiauthoritarian streak. In DeBoer's view, Pittman's experience in Vietnam and exposure to antiwar protests, though he didn't participate, made protests in general something that he did not consider "off the wall."[25] Equally important, Pittman saw sports as central to his own identity, having participated in three sports at the high school level: track, football, and basketball. He liked them all and noted that "there were no girls' sports." So he thought, "Why would you possibly deny that to another group of people? What's the deal?"[26] In DeBoer's view, Pittman felt "comfortable with and supportive of women athletes," appreciating their competitiveness and grit. As she recalled, he dated several women athletes at the time, including her, and she thought that the emotion of being with a successful athlete motivated him to some extent. "I think he thought he was in love and that kind of thing . . . I mean when we really care about somebody, and they're carrying a flag or banner or whatever, it's like, yeah, I'm with you."[27]

During MSU's 1977 fall quarter, Pittman's friendships with DeBoer and with the team's coaches, including head coach Langeland, made him an increasingly strong supporter of MSU women's basketball. On occasion, Pittman continued to meet DeBoer, together with other friends, for a meal or drinks. He also worked with her to sell car decals at a football game to raise money for the women's basketball team's desired trip to a highly competitive invitational tournament in New York. The Queens College Holiday Tournament would include the highly ranked Old Dominion, with All-American player Nancy Lieberman.[28] As a writer for the *Lansing State Journal* put it, the tournament offered the team the "first-class competition" it needed to "make them the national contender a lot of observers [said] they [could] be."[29]

In fact, the whole practice of nationally ranking teams in a weekly coaches' top-twenty poll—a practice critical to the visibility of the game and to creating national rivalries—was still new for women's basketball. The women's poll, published by the Associated Press, was initiated by *Philadelphia Inquirer* sports reporter Mel Greenberg, a strong, early supporter of the women's game. Greenberg's articles in the *Inquirer*, the *Sporting News*, and his own *Women's Basketball Report* framed the growth of the game for his readers. He commented on topics including increased attendance, greater size and experience of players, improved caliber of coaches, the ambitions of big schools to challenge the dominance of small school powers such as Wayland Baptist or Delta State, the impact of media coverage (for instance, of the 1976 Olympic women's basketball team), and fundraising strategies. Several of Greenberg's articles are among the papers Pittman collected and saved from 1977, which indicates that Pittman followed some of these larger trends in the women's game.[30] For Pittman's part, when it came to fundraising, he and others at MSU found that approaching some of the wealthiest Spartan donors in their reserved parking places at football games to sell them candy bars was a successful fundraising tactic. However, Pittman recalls that administrators eventually discouraged this practice when the donors began asking questions about why those teams needed to sell candy bars to raise money for their sports.[31]

These small efforts, while they were helpful in the short term, were largely ineffective compared with more coordinated, higher-level efforts in select women's programs elsewhere. Although virtually unheard of in the Midwest, in other regions of the United States during this time period a few institutions started to see "name" boosters supporting women's athletics. One of Greenberg's news articles touted several well-known football coaches, including those who strenuously opposed applying Title IX to athletics, as supporters.[32] Women deserve "to go first class just like we do," Johnny Majors at Tennessee reportedly attested while participating in a fundraiser during which he was held for ransom by a UT sorority. Tennessee women's basketball coach Pat Head (later Pat Head Summit) underscored Greenberg's point that prominent male coaches served as "magic name[s]" that became "magnets for support." She claimed, "He [Majors] really helped us out by his involvement. . . . We're getting help now from a lot more people in the state."[33] At UCLA, the women's program hired its first professional fundraiser and promoter to capitalize on their All-American player, Ann Meyers. Even the most notably outspoken opponent of Title IX, Darrell Royal, drew praise for his support from women's basketball coach Jody Conradt (who still contended with the constraint of high school players in Texas having played by only the six-player girls' rules).[34]

Women's sports leaders may have acknowledged gestures of support from prominent football coaches as a rhetorical strategy. Suggesting that icons of the men's sports establishment were beginning to support women's athletics encouraged public support for Title IX through a bandwagon appeal. Behind the scenes, though, the NCAA was hardly supportive. In fact, they were readying a lawsuit to file against HEW by July 1978 when the Title IX regulations were to take full effect for university athletic departments. The suit claimed that the regulations impinged on the independence of universities and that the US Department of Education had overstepped its bounds.[35] While the support from some football coaches may have been authentic, the experience of the women's basketball team at MSU was certainly more common. For them, fundraising depended on less visible, more ad hoc efforts by coaches and team members who lacked the draw of a "name" booster.

At MSU, Pittman's friendship with DeBoer and the women's basketball coaching staff and his general support for women's athletics made him a regular in the sparsely populated stands at the team's games. At one game, he recognized a fellow sociology graduate student, Bruce Alexander, who had seen an article in the school newspaper about a women's basketball game and decided to attend. Alexander hoped to distract himself from thinking about the depressing fact that his entire master's thesis had been lost when his car was broken into. Surprised at the nature of the competition, he remembered thinking to himself, "This isn't pretend. This isn't six-player [basketball] like they played in my high school. This is the real game, and they're playing."[36] Because he enjoyed himself, he took a look at the schedule and decided to come to another game.

As friendships—and a soon-to-be rhetorical coalition—developed among Pittman, Alexander, and DeBoer, Mary Pollock began to make her voice heard on the MSU campus and beyond. A December 21, 1977, article in the *Coldwater* [Michigan] *Daily Reporter* conveyed Pollock's perspective on the relationship between personal assertiveness, success in the workplace, and contact sports for women. The article, "MSU Official Says: Contact Sports Good for Women Too," reported Pollock's contention that women often avoid direct confrontation at home and work, limiting their complaints to female friends rather than engaging in rational discussion to achieve desired change. Men, in turn, Pollock asserted, are not used to confrontations with women at work and may become defensive until they see that women can "perform as professionally as themselves." Women can do so especially "when competitiveness and competence have been given early encouragement." Pollock spoke, too, about Title IX, explaining that the law covers not only athletics but also "working conditions, wages, promotions, and a variety of other 'equals.'" She explained that federal sex discrimination complaints gained new attention in the Carter administration, but she encouraged women to protect themselves from reprisals by working as a group with other women if they chose to take action. (She suggested working with organizations that allowed them to "hide their identity.") The article concluded with a warning: "[When] acting alone in a legal setting . . . a woman must be prepared to spend time and such funds as she has in action through one or more courts. She must also be ready to use up a lot of patience and emotion."[37]

Pollock's discourse on the relationship between athletics and workplace performance reflected a growing awareness by prominent feminists that sports mattered for women. In March 1977, the *Minneapolis Tribune* ran an article highlighting Betty Friedan's attendance at the first game of the national AIAW basketball tournament, between the University of Minnesota and Delta State (a Southern powerhouse in women's basketball). Friedan, head of the National Organization for Women, commented, "Tomorrow will be the first time I've seen women play baseball, er, basketball, and I don't know whether I should cheer for the Golden Gophers or the Lady Statesmen, ah, Statespersons." She acknowledged that sports was "not her bag," but like Pollock, she emphasized that "athletics offers something that many women have never had a chance to learn. . . . Now they are learning how to fight and win, to compete, yet not make enemies." Friedan observed, "Now all of you [athletes] are on a frontier. We used to think that only textbooks for boys and girls were relevant. But now we're finding that athletics are relevant too."[38]

The pioneering athletic experiences of the MSU women's basketball team continued to engross Mark Pittman and Bruce Alexander. By the 1977 winter quarter, the two men considered themselves dedicated fans of Spartan women's basketball. Alexander enjoyed getting to know the coaches and players through his friend, so when Pittman volunteered his time to keep the MSU official game/score book, Alexander recorded and kept a record of the "official" statistics.[39] Their friendship and common connection with the women's basketball program made it natural for Pittman, DeBoer, and Alexander to discuss Pollock's presentation on Title IX for MSU coaches that Pittman had heard in the fall. In a 2011 interview, DeBoer described Alexander as "really a smart, smart guy." She laughed and recalled, "I mean, Bruce was always the one you wanted on your team for trivia because he just knew more and remembered things." She also saw him as someone who would have understood campus politics far better than any of the athletes.[40] A self-described "political junkie," Alexander had followed the controversy over the government's development of regulations for Title IX and athletics in the news. In particular, "the parade of football coaches" that went before Congress to oppose Title IX's application to athletics astonished him.[41] So he listened with interest when Pittman shared his impressions of the newly hired Title IX coordinator shortly after her talk in May 1977: "Excellent rhetoric," Pittman wrote in his "Chronology." "[She] knew Title IX information, aggressive, would speak out/up, ardent feminist (not a separatist)." And, he continued, she "would NOT be around MSU long if she pursued sex discrimination as practiced in MSU's Department of Intercollegiate Athletics." He found Pollock witty, with a "draconian humor": when asked in the meeting what she was most proud of, she replied, "My ovaries."[42]

Thinking back during a 2011 interview, Pittman speculated that the assistant director of athletics for women, Nell Jackson, had probably invited Pollock to speak to the coaches in her program (Jackson, after all, had spoken to Pollock's NOW group in Illinois).[43] Alexander, in an interview the same month, thought it possible that Pollock had set up the meeting on her own. He remembered Pollock as "very much somebody who was gonna' make sure that she opened doors that she felt needed to be opened on her own." He saw her as someone with a unique take on what it meant to be a compliance officer. He also viewed her as someone who, instead of taking a somewhat neutral position typical of administrators in such positions, was "looking for situations and advocating that people seek remedy."[44] What's certain is that Pollock's speech successfully planted a seed for Pittman, and Pollock convincingly sowed that seed through action and rhetoric.

At this meeting, according to Pittman's "Chronology," Pollock "handed out [an] excerpt from the Federal Register, Vol. 40, No. 108-IX. She read, interpreted, and discussed Title IX. She pointed out what sex discrimination 'might' be. She also discussed University grievance procedures." Pittman noted that "those present discussed at length, with Mary [Pollock], their problems and observations concerning their individual sport situation and the women's athletic program in general."[45] Alexander, who attended subsequent meetings with Pollock, characterized her as "very professional, very self-assured and very confident in what she was saying." In his view, her demeanor allowed listeners to "understand that they could feel the same way. It was alright."[46] Honed by her work with students concerned about injustices at Illinois, Pollock's calm rhetorical style gave her credibility with responsible young people who sought reassurance. Had she come across as an agitator or a volatile personality, those particular students would not have been as open to her message.

Pollock's explanation of Title IX and the options available to people for filing for redress of grievances found a receptive audience in Pittman, DeBoer, and Alexander. DeBoer was taking a philosophy of feminism course from MSU professor Dr. Marilyn Frye, and Pittman audited the class (which, despite his feminist sensibility, he found disturbingly extreme because of Frye's sex-separatist philosophy).[47] DeBoer had not been politically active about equality in athletics until her senior year, when she switched her major from music to humanities (after realizing she was "never going to be a diva"). She took courses in women's studies, sociology, anthropology, and philosophy. These classes, she said, brought her the benefits that a well-rounded higher education ideally provides— "expanding your mind, getting you to think about things you didn't think about before."[48] As she read books such as Marilyn French's *The Women's Room*, she began to view athletics at MSU through a lens shaped by feminist discourses. Although in the past she had wondered why, just once, the women's team could not practice on the main gym floor instead of a side gym, she "wasn't politically motivated to protest it." Her course with

Professor Frye at the end of her college career made her think, all of a sudden, "Hey, wait a second! I'm being cheated!"[49]

DeBoer's emotional reaction resonated with both Pittman and Alexander as friends and as fans of the women's basketball players and staff. Alexander was also drawn to conversations surrounding Title IX from a sociological perspective; he was interested in higher education as a complex sociological organization. As he learned of inequities suffered by the women's basketball team, he viewed the sequence of events that followed as an opportunity to observe, and perhaps assist in, a social movement beginning to take place within one such organization. Alexander recalled that he and Pittman considered it an opportunity "to figure out what's going on and why."[50]

Alexander, DeBoer, and Pittman all learned from Pollock that the university had one more year, until July 1978, to institute equality under Title IX. Assuming that institutions must follow the law, DeBoer took the federally mandated compliance date for universities and colleges seriously and literally. When she conveyed this timeline and her understanding of the team's rights under Title IX to her teammates, what she had to say resonated initially with some players more than others. A process of consciousness-raising began.

1. Women played organized basketball at MSU well before 1972 when Title IX was enacted. This Spartan team competed in 1932 under MSU's Women's Athletic Association, established in 1925 and led by the director of physical education for women. Photo courtesy of Michigan State University Archives and Historical Collections.

2. Between 1973 and 1981, Dr. Nell Jackson, a former Olympic track athlete and coach, served as assistant director for women's athletics at MSU, associate professor of physical education, and women's track and field coach. In the wake of Title IX, like other leaders of women's programs, she negotiated conflicting values between the AIAW's educational model of sport and the commercialized model embraced by men's athletics. Photo courtesy of Michigan State University Athletics.

3. In 1977, Kathy DeBoer mobilized her women's basketball teammates to alert MSU that the institution was not complying with its obligations under Title IX. Photo used with permission of *MLive*, the *Grand Rapids Press*, and Michigan State University Athletics; courtesy of the Grand Rapids Public Museum Archives.

4. Mary Pollock served as MSU's Director of Women's Programs and Title IX Coordinator from 1977 to 1978. A feminist activist, she took seriously the charge to guide MSU toward compliance with Title IX when most colleges and universities were slow to make serious progress toward gender equity. Photo courtesy of Michigan State University Archives and Historical Collections.

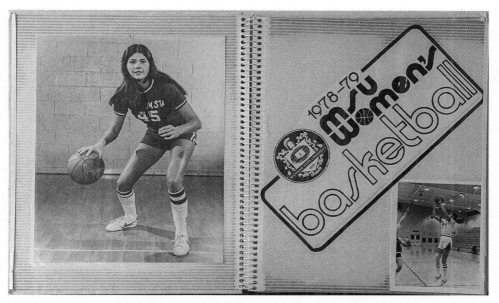

5. Pages from the scrapbook of Lori Hyman, co-captain of the 1978–79 MSU women's basketball team, preserve memories of playing for love of the game, without full scholarships, in a near-empty gymnasium with a warped floor. The team sold bumper stickers to raise funds for travel in station wagons to games outside the state. Photo courtesy of Edward Byrne; images of Lori Hyman courtesy of Michigan State University Athletics.

6. When MSU and star player Earvin "Magic" Johnson won the 1979 NCAA National Championship for men's basketball, the men played and practiced in Jenison Fieldhouse. The women's team rotated between intramural buildings, where subpar conditions became one basis for the 1978 team's Title IX and Michigan Department of Civil Rights complaints. Photo courtesy of Michigan State University Archives and Historical Collections.

7. Mariann Mankowski, known as "Cookie," was the MSU women's basketball team spokesperson and co-captain in 1977–78 when the team filed an internal Title IX complaint. Photo courtesy of Mariann Mankowski and Michigan State University Athletics.

8. Mark Pittman was head coach of the MSU women's cross-country team and assistant coach of women's track and field, 1977–79. His document, "Title IX: Chronology and Comments and Complaints," records details of the women's basketball team's Title IX struggle. Photo courtesy of Mark Pittman and Michigan State University Athletics.

9. Mary Jo Hardy, MSU volleyball and track student athlete, 1973–77, assisted with the MSU women's basketball team's struggle against sex discrimination. No other athletes on women's teams participated, some of them fearing that formal complaints could mean losing existing resources. Photo courtesy of Mary Jo Hardy and Michigan State University Athletics.

8
December
1978

We, the undersigned members of the 1978-79 Michigan State University women's varsity basketball team, wish to file a complaint under the relevant federal and state laws about specific sex discriminatory practices in public education to which we are subjected. We understand these laws to include Title IX of the federal Education Acts of 1972, the Michigan Elliott-Larsen Civil Rights Act of 1976, and the Michigan Public Accommodations Act of 1972.

The practices of which we complain concern our health, our safety, and minimal fairness. They are specific and relate to certain facilities, equipment, travel arrangements, per diem, and personnel with which the MSU men's varsity team of 15 members is provided and which our team of 11 members does not receive.

The specific complaints are listed on the attached chart grouped according to whether they are issues of health, safety, or fairness.

We are limiting this complaint to these issues. We understand that the total budget for varsity men's basketball at MSU, apart from coaching salaries, and athletic aid, is $116,000 and that the analogous amount of money available to our team this year is $13,500. We think this allocation is inequitable but we do not include it in this complaint. We are seeking an immediate remedy for unhealthy, and grossly unfair practices. We believe that attempting to address the money problem here would delay relief far beyond 1979. We want changes made in current practices soon enough so that our team can benefit from them while we are still MSU students and team members.

Nancy Hannenberg

Laurie Reynolds

Dawn Hertz

Ann Sober

Carol Hutchins

Deborah Traxinger

Lorraine Hyman

Gale Valley

Mary Kay Itnyre

Mary Vielbig

Marianne Jones

10. After MSU's 1977–78 women's basketball team filed an internal Title IX complaint charging widespread violations of Title IX, players on the 1978–79 team adopted a strategy of filing a more narrow complaint with federal and state offices of civil rights. Students and coaches were beginning to lodge complaints about sex discrimination in athletics at other colleges and universities across the United States. Document and photo courtesy of Deborah Traxinger.

11. The 1978–79 MSU women's basketball team filed one of the first Fourteenth Amendment and Title IX lawsuits by college students. Their case, filed in 1979 and settled in 1987, shows the challenges that plaintiffs and attorneys faced in Title IX's formative years. Photo courtesy of Michigan State University Athletics.

12. Carol Hutchins played basketball and softball at MSU from 1976 to 1979. As a starting shortstop, she helped MSU win an AIAW national championship. In her senior year, she became the named plaintiff for the women's basketball team's lawsuit. Photo courtesy of Michigan State University Athletics.

13. The 1978–79 MSU women's basketball team juggled homework, hearings in court, and basketball games as their Title IX battle unfolded. Coach Karen Langeland supported the team's activism without becoming directly involved. Photo courtesy of Michigan State University Archives and Historical Collections.

14. Deborah Traxinger, an MSU Academic All-American in women's basketball, served as class representative in the *Hutchins v. MSU Board of Trustees* class action lawsuit. Photo courtesy of Deborah Traxinger and Michigan State University Athletics.

15. Rollin Haffer, a Temple University student, was the named plaintiff in a Title IX lawsuit filed one year after *Hutchins v. MSU Board of Trustees* and settled one year later. The Temple case, like *Hutchins*, shows challenges faced by the first groups to sue under a new law being interpreted, contested, and implemented. Photo courtesy of Rollin Haffer.

16. Kelly Belanger played basketball and majored in English at MSU from 1982 to 1986. The 1982–83 season marked the first Division I women's basketball tournament sponsored by the NCAA. The Big Ten Conference also sponsored women's basketball for the first time that season. However, Title IX did not apply to college athletics programs between 1984 and 1988. Photo used with permission of *MLive* and the *Grand Rapids Press*, courtesy of the Grand Rapids Public Museum Archives.

17. Beginning in 1989, MSU women's basketball found a home in the state-of-the-art Breslin Student Events Center, the same venue where the MSU men's basketball team competes. Photo courtesy of Anna P. Chlopeck (Own work) [CC BY 3.0 (http://creativecommons.org/licenses/by/3.0)], via Wikimedia Commons, https://commons.wikimedia.org/wiki/File%3ABreslin_Center_Upper_View.

18. Girls and women today enjoy opportunities resulting from the work of the women's sports movement's pioneers. In 2014, Jaycie Fetter played offensive tackle on her middle school football team in Perkasie, Pennsylvania. Girls who wanted to play on teams reserved only for boys were often plaintiffs in early gender equity cases. Photo courtesy of Gerald Fetter Jr.

PART THREE

Students Take Action

The discussions about sex discrimination sparked by Mary Pollock's outreach efforts were not the first time women athletes and a feminist activist at MSU had engaged in a shared consciousness-raising process. Likewise, although the MSU women's sports program led the Midwest in budget and number of women's teams in the mid-1970s (before Title IX spurred other institutions to increase their commitments), it wasn't always that way. The growth of MSU women's athletics to the point that it could attract a multisport player of Kathy DeBoer's caliber or an administrator/coach with Nell Jackson's credentials came about in part through the efforts of an activist organization called the Alliance to End Sexual Discrimination at MSU. One of its founders, Vicki Nyberg, traced the organization's origins to a women's restroom in Flint, Michigan.

In 1970, Nyberg was a young mother with a spouse teaching at the University of Michigan's Flint campus when she overheard a conversation in the restroom. She was in a stall changing her baby's diaper (there were no changing stations in those days). As Nyberg recalled, "Almost everything about the women's movement went on in bathrooms. . . . In part, they were the only private place where women could talk with one another."[1] As Nyberg juggled her infant in the stall and tried to keep quiet, she heard one woman ask the other, "Did you get a call from main campus today?" The other said she had. They were both laughing and expressed their complete surprise because, as one put it, "Ann Arbor [the main campus] is finally going to recognize how important we are because someone finally sued them, and they are trying to find every woman on the faculty." They noted the irony of the main campus not wanting to hire women and then, in the light of the lawsuit, urgently seeking out any of them who happened to be teaching. Nyberg recalled, "I was very quiet trying to hear what was going on. . . . One of them said, 'Her name is Jean King.'" The other one asked if she ever heard of her. Nyberg heard the woman's colleague say, "No, but I guess she's an attorney in Ann Arbor, but I don't know, maybe she's from New York or California." They agreed that it would be very interesting to see how it all turned out.[2]

Nyberg herself had no idea what the lawsuit was about. She knew "only that it had something to do with U of M and something to do with women and something to do with Jean King." However, she recalled the conversation a year and half later when she moved with her husband to East Lansing so he could attend medical school at Michigan State. Almost immediately upon arriving, she was recruited by a graduate student to attend an MSU Board of Trustees meeting called to discuss an affirmative action plan for the university. Women's groups needed large numbers of women at the meeting, Nyberg was told, and they needed to leave in ten minutes. So in shorts and a t-shirt with a baby in a wet diaper, Nyberg attended the board of trustees meeting on affirmative action.

After being almost literally dragged to the affirmative action meeting, Nyberg found herself drawn deeper into the women's rights issues emerging at MSU. She did not get involved initially as a self-identified feminist or activist, and one appeal may have been simply the opportunity as a primary caretaker for an infant to engage in adult, intellectually stimulating interactions while her husband studied medicine. Whatever Nyberg's motivations, after the board meeting, she took it upon herself to start writing a university affirmative action plan. Functioning in "graduate school mentality," she just started researching and writing.[3]

As Nyberg worked on a plan for MSU, she learned that the law had required an affirmative action plan at the University of Michigan as a result of the sex discrimination lawsuit Jean Ledwith King had brought against the institution. The suit had sent shock waves across the state, even the country, because it held up millions of dollars in federal research funds. As Nyberg wrote, people gave her materials, and she began wondering whether "that attorney in Ann Arbor would talk with her." Nyberg remembered, "I called and explained who I was, which was difficult to do because [she laughed] I wasn't anybody. But there was this person on the other end who said what I was doing was very important." King even offered to come to East Lansing. She asked Nyberg where she lived.[4]

An Alliance Formed

In 1971, King came to East Lansing for a meeting at Nyberg's house. Nyberg had called every single name in the campus directory that appeared to be a woman's name. She was heartbroken when only twenty-two women showed up. By the time King arrived after ten o'clock in the evening, only five women remained. When King heard that three of them worked at the university, she informed them bluntly that anyone who worked at the university or had spouses who did should not get involved. When Nyberg protested and asked what she meant, King warned them about pressure the institution would exert. According to Nyberg, King said she would help in any way, but she didn't want anybody involved who could not afford to lose. She said, "Because you will lose and there will be a lot of pressure." But she added, "I can't protect you against yourself; if you insist on this, I will help."[5]

By the end of the night, only two women remained, Nyberg and Mary Craypo, who was married to a graduate student studying labor relations. Together, the two of them formed the Alliance to End Sexual Discrimination at MSU. Nyberg published her phone number in the paper, and women started calling. They reported females getting served less food for the same money as males in the dorms, so the two founders of the Alliance "went over and counted what was on everyone's plate as they went through the line and made our article for the next day. That's how we created articles for the student newspaper." They discovered sex-specific academic classes, a male-only marching band, and male-only cheerleading and flag squads. Nyberg explained, "The band issue boggled our minds and got us into sports." Sports led them to budgets. It shocked them to discover that some male coaches were still receiving millions of dollars a year to pay out their contracts after being fired. They got into philosophical conversations about whether single-sex teams should exist. They discussed whether the university should spend so much money on relatively few elite athletes as opposed to sports participation for students as a whole (here, they echoed long-standing concerns of physical educators). They continually wrote and published articles while also working on an affirmative action plan for the university.

At first, they assumed the university would be grateful for their voluntary work, would find their plan reasonable, and would implement it—a series of assumptions they later saw as naïve. Nyberg had limited clerical skills, so she found typing everything out to be very tedious. More comfortably, Nyberg went on radio shows and tested her verbal rhetorical skills. On the air, she refuted arguments that women were not interested in sports. She drew an analogy with her uncle's experience in the 1930s when he was told that Jews couldn't practice as OBGYNs because "they didn't like all that blood and they don't want those positions." When "those positions" opened to Jews after World War II, they joined the professional work force in great numbers. She contended, "It's the same with what you are saying about women athletes. Open up the slots—you'll see women will fill them. No matter how many slots you open, women will fill them." She added that, as with anything, "you have to create an atmosphere." She also argued that more than just a coach, a mentor, or even funding, if you want to encourage something in society, you need affirmative action, which she defined as a "booster kind of atmosphere." As a result, she said, members of some groups won't automatically think something just isn't for them. They need to be told in all kinds of subtle and clear ways that they are welcome.[6]

To kick the door of opportunity open for women athletes at MSU, the Alliance became "very annoying" to MSU President Wharton, according to Nyberg. Along with writing articles for the student newspaper, the Alliance began copying informative flyers and dropped or posted them around campus. They focused on women's basketball because there was no intercollegiate team, and women at the university called the Alliance to say they wanted more than intramurals. Nyberg said she spoke frequently with the director of intramural programs for women, Carol Harding, whom she described as a strong supporter of athletics for women. Harding passed along inside information about how male administrators perceived their efforts on behalf of women's athletics. Through Harding, Nyberg learned how MSU administrators responded to activism on behalf of female athletes. On the one hand, administrators argued that finding five girls who would want to play was impossible. "They told us that over and over again," she said. On the other hand, Nyberg claimed that Underwood and at least one other administrator viewed addressing the women's efforts as a lower priority than addressing problems faced by black male athletes.[7]

As Nyberg saw it, discrimination was discrimination, and she did not distinguish among groups. So as she and Alliance supporters heard women's stories, they continued to make them public as much as possible. They also prepared for a lawsuit, which for Nyberg included continued conversations with Jean Ledwith King. In those talks, King continually warned of repercussions. Nyberg held up to her the term MSU administrators used to attack them—"bored housewives"—as an example of what she thought was the worst that would happen in retaliation. Nyberg said, "There weren't a lot of words to put women down at that time. To really put them in their place. One was prostitution, being a slut, and one was being a lesbian. . . . They had a hard time, and that was why they came up with the word housewife." But King kept warning that things would get worse.[8]

The Alliance publicized a board of trustees meeting in which, according to Nyberg, more than five hundred people testified either in person or in writing. They sent out flyers encouraging women to tell their stories. Support for their efforts grew, but Nyberg and her supporters felt frustrated with the pace of change because they sensed that information they assumed was private—regarding budgets and salaries, for example—shielded discrimination from exposure. Her conversations with King expanded to include the ACLU and politicians with Michigan's attorney general's office. She was advised to find "the little red book" in which MSU employee's salaries were published. She was told, "If that little red book disappeared overnight but was back in the morning, nobody would know what happened to it." So, she said, "That book did disappear." Nyberg released photocopies to the newspapers, and before long, she said, "You could see how much everybody made, including the athletic department."

The information made it obvious to community members and alumni that "a lot more money was being spent on men's athletics." It also made clear that the director of women's intramurals acted as the only real paid staff member in women's sports at the university. As Nyberg put it, "She is it. She is all there is. There ain't no more. There's not a women's basketball coach and an assistant coach, not a tennis team. They don't exist. And all of a sudden it is clear they don't exist."[9]

When it came to sports, the debates were complicated, as always, by the conundrum of physical differences between males and females. Nyberg herself was not an athlete, so she could not imagine legitimate objections to mixed-sex teams. She argued boldly for a sex-integrated ice hockey team, for example. She remembered asking, "What do you mean it has to be all men and it's rough? I thought the rules were you weren't supposed to touch each other?" And she argued, "If you really believe no woman would ever make the team, then what do you care? Open it up to everyone—obviously you think there are some women out there who could make the team or you wouldn't be keeping it closed down." Whatever they thought of Nyberg's points if they heard them, people at every level began asking practical questions about scholarships and teams. In Nyberg's view, enough people began to think about the fact that perhaps their daughter could be excellent in softball—good enough to have her way paid through college. That thought crossing their minds made parents care about sex equity in athletics. And there was still the threat of a possible lawsuit, a credible threat in light of the University of Michigan suit. As a result, even before Title IX came about in 1972, the university opened doors, created positions, and made administrators increasingly accountable for prohibiting discrimination.[10]

The two years when all this happened, between 1971 and 1973, were "naïve times for all of us," Nyberg recalled. "To think that two bored housewives would be able to disrupt [the university's] whole pattern and undo everything they believed in within two years." But as unlikely as it all seemed even to Nyberg in retrospect, a process of change had been set in motion.[11]

9 Consciousness-Raising

24 Feb to 7 March 1978—A continuation, at a more fervent level, of informal, spontaneous and conscious[ness]-raising discussions among the various basketball team members themselves and with variously associated individuals about the general situation of sex discrimination in athletics at MSU.

—Mark Pittman, *Title IX: Chronology and Comments and Complaints*[1]

The position of director of women's programs at MSU that Mary Pollock accepted in 1977 was a product of pre–Title IX activism. In Nyberg's view, by the time Pollock came, the university had come a long way. The Alliance had secured increases in salaries for women, the Spartan marching band was integrated, and "ladies portions" were abolished so that the size of meals served in dorms to women were increased to equal the portions served to men. There was a clerical union and intercollegiate athletic teams for women. Sex-segregated classes no longer existed, and men and women lived together in the same dorm buildings (though on different floors).[2] Although the Alliance saw MSU President Wharton as a target of the activism, Nyberg described his replacement, President Harden, as far more invested in the status quo, in her words, "a white man and an ineffective white man."[3] In her view, many of the tensions had died down and the administration had figured out how to put forward "the right rhetoric" and to hire leaders who would make the institution look good without pushing for real change. According to Nyberg, "There were people who really knew this campus and applied [for the job directing women's programs] and would have really run with it." Women's groups assumed Mary Pollock was "a weak person" because she lacked institutional clout and knowledge and because of their observation that "the women who really fought to open up these positions were never the ones who got the positions." As Nyberg put it, institutions preferred to hire people who "were involved, but they were tangential to the whole thing—they never created havoc or spoke up, but they could say they were a member of NOW or a member of the political caucus or a member of the alliance."[4]

Of course, Pollock did not fit that mold. Although she paid attention to athletics because she thought of it as an interest area and a focus of Title IX, her already strong interest in sex equity in athletics at MSU was heightened by what she observed every day. As director of women's programs, she worked across from the office of the assistant director of minority programs. That individual, it happened, was responsible for making certain that one very important minority student who was new to campus that year felt as comfortable as possible: Earvin "Magic" Johnson. As Pollock recalled, the assistant director of minority programs had a huge telephone board of phone lines, and "what he did in a lot of his time was manage Magic Johnson." Pollock liked her colleague a lot, but she wondered about the fact that he drove a Cadillac on his modest assistant director's salary and wore expensive clothes. She understood that "Magic brought a lot of spotlight to the university," but as far as she could tell, the star men's basketball player received a special personal assistant, something that to her knowledge no female athlete received. For her, this provided another example of illegal disparate treatment, not to mention something she assumed must be unacceptable under NCAA rules.[5]

As Pollock's sense of injustice was upset by the special assistance the university provided to the men's basketball star, the Spartan women's basketball team started strong on the court. The early success they experienced in the 1977–78 basketball season must have heightened team members' sense that the inequitable conditions in the MSU athletic department were unfair. They had raised enough money to help support travel to the Queens College Women's Holiday Tournament held December 27–29, and the Spartans won their first game decisively, 94–41. A *New York Times* headline announced their success: "Mich. State Women Easy Victor in Women's Basketball." According to the *Times*, "Michigan State brought its finely tuned fast break and unselfish teamwork to New York and quickly earned the role of favorite during its game with Concordia of Montreal." The couple of hundred fans attending the game, however, consisted mostly of Queens College students. The reporter noted that six hundred fans attended the second game of the night between Queens and Southern California, a number considered at least respectable for the time.[6] Although MSU lost to national power Old Dominion in the tournament's final game, the Spartans made a respectable showing that helped establish DeBoer as a top player in the country. At the end of the season, she was one of thirty finalists for the Wade Trophy, a prestigious honor given to the top women's basketball player in the nation.

Trustees of the Golden Egg

While DeBoer had an outstanding senior year on the court, off the court she learned about methods of social change activism. In Dr. Frye's Philosophy of Feminism course, she and Pittman were asked to sign a petition that was distributed to the class. It had been developed "as a result of the recent knifings of women students on and around campus" and in response to news coverage of a rape and murder in Florida.[7] The petition was to be presented at the next MSU Board of Trustees meeting, and the class was encouraged to attend. Even before the full board meeting, Pittman, DeBoer, and their friend Bruce Alexander decided to attend a meeting of the board's affirmative action committee, a group whose existence likely had roots in Nyberg's activism half a decade earlier. The February 3, 1978, meeting, it turned out, focused on Title IX and athletics.[8]

According to Pollock, she had requested the meeting for two purposes: "to find out whether [MSU] policy makers wanted to continue the kind of program [already in place] or make changes," and to alert them that she had "probable cause to believe that there were problems." She envisioned herself leading this meeting that she had initiated, but "it was decided that Dr. Kearney would give a report to the Committee." She recalled that she "did get to say a few words, but the agenda was controlled by others."[9] In her recollection, "Dr. Kearney used the opportunity to lobby for a new football facility," and one of her supervisors, Vice President for University Relations Robert Perrin, "said he wanted [her] to draw up a list of questions she wanted to ask rather than let [her] look at salary, scholarship, or expenditure information for a program audit."[10]

MSU's *State News*, a student-run newspaper, covered the meeting under the headline "U May Lose Funds if Sports Renovation Demands Unheeded." Despite Pollock's frustration about not controlling the agenda, she communicated the urgency of the July compliance deadline effectively enough that the school paper used it as the frame for their article. Speakers quoted in the article included athletics director Joe Kearney, Mary Pollock, and Nell Jackson. Pollock, true to her background in student affairs, emphasized student's rights. She explained the need for a "comprehensive survey of student athletic interests and abilities." Title IX required finding out what "level of competition" they wanted, she explained. "Student opinion would probably justify existing big-time football, basketball and hockey programs," she said, seeking to mitigate any fear that Title IX implementation would harm men's sports.[11]

Jackson likewise delivered the message that the university needed to make changes but that men's sports would remain protected. She pointed out that although MSU had recently led the nation in women's athletics, they were quickly falling behind. As portrayed in the *State News* article, Jackson allied herself more with Kearney than with Pollock (perhaps a purposeful and political move on her part). Jackson noted that women's teams desperately needed budget increases but also acknowledged that funds from the "three money-making teams" helped support women's teams as well as men's. She even reportedly agreed with Kearney that some women's sports could make money "if they were financed and 'marketed' right."[12] Presumably, this discourse of commercialism came primarily from Kearney, as Jackson's independent use of such language would have been uncharacteristic given her grounding in physical education values. She apparently assented, though.

One of the trustees described the strategy more colorfully: "We don't want to kill the goose that lays the golden egg. . . . It would be more advisable to fatten it up."[13] This golden egg metaphor functioned as a powerful rhetorical tactic that worked in concert with a second defining metaphor of the men's sports establishment: the family metaphor. By the logic of this metaphor, in the college sports family, men's sports (the golden geese) were and must continue to be the breadwinners. Any extra privileges or benefits they received simply kept the breadwinner healthy enough to support the others, or so this rarely contested logic went.

According to Pittman's notes, Kearney's handouts focused on budget issues related to the law. In language echoing that of his NCAA colleagues, Kearney warned that the university needed to find more sources for funds "or drastic changes might be forthcoming." Pittman's view of the athletics director was that he was "all PR."[14] In fact, upon arriving at MSU, Kearney voiced support for women's athletics, noting a large and growing budget. Like athletic administrators at Illinois, Kearney routinely compared MSU women's budgets with women's budgets at other schools, not with budgets for men's teams at their own institution.

However, Kearney was familiar with female-male comparisons. In 1972, as the athletics director at the University of Washington (UW), he noted in a student newspaper interview that women's athletic programs would inevitably develop beyond "club team status," a neutral-sounding statement that could be interpreted as supportive, whether or not he really meant to voice approval of that inevitability.[15] Two years later, Kearney was confronted with a budget request of "nearly $200,000" for UW women's athletics programs, and he faced public criticism because women athletes received half as much money as male athletes for food on road trips. A 1974 *Seattle Post-Intelligencer* article reported that, unlike their male counterparts, women athletes at UW slept two people to a bed on road trips and in the basketball program had to purchase their own shoes.[16] After Kearney came to MSU in 1976, Pittman observed him in action and believed he understood Kearney's signature rhetorical strategy all too well. As far as Pittman was concerned, the athletics director had perfected the art of making neutral-sounding statements that belied his lack of actual intent to support change. His assessment of Kearney's presentation to the MSU Board's affirmative action committee in the spring of 1978 was brief and sarcastic: "Kearney at his best!!!"[17]

Inequities

On February 23, 1978, Pittman, DeBoer, and Alexander returned for the full board of trustees meeting. According to Pittman's notes, "The group presenting the petition and speaking out concerning women's safety on campus was not allowed to appear before the Board."[18] The experience of attending the affirmative action meeting, however, seems only to have whetted the trio's appetite for continued involvement in a social and institutional change effort. They participated in conversations with the women's basketball team that continued "at varying degrees of intensity" as the basketball season hit full swing in late February 1978.

During that season, some of the inequitable conditions that the Spartan women's basketball team faced, such as unequal per diem for road trips, resembled what women experienced at UW or Illinois, while other problems were unique to MSU. The Spartan women practiced in the poorly heated Women's Intramural Building (women's IM) and played their home games on the buckled, warped floorboards of the Men's Intramural Building (men's IM). On occasion, they practiced in Jenison Fieldhouse and sometimes played a home game there, while the men's team consistently practiced and played on their home court in Jenison. Team member Lori Hyman recalled that in at least one season, she played more games in Purdue University's Mackey Arena than she did on any single court on the MSU campus. Purdue's main court began to feel more like a home court than the gymnasium at MSU.[19] Signs of inequity abounded:

- When the women's team played in the men's IM, they had no permanent lockers to store their belongings (and no hair dryers or other basic conveniences taken for granted by today's athletes).
- Little heads of nails protruded from the men's IM floor, presenting a safety hazard.
- Players recalled that during course registration, long lines of students wound through the gym during their practices.
- When they practiced in the women's IM, some of the players wore hooded sweatshirts to ward off the chilly Michigan winter—and when the thermostat broke one winter, no one was available to repair it.

- Practice stopped briefly every few minutes for one of the players to wipe the dust off the basketball since no university employee swept the court before practice as they did for the men's team.
- When the one pair of shoes provided by MSU to each player wore out, the athletes used masking tape to bind the soles to tops of their shoes or spent their own money to buy a new pair.
- The university did not provide a laundry service for the women but laundered the men's athletic clothes.
- "Sparty"—the muscular, armor-clad mascot who strutted in front of the visitor's bench at men's games—never made an appearance at women's games.
- On occasion, one or two cheerleaders came to their games, but never the pep band that regularly supported the men's team.
- While the men flew or took buses to away games, the women players squeezed into their own station wagons to make the five-, six-, sometimes ten-hour drives to hotels where they slept four players to a room, two players to a bed.
- Carol Hutchins recalled a particularly outrageous incident when University of Indiana Coach Bobby Knight told them to leave the court in Jenison Fieldhouse because his visiting men's team needed the court to practice.[20]

Unknown to the Spartans, women's teams elsewhere increasingly refused to accept such conditions and treatment. As early as 1975, athletes and coaches at Washington State University (WSU, not to be confused with UW, where Kearney worked), spoke before campus organizations and university officials about correcting inequities much like those the women players experienced at MSU. Women athletes and coaches at WSU contended that "general social policies support[ed] prioritizing men's athletics, especially football, over women's athletics" (their actions led them to file one of the first gender equity in college athletics lawsuits, *Blair v. Washington State University*, 1979).[21] The defeat of the two Tower Amendments notwithstanding, WSU leaders decided that Title IX should not apply to football revenues and the sport of football in general. Charges of discrimination made against WSU came from two different groups that included athletes, student managers, graduate assistant coaches, and four-teen coaches of teams between 1963 and 1982.[22]

At MSU, the activist stirrings were less broad. They focused on a single team and a core group of outside supporters whom Pittman referred to as the "cabal."

The Cabal

When asked to define the term, Pittman evoked the notion of a cell; that is, a small, highly motivated group "that was taking on something that needed to be taken on."[23] Decades later, however, Alexander eschewed the term "cabal," laughing at Pittman's dramatic flair. He said it sounded too much like "we were thinking it up, and we were scripting what other people were doing, and that's not what was happening." As Alexander saw it, "We were trying to provide support, we were trying to help, and we were trying to clarify, but we were not trying to lead it."[24] He perceived that the people associated with the women's basketball program "were trying to do something that, on its face, looked like the ordinary activities of daily life, but it was a world-changer all at the same time." These people had become his friends, and for Alexander, "Sometimes friends need help getting something done, and . . . these were people worthy of having the help."[25]

Volleyball and track athlete Mary Jo Hardy was the third member of this core support group. After starting out at Delta Community College and then attending Central Michigan University, Hardy transferred to MSU in 1973 to try out for the volleyball team with her sister. Under AIAW rules, players could transfer without the penalty of sitting out a year (as the NCAA required). The idea was that if athletes were students first, then presumably they would make decisions based primarily on academics. Recruiting, as Hardy explained, "was actually outlawed, so you really couldn't find out ahead of time if [a coach] even wanted you to play [at a school], or if you would fit in." This idealistic AIAW philosophy began to appear naïve under Title IX. A 1978 "Women's Review" article for *Basketball Weekly* noted that "once women began receiving athletic grants and increased budgets, an unspoken pressure existed to produce results." The added pressure to win and the accompanying promise of scholarship money or more visibility led some outstanding athletes to migrate from smaller schools like Immaculata to larger programs.[26] DeBoer's move from Calvin to MSU reflected that trend.

In 1977, Hardy and DeBoer played volleyball together at MSU, though they first met as opponents in previous years when DeBoer still played at Calvin College.[27] Hardy recalled DeBoer as tough and very competitive, with leadership skills that bettered any team on which she played.

Hardy's exposure to Pittman came when she observed him coaching the long distance runners while she practiced javelin throw. She remembered him as headstrong, outspoken, and someone probably difficult for the "higher-ups" to deal with. But her favorite memory of him coaching shows a humorous side of his personality: he wore a pioneer ladies' bonnet, a prize the team received for winning the Becky Boone Relays. He was "running around the track, just hollering at different people and exhorting them to 'run faster! Pick it up! C'mon you!'"[28]

Hardy returned to graduate school in 1977 after graduating from MSU and searching unsuccessfully for a full-time job. She had met Bruce Alexander the previous spring at an MSU softball game, which she sometimes attended to support track or volleyball teammates who also played softball. Not recognizing Alexander as a familiar face among the tightly knit group of fans and players, Hardy wondered, "What's his reason for being here, and who is this guy?" The response she got was, "Well, his name is Bruce, and we're not really sure why he comes here, but he's really nice."[29] Eventually the two met, talked, and later became a couple. The cabal was complete.

As a self-described "gopher" ready to do whatever the cabal needed, Hardy had the most behind-the-scenes role of the four friends. But her low profile belied her strong feelings about the cause; since high school, she had waited for an opportunity to participate in the movement for gender equality in athletics. She remembered when Title IX was enacted during her senior year in high school; her high school basketball coach showed players a small article claiming that the new law would bring an end to sex discrimination in school athletics. Tired of playing in the smaller "girls' gym" and frustrated with differences in uniforms and literally every other resource, she was elated by the news. She and her teammates assumed that things would change immediately. "OK, great! Where's the stuff?" Hardy remembered asking. They soon realized that "just because the law says they have to give it to ya', doesn't mean they have to give it to ya'." She laughed, and said, "You have to fight for it."[30]

As a high school student, her protests took the form of changing the sign on the small gym that said "Girls' Gym" to "Small Gym." Hardy and her teammates reasoned that "the boys' gym, the main gym, didn't say 'Boys' Gym,' so why was the small gym labeled 'Girls'?" The labels reinforced the assumption that the large, main gym naturally belonged to the boys, so for several years, Hardy and her friends switched the sign every day, and every night someone switched it back. When she went back around 2010, she could still see where they had finally wiped out for good where it said "Girls' Gym." But, she noted, "You could still see it very faintly, still in the door." This high school experience with a small protest made her eager to help her former college teammates when they began fighting to enforce Title IX.[31]

Athletic Funding: Cracking Open the Golden Egg

As the cabal solidified, Pollock discovered a potentially useful document in her quest for information on exactly how MSU funded men's and women's athletics programs. For several months, Pollock had requested sensitive information that she needed "in order to effectively audit and evaluate sex equity in regard to intercollegiate athletics." In a February 1, 1978, memo to Vice President for University Relations Robert Perrin (the VP responsible for her program), she wrote, "I would like to see the ledger sheets for 1976–77 fiscal year for the intercollegiate athletic accounts which are numbered 21–1700 through 21–1899. What will be the quickest way to get that authorized?" She needed them, she explained, "to inspect vouchers and other details which might help in a comparison of the various athletic programs. Personnel files might be the most sensitive area but will be needed."[32] On February 14, 1978, MSU's vice president for business and finance, Roger Wilkinson, sent Pollock a memo, copied to Perrin, containing some of the information she needed. Wilkinson also attached to the memo a special report completed by MSU's financial analysis staff, along with additional memos that highlighted "various funding relation-ships." Schedule C, for instance, documented "Repair and Maintenance Projects Funded from Sources other than the Athletic Department."[33] A 1977 memo from the assistant controller listed seven areas in which "rev-enues or expenditures could be considered attributable to the athletic pro-gram but are not credited or charged to the program."[34] The documents that Pollock received exemplify hard-to-come-by information that gender equality advocates needed (and still need) in order to study in depth the relationship between the "goose," its "golden eggs," and the university out-side of athletics.

The financial report offered evidence that Pollock could use to challenge narratives about revenue and intercollegiate athletics that the public routinely accepted as conventional wisdom. The sight of all the fans in Spartan Stadium on football Saturdays offered proof enough to most people that the "bootstraps" narrative surrounding the big three sports at MSU (football, men's basketball, and ice hockey) was the simple truth. In this narrative, people viewed the big three sports at MSU as self-sufficient, consistently lucrative revenue producers. In reality, the finan-cial report showed that ice hockey depended on football ticket revenues to pay down the debt on the Munn Ice Arena. The athletics department as a whole received money from the university general fund to renovate Spartan Stadium, which meant football itself benefited from university resources. Other projects for both men's and women's athletics received general fund support—for example, an office remodeling for the assis-tant director of women's athletics, renovations to Jenison Fieldhouse, and work on the men's and women's intramural buildings. Six full-time MSU employees who devoted 100 percent of their work to athletics—and disproportionately to the "revenue sports"—in the areas of sports broadcasting, sports information, and fundraising were paid entirely from accounts outside the athletics program. MSU's general fund paid $280,000 to retire debt associated with the Student Activities Center and Stadium Revenue Bonds.[35]

This information demonstrated that general university funds partially supported MSU athletics, including the supposedly self-sufficient, "reve-nue-producing" sports. With such information, Pollock could readily show that the big fat goose's golden eggs were less valuable than people thought and that the "revenue-producing" sports relied on complicated, interconnected funding relationships. The report did not even begin to address all the ways in which athletes as students benefited from university-funded resources, staff, and infrastructure that enhanced the value of their scholarships, learning experiences, and degrees when they graduated (e.g., the library, bookstore, student health center, parking lots, research, and professional development for faculty). Perhaps most significantly, because the athletics department was legally part of the institution, it operated on a tax-deductible, nonprofit basis. When it came to Title IX, however, including the three highest revenue-producing sports in MSU's compliance plan was quite simply inconvenient. Doing so would threaten the cozy relationship between academics, athletics, and a taxpaying public that seemed satisfied to believe whatever the athletics department wanted to tell them, as long as it didn't interfere with their tail-gating parties.

In March 1978, Pollock continued to ask questions about budgets, revenues, and expenditures. She also made herself available to talk informally with anyone on campus who had questions or complaints related to sex discrimination. During this time, a series of "mini-crisis incidents" intensified the women's basketball team's intermittent conversations about inequities. Pittman listed them in his "Chronology":

1. Having to sell decals for needed funds to go to New York for the Queens Tournament,
2. Having early season games cancelled due to strict enforcement of university policy while the men's team still played,[36]
3. Having to drive to away games in cars,
4. Not receiving the full per diem allowance permitted by the University,
5. Not having a team physician at all games,
6. Because of budget limitations, having to play back-to-back road games,
7. Having to play three back-to-back games,
8. Obvious scholarship differences from the men's basketball team and even more increasing differences from women's basketball teams at other universities,

9. Tremendous facility discrepancies,

10. *Ad infinitum.*[37]

These incidents led DeBoer to approach Pollock about filing a complaint. Pollock suggested that in order for the university to take a complaint seriously, the whole team should sign onto it, so within a day or two DeBoer initiated a team meeting after practice. By the end of the meeting, which took place on the floor of Jenison Fieldhouse, DeBoer and Cookie Mankowski were designated team representatives. The team members had voted unanimously to file a complaint as a team with Pollock's office.[38] Inevitably, though, some players felt ambivalent. A few may have spoken with their parents, who perhaps expressed fears that their future employment prospects might be affected by signing onto a complaint against the university. But the team remained remarkably unified.

In Alexander's view, DeBoer must have "had a very significant role in pulling this together." He pictured her saying to herself, "This is my team; these are my people; this is me; and we are being disadvantaged here. And there oughta' be something we can do about it." He viewed her as an inspiring individual who successfully urged others to think about things differently.[39] Mankowski was especially receptive to the challenge. According to DeBoer, "This was all her. . . . I think she relished these types of [situations]. . . . She felt she was on the right side, and on the side of justice, and I think that's a little bit of what she's always been about."[40] Other team members gained confidence from Pollock. When she met with the Women's Varsity Club, her discourse conveyed strongly the idea that "if we don't like it, we don't have to do nothing about it or wait for other people. We can take some action; we're entitled to do that." To be clear, Hardy pointed out, "It isn't like [the women's basketball team] immediately went racing out of the room to storm the athletic department demanding redress of grievances. But [for them], it was the beginning of conversations that started around the idea that 'it doesn't have to be like this. And it doesn't have to be like this *for us.*'"[41]

10 Fighting Words

> The one thing that we've learned about social change—it doesn't happen because good people *wish* it to happen. It happens because people organize and get active politically.
> —Roscoe Brown Jr., President, Bronx Community College, "Minority Women in Administration"[1]

To move from wishing for change to making it happen calls for the use of rhetoric. What's more, organized change requires the *strategic* use of rhetoric—that is, language appropriate for a particular speaker in a given role and situation. Inevitably, then, local struggles for organized change under Title IX took on different tenors depending on the individuals and athletic department organizational structures involved. Schools such as Yale, Ohio State, and Texas faced problems similar to those at MSU, but effective strategies for addressing those problems could not follow a single blueprint, considering the different individuals in leadership roles and differently structured athletic departments. Yet even across local differences, a general rule held true: while many women's sports administrators guided organizational change with carefully constrained speech and writing (hopeful to retain their jobs and a positive work environment), youthful athletes often felt freer to take a straightforward, sometimes blunt approach. Both groups chose fighting words that best suited their standpoints, contexts, and purposes.

For the student athletes at MSU, the challenge became to juggle competing demands of their academic work, basketball season, and social lives with time invested in making change for the future.

Balancing the Present and Future at MSU

In early March 1978, when the MSU women's basketball team voted to file a Title IX complaint with Mary Pollock's office, they were preparing for the Midwest AIAW postseason tournament play. The Spartan women had just completed a winning regular season, finishing with a 21–6 record, with four of their six losses by just a point. In a loss to Northwestern University in mid-January, Lori Hyman, a key player, suffered a season-ending knee injury. Noting that knee injuries had also afflicted the men's team, a *Lansing State Journal* article lamented the MSU women's loss of the "slick shooting" Hyman, a "bubbly 5'10" forward."[2] She was replaced in the starting lineup by Mary Kay Itnyre, who had transferred from Arizona State and hoped the team could still contend for a national championship.

Coincidentally, the women's regular season record nearly paralleled the Spartan men's final season record of 25–5. But the men's team captured the Big Ten championship, an accomplishment heralded by three separate concurrent resolutions presented in the Michigan state legislature. The resolutions praised the men's basketball team for unselfish team play, commended coach Jud Heathcote, recognized the leadership of four Michigan natives, and praised Earvin Johnson for making the All-Big Ten team as a freshman. One resolution declared: "His leadership, pinpoint passing, amazing ball handling, scoring ability and rebounding skill have earned him a unique place in Michigan athletic history even though he is only a freshman. . . . With his unique style of playing basketball, he has been a catalyst to turn around the basketball program at Michigan State University and has brought national attention and prestige to the University."[3]

The MSU women's team members enjoyed the men's success as much as anyone, but they also wondered how it would feel to be so warmly embraced by the campus and community. When asked what it was like to be on campus as excitement over the men's program grew, DeBoer said: "It was great fun, is what I remember. I don't ever remember taking the situation that we were protesting in the athletics department and making it feel like it was ever us against the men's team. We were fans. We went to the games. Magic Johnson, it was his freshman year. Gregory Kelsor . . . I mean it was exciting. If anything, we were envious. We wanted people to care about *us* like that."[4]

After making the critical decision to take action and report areas of unequal treatment, the women's team had to first focus on basketball. In the AIAW state championship tournament, DeBoer had put on a "virtuoso performance," with teammate Itnyre showing signs of "magical" potential, according to the *Detroit News.*[5] But in the regional, the Spartans, for the third time that season, could not get past Ohio State. According to one news account, "the game was tied eight times and deadlocked at 49–49 with seven minutes to play when the Buckeyes . . . pulled ahead to stay at 53–51."[6] MSU's defeat by the Buckeyes dashed the team's hopes of a trip to the Texas regional and the Final Four in Los Angeles. Disappointed with the ending to their season, DeBoer and Mankowski turned to the unfinished business of the team's Title IX complaint.

In late March, the two team representatives went to see Pollock, who asked them for specific evidence to support their claims, taking notes as they spoke. Mankowski recalled that she and DeBoer did not weigh alternatives or deliberate over whether to file a complaint with Pollock's office. The matter seemed straightforward at the time; they considered it the best way to proceed. As the university's designated Title IX coordinator, Pollock had educated them about their rights and explained the procedure for filing a complaint. In Mankowski's view, the team members were simply following the proper procedures one step at a time. Because Pollock had informed them of their right to file a complaint on their own behalf, they did not expect their coach to address their concerns for them. After all, Langeland was at the time a relatively inexperienced college coach whose career, if she stirred up trouble, could end when it had barely even started.

Langeland, in her late twenties at the time, was not much older than the seniors on her team. She explained that "there were some very strong people on that team," and without them, no action would have been taken. She remembered that team members initially came to her asking some questions—for instance, about why the women's team had to sleep two people to a bed on road trips. "My recollections are the one thing that was so striking was having to stay four to a room," Langeland said. "It was the lodging piece that started the questioning and then watching the men get on buses as we piled into—not SUVS—but station wagons. Those were probably the two most glaring things, and then I think women on that team starting looking into it. Then more and more things started popping up." Langeland perceived that the team members "were very aware they were treading on some thin ice." She recalled, "They didn't want my job to be in jeopardy, so it very quickly turned to them keeping me out of the loop." But, she said, "I pretty much had my sources, and I knew pretty much what was going on." Although she didn't know whether the university would have fired her if she had taken a more active role, Langeland greatly appreciated her players' concern for her.[7]

How to Tread on Thin Ice: The Dilemma of Women's Sports Administrators

In truth, women's sports advocates *were* being fired—coaches and administrators risked quickly losing their jobs if they lobbied too strongly for women's athletics. Mary Alice Hill is a case in point. An early plaintiff in a lawsuit charging discrimination in athletics, Hill was repeatedly harassed and finally fired from her position at Colorado State University after strongly lobbying for increased funding.[8] She shared her advice to colleagues in an interview for the 1980 book *Women Who Win: Exercising Your Rights in Sport,* urging others to work for change within the university and avoid the courts if at all possible: "The fastest, most efficient way of bringing about equality is staying out of the courts, but an implied threat of a suit can be a tremendous incentive to bring a program into line."[9] Even implied threats, however, could upset relationships within an athletic department or the larger institution.

DeBoer and Mankowski had never heard of Alice Hill. What's more, as students, they had little reason to concern themselves with athletic department or intra-institution relationships. Remarkably, they even had no idea that in her previous position at Illinois, Pollock had led the group called Concerned Women Athletes. In those pre-Internet days, coverage of local Title IX struggles rarely made the national news. Player Deb Traxinger still attended high school when DeBoer and Mankowski began the process of filing a complaint with Pollock's office, and she had never even heard of Title IX. When she met her new teammates at MSU in the fall of 1978, she found herself, most unexpectedly, in the middle of a struggle she could not have imagined. She recalled, "We didn't hear about any other teams doing this. I don't think anyone on our team was politically ambitious. We were really kids. Very, very young adults." In her view, "It wasn't a political movement. It wasn't necessarily a women's movement. It was just, 'We're a bunch of basketball players that play for Michigan State University. Why are they treating us so differently than they are treating the men?'"[10]

Traxinger remembered her impressions of MSU's 1976 AIAW national championship softball team: "They were just a tremendous group of athletic women and very impressive. My thought at the time was WOW—if that's what Michigan State puts out for women's athletics, then I wanna' be one of them!" Behind-the-scenes struggles, of course, were invisible to her. But not for Nell Jackson. As assistant director of women's athletics, Jackson had an inside perspective. Her advocacy role for women's sports included trying to explain to news reporters the significance, for instance, of the softball team's accomplishment. She and her counterparts at other institutions faced questions about whether a women's championship was the same thing as if the men's basketball team won a national title. It took more than a week for even the East Lansing papers to cover the MSU softball team's national championship, and then coverage was minimal.

To address such inattention, most gender equality struggles involved decades of quiet, behind-the-scenes advocacy. Usually, women's athletic administrators guided an incremental process of change. They had to seek out and take advantage of opportune moments for persuasion—and sometimes those moments were forced upon them.

Women's Athletics Director Pressured by Yale Students

In March 1976, the administrator responsible for women's athletics at Yale, Joni Barnett, did not move fast enough to suit members of the women's crew team. Led by athlete Chris Ernst, the students launched a dramatic protest. The 1999 documentary film A Hero for Daisy dramatized their activism: nineteen women stripping to the waist and reading aloud a statement with the words "Title IX" painted across their naked backs. Their March 3, 1976, statement, the whole of which is preserved in the Yale archives, begins as follows:

> Mrs. Barnett:
>
> These are the bodies Yale is exploiting. We have come here today to make clear how unprotected we are, to show graphically what we are being exposed to. These are normal human bodies. On a day like today the rain freezes on our skin. . . . We're human and being treated as less than such.[11]

Their eloquent statement offered a compelling set of emotional appeals, emphasizing threats to the athletes' physical health and the fact that, in order to protect their coach, they took action without his knowledge. The athletes emphasized their rights as human beings, and their powerful bodily rhetoric formed a dramatic tableau. Their protest proved effective. At a private university dependent on alumni for its endowment, Yale administrators certainly did not want the negative media exposure created by the students' spectacle. When Yale alums began contacting the university in support of the women, the team's demands were met in short order, and the team suffered no backlash for speaking out. They had read the rhetorical situation well and staged an effective protest. As students at a well-endowed private institution—one more concerned about its reputation than its football team—they had some leeway to speak out forcefully and get away with it.

The same luxury of (relatively) fearless speech, however, was rarely afforded to women's athletics directors at most institutions. The fact that the Yale students directed their statement to Joni Barnett, the women's athletics director, reflected the difficult position in which women's athletic administrators found themselves. In their statement, the Yale women softened their critique of Barnett by positioning her as a symbol they used as a means to an end. When they most directly accused her of failure, they couched the beginning of their sentence in a passive construction ("There has been a lack of concern and competence") although still directly attributing some responsibility to her ("on your part").[12] They seemed aware that she did not herself hold the power to make change.

Rhetorical Advice

In the late 1970s, explicit rhetorical advice for women such as Barnett at Yale, Jackson at MSU, and other women's sports administrators circulated among networks of women's athletics directors. Bonnie Parkhouse, a scholar of physical education and business administration and coauthor (with journalist Jackie Lapin) of *Women Who Win*, observed that male administrators often made women who sought change under Title IX the brunt of jokes. In the face of ridicule and resistance, many women seemed ready to "throw in the towel."[13] Parkhouse, who once served as executive director of the National Association for Girls and Women in Sport and the AIAW, urged women to speak up but to do so strategically. She and Lapin included three chapters in their book with detailed advice on effective organizational communication for women athletics administrators: "Getting Along with the Men's Department (She's Really Just One of the Boys)," "Manage Men," and "Persuasion: Getting It from the Administration." Their main point was that "survival for the woman athlete means ACTION—exercising her rights of free speech."[14] They believed that without action, programs would stall or wither away despite the backing of Title IX. They observed, "There is little question that women are getting the least of their needs met at schools where they have been afraid to speak up."[15]

When "speaking up," however, Parkhouse and Lapin advised women to remember that in "the carousel of institutional politics, a thorough knowledge of the workings of the male innerarchy is a must; naiveté can be fatal." They urged women's sports administrators to work together with allies and "painstakingly [nurture] relations with influential people."[16] In social movement rhetorical terms, women's athletic administrators needed to "bore from within."[17] That is, they needed to connect with the cultural values held by resistant audiences they faced. Without sacrificing their own values, women leaders needed to demonstrate to male leaders that they were one of them.

Parkhouse and Lapin also warned that no matter how careful women were in protesting, those "who are the first to speak up become the martyrs—these women must suffer the initial indignities so that others after them will never know discrimination."[18] For these authors, the risk to women's "integrity, dignity, and pride" if they failed to speak out outweighed the very real risk of being fired, at least for those women without tenure.[19] Along with these emotional appeals, they offered two strategies for self-protection: First, they advised, "Doing a near flawless job is the best protection against discrimination and prejudice." Second, they urged women to remember that "more doors can be opened with a smile than with a fist."[20] This advice urged women to capitalize on traditional feminine characteristics that men would find appealing and unthreatening: the hardworking, perfectionistic good girl and the happy and smiling (as opposed to angry and frowning) woman.

Testimonials in the 1979 publication *Out of These Bleachers: Writings on Women in Sport*,[21] a collection sponsored by the Ford Foundation and published by the Feminist Press, offer similar advice. In a chapter called "Shedding Light on Title IX," one woman warned, "If you start out by bucking them, you're in trouble."[22] Another individual offered an example of a strategy she found effective: "I went over and sat down with the guys on the men's team, smoked a couple of cigarettes and we got to know each other. From then on I'd go every afternoon and have the gym all to myself for the women's team."[23]

Along with encouraging a commonsense approach to relationship-building, combined with some traditionally feminine rhetorical tactics, Parkhouse also counseled patience. She quoted respected AIAW leader and women's athletics director at Iowa, Christine Grant, who urged women to set reasonable, incremental goals. Toward this end, Grant offered two questions women should ask themselves to guide their actions: "(1) Will the action enable the disadvantaged to move expeditiously in a positive direction toward equality? [and] (2) Will the action in any way further disadvantage the previously disadvantaged group?"[24] This formula of cautiously speaking out in a carefully planned, rational way was tailored to realistic constraints of the situation faced by women's athletic leaders in the late 1970s. That Grant's advice did not reflect a rights-oriented feminist rhetoric is not unusual considering her late-blooming self-identification as a feminist. But Grant's advice—like that of Parkhouse and Lapin or Hill—missed an opportunity to address a critical constraint that affected decision making and available means of persuasion: the departmental structure within which an administrator of women's athletics functioned.

The enactment of Title IX led many women's athletic programs to separate from academic departments of physical education (where men's programs also originated). When women's athletics programs merged with the men's programs, a pattern previously established in another civil rights context repeated itself. Racial integration of schools in the South often meant the black principal became the assistant principal and the black coach became the assistant coach.[25] In the Title IX era, two primary departmental structures predominated: (1) separate departments for men's and women's athletics with their own directors, and (2) merged departments in which the women's athletics director was an assistant director, subordinate to the primary athletics director, who directed men's athletics. Some merged departments integrated women's athletics into the department as a whole, while an assistant director of women's athletics worked closely with and for the head athletics director. In other departments, women's athletics essentially existed as a separate but unequal entity in which the assistant director of women's athletics maintained significant autonomy over budgets and philosophies for women's teams (such was the MSU model under which Jackson worked). Other situational factors came into play as well, including the relationships among female faculty, activists, and students on campus. Each department also needed to adapt for local situations the general rhetorical advice circulating through professional networks and publications.

The issue of merged versus separate programs under Title IX felt like a catch-22 for most women's athletic administrators. A separate model worked better with the AIAW-endorsed value of self-determination and control for women's programs, but it risked continued inequality. A merged department offered the benefit of more easily making the kind of direct comparisons that would effectively shine a light on inequities. Yet if women joined athletics departments led by the men's athletics director, then women administrators, coaches, and athletes risked becoming colonized, subordinate, second-class citizens. Even so, a merger with men's athletics might provide increased access to funding sources tapped by men. For example, in 1973 (the same year Jackson began working at MSU), Frances Schaasfa became the women's athletics director at the University of California, Long Beach. She sought to move women's athletics away from physical education, an academic unit, thinking that greater financial support would be available if women's and men's athletics were combined under the university's Student Services unit.[26] By contrast, the vice president at Southern Illinois threatened Charlotte West with a merger as a form of punishment because she pushed too hard for reforms. She recalled him saying that she would "no longer be the director, and [he would] just go ahead with this merger."[27] Varying local circumstances and personnel, then, called for savvy leaders who could identify the most advantageous path and employ the language strategies needed to implement a coherent vision. That path was almost never clear-cut, as illustrated by the case of The Ohio State University.

A (Sub)merged Department: Ohio State

In 1973, Ohio State offered Phyllis Bailey the position of assistant athletics director of women. Her appointment came a year after she first alerted OSU Athletics Director J. Edward Weaver that Title IX meant the university "was going to have to deal with women's sports." She recalled, "Of course, he just laughed at me, because he thought I was pushing for something no one else was going to have, and he wasn't going to have any part of this." However, after the NCAA's attorneys confirmed for its members that the university needed to address women's sports, the OSU president called Bailey into his office. She explained, "I didn't very often get to his office" because, ever since she began working with women's sports club teams in 1956, she was "always under two men." She remembered the OSU president asking her, "Would you be terribly upset if the title was assistant director of athletics?" She looked at him and said, "Well, you know that isn't really what it ought to be, but I don't care what you call it as long as you call me." She understood that putting her on equal footing with the men's director would upset power relations in the athletics department, so she knew from the beginning that she would have to work from a colonized position.[28]

Like many women in her position, Bailey considered contending with resistance to change from men's athletics for a subordinate position as simply part of the job. In that position, she constantly dealt with resistance based on misinformation and false assumptions, especially the idea that "if women got any grants in aid, it would be taken away from the men." Men also resisted in indirect ways. For instance, before softball games, "it was difficult to get the field in shape." She recalled, "It would be an hour before a game and nothing had happened. Then they would appear—they would always do it, but they would always try to make it difficult before they got it done." Bailey said, "It was very obvious from the beginning that our athletic director did not want Phyllis Bailey in that position. He knew that I had been around [OSU] since the mid-1950s and had been building our program and that I wouldn't let him make all the decisions." She speculated, "He wanted to bring in someone who didn't have any vested interest in what was going on, preferably someone young who would just say, 'Yes sir,' and let him do primarily what he wanted with the program."[29]

When feminist women on campus strongly protested Grant's cautious approach to addressing men's resistance, it initially surprised Bailey, who described her own rhetorical style as a "people approach." That is, she presented herself as (and most of the time genuinely was) a patient, reasonable woman who pushed for change incrementally. But self-identified feminist women—the counterparts of MSU's Mary Pollock and Marilyn Frye—expected her to act more aggressively. She felt she made enemies among these women for accepting trade-offs and for letting men take credit for changes created largely by her actions. She sought to persuade her supervisors by "plowing a field" rather than "using a sledge hammer." She got to know the wives of the men's coaches and administrators, hoping they would influence their husbands' receptiveness to her requests. She expected the athletics director's first response to any of her requests to be "no." Then she waited a few weeks and went back again ("plowing the field"). A little later, she went back a third time to "plant the seed." Finally, she laughed, he would say "You know, we really need to do such and such," as if it had been his own idea. Meanwhile, Bailey had the task already half done because she'd been working on it all along.[30]

At times, Bailey took an even more proactive approach. Shortly after MSU hired Jackson as assistant director of women's athletics and women's track and field coach, Bailey recalled being told that Ohio State didn't have the funds to hire a coach for women's track. But she wanted very much to hire a talented young coach whom she knew to be looking for a position, and she felt that she had to act quickly. Bailey feared losing this individual to MSU, where the opportunity to work with and for the Olympian track athlete Jackson would be a strong draw. Without waiting for approval, Bailey brought the young woman in for an interview, only to find the candidate wearing green and white, the Spartans' colors. However, when directly asked whether she was considering a position at MSU, she denied it. Regardless, Bailey acted decisively—that very day, she used her connections in the personnel department to implore the senior associate athletics director to come up with a position for the outstanding candidate sitting right in her office. Within half an hour, Bailey recalled, she got a call saying that she could make an offer. The next day, former OSU men's track star Jesse Owens called the athletics director to congratulate him on making such a fine hire. Astutely, Bailey did not contradict her boss when she heard him on the phone taking the credit. In fact, she had planted the seed for this development not only through her connection with the personnel department but also through talking with Owens at a convention, where he had made a point of saying, "We have to do something about women's track at Ohio State." Bailey recalled how much it meant to her that Owens had said "*we*, not *you*." The extra time she took to get to know people when she had the opportunity invariably smoothed the way to accomplishing her goals.[31]

Bailey's experiences underscore the additional rhetorical advice offered in *The Woman in Athletic Administration*, a second book by Parkhouse (again with Lapin). The book identified challenges facing women leaders during the Title IX era as primarily communication based. The authors urged women to speak and write "with care and understanding" to dispel suspicion and earn respect.[32] When working from subordinate positions in a male-run hierarchy, they asserted, women must learn the art of compromise while also acting proactively and assertively. Parkhouse and Lapin listed twenty-two different common failings of women in management, such as not accepting criticism well, trying too hard to please, taking on too many responsibilities, and not trusting others to do a job right. In short, for these authors, women needed to figure out how to use language effectively in order to gain the financial and moral support they and their programs needed from men. They explained that as a first step, women needed to identify men with the most influence in the "informal power network" and analyze them, perhaps seeking them out as mentors: "A woman must begin by establishing who they are, how they view her, which are sympathetic and which are antagonistic, what their pet projects are, what their likes and dislikes are." The authors asserted that other women who "have been able to infiltrate the group" proved a valuable source for this information.[33] For Bailey, one such woman was the secretary to the head athletics director. Bailey recalled an occasion when this wise and protective staff member locked her in a room until she "cooled off" before meeting with her boss.

In merged departments such as OSU, women's athletics administrators acted as middle managers. They faced the ongoing challenge of mediating between highly competitive women athletes and coaches—such as Kathy DeBoer and Mark Pittman at MSU—who wanted immediate results, and their own supervisors, who were strongly invested in the status quo. At Ohio State, Bailey recalled a particularly startling incident when she could not maintain distance between a strong-willed women's field hockey coach and a key "power coach" in the men's program, football coach Woody Hayes. Bailey remembered Hayes as a man known to think women "couldn't be athletes because they didn't have bull necks and that sort of thing," and that "nothing else quite added up to football." At the time, the field hockey team practiced on the football field, and managers for the football team increasingly encroached on the women's time by coming earlier and earlier to set up. Bailey recalled that the managers were "scared to death of Woody," which was likely why they wanted to get set up well ahead of time. The field hockey coach, though, finally couldn't contain her anger. She confronted Hayes on the field, saying, "Haven't you ever heard of Title IX, and don't you believe women have any rights at all?"[34]

Such an approach was unthinkable for Bailey, who never saw herself as "a great fighter for Title IX or women's rights." But she had made a point of getting to know Hayes, had gone to his team's Bowl games, and had gotten to know his wife, Ann. Bailey noted that Hayes had observed how tough the women's track coach was and how the players "practiced like athletes, they thought like athletes, and they were real competitors because [their coach] was that way." In Bailey's view, these observations impressed upon Hayes how serious Ohio State's women athletes could be, so he was unexpectedly receptive to the field hockey coach's complaint. Bailey recalled that when they sat down and talked, Hayes said he had no idea that the managers were encroaching on the women's track practice time, and that after he gave them a tongue lashing, it would never happen again.[35] Bailey's point in this story seemed to be that direct confrontation may be effective at times, but it could be most successful if the field had been plowed ahead of time to make the person at whom it is directed as receptive as possible.

Bailey's longevity at Ohio State, combined with OSU's highly successful women's programs, suggests that in the long run her rhetorical approach proved effective. She seized available moments for persuasion when she could and made the most of them. In retirement, she has been recognized as a quiet hero for OSU women's sports, a patient architect of what is today a vibrant program. A modest woman, Bailey made only one request when her boss retired: she wanted his office chair. It was the one prize she claimed as a symbol of hard-won accomplishments that belied the title "assistant director."

Seeking Separate but Equal: Texas

The process of institutional change under Title IX played out much differently at Texas, where a highly competitive, outstanding female athlete fulfilled the role of director of intercollegiate athletics for women. Like Nell Jackson at MSU, Donna Lopiano was a world-class athlete, a college All-American who played professional softball after graduation. In 1975, at age twenty-seven, she left her position as assistant athletics director and assistant professor of physical education at Brooklyn College of the

City University of New York and arrived at the University of Texas, Austin (UT).[36] Lopiano spent nearly two decades building UT's women's athletics into a signature program separate from the men's program. By the time she stepped down in 1992, Texas was widely considered the most financially and athletically successful women's program in the country. She had even developed a women's basketball program that attracted enough paying spectators to be considered "revenue producing."[37] In developing a separate program, she nevertheless employed techniques of "boring from within" by emphasizing values common to both the men's and women's programs. She also used more confrontational strategies when necessary. Her combination of "foot in the door" and "door in your face" strategies effectively accelerated the pace of change for women's athletics.

A 1994 interview study of women's athletic administrators conducted by Gail Maloney and a 2010 rhetorical analysis of Lopiano's administrative discourse by Meredith Bagley offer important insights into Lopiano's professional communication. Bagley analyzed Lopiano's testimony before Congress in opposition to the Tower Amendment, which took place in the summer of 1975, just a few months before she arrived on the Texas campus. Like N. Peggy Burke from the University of Iowa and others who testified in opposition to Tower, Lopiano knew how strongly men's athletic administrators associated Title IX with outside interference and unwelcome mandates. She adopted a positive tone and took this information into account with her subsequent rhetorical strategies. Although she had referenced "blatant discrimination" in her congressional testimony regarding the Tower Amendment, her written discourse at Texas avoided such charged language. Instead, she developed appeals to common athletic and human values, seeds she planted during her congressional testimony.[38] When she arrived in Texas, Lopiano adopted an approach resembling one articulated by Christine Weller of the University of Maryland, whose strategy involved never invoking the words "Title IX." In an interview with Maloney, Weller explained, "I use the term 'fair.'" Specifically, in appealing to the director of athletics, she pointedly referred to him as a "fair man" who "[loved] sports for people."[39]

According to Bagley, Lopiano elaborated on Weller's rhetoric of fairness, employing a more complicated, even contradictory rhetoric of fair play. In her work at Texas, Lopiano defined "fairness" as balancing "the seemingly opposite claims that female athletes were just the same as their male counterparts [and] that women's programs deserved legal protection from their richer, bigger male opposites."[40] By "just the same," Lopiano referred not to physical attributes such as strength, quickness, or flexibility but rather to the reality that both women and men athletes confronted the same psychological and physical challenges posed by competition. She emphasized an experience common to all athletes: they continually "battled evaluation and comparison." Lopiano's memos and mission statements conveyed her assumption that both men's and women's programs had the same aim: to support skilled athletic performance and excellence that transcended the sex of the athletes.[41] She emphasized "the universality of the athlete" regardless of gender and invoked a "humanistic" vision of sports. This humanistic vision—meant to create a sense of identification between men's and women's athletics—became her primary argument for why the women's athletic program needed additional resources. Strategically, Lopiano's language and rhetorical vision "downplayed the disruptions that new women's varsity programs would cause."[42]

Whether or not Texas's athletics director and football coach Darrell Royal fully understood or accepted Lopiano's paradoxical argument, he must have noticed that Lopiano did not directly confront him with the threat of Title IX. Nor did she use terminology in her administrative communication that he would have associated with radicalism and unreasonableness (e.g., terms such as "discrimination" and "sex-equity," frequently heard in more overtly feminist discourses). She did, however, praise and acknowledge Royal. Like Jackson at MSU, Lopiano understood the psychology of affirming a potentially resistant individual targeted for her persuasive messages. Just as Jackson routinely expressed public gratitude for support provided to women's athletics, Lopiano described Royal as "a humanist" for his ability "to put himself in the position of the 'other guy.'"[43]

Along with establishing her own "tradition of tact," Lopiano's successful rhetorical efforts may have benefited from Ellen "Lennie" Gerber's visit to the Texas campus.[44] Gerber was a physical education professor who traveled the country to meet with higher education faculty and administrators to advocate for gender equality. In 1974, just a year before UT hired Lopiano, Gerber "plowed the field" (to use Phyllis Bailey's phrase) for Lopiano's subsequent discourse emphasizing the universal athlete. Recall that Gerber believed males and females had more in common than not, and she communicated her message through indirection, humor, and logical reasoning. Gerber's discourse may have served as a "foot in the door" tactic, providing a relatively low-stakes precedent for Lopiano's later, higher-stakes persuasive discourse.

Still, Lopiano needed to establish her own legitimacy at Texas as a change agent to be reckoned with. She did so by combining coactive discourse—appeals like the universal athlete that emphasized a common cause—with calculated confrontational strategies. Confrontational, or conflict strategies, as the name implies, "emphasize dissimilarities, diverse experiences, and conflict with target audiences."[45] When strategically combined, these two approaches can be an effective strategy for establishing legitimacy as a social change agent.[46] Lopiano used the term "reverse psychology" to describe a confrontational strategy that she used early on to achieve her goal of maintaining separate departments for women's athletics. Contrasted with the more gentle "foot in the door approach," Lopiano's reverse psychology was a "door in your face" tactic designed for a strongly resistant target audience. In the case of athletics director Royal, she had to deal with a powerful, high-profile administrator who had lobbied strongly and publically for excluding football from Title IX. Lopiano capitalized on Royal's fear that women wanted access to what male athletic administrators thought of as "their money" (in truth, women's programs did need money from somewhere in order to grow). Lopiano described her initial confrontational move as follows: "I pretty much insured, at least for a fifteen-year period, that athletic departments would remain separate. The first year I was [at Texas], I walked in to a meeting with [Darrell] Royal, who was the athletic director, and Jay Neals Thompson the [NCAA] faculty rep. And just point blank told them that we didn't have any money, they did, and I wanted to merge the departments, so I could get the men's money."[47]

As she expected, "It did not go over very well, there was a real anti-merger mentality there just because they figured, my God, she's after our money."[48] By establishing an initial demand that she expected the men's athletic department to reject, she created an anchor to which they would compare future requests. Thus Lopiano paved the way for subsequent smaller requests that she would need to make in developing a viable separate program.

Lopiano also employed coactive strategies when she rejected the idea that men's athletics must play the breadwinner role in a redefined relationship between men's and women's programs. After implementing her reverse psychology and securing a separate program for women, Lopiano emphasized that she did not want the men's and women's athletic departments competing for limited financial resources or for women's sports to fully rely on men's sports for financing. Instead, she offered new ideas for fundraising to benefit both programs. Her frank language on the subject showed that she understood and accepted as legitimate the most common source of resistance from men's athletics. In a 1975 internal athletic department document called "Recommendations for Implementation of Philosophy and Objectives," she wrote:

> One of the most prevalent fears of administrators of athletic programs for men has been that the next "knock on the door" will be a woman athletic administrator demanding "what women deserve" and making no effort to contribute to the financial stability which has taken so long for men to achieve. Such demands only detract from the solvency of the total athletic program and create unnecessary antagonisms between the men's and women's program. Women must be willing to carry their own weight in the production of revenues to support intercollegiate athletics. The quickest and easiest way to reassure male administrators of good intentions and budgetary competence is to jump into the fundraising effort.[49]

With this discourse, Lopiano identified herself as a team player, a role she could afford to play, having already carved out her own space to develop women's athletics in a separate program. She also separated herself from many of her women's athletic administrator peers with her unabashed embrace of commercial discourse surrounding the men's sports model. Although she insisted that she considered the welfare of students paramount, she adopted a vocabulary that would have horrified her physical education foremothers. For Lopiano, women's sports were a "product" and a "revenue-producing resource" in a "new market."[50] The terminology of economics became integral to her administrative vocabulary.

A Hybrid Structure: MSU

The coactive and confrontation approaches that Lopiano effectively combined at Texas were employed at MSU as well, except by different individuals rather than as part of a single leader's rhetorical strategy. Whereas Jackson routinely employed coactive strategies, Pollock gravitated toward more confrontational approaches. Other than Jackson organizing initial meetings for coaches and women athletes to hear Pollock's presentation on Title IX, the two women did not work together. Typically, across the country, directors of women's athletics became the point person in responding to Title IX and were primarily responsible for managing and advocating for women's sports programs. However, Jackson's voice was relatively subdued during the escalating conflict at MSU. By all accounts, she quietly supported the efforts of Pollock, DeBoer, and the others. According to Pittman, she knew he was assisting the women's basketball team. Pittman recalled that when a higher-up asked Jackson about his frequent associations with the team during the growing conflict, she covered for him by explaining that he was in love! Apparently, in 1978 a young coach's romantic interest in an athlete was more acceptable than joining a campaign against sex discrimination. Jackson herself occasionally met in private with Pittman, not to discuss his cross-country coaching duties, but to share information she thought the women's basketball team would find useful in their activism.

Unlike Pollock, DeBoer, Mankowski, and their supporters, Jackson struggled with a delicate balancing act. Her roots in the AIAW's educational model of sport and her identification with the traditional values of physical education tempered her appeals for sex equity under Title IX. She harbored conflicted feelings about how much equality with men's athletics was advantageous to women and how quickly change needed to happen. Like Pollock, she felt limited by her lack of institutional knowledge or a network of personal relationships of the sort that Bailey brought to her advocacy work at Ohio State. When Title IX was enacted, Bailey had already been building women's programs at OSU since the 1950s, beginning in physical education and intramurals, then moving into the athletics department. In contrast, Jackson and Pollock were both relatively new to MSU. Complicating matters further, Jackson did not operate in a clear-cut role. Like Bailey, she held the title of assistant director of women's athletics, but Jackson had considerable freedom to act as a de facto director. Although she needed to make a case for budget needs to athletics director Joe Kearney each year, it was not entirely clear that he was her supervisor in all the customary ways. She held full responsibility for determining the allocation of those funds and for setting the philosophy of sport that guided her program. When she was first hired, she said, she encountered an attitude of "do whatever you want, but don't rock the boat."[51]

Following that advice came easily at first. When hired in 1973, Jackson held a position that distinguished her from peers across the country: the first woman in the Big Ten Conference to hold the title of assistant director of women's athletics. In 1975, two years before Pollock's arrival, Jackson publically expressed satisfaction with the MSU women's program, citing strong administrative support and calling it "the overall best progressive program in the Big Ten."[52] She had good reason for this glowing assessment. The fact that she requested budget increases each year for women's athletics at MSU and received them reflected her positive relationship with administrators. Her warm relationship with Wharton and vice president Jack Breslin, with whom she sometimes played racquetball, offered her a unique advantage. When she lobbied the president and vice president of the university for support, she subverted the athletics hierarchy by not working directly through the men's athletics director. However, given the hybrid nature of MSU's athletic department structure, she likely felt comfortable advocating for her own program.

Jackson might have found it easier to maintain positive relationships with upper administrators because she never challenged the inequities surrounding the three most well-supported men's sports: football, basketball, and ice hockey. In its 1976 self-evaluation for Title IX, conducted under Jackson's watch, the university completely excluded these three sports from program comparisons. When Pollock learned of this exclusion a year later, she viewed it as a blatant defiance of Title IX. Jackson seems to have accepted it, though, perhaps convinced by the argument that all the other sports depended on revenues from these three. In any case, in a 1975 article, Cynthia Meagher, a *Detroit News* reporter sympathetic to the women's movement, noted Jackson's remarkable lack of bitterness in light of glaring inequities.

While Jackson may have felt more bitterness than she revealed, in her public comments she espoused a patient approach to developing the women's sports program. In the article, Meagher observed that Jackson's budget for women's athletics had grown to $160,000 for 1975–76, more than twice what it was when she was hired. Meagher pointed out, however, that the new budget for nine women's varsity sports was "also $10,000 less than the sum spent to install Astroturf in the football stadium last year." When asked whether "the movers in women's intercollegiate athletics would like to see one of their sports receive the same treatment as football," Jackson responded that she would not. True to her foundational physical education values, she described a vision of women's sports as one that emphasized education and "developing ability," rather than focusing on winning. Yet somewhat paradoxically, she also expressed her desire for more assistant coaches, an expanded schedule, and athletic scholarships.[53]

When it came to scholarships, Jackson's public remarks often revealed inconsistencies. Her ambivalence about whether they were good for women's athletics must have made it easier for MSU to delay significant increases in scholarship funding for women athletes. MSU's 1976 Title IX self-evaluation cites the university's "lack of athletic scholarships for women students as a shortcoming."[54] However, just five months later, Jackson again communicated her ambivalence toward scholarships. "Now we have competition for the fun of competition," she said. "When you have scholarships then you can develop a whole new attitude with the problems of overemphasis on winning."[55]

Although Jackson's praise for administrators and her program likely helped build and maintain goodwill with her supervisors and other administrators, her contradictory discourse surrounding the scholarship issue sent mixed messages. The *Detroit News* reporter, Meagher, summed up what she understood of the difficult balance informing Jackson's stance: "Women's sports must count, but not so much that there's a temptation to teach rule-breaking along with athletic discipline—and not so much that a team's winning season means more than an individual's future."[56] As for many physical education faculty and women's athletics administrators, Jackson found it difficult to maintain this balancing act and to advocate wholeheartedly for equality as defined by the 1975 Title IX regulations. She recognized, however, that "the young girls take what we've done for granted and want more. It keeps us on our toes."[57]

Given her grounding in the traditional values of physical education, Jackson's often conservative discourse extended beyond what might have been expected. As a black woman who was a trailblazer throughout her career, she was accustomed to adversity. Often, instead of fighting against obstacles or simply giving up, she went around them. When Jim Crow policies in Alabama prevented her from attending a graduate program there, she moved first to Massachusetts to earn a master's degree and then to Iowa to earn a doctoral degree in physical education. When her professional association's chapter in Alabama prohibited her from joining, she gained access to national conferences through a mentor from Iowa. When women were prohibited from competing in races over two hundred meters (the middle distance events that Jackson believed were ideal for her strengths), she focused on the two hundred meters—and broke the American women's record.

A brief article Jackson wrote after returning from the 1972 Olympic Games in Munich, where she served as head coach for women's track and field, offers further insight into her attitudes and discourse. In her article, included in the 1974 book *Women's Athletics: Coping with Controversy*, she asserted that "no excuses can be made for the lack of success of the United States in women's track and field." Although she noted that the program "needs a financial shot in the arm," she emphasized even more strongly that "U.S. sports programs can no longer allow social permissiveness to have the kind of influence that it has seen over the past five years."[58] Jackson's comments sharply contrasted with those of the article that followed hers in the book, in which a 1972 Olympic competitor in women's discus passionately objected to the social prejudices constraining America's female athletes.[59]

In Jackson's well-respected academic research on the physiology of women athletes, her balancing act again revealed itself. She supported the apologetic imperative, perhaps inadvertently, by acknowledging female athletes' frequent concern about developing large muscles. Rather than critiquing traditional ideals of femininity, she assured female athletes that physiological differences would prevent them from developing muscles to the extent that males could. She intended for her message to encourage women athletes, which it did, but it also subtly undermined efforts to support a new socially acceptable aesthetic for athletic women.[60]

Along with presenting her scientific research in publications and at academic conferences, Jackson also occasionally spoke on social and political topics.[61] In 1986, two presentations at the American Alliance for Health, Physical Education, Recreation and Dance conference demonstrated her rhetorical strategies as an administrative change agent. Although her remarks were recorded for future audiences, Jackson directly addressed a close-knit community of professional colleagues. On the recording, comments from members of that community reveal their respect for her as a groundbreaking leader, a mentor, and role model. For example, one longtime colleague, Roscoe Brown Jr. (then president of the Bronx Community College in New York City), followed Jackson on the program. He began his own talk by expressing admiration for her rhetorical abilities and by noting, "She uses all the strategies that she talks about—and she usually wins."[62]

Despite Brown's compliment, Jackson felt the burden of struggle. She observed that "the process of education takes a toll on all of us." That toll seemed especially high for the leaders who guided women's athletic programs in the tumultuous first decade of the Title IX era. For Jackson and her colleagues, the conference itself offered a brief respite from the daily struggles they faced in education administration. For a panel on "Minority Women in Athletic Administration," she noted, "I am not a person who gets angry easily, but I will use anger as a strategy." Especially when it came to racism, she declared herself "willing to take risks in an effort to face some confrontations." She observed frankly, "Whites tend to believe what other whites tell them about blacks. So you have to work sometimes with a racist listening to a racist."[63]

Although she spoke bluntly to her professional colleagues who attended the panel, Jackson avoided such forthright speech on sensitive issues in her professional discourse at MSU. In her public comments, like some (perhaps most) of her women's athletic administrator colleagues, she avoided terms such as "discrimination" and "Title IX." For example, Jackson represented MSU by participating in a study of the experiences of minorities in college sports for the American Council on Education's 1974 Hanford Report, which examined moral, financial, educational, and philosophical issues concerning intercollegiate athletics. In news accounts of the process, Jackson's comments mirrored the cautious strategy that shaped her public rhetoric at MSU: she asserted in general terms that she wanted to ensure that the situation of women athletes received the attention it needed.[64]

Generally, Jackson summed up her rhetorical approach in a simple statement: "I try to be amicable to people." She explained that she showed interest in people as individuals and presented herself to them with "a relaxed affect." On one hand, she conceptualized such efforts as "external strategies" that she used in dealing with others. On the other hand, she used "internal strategies" to assess her personal development and progress toward attaining goals. However, she noted that no amount of self-reflection allowed her to sort out whether she encountered resistance due to her race, her sex, both, or neither.[65] These layers of complexity unknown to her white, female counterparts at other institutions influenced her rhetorical choices. By consciously controlling her affect, she sought to maintain a calm, dignified, confident self-presentation. At MSU in 1978, other individuals who felt more able to speak freely could express some of the emotions that Jackson intentionally held in check.

Confrontation at MSU

Whether pursuing merged or separate programs, almost all women's athletic program administrators accepted a timetable even more gradual than Title IX's generous three-year adjustment period. Doing so demonstrated the ethos of reasonableness that women leaders believed it essential to cultivate. Reasonableness also meant choosing allies carefully. In short, "reasonable" female athletic administrators avoided feminists like Pollock. One female senior associate athletics director interviewed by Maloney kept a distance from anyone within the women's movement who tried to intervene in athletics. She observed that "they [were] not particularly successful because . . . they [were] a little too brash."[66]

This lack of appreciation for activist groups outside the athletics department was shared by Karol Kahrs, the former Illinois volleyball coach who, in 1977, was hired into a newly established position as Illinois's assistant director of women's athletics. In a 1994 interview, Kahrs did not acknowledge that her administrative position resulted from the successful campaign conducted by the Concerned Women Athletes group that Pollock helped lead. Kahrs recalled, "We had a Title IX group on our campus early as well and they did not represent the majority of campus. . . . They were a pain in the neck because you had to spend a lot of time getting stuff generated for them."[67] She viewed such organizations as "interfering groups."[68] In general, women in athletics viewed women's rights groups as more extreme than male athletic administrators who wanted to exclude football from Title IX. Conversely, activist-minded women such as Pollock viewed those who wanted to exclude football as the true extremists. At MSU, DeBoer and Mankowski had little sense of these divisions among university administrators and assumed it perfectly appropriate to take their complaint to Pollock.

In spring 1978, Pollock's second semester at MSU, she was a complete outsider to the athletics department. She had never worked in athletics, knew little of its culture, and as director of women's programs reported to the vice president of federal and public relations. In early March, Pollock was not developing behind-the-scenes relationships with decision makers in athletics or strategizing about how best to work with Jackson to approach athletics director Joe Kearney. Instead, she developed connections with other Title IX coordinators and planned trips to national conferences related to her administrative responsibilities. For example, on April 3, 1978, she attended the National Women Dean's conference, and on May 4–5, 1978, she attended the Women's Equity Action League convention.[69]

True to her instincts for grassroots organizing, Pollock also enlisted the support of student organizations, three of which came together to draft a resolution asking administrators to support her initiative to survey students' needs and interests regarding physical recreation: the Associated Students of Michigan State University, the Council of Graduate Students, and the Student Council. A *State News* article covering the initiative prominently conveyed Pollock's urgent message to the campus community: the July 21, 1978, deadline to comply with the Title IX regulations fast approached.[70]

On March 28, Pollock sent a letter to athletics director Joe Kearney and women's athletics director Nell Jackson. The letter, carbon copied to Kathleen DeBoer, read as follows:

Dear Joe and Nell:

Last week a captain of one of the women's teams filed a complaint on behalf of the entire team alleging sex discrimination in the provision of athletic opportunities to the women's team. In addition, a coach filed a complaint alleging sex discrimination in the terms and conditions of employment for the coach of the women's team. Although separate complaints, the kinds of treatment alleged by both have serious implications if investigated and found to be accurate.

As Title IX Coordinator, I will attempt to research the issues around the accusation of sex discrimination in athletics and try to find some amenable solutions if problems are discovered. If we cannot seem to come up with adjustments which seem to be reasonable to the complainants, the respondents (you), or to me, I will refer the matter to the Anti-Discrimination Judicial Board for their formal investigation and findings.

I will be in Detroit at the National Women Deans conference and will return to my office on Monday, April 3. I hope by then that my secretary, Jean Grifka, can find a convenient time when the three of us can meet.

Sincerely,
Mary I. Pollock, Director
Women's Programs and Coordinator, Title IX[71]

The complaint from a women's coach mentioned in Pollock's letter referred to one filed by Pittman. In his "Chronology," he noted that "KDB [Kathy DeBoer] and MHP [Mark H. Pittman] went to see Mary Pollock in her office and file their complaints." Jackson likely knew from talking with Pittman that complaints were forthcoming because he noted a conversation with her in the winter of 1977 about inquiries he made regarding coaches' salaries. However, Pittman carefully shielded Jackson from association with either complaint. He respected her and did not want to compromise her job or effectiveness as an advocate from within the athletic department.[72]

Pollock's letter to Kearney and Jackson, while clear and informative, may have come across as an affront to Kearney. In the culture of big-time intercollegiate athletics, athletics directors exercised considerable authority over their programs and prized their autonomy—a culture that remains prevalent today. Pollock's discourse projected a strong sense of agency. She presented herself as the person in control of the process, taking action to research and problem solve in order to avoid possibly turning the matter over to yet another unit outside of athletics. She positioned the athletic administrators as "respondents" to a complaint rather than as powerful authority figures. Pollock may have chosen to send a letter in order to document her handling of the complaint process (especially as she prepared to leave town). However, delivering this news in writing before approaching the administrators through a phone call (perhaps to initiate a meeting even before the complaints were actually filed) undermined the personal touch implied by addressing the letter to "Joe and Nell." In particular, deferring a meeting until she returned from a conference seems unlikely to have set the tone for mutual problem solving, collaboration, and goodwill. In the letter, Pollock presumed herself responsible for determining the validity of the complaints and that she would play a significant role in assessing the acceptableness of proposed adjustments.

However presumptuous Pollock's sense of her role may have seemed to Kearney, he initially responded by delegating the whole matter to Clarence Underwood, who was responsible for NCAA and AIAW compliance. On the surface, the decision made sense, except that Underwood's experience or responsibilities with compliance did not include Title IX. On April 6, Underwood, Pollock, and Jackson met from 9:30 in the morning until 12:30 in the afternoon.[73] In the meeting, they agreed to put their questions in writing. Afterward, Underwood communicated his personal perspective on the whole matter in a memo he sent to Kearney, without copying Pollock or Jackson.[74] Underwood's memo, in effect, positioned Pollock herself as the complainant. He listed items that Pollock brought up as though they were her own concerns; for example, "She indicated that the department should develop an equitable formula for awarding athletic scholarships for men and women." Moreover, he represented her as hostile to men and unreasonable: "She further indicated that if present surplus money was not available at this time to provide equitable funding for women's scholarships comparable to that of men, she suggested that the men's scholarships be cancelled and given to the women." Further undermining her credibility, he referred to the male coach of a woman's sport in her letter as an "alleged complainant" and the woman as the "alleged female complainant." This language suggests that Underwood, at that point, believed Pollock herself was the true source of the complaints. He asked that the complaints be put in writing and made formal, perhaps to ensure that the complainants did actually exist.[75]

Underwood's concluding assessment of Pollock's ethos emphasized her outsider status. He noted that "she displayed a limited knowledge of athletic programs and their operations." Further, he was put off by her citing unspecified "grave consequences" if the compliance deadline was not met and by her expressing a hope that the athletic department would comply with the law "so that nobody would get fired." He took that statement as "a scare tactic." To sum up his assessment of her, he wrote, "In conclusion, I was not particularly fond of her disposition in our discussion and told her that I personally did not appreciate her threatening manner. My opinion is that she is full of bluff."[76] In combination, Kearney's delegation of the matter, Pollock's zeal in presenting Pittman's and the team's concerns (which she undoubtedly shared), and Underwood's assessment that she was simply bluffing served only to escalate two informal complaints into a full-blown battle. Although Underwood did not copy Pollock on his letter, she undoubtedly left the meeting understanding that their discourse was on an uneven keel, a fact she likely communicated to the team representatives.

Within a week of the meeting between Pollock, Underwood, and Jackson, an article appeared in the *MSU News-Bulletin* that highlighted Nell Jackson's role as the more tempered spokesperson for MSU women's athletics. In "Jackson Assesses Women's Athletics," she represented herself as a team player committed to an ideal of the athletics department acting together as a unit. She credited Title IX for "much of the financial growth" of women's sports but noted that "the university's own commitment to women's athletics has also been a factor."[77] Ever tactful, she packaged praise with gentle criticism that came across as unemotional, carefully qualified, and even empathetic toward the administration. A reader fully identified with the institution might miss her gentle criticism altogether.

After citing accomplishments of MSU's women's teams, Jackson observed that "as other schools added programs [after Title IX], some of them did a hop and a jump over us in some sports." She first praised the athletic department for creating more equity between men's nonrevenue and women's sports "than most people think." Then she noted that "total compliance may be a problem if that means equity between all men's and women's sports."[78] By 1978, given the discourse from Pollock's office and Jackson's own professional organizations—not to mention from conversations with Pittman in which they discussed the women's basketball team's campaign—Jackson would have known very well that Title IX applied to all men's and women's sports, not merely to nonrevenue-producing teams. Reading her comments in that context suggests that she may have employed carefully veiled sarcasm. Similarly, the following statement could read as a genuine statement of common cause with Kearney or as a mild critique of her boss's emphasis on big-money sports: "Dr. Kearney plans to keep revenue and non-revenue sports separate until mandated to do otherwise. . . . The reason is that revenue sports are bringing in money and we don't want to interfere with that."[79]

When Jackson did directly critique the MSU administration, she used a passive sentence structure that allowed her to avoid affixing blame to any individual. For example, after acknowledging problems with facilities, she commented, "We'd really like to feel like an integral part of the program but *funds haven't yet been made available* to make us an equitable member of the group." Meanwhile, she continued her balancing act by offering the players who wanted immediate equality a longer-term perspective: "I have been in the program since the start, and I've seen tremendous improvement. Those coming in now may say we aren't anywhere, but I'm a former athlete who knows what we had way back then."[80]

During the week when the article featuring Jackson appeared, DeBoer and Mankowski stopped by Pollock's office several times for consultations. DeBoer then submitted an open letter to the *State News*, making the team's complaint public. On April 19, the paper published DeBoer's letter in full under the heading "Probe MSU on Title IX":

> An area of discrimination which has been tacitly overlooked for many years is that suffered by women athletes. The members of MSU's Women's Basketball team would like to make public the fact that they are charging the University with outright violation of federal law. Title IX of the Higher Education Amendment of 1972 forbids discrimination on the basis of sex in higher education institutions receiving federal funds.
>
> Michigan State annually receives millions of dollars in federal funds, yet its intercollegiate athletic program is discriminatory in virtually every area examinable. Unlawful discrimination is practiced in the division of facilities, the quality thereof, the size of budget allotments, the size of coaching staffs, their salaries, and the amount of scholarship compensation available.
>
> Michigan State has had six years to implement a program which complies with Title IX regulations. There has been no serious attempt to do this. In fact, University officials have only recently begun to even estimate the scope of Title IX implications for their program.
>
> As members of an intercollegiate team we have unanimously filed a complaint against the University with Title IX coordinator Mary Pollock. Further, we will send this complaint to the Office of Civil Rights and request a federal investigation of the University.

Blatant discrimination against women has existed in intercollegiate athletics for many years. If the University will not
voluntarily act to remove it, we will force their hand.

Kathleen J. DeBoer
Co-Captain Women's Basketball Team
1136 Frye St.
East Lansing[81]

Obviously DeBoer did not subscribe to the Parkhouse and Lapin
approach to organizational communication. Her discourse resembled her
approach to athletics—strong, unrelenting, and sometimes a little reckless.
She often led the 1978 women's basketball team in scoring and rebounding; she also set a record by fouling out six times that season, a result of
her aggressive play. Her letter on behalf of the team was a blistering hit
like those her volleyball opponents knew well—it was aimed straight at
university administrators who doubted the existence of a real complaint.
These were fighting words, and with them, the battle began.

11 A Plea for Unity

Women students all over the country are taking matters into their own
hands. They are tired of being told what they can and cannot have,
so they unite in an effort to make the institutions stop ignoring them.
—Bonnie L. Parkhouse and Jackie Lapin, *Women
Who Win: Exercising Your Rights in Sports*[1]

DeBoer's assertive rhetorical style was not typical of student athlete leaders of the early Title IX era. Young women who emerged as leaders in the
struggle for equality needed to unify athletes from across the women's
sports program, and to do so, they needed to consider how their appeals
would be received by a variety of other audiences—from their coaches,
to university administrators, to their own sports administrators, many of
whom practiced the apologetic discourse widely adopted by female athletes
and physical educators. When an athletic female student spoke assertively
and unapologetically, she risked alienating almost everyone. The gender
transgression already committed by women who played sports—especially
a contact sport such as basketball—was amplified when a female basketball player eschewed a feminine rhetoric of humility, indirectness, and
compliance for a more forthright, demanding style.

As student athletes across the country appealed to their peers and
other supporters for unity in the face of institutional opposition, gender
stereotypes also determined how their arguments were received in other
ways. For example, arguments opposing pro–Title IX rhetoric often mirrored the protectionist discourse of anti-ERA activists. That is, institutional leaders—especially the men's athletic power structure—made
their own appeals to unity by emphasizing that if women's sports and

lower-revenue-producing men's sports would simply accept their place in the athletic hierarchy, they would be taken care of. Arguments for excluding football from the gender equality equation rested on that protectionist logic: provide football all the resources it needs to be a successful bread-winner and to bring in funds to support the whole program well, though not everyone equally. The good of football, so the argument went, was also the common good.

Outside of universities, similar arguments and supporting gender stereotypes circulated in the corporate world. The prevailing ideology of the time presumed that certain kinds of work befitted men and other work better suited women. It just so happened that the men's work, like football, held a higher status and paid more. Just as women athletes were challenging these status quo ideas in universities, women began to question these inequalities in the business world. And like athletic women, they had civil rights law on their side. Although the federal government failed to act as decisively and assertively in communicating and enforcing these laws as feminists would have liked, HEW's Office for Civil Rights at least offered another interpretation of the common good. The OCR's version of what was best for society included gender equity rather than gender hierarchies as a social good.

Whether in business or higher education athletics, however, women needed to find support networks to fight discrimination. Neither civil rights law nor solitary individuals fighting an established system of values could accomplish change by themselves. Teamwork was needed. To build a team, change agents needed strategic appeals for unity that could attract both eager and reluctant potential allies without completely alienating members of their opposition who might be persuaded to offer a measure of support at critical junctures. To achieve the restraint needed for such artful rhetoric called for women to manage the same wellspring of anger that had propelled them to speak up for themselves at all.

Team-Building at MSU

When Kathleen DeBoer indicted MSU in her open letter, she had not yet formulated the theories of gender and leadership that she wrote about later in life. In her 2004 book on gender, competition, and the workplace, she recalled that in college she had not been elected captain of the MSU volleyball team, losing out to a teammate with an "easygoing manner" and "quiet confidence." Her self-described "in-your-face-assertiveness" was, in her view, a leadership style less well-suited to what she came to view as "the tenuous interpersonal fabric of female teams." Her basketball team-mates may have found her rhetoric and leadership style more acceptable than her volleyball teammates, perhaps because those women who had chosen to play a contact sport could better appreciate a more confronta-tional style. In any case, DeBoer's public statements communicated out-rage rather than an attitude of patient consensus-building. As she wrote later, women have a tendency to "punish our peers" who "tell others what to do in a direct and unambiguous manner."[2]

Although the women's basketball team had elected DeBoer and Mankowski their spokespeople, other women athletes at MSU had not yet been invited to offer their opinions or become part of a broad-based collective action group. In her open letter, DeBoer had represented her-self as a member of the women's basketball team, but she also acted as an individual. Her name and address on the letter underscored that she took personal responsibility for the complaint. Perhaps with access to informa-tion about other "student pressure campaigns," as Parkhouse and Lapin termed them, she would have sought allies in a student organization or created an ad hoc social action group.

As it was, Mary Pollock tested the waters with MSU student organiza-tions to gauge their willingness to exert pressure on the administration. Of course, she had experience with an organized group of student athletes across many sports at Illinois. She was, however, in a completely different role at MSU, and she found MSU's culture different than that of Illinois, even though both are large, public, land-grant institutions. In retrospect, she observed that she "found Michigan State to be a lot more conservative than Illinois, much less dedicated to free speech and academic freedom, more entrenched." Not referring only to the weather, she noted, "It was colder than Illinois."[3]

Pollock recalled, "Under Title IX, [the team] didn't have to file a com-plaint with the university. I was thinking if I could get [the compliance problems] solved, they wouldn't have to file a HEW complaint, and we could get this thing solved in-house." Initially, with youthful idealism and ambition, she imagined that she would guide MSU into Title IX compliance, and that the institution would then represent a model for the whole Big Ten. So she specifically asked the team to promise not to file with the US Department of Health, Education, and Welfare. In turn, she served as the team's internal spokesperson and advocate, communicating their complaints to athletic administrators and seeking redress on the athletes' behalf. As she listened to the details of the inequalities they experienced, she shared materials with them from workshops, "page after page of the kind of things you would ask in an investigation." Although Pollock did not fully orchestrate the women basketball players and their actions, she continually alerted them to their rights and encouraged team members to contact the press when the athletics department acted uncooperatively.[4]

Meanwhile, Pollock told her boss, Ralph Bonner, that she encountered resistance in getting information from the university. Bonner initially assisted her by sharing what she described as "a board of trustees public document about the budget." Then, she recalled, "I started calling to ask what does this mean." She was "seeing things" that she later interpreted as "subsidies to the athletic program, to football and basketball." She kept insisting that she could not assess how much the institution spent on women until she could see how much it spent on men. Looking back, she observed, "They did not want me asking about that." She recalled, "I think I even asked the women to go over to the men's training table. I said go over there and ask to eat. We need proof that they won't let you have equal food." She listened with great concern as the women told her stories about "crowding into these vehicles and driving places, getting out and playing. The men were flying to places; there were just huge disparities in treatment." Player Carol Hutchins recalled that after the team's car ended up in a ditch one time after a snowstorm, her mom "had a cow." She "called the university and was just furious that we were driving those cars in the winter. . . . We could have been killed, obviously."[5]

Although Pollock was a sympathetic and determined advocate, she realized in retrospect that it was unrealistic to think that the university would accept a vision for gender equality from "a thirty-three-year-old from out of town," especially a young woman in her first year at the institution. Before long, she felt isolated, experiencing what she believed to be stress-related asthma attacks. Throughout spring 1978, she felt increasingly overwhelmed by "competing demands and impossible situations and feelings like [she] had to get justice for these women." She felt that the burden of dealing with a resistant university rested entirely on her shoulders. In a 2005 interview, she painted a stark picture of the situation when she said, "I had no ally. None. Zero."[6]

Of course, the players had no idea that Pollock felt so isolated. For their own part, they wondered how to find allies among the other female athletes. As Cookie Mankowski recalled, they brainstormed a range of strategies to gain attention for their cause, including mooning the media with Title IX written on their butts, an idea they abandoned after "someone said, 'no, no, don't do that!'" They sensed that they needed a unified effort to achieve their goals, but they had no idea that student athletes at other schools had already found ways to work together and take action.[7]

For successful models of student athlete activism, the team would have needed to look beyond their own campus. Pollock's experience at Illinois would have been useful had she shared it with them. Students at the University of Minnesota; the University of California, Los Angeles (UCLA); and Vanderbilt University also established early strategies for claiming their Title IX rights. However, communication channels for sharing information and strategies—whether successful or not—were virtually nonexistent. Although student groups employed a range of social protest tactics to make their voices heard, they lacked networks through which they could share strategies or support. With this lack of coordination, large-scale change came gradually, but local conflicts could escalate quickly. Experiences of discrimination and exclusion generated strong emotions; administrators under pressure from students felt attacked and resentful. Language used by parties on both sides of a conflict set a tone that determined, in part, the progression of events set in motion by an initial complaint.

Student Activism: Minnesota, UCLA, and Vanderbilt

In 1974, before legislators issued Title IX regulations, the first female president of the student government at Minnesota heard a speech about the new law. She subsequently led the student government organization in a campaign to investigate sex discrimination in all departments on campus. The group found athletics to be the most noncompliant department and eventually filed a lawsuit as a student organization.[8] By 1978, clear signs emerged that the campaign and pressure from the lawsuit had made a significant impact. At the time, female students comprised more than 50 percent of those enrolled in the university—the highest percentage in the Big Ten—and Minnesota led the conference in its budget for women's athletics, allocating more than $750,000.[9] By suing under the protection of a recognized organization, the students benefited from its already established legitimacy. Individuals also shielded themselves from possible retaliation against a single named complainant or possible damage to their reputation.

The impressive success of this groundbreaking group at Minnesota seems to have gone largely unnoticed by other college students or even women sports administrators and coaches. In the same year that the Minnesota group filed suit, swimmer Jan Palchikoff at UCLA created an official student organization called the Union of Women Athletes to provide an institutionally recognized entity under which she rallied support from across campus. In *Women Who Win: Exercising Your Rights in Sport*, Parkhouse and Lapin used the UCLA group to illustrate recommended tactics for student pressure campaigns (recommendations that came too late to the MSU women, even if they had decided to consult a book on activist strategies). *Women Who Win* includes the letter Palchikoff wrote to mobilize students, which remains one of the few published examples of student athletes' activist discourse from the period:

Dear UCLA Athlete,

As a participant in the UCLA Women's Intercollegiate
Sports program you are probably aware of the current state of
affairs. You are aware of the lack of facilities for practice. You are

aware of the lack of training rooms and meets and tournaments. You know that some of our coaches work for no pay and that the rest of them work for very little pay. Preferential enrollment is not provided for women athletes (as it is for men) to facilitate regular practice attendance. No doubt you are aware that we do not receive financial assistance in the form of athletic scholarships. Nor do we receive publicity in the general press (and more specifically the *Daily Bruin*) which is representative of our involvement in the world of sports.

We can do something about this situation. We can organize in the form of a union of student athletes and begin working together to help build the intercollegiate sports program and develop it to its fullest potential. As a large group, we can make demands which will help up-grade the program and to obtain the things we as athletes need to perform to the best of our ability.

I have spoken to women from several of the sports about the possibility of organizing such an effort. All of them felt it was necessary.

Please come to our first meeting to discuss the problem and possible courses of action. The meeting will be on Wednesday, February 20 in the evening somewhere on campus and after practice. Please call me for the details and to tell me whether you will be able to attend or just to gripe! I can be reached at 837-7697 between 7:00 pm and midnight on week days and all day on Saturday or Sunday or leave a message for me at the Women's Resource Center 825 3945 or at the Women's Intercollegiate Athletic office MG 118 (address the note to Shirbey Johnson). I'm looking forward to hearing from you!

> Sincerely,
> Jan L. Palchikoff
> member, UCLA swim team[10]

Palchikoff learned some of her activist strategies when, for a time, she gave up sports and became politically active in the women's rights movement. She understood the importance of soliciting feedback and bringing people on board with her cause gradually. Her tone communicates confidence, efficacy, and optimism. Like Lopiano at Texas, she emphasized a goal that any athlete or sports administrator could embrace: to develop as athletes to their fullest potential. She offered a chance to "gripe," but kept her diction on an even keel as she described "the current state of affairs." She avoided inflammatory language about rights, injustice, or discrimination. She even avoided the relatively innocuous references to "fairness" frequently used by women's athletic administrators. As a result, Palchikoff's initial meeting at UCLA yielded forty attendees and a core group of five leaders who conducted research on campus budgets, wrote letters to campus committees, and contacted influential individuals.[11]

Seen as a "radical" group, they wrote position papers to correct misrepresentations of their stances on issues, published editorials in the student newspaper, circulated petitions on critical issues, and kept in touch with the local press. When UCLA fired a women's crew coach, a law student making $750 dollars, for requesting a salary raise to $2,000 after finishing sixth in nationals, the group protested, insisting on a meeting with the vice chancellor.[12] When their requests went unanswered, they asserted themselves further, presenting him with a letter listing their questions that stated, "The questions are specific and we would appreciate specific answers. If you cannot answer the questions now, we will be happy to wait in your office or come back in a half an hour to receive the answers." When they received a response, they confirmed it in a letter that concluded with the statement, "If we do not hear from you by Monday November 11, 1974, we will assume you are in agreement with the contents of this letter. Thank you for your consideration."[13] Ultimately, Palchikoff filed an official complaint with HEW, a step she came to believe that student activists should take at the very beginning of a campaign.

Although Palchikoff herself never benefited directly from her efforts—despite working six-hour days to keep issues alive for most of her senior year—her group prompted the university to establish and take seriously an athletes' advisory council and, for a time, created a culture in which student athletes participated in campus politics. Although few people probably realized it, she also influenced the language people used to describe women athletes at UCLA; after her conversation with the student newspaper editor, the paper no longer referred to them as the Bruin Dolls.[14] She was, however, recognized with the outstanding senior award from the Alumni Association, a testament to how well she followed her own primary recommendation to student activists: "DON'T GIVE UP. You may be surprised and offended at the number of people who will tell you that you are only hurting women's athletics. 'Don't rock the boat.' Experience tells me that the only way to get what we want is to demand it, especially where women's rights are concerned. The trick is learn how to demand in a diplomatic manner."[15]

Demanding with diplomacy, a tricky rhetorical challenge for anyone, presented a tall order for the eighteen- to twenty-one-year-old college students who first asserted their rights under Title IX. After all, they addressed an audience of university administrators well aware that, as a resistance tactic, they could simply stall until activist student leaders graduated.

Involving first-year students in gender equality struggles turned out to be critical. At Vanderbilt University in 1977, freshman track athlete and engineering student Peggy Layne became the named complainant in the Vanderbilt women's Title IX struggle. The senior leaders of the activist group wanted to use Layne's name on the group's formal complaints to ensure its continued validity even after the juniors and seniors graduated. In 1977, Vanderbilt's women's track was a student-organized club sport. Their uniforms had no school logo, and they had to create their own varsity "letters," a little pin that said "Vandy '77" made by the student who organized the team. As an engineering student, Layne had limited exposure to academic feminism, but she read about the women's movement in newspapers and felt that she was part of "a national story related not only to women's athletics but women's rights in general." But, she explained in an interview, "Vanderbilt is a very conservative campus, I mean, we were the radical fringe at Vanderbilt, and we were not that far out there, let me tell you."[16] Unlike Palchikoff at UCLA or DeBoer at MSU, Layne had not come to college expecting a highly competitive athletic experience; instead, she sought a competitive academic experience. However, she was willing to play a role in helping to move women's sports to a competitive level—even to the point where she could not have participated at the varsity level. She explained her perspective and what motivated the Vanderbilt activist this way: "Club sports are fun. In fact, they're more fun than varsity sports because you don't have the pressure. But certainly at the time that I was at Vanderbilt, we were very conscious of being treated differently. We wanted to have what the guys had; we didn't want to be second-class citizens. We wanted to have the college logo on our uniforms and not be wearing ratty tee-shirts when we went to a meet. We wanted to be official; we wanted to be part of the institution."[17]

In a meticulously organized notebook that she compiled as events unfolded, Layne preserved news clippings, letters, and other documents related to the athletes' campaign. Layne recalled that the vice chancellor took the position that "women are just not interested." She suppoted her recollection by citing a clipping that she had saved from the *Chattanooga Free Press* with the headline, "Vandy Women's Group Says SEC Is Sexist." In the article, university administrators claimed they didn't know what they needed to do in order to comply with Title IX. But the students themselves had answers, backed by mimeographed copies of the code of federal regulations. Like Pollock, DeBoer, and the MSU women's basketball team, the Vanderbilt group reminded administrators of the July 1978 compliance deadline. And like MSU and many other institutions, Vanderbilt did not take the deadline seriously.[18]

The Vanderbilt group was effective, in part, because they had successfully built a collective identity before taking action. To make their thirteen demands known, Layne and other Vanderbilt students sent a letter to Vanderbilt's opportunity development officer and to HEW's Office for Civil Rights, stating, "We represent an ad-hoc committee of students concerned about the continuing non-compliance of Vanderbilt University's athletic program, with federal regulations which prohibit sex discrimination." In an interview, Layne read aloud the key statement at the end of their collaboratively composed February 1977 letter. "Quoting chapter and verse," she said with a small smile: "We're prepared, if necessary, to take legal action against the university. We hope we won't have to choose this course." They named their group TNT: Title IX in Tennessee Committee. The group's press releases stated confidently, "We are informed, we are strong, and we are right."[19] Parkhouse and Lapin approved of TNT's rhetorical approach, stating that their efforts resulted in HEW demanding the institution submit its required self-evaluation. TNT secured meetings with the university legal staff and administrators by taking the step of hiring an attorney. Notably, for Parkhouse and Lapin, "the women did not demand equal support—just some." Their efforts resulted in gradual program improvement, including the university hiring a woman for the assistant athletics director position.[20] Certainly, it was important that an advocate for women's sports was placed in that position. However, like her counterparts across the country, the newly hired assistant athletics director would face an ongoing, often lonely struggle to make change from an administrative position as a newcomer within the athletics department.

Athlete-Activists Gain a Network

In 1978, the national movement for change in college sports gained a much-needed communication medium: a clearinghouse for news and information related to women's sports. As sociologist John Markoff noted in *Waves of Democracy: Social Movements and Political Change*, communications media are critical for "leading people separated in space to feel themselves moving to a common rhythm."[21] Toward that end, HEW awarded grant funding to the Women's Equity Action League, in part to create a Sports Referral and Information Network (SPRINT). SPRINT "collected and distributed information on women and girls in sports, particularly in educational institutions, and monitored legal and political developments, model programs, and trends in women's physical education and athletics."[22] In the spring of 1978, the network began publishing a quarterly newsletter called *In the Running* to which women's coaches and administrators, including Nell Jackson and Mark Pittman, subscribed. The newsletter published articles related to activism and advocacy as well as up-to-date information about events related to women's sports. As an organization, WEAL provided an important link between the women's sports community and the women's rights movement.

In 1974, WEAL leaders saw that Title IX and other anti–sex discrimination laws were not being enforced. With the National Organization for Women, the National Education Association, the Federation of Organizations of Professional Women, the Association of Women in Science, and four individual plaintiffs, WEAL filed a complaint against HEW, HEW's Office for Civil Rights, the US Department of Labor, and the Office of Federal Contract Compliance. In 1977, the suit resulted in an order, known as "the WEAL order," requiring that HEW respond in a "timely manner." (By March 1982, however, the group of plaintiffs charged that the government was still not complying with the WEAL order.)[23]

Beginning in 1977, WEAL kept records related to federal complaints and litigation related to sex discrimination in college sports and academe in general. The archives at the Radcliffe Institute's Schlesinger Library document hundreds of complaints, news clippings, and correspondence related to sex discrimination at universities and colleges, many of them contemporaneous with the internal complaint filed at MSU in 1978. The library contains documentation related to MSU athletics beginning in 1977, archived in alphabetical order among a long list of reference files on sex discrimination in college sports. Just a few of the file headings listed in the extensive WEAL archive are excerpted here to suggest the wide range of institutions involved in complaints or litigation:

- 69.27. SPRINT. Reference files. [Litigation. Colleges and universities.] Louisville, University of [letter, clippings], 1980.
- 69.28. SPRINT. Reference files. [Litigation. Colleges and universities.] Marian College (Indiana) [letters, copy of complaint], 1979.
- 69.29. SPRINT. Reference files. [Litigation. Colleges and universities.] Maryland, University of [notes, clippings, etc.], 1978.
- 69.30. SPRINT. Reference files. [Litigation. Colleges and universities.] Massachusetts, University of (Amherst) [correspondence, documents supporting complaint], 1974–75.
- 69.31–69.33. SPRINT. Reference files. [Litigation. Colleges and universities.] Michigan State University [correspondence, clippings, etc.], 1978.
- 69.34–69.36. SPRINT. Reference files. [Litigation. Colleges and universities.] Michigan, University of [notes, clippings, press releases, etc.], 1977–82.

• **69.37.** SPRINT. Reference files. [Litigation. Colleges and universities.] Minnesota, University of [letters, clippings, etc.], 1978–81.

• **69.38.** SPRINT. Reference files. [Litigation. Colleges and universities.] Missouri, University of [request for information, clippings], 1978.[24]

Of course, in those pre-Internet days, information related to these cases was available primarily through the newsletter *In the Running*. No case law existed at the time, in part because the cases were either settled out of court or argued under the Fourteenth Amendment and state sex discrimination laws. In some cases, complainants simply gave up because their complaints went unanswered.

A Glance at the Bigger Picture: Sears and Sports

WEAL also tracked sex discrimination cases unrelated to sports, at least one of which concerned a complex set of gender issues, and many of which overlapped with arguments that became integral to the movement to upgrade women's college sports under Title IX. In a case that originated in 1973, the US Equal Employment Opportunity Commission (EEOC) filed suit against Sears, Roebuck and Company in 1979.[25] The Sears case was filed under Title VII of the Civil Rights Act of 1964 (legislators used language in another part of the 1964 Civil Rights Act as a model for Title IX), and key arguments in the case highlighted ways in which athletics and career training and opportunities are often linked.

The Sears case revolved around two related questions: "Are women's interests best served by public policies [including corporate and institutional policies] that treat women and men identically, ignoring the social and cultural differences between them?"; or, conversely, "[Should] we view those differences positively and seek greater recognition and status for traditionally female values and behavior?"[26] Indeed, throughout the 1970s, the entire country pondered the same questions when considering whether or not to support ratification of a constitutional Equal Rights Amendment. The EEOC charged Sears with discriminating against women and minorities in hiring and in promoting individuals for the most lucrative "big ticket" sales positions. The company required applicants for such positions to take a temperament test that included questions desired to measure their "vigor"—a quality often equated with sports participation. These questions included the following:

"Do you have a low-pitched voice?"

"Do you swear often?"

"Have you ever done any hunting?"

"Have you participated in wrestling?"

"Have you participated in boxing?"

"Have you played on a football team?"[27]

For the potentially lucrative commissioned sales positions, experience and comfort with competition was paramount. The company highly valued the kind of experience that pre–Title IX athletic opportunities discouraged for women. Before Title IX, playday-oriented college sports experiences offered to women emphasized a female culture that actually fostered social attitudes unsuited for highly competitive positions. Attorneys for Sears argued that women were more suited for and interested in jobs requiring "a sociable person with a pleasant, helpful personality." Conversely, they also contended that women held a "fear or dislike of the competitive 'dog-eat-dog' atmosphere of most commission sales divisions" and a "fear of being unable to compete, being unsuccessful, and losing their jobs."[28] A historian who served as an expert witness pointed out that "men's more extensive experience in competitive sports . . . prepares them for the competitiveness, aggressiveness, teamwork, and leadership required for many jobs." In rebuttal, another historian pointed out that "the argument that women are only interested in certain kinds of work reflects women's perceptions of opportunities available to them which are themselves products of employers' assumptions and prejudices about women's roles."[29]

Sears's expert contended that women simply were not as interested in sales commission jobs, a claim that mirrored the Vanderbilt vice chancellor's explanation for lack of athletic opportunities offered for women at his institution in the 1970s. The claim that "women just aren't that interested" was a rhetorical commonplace—that is, a readily available argument used in a variety of contexts. The Sears case also underscored another frequently made claim: the contention that traits cultivated in sports create workplace opportunities. Whether or not such a claim can be proven, its persistent circulation meant more was at stake in women athletes' struggle for sporting opportunities than simply the chance to have a more well-supported college sports experience.

Indeed, college athletics directors seem to have resisted support for women's sports for many of the same reasons corporate managers resisted policies to speed the advancement of women and minorities. In her work on charges of sex discrimination at AT&T in the early 1970s, economist Phyllis Wallace offered these possible explanations for managerial resistance:

> The threat of increased competition from individuals they perceive to be less qualified than themselves is part of the reason for managerial reluctance. Basic prejudice may be another reason. And some managers feel they are losing some of their hard-earned management prerogatives. However, the main cause, I submit, is simply a resistance to change. Line managers at all levels of most corporations really don't understand the significance of new equal opportunity regulations, labor laws, OSHA [Occupational Safety and Health Administration], or a host of other external impingements on their primary responsibilities. And further, they tend not to view these external forces as their problem but as a personal or legal matter.[30]

Men who ran athletics departments in the 1970s certainly viewed Title IX as an "external impingement" on the primary responsibilities of the department. It seemed inconceivable to most athletics directors that they should have to factor their higher revenue-producing sports into any Title IX compliance picture. As a result, they continued to treat the issue as open and unresolved, despite the failure of the Tower Amendments that sought to exclude those sports. Their presumption that departments generating revenue had the right to control their spending reflected athletic departments' ownership mentality. Athletics directors promulgated the idea that they properly functioned as owners of college sports departments and programs, just as professional teams have owners. It followed from this ownership paradigm that managers could reinvest any revenue produced or profits made as they saw fit, although talk of "profits" as opposed to "revenue" was rare. Along with an ownership perspective, attitudes toward athletic departments also reflected the still-prevailing gender ideology of the time—the idea that the "natural" male role is as the breadwinner who pays the bills for the women.

Back in East Lansing

DeBoer's open letter charging MSU with sex discrimination never directly confronted the breadwinner ideology or the capitalistic "ownership" mentality of athletics departments. Rather than functioning as an integral part of undergraduate education, athletic departments viewed themselves, and were often viewed by university presidents, as more akin to an arm of university development—a fundraising, image-creating part of the institution. Although much later DeBoer came to understand this perspective well (when she worked as senior athletics administrator at the University of Kentucky), in 1978 she had little access to that viewpoint. As a student activist at MSU, her rights-oriented discourse did not address the fact that athletics departments viewed themselves as commercial-like entities entitled to invest their resources as they saw fit in order to maximize revenue.

Instead, DeBoer's uncompromising insistence on "equality" communicated high expectations that MSU would follow the letter of civil rights law. Her rights-oriented discourse reflected the influence of Pollock, Frye, and feminism rather than the rhetorical advice circulating among athletes and physical educators. Her rather undiplomatically presented demands, combined with Pollock's investigative approach to her Title IX coordinator duties, prompted the East Lansing community to confront issues regarding the relationship between revenue and equality and between interest and opportunity. Policymakers had already addressed these issues, but people began to redeliberate them in public and private forums. Eventually, public opinion would either catch up with policy and the law or women's advocates would have to recalibrate their rhetorics for influencing social values.

The Campus Responds

The day after the *State News* published DeBoer's April 19, 1978, open letter, the paper followed up with an article on the women's basketball team's
complaint. The article extensively quoted Mary Pollock, who explained
that the complaint process was in a fact-gathering stage, with Underwood
heading up an affirmative action committee within the athletics department. A hint of the behind-the-scenes tension appeared in Underwood's
statement that "he [had] not seen the complaint filed by the women's basketball team and [could not] comment on it until he [did]."[31] On April
24, another *State News* article quoted Jackson noting the problems facing women's teams in a matter-of-fact way, acknowledging small improvements but also pointing out remaining problems.[32] For example, instead
of using an old training room in the men's intramural building to change
before and after games, women's teams would move into their own locker
room; however, they would have to share it with the opposing team. Coach
Langeland, too, backed up the team's complaints, agreeing that "her multiple roles" as teacher, administrator, and part-time coach with no assistant
left her "no time to develop an important relationship with the team."[33]

DeBoer shared more pointed observations, citing problems with getting their uniforms cleaned after practices, as the men's teams customarily
did. The *State News* quoted her as saying, "The school doesn't provide
us with any underclothing. . . . But it provides the men with jocks—they
make things so convenient for the men."[34] This sarcastic comment was not
entirely logical because jocks, more than "underclothing," provide protection, but also because the sports bra had not been invented yet, so schools
could hardly have been expected to provide them. In fact, the provocative comment—and the choice to print it—probably escalated the growing
tensions at MSU. DeBoer's tone likely undermined her ethos with some
readers of the *State News*, especially if she intended, like Phyllis Bailey at
Ohio State, to come across as a reasonable woman. Others, perhaps, found
her irreverent tone empowering or amusing. As a student about to graduate, she may have felt freer to speak out than university employees such as
Bailey or Jackson. DeBoer probably did not know or consider how activism

could potentially affect her post-graduation employment opportunities, especially if she stayed involved with athletics. Her role, in the last semester of her senior year, was to mobilize, provoke, and call attention to her cause. Before then, she had used an indirect line of communication with university administrators—through Pollock and the press. That distance between her and university administrators likely contributed to the sense that DeBoer spoke to no particular individual for whom she needed to adapt her discourse, just to "the institution."

The same *State News* article quoted Jackson, who used more guarded language than DeBoer. However, instead of talking about specific matters such as underclothing, Jackson honed in on the root of the problem behind the array of symptoms others pointed out. "The athletic department has been reluctant to include revenue-raising sports (football, basketball, and hockey) in Title IX regulations," she explained, using an odd choice of words that implied the department thought it could decide for itself what to include in the federal regulations.[35] Her wording, though, reflected the attitude of many men's athletic leaders at the time. She later invoked a biblical phrase to describe her inability to make herself heard: "I've been like a little voice in the wilderness."[36]

On the following day, April 25, women's basketball team members removed all doubt about whether a complaint existed. At Pollock's insistence, all thirteen of them signed the complaint, a one-page memo to Mary Pollock claiming sex discrimination. That same day, complainants around the country received a boost from HEW. In a document dated April 25, 1978, and made public several days later, Joseph Califano, the HEW secretary under President Jimmy Carter, requested in writing that his general legal counsel clarify HEW's stance on the relationship between revenue-producing college sports and Title IX. The secretary's instructions clearly stated the compliance deadline of July 28, 1978, in the first sentence and instructed the Office of Civil Rights to "arrange for a review of the implementation of Title IX with respect to athletics with particular attention to revenue-producing sports." In an appendix, the memo included a list of "Congressional Attempts to Exempt Revenue-Producing Sports from Title IX." The page listed proposals and resolutions by Tower, O'Hara, and others—all of them clearly labeled as "unsuccessful attempts."[37] However, even though the memo's authors likely intended it to pacify resistant administrators, the memo also offered up discourse that administrators could use to claim continued confusion. That is, the secretary noted that universities could exercise flexibility in the treatment of revenue-producing sports, a reference to the Javits Amendment. This addendum offered just enough ambiguity to keep alive and well the idea that, in complying with Title IX, revenue production could and should trump other considerations.

Controversy surrounding the MSU women's basketball complaint centered on the issue of whether the amount of revenue a team produced could justify treating women's teams differently from men's teams. On April 25, the *State News* published the first student response to DeBoer's open letter:

One on One

An open letter to Kathleen DeBoer:

Please realize that this letter is not intended toward you personally nor toward women as a group, but to show you that because of your subjectivity, your statements simply have no foundation.

The purpose of Title IX legislation should have been an attempt to help upgrade women's programs and to provide for a fair opportunity. In reality, what Title IX is, is ridiculous. Women's programs here or anywhere else will never be on par with their male counterparts. In no way can it be expected to bring about the equality between men's and women's programs that you profess. An attempt to do so would bring about the demise, not only of women's athletics, but of men's too! It is financially inconceivable and impracticable to have a balance between the two.

The interest generated by women's athletics, either in the number of participants or spectators, is nowhere near that of men. Never have I seen 9,000 people attend any of your games.

Granted, not everything is as it should be with your programs, but to expect an equal amount of money, coaches, and

scholarship competition is as absurd as believing you could beat
Earvin Johnson one-on-one.

John Hoekje

Lansing[38]

This writer did not spell out all parts of the familiar claim upon
which he made his argument; perhaps he felt confident that readers
could fill in the familiar missing pieces. In full, the often-repeated claim
goes something like this: women's sports attract fewer spectators than
men's sports do; more spectators lead to more revenue; and more revenue entitles the highest producers to the lion's share of resources (both
those funds generated by revenue they produce and, in many cases, institutional resources as well). One counterpoint to this argument includes
the claim that programs need investment and promotion in order to produce revenue and, unlike men's basketball and football, women's sports
had not received such investments, so they could not be expected to
have produced.

A subsequent letter printed in the *State News* pointed out the limits
of Hoekje's perspective, exhorting him to "open his eyes" to the fact that
women's basketball in some cases attracted large numbers of spectators,
citing nine thousand fans per game at schools such as Tennessee, UCLA,
or Delta State. "If we want our women's program to be on the same level as
these schools, even with the many super athletes we have, they still need
more money," Bill Christie, the editorial writer, asserted. "Title IX was
supposed to do this but apparently MSU has chosen not to honor it," he
continued. Christie concluded with a pledge of support for the women's
basketball team: "I stand behind them all the way."[39]

These opposing perspectives published in the *State News* reflected
the nationwide transitional period for women's basketball. In truth,
women's basketball games in the state of Michigan did have low attendance. A *Detroit News* article covering the state's AIAW women's championship tournament in 1978 lamented how few fans turned out for the
event: "When [six-foot center Mary Kay] Itnyre goes in for a turnaround
jumper and effortlessly makes the basket, she's obviously just a plain
good basketball player, with no qualifiers. The Detroiter may be the

Spartan women's 'Magic' by next season, but is anyone interested? Does anyone care?"[40]

Yet that same season, more than ten thousand fans attended the women's AIAW national championship, and an invitational tournament earlier in the year in Madison Square Garden drew more than twelve thousand people. A May 20, 1978, *New York Times* article, "Women's Basketball Arrives," announced that the women's game followed too well the steps of the men's game: "Money has propelled women's basketball out of infancy and into a tumultuous adolescence," driven by "bountiful scholarship money [and] growing gate receipts."[41] The article cited increasing skill levels, physical play, and talk of a new professional league as signs of development, but also highlighted how the infusion of money into the women's game had already led to exploitation.

Coaches alleged that higher stakes for themselves and players led to recruiting violations and a changed relationship between coaches and players, who no longer played just for school spirit and pride. With coaches' higher salaries, former Immaculata coach Cathy Rush noted, athletes increasingly played for the coaches themselves, whose careers and personal incomes were at stake when win-loss records were assessed at the end of each season. Rush also observed, astutely, that women were just as susceptible as men to the dangers associated with commercialized higher education athletics: "I thought we could stay away from [the pressures and problems men have]. I thought women were probably more honest than men. Men are out wheeling and dealing, but we wouldn't do that. But it's not true. In all business spectrums everybody's the same."[42] Despite this commentary on the negative aspects of increased funding, most players and coaches had yet to have a chance to show how they would handle it. At the grassroots level, players such as those at MSU had only begun their struggle for visibility.

Within a day of the MSU women filing their internal complaint, the *State News* itself announced its support of the team. A prominently placed editorial, "Voices in the Wilderness," condemned MSU's neglect of Title IX orders.[43] The editorial writer agreed with Jackson's characterization of the university's insistence that "revenue-raising sports such as football, basketball, and hockey do not fall under the purview of Title

IX" as "faulty reasoning." At the same time, the piece acknowledged, "it seems likely that the women's team can never achieve parity, in terms of publicity and media interest, with the men's team." However, rather than citing the men's team and Magic Johnson's outstanding skills as a reason to support the women's team less, the editorial made the opposite assertion: "[The] fact that Jud Heathcote's troupe did so well this year—almost winning a national championship—forcefully underlines the necessity for closely scrutinizing inequities between men's and women's sports." The editorial concluded: "The rush of praise and self-congratulation that has followed the success of the men's basketball team is all well and good, but the complaint filed with Pollack [*sic*] puts everyone on notice that sport is more than just fun and games."[44]

A Memo from HEW

On April 27, 1978, HEW released a copy of an April 25 memo regarding revenue production, college sports, and Title IX, along with a longer memo from the HEW attorney that offered a legal basis for HEW's official statement "reaffirming the applicability to revenue-producing intercollegiate athletics of Title IX of the Education Amendments of 1972."[45] These documents offered four primary reasons to support HEW's official opinion that Congress did not intend to exempt revenue-producing athletics from Title IX. In the shorter memo included in the press release, HEW secretary James Califano first noted that Congress had rejected the Tower Amendments that sought to exclude revenue-producing sports. Second, Califano pointed out that some revenue-producing sports "clearly receive direct Federal financial assistance." Third, Califano's memo noted, "Historically, intercollegiate athletics have been described as an integral part of general undergraduate education." Student loans and grants from the federal government that support undergraduate education constitute federal financial assistance to an institution. Therefore, the argument went, support for undergraduate education also supports athletics if athletics are treated as truly integral to general undergraduate education.[46]

Citing page five of the NCAA's manual, the Califano memo included in HEW's press release piggybacked on the NCAA's authority in the eyes of men's athletics administrators. Califano called attention to the NCAA manual's assertion that maintaining intercollegiate athletics' integration into "the student body" was critical to "retain[ing] a clear line of demarcation between college athletics and professional sports." Finally, Califano's memo cited the "infection doctrine," which applies to Title VI of the Civil Rights Act of 1964 as well as to Title IX. The doctrine's logic as applied to intercollegiate athletics went like this: "Revenue producing intercollegiate athletics [are] so integral to the general undergraduate education program of an institution of higher education that sex discrimination in the administration of a revenue producing athletic activity would necessarily infect the general undergraduate education program of the institution."[47]

A Petition

Shortly after HEW nationally released Califano's April 25 memo, MSU was hit with what must have felt like a one-two punch. First, the women's basketball team attended the annual Women's Sports Banquet and caused a stir by greeting people at the door with a petition that implored other MSU women athletes to join in their complaint. On May 11, two days later, the *State News* covered the banquet in an article that began with an understated hook: "The fourth annual MSU women's sports banquet got off to a slightly different start this year." It continued: "Those attending the awards dinner Tuesday night . . . were greeted with a written appeal for the Spartan women's basketball team. The appeal, which was being handed out to the crowd by cagers Kathy DeBoer and Mariann Mankowski as they filed into the banquet room, asked for support from other women's athletic teams."[48]

Pittman's "Chronology" added another detail: as DeBoer and Mankowski handed out the petition, Pittman "asked attendants to sign [it]." Accompanying the signature sheet, DeBoer and Mankowski included a plea for unity—a call for action that seemed to have the opposite effect. Fewer than a dozen people signed the petition (and one of those signatures was from women's studies professor Marilyn Frye).

The petition reached out to prospective supporters with an imperative, uncompromising, sometimes youthfully outraged tone:

You are all probably aware of the fact that the Women's Basketball Team has filed a public complaint against Michigan State University charging them with flagrant violations of Title Nine of the Equal Education Amendments of 1972. All of us as women athletes have suffered from blatant discrimination because of our sex. This University has cheated all of us out of our legal rights for the past 6 years. They have choosen [sic] to follow a policy which not only disregards our rights as athletes but has also caused a steady depreciation in the quality of our total program. We can no longer be passive in pursuing our rights. Obviously legal sanctions are not enough; we must coerce the University into obedience with them. We must collectively fight the self-denigrating attitude which makes being treated as second class athletes unacceptable. Become familiar with your rights as an athlete. Examine your own programs for discriminatory practices. Contact Mary Pollack [sic], the Title Nine Coordinator, and familiarize yourself with the procedures to follow in filing your own complaint. Sign our petition. Show your support by helping us circulate it. This is for all of us; it will not be done for us; we must do it together.

> Mariann R. Mankowski
> Kathleen J. DeBoer
> Representatives of the Women's Basketball Team[49]

The charged language of these paragraphs likely eclipsed the more matter-of-fact statement below it that the women asked supporters to sign. On a lined, legal-sized sheet of paper, with space below it for signatures and local addresses, the statement read:

We as students, faculty and staff of Michigan State University support implementation of measures to bring overall equality in athletic opportunity and full compliance with Title IX of the Educational Amendments of 1972 at Michigan State University.

We support implementation of measures to remedy the
effects of past and present discrimination in athletics at Michigan State University.[50]

Mankowski recalled that team members chose the petition as "one of
[their] civil disobedience things" after more extreme ideas such as mooning the media had been dismissed. A political science major, she called
the document their "Title IX Manifesto" and laughingly attributed its
strong language to their age: "That was like '78; we were kids, you know!"
She remembered her dad felt concerned that their actions might affect
their employment opportunities after graduation, but at the time, few of
them imagined coaching careers for themselves.[51]

In a 2005 interview, Mankowski remained puzzled at the resistance
the team faced from university administrators. She recalled that administrators who attended the banquet severely chastised her and other members
of the team for their efforts in the lobby—they called her a "rabble-rouser"
and informed her that "complaints of the type she and her team were
making were not the way to get results in a bureaucracy."[52] Mankowski felt
profoundly misunderstood. She and her teammates were following both
institutional procedures and their own higher sense of principle. In that
sense, they fit at least one profile of university student activists: a study of
the 1960s Free Speech Movement found that young people who actively
participated exhibited a higher level of moral development than their
inactive peers. That is, they demonstrated an allegiance to general human
values and principles of justice rather than simply trying to maintain adult
and peer approval. This profile contradicts the stereotype of a rebel simply
out to cause trouble and "trash the system."[53] And as Mark Pittman and
Bruce Alexander knew from their studies in sociology, circulating petitions to generate and demonstrate support for a cause is a standard tactic
in social movement persuasion. Considering the full repertoire of tactics
available to change agents, petitioning was a respectful approach to exerting influence through exercise of free speech. Likewise, the team sought
to work within the system by taking their complaints to the university's
board of trustees. As Mankowski later testified, on the day of the sports

banquet, she "went to the Board of Trustees' office on the fourth floor of the Administration Building and got on the Board of Trustees' docket . . . for the May 25 meeting."[54]

Women athletes also resisted DeBoer's and Mankowski's fighting words, which disappointed the team spokeswomen even more than the administrators' unsupportive response. Certainly, though, a public venue like the sports banquet did not provide the comfortable, private space for dialogue and reflection where feminists typically introduced conscious-ness-raising discourse. Inexperienced with such strategies, the women's basketball team and their supporters underestimated the degree to which other women athletes might fear allying themselves with perceived "rab-ble-rousers." DeBoer had grown accustomed to her role as the assertive team leader who spurred others to increased effort and competitiveness, often with great success. Off the court, however, definitions of winning and losing, and the stakes involved for each, were less clear-cut. Although discontent with inequities extended to women's teams in other sports, those athletes may have perceived the basketball team as privileged among the women's teams. In fact, DeBoer speculated later that the perception of basketball's place on a women's sports hierarchy might have made other women athletes reluctant to join their protest campaign. A psychology of scarcity likely came into play: because women athletes had relatively few resources, losing any of the support the institution gave them could leave them with almost nothing.

Certainly the strong language in the petition put these women on the spot. With a few exceptions, they expressed a passive form of resistance — perhaps best described as inertia — by choosing not to sign the petition. Staying in place must have seemed the safest route, especially since MSU still surpassed many other institutions when it came to women's sports. They did not want to lose what little they had.[55]

Pollock, by contrast, was energized. On May 12, in a handwritten note to MSU's President Harden after the banquet, she told him she enjoyed his comments during the gathering and thanked him for his support "in lessening some of the attitudinal as well as behavioral barriers to achieving sex equity in athletics at MSU" by taking action to include women's sports in the athletic council's jurisdiction. In a footnote to the friendly note was a shocker: "I will copy you on future items about this complaint as the students seem to be heading for the political arena."[56]

On May 9, just a few days before her May 12 note, Pollock had copied Harden, MSU vice president Robert Perrin (her boss's supervisor), Bonner, Jackson, and Underwood on a two-page, singled-spaced letter addressed to athletics director Joe Kearney.[57] In it, she outlined her plan of action regarding the women's basketball team's complaint. She noted that "[w]ith the recent Califano statement about revenue sports, we need to re-do our 1976 self-evaluation since revenue sports were excluded in that assessment." In a determined, professional tone, her letter listed fifteen areas she would cover in a written questionnaire she developed. The areas included student enrollment; student participation in varsity athletics; revenue sources for intercollegiate athletics; general overhead costs; budgets by sport; total expenditures and per capita participant expenditures; budget requests from coaches; corrective actions taken or projected; remedial actions; post-season invitations (1972–78); equipment, supplies, and uniforms; and scheduling of games and practice times. Pollock wrote of her meeting with Underwood and Jackson, "We seemed to be making progress on the facilities problem, length and intensity of the season, travel expenditures and a few other items, but coaching and scholarships just seemed to be areas where Clarence wouldn't budge." She explained that she preferred an informal approach "to see if we can clear up misunderstandings or get the issue resolved." However, she wrote, Underwood "insisted on written questions and I finally agreed."[58]

Pollock's questions, and her letter in general, probably made the memo written by HEW secretary Califano look comparatively innocuous. Pollock warned that she would launch an in-depth Title IX investigation, one that focused like a laser beam on the most sensitive issues. She explained that she based her questionnaire "on the HEW technical assistance document by Margaret Dunkle," adding that she hoped her document would even be "an improvement upon it" and that "we should move carefully and be very thorough."[59] In short, Pollock used discourse that the institution surely did not want from its Title IX coordinator, or expect from the woman in the pink suit they hired, without tenure, to direct women's programs.

However much she felt the growing tension around her at MSU, Pollock seemed to have been buoyed by the changes happening nationally. In a postscript to her May 9 letter to Kearney, she added the following:

> I met the woman A.D. from Yale last Friday. The women's program has a $600,000 budget (scholarships are based on need, not talent, so this figure excludes scholarships) for 16 sports, 250 participants out of a total population of 1700 women students. Of course the male budget is greater as there are more male students still being admitted to Yale, more males attracted to sport, more teams (19), etc. Rosa Weiner at HEW recommended their program as approaching a model higher education sports program. Apparently they will be featured in a TIME magazine article very soon.[60]

In contrast to "the stick" represented by the team's threatening language, in this ebullient footnote, Pollock used a "carrot" appeal. Pollock's note seemed designed to motivate MSU to compete with Yale, to work together to become a model program, make positive national news, and feel good about having done the right thing.

Pollock did not know then that no athletic department in the nation cared about winning the national championship for Title IX compliance. Nor were they too fearful of actually facing real punishment for noncompliance. Based on her experiences in Illinois, Pollock likely imagined support could come from the political arena. After all, in Illinois, she and the group of Concerned Women Athletes found strong support for their cause, including state-level hearings on sex discrimination in athletics. But in the state of Michigan, legislators had other agendas. On April 27, the state senate passed a resolution to approve construction of a one-million-dollar football training facility for MSU funded by athletic revenues.[61] And Michigan's legislature included one of the nation's strongest opponents of Title IX, Representative James O'Hara, a politician who saw the futures of college football and women's intercollegiate athletics on a collision course.

Media Framing

By mid-May, Pollock realized that the resistance she faced in conducting a Title IX audit of the athletics department was insurmountable. Although she finished assembling her questionnaire by May 15, she delayed delivering it because she had encouraged the team to notify the East Lansing media about their complaint, and she wanted to give them time to do so. She recalled, "I had to admit I was using the media as a way to pressure and get information and telling the kids to talk to the newspapers. They were doing things—I don't know what all they were doing."[62]

Shortly after the Women's Sports Banquet, the May 17 issue of the *State News* included three headlines related to the women's basketball team's complaint—two of them were on the editorial page, and both cast the women's basketball team's campaign in a somewhat negative light. The headline of one of the articles used neutral diction: "Women Cagers Address Board." That article quoted DeBoer extensively, and she provided her own framing for Pollock's soon-to-be-released Title IX questionnaire. As DeBoer phrased it, Pollock did not prepare her questionnaire *at the request of* the athletic department but rather as a document "to be answered by the athletic department's Affirmative Action Committee." In DeBoer's framing, the document's purpose was to "[examine] areas of discrimination specified in the complaint."[63] Whether this framing echoed how Pollock represented the document to her (and Pollock's own understanding) or whether it was her own interpretation, DeBoer's comments implied that the athletic department committee must answer to Pollock and the women's basketball team. To say the least, the department of intercollegiate athletics did not welcome this audacious reversal of institutional power arrangements (university administrators answering to students; the athletic department answering to the director of women's programs). At least for the moment, activist rhetoric had reversed the hierarchy.

Throughout this *State News* article, DeBoer represented the team as possessing a strong sense of agency and initiative. In a series of "if-then" statements, she painted a picture of the team in full control with plenty of options to exercise. For example, after noting that the team wrote to the

Office of Civil Rights "to establish contact . . . which could eventually prompt compliance procedures," she introduced the possibility of legal action. She said, "If no progress toward ending discrimination is made through University and federal channels . . . and if we feel we're running into road blocks . . . if they [administrators] try to lose us in the system . . . we may go in that direction [getting a private lawyer]." The article concluded with a few characteristically guarded-sounding statements by Jackson, who observed that the affirmative action committee (that she headed along with Underwood) had met for a month to address "the issue of Title IX." Guarded as her statement appeared—that an athletic department committee had met for a month to address Title IX as a three-year adjustment period came to an end—it could have been read as damning by informed readers. Moreover, the article ended with Jackson's statement that "the committee cannot release findings on discrimination in the women's athletic program until the questionnaire has been answered and a formal report has been completed." Even this innocuous statement afforded more weight to Pollock's questionnaire than Underwood likely intended it to have when he requested it. What weight it would in fact have remained to be seen.[64]

On the "Letters" page of the May 17, 1978, issue of the *State News*, student journalists provided a negative frame for the women's actions at the sports banquet. Instead of "A Plea for Unity" (as Pittman had labeled the statement circulated with the petition), the paper reprinted the statement underneath an inflammatory headline, albeit one DeBoer herself had introduced into the discourse: "Coerce MSU into Compliance." Above that heading, an even larger one posed the question, "Are Title IX Demands Reasonable?" A subheading answered that question: "Women Cagers Ask Too Much."

Finally, an "open letter to Ms. Kathleen DeBoer and Ms. Mariann Mankowski" appeared below the third headline. James Madaleno, the writer, identified himself as "an auxiliary member of the athletic program." He began by acknowledging that women athletes should not be expected to double or triple up on lockers. Presumably to show his own reasonableness, he graciously asserted, "You deserve a separate locker space, or at least a section of lockers in the Women's IM." However, Madaleno quickly moved on to his primary arguments. He contended that women, or any athletes, who do not bring in revenue have no right to expect the same treatment as those who do. He argued that sex discrimination was not the issue because "men's track, lacrosse, tennis, cross country, golf, swimming and even wrestling all travel by University station wagons to away events." Finally, he attacked the women's ethos as relative newcomers to competitive, organized athletics. He asked, "How can you expect to do in less than 10 years what took men approximately 100 years to achieve—a superior program of athletics?" He critiqued the team for "extreme lack of class," called them "irresponsible," and advised them to "quit being so demanding of University athletic officials with deadlines for decisions and ultimatums."[65] Madaleno never mentioned Title IX or the federal government's own deadline, which an editorial note above the open letter did mention: "The controversy promises to become even more pressing as the federal deadline for Title IX compliance, in July approaches."[66]

Madaleno's letter underscored that the often unclearly defined distinction between "revenue and nonrevenue" sports was not just another argument; it was (and still remains today) a powerful ideology. Like any strong hegemonic idea, the argument that revenue production must drive resource allocation was continually represented as in everyone's best interests, not just in the interest of the most privileged men's teams, coaches, and administrators. As one of the MSU trustees had quipped, "The goose that lays the golden egg must be preserved."[67] To conclude his open letter, Madaleno put it more bluntly: "Lately your actions have shown definite lack of thought, and you should think before you further damage yourselves, the whole women's athletic program, and MSU."[68] Indeed, women's sports advocates have continually faced the challenge of discovering ways to dislodge this dominant ideology and reframe the discourse.

Toward that end, on May 16, 1978, DeBoer, Mankowski, Jackson, and Pollock appeared on WELM TV, Channel 11, to discuss the team's complaint. Meanwhile, Pittman noted in his "Chronology" that Bruce Alexander stopped by Pollock's office to give feedback on her questionnaire. Pittman also observed, somewhat ominously, "From discussions with KDB [Kathy DeBoer] and MRM [Mariann Mankowski], it is becoming apparent to me [MHP] and Bruce [BKA] that internal institutional power arrangements are being disturbed by Mary Pollock. She [Mary] is being blocked from finding information and her questionnaire is too threatening to (1) Perrin, and (2) Department of Intercollegiate Athletics, and (3) perhaps President Harden."[69]

Pittman's notes for May 16 also introduced a new and important individual into the mix. At an athletics booster club meeting, he ran into Lou Anna Simon, a thirty-year-old assistant professor proficient in statistics, who was also a trusted number-crunching assistant to President Harden and a member of the athletic council (by 2005, the board of trustees appointed her as the first female president of the university).[70] She understood how MSU worked—and she had some advice for the women's basketball team.

Female Power Brokers

Shortly before the Title IX controversy erupted on campus, President Harden had pulled Simon up to his office to handle an affirmative action compliance audit that the university faced in the employment area (the federal government would withhold a major contract until the university demonstrated compliance). An administrator who knew Simon well described her as "a basic, go-by-the-numbers person, not someone viewed as a card-carrying feminist of the network that Mary [Pollock] and others were a part of."[71] She did, however, participate in a close-knit women's club that included behind-the-scenes power brokers such as Gwen Norrell, who held a doctorate in education and since 1945 had worked in the MSU counseling center. Norrell, an independent, tough-minded woman who mentored Simon in MSU politics, observed in an MSU oral history interview that she "was taught, [from] early days, that you have to be political on campus. People don't think a campus is political. My god, it's the most political place that I know anything about!"[72] According to Pittman's notes, Simon tried to warn him that "the women's basketball team was being led down the wrong path." She didn't tell him that, behind the scenes and unknown to Pollock, Norrell felt upset that the women's basketball players had not sought her counsel. Pittman failed to understand Simon's warning as an invitation to accept guidance from powerful women working behind the scenes, probably because of its indirectness, or perhaps because he already felt distrustful toward anyone connected with the university's higher administration. He heard only a vague suggestion that the team use "internal University procedures." Ironically, both the team and Pollock, unaware of the nuances of MSU's institutional politics, thought they were doing just that.[73]

As Mankowski later described the women's basketball team's approach, "We followed all the rules until there were no more rules left to follow."[74] But a web of tacit rules and power networks remained invisible to them. A group of interested athletes proceeded to meet at Mankowski's apartment to plan their next step, with both Pittman and Alexander present. Their plan certainly did not follow Simon's advice to pursue things internally— they set to work on another petition and a presentation they intended to deliver at the next MSU Board of Trustees meeting.

PART FOUR

Escalation

In summer 1978, the women's basketball team at MSU had reached a pivotal point. By August, the team leaders had decided to put their complaint in the hands of attorney Jean Ledwith King. In doing so, they abandoned their own self-styled rhetoric of protest—discourses influenced by their college courses in women's studies and sociology.[1] Instead, they put their trust in the legal rhetoric of their attorney. At precisely this time, a similar chain of events was taking place at another school known for its strong women's physical education program, Temple University. Like at MSU, the July 1978 Title IX compliance date proved to be a powerful exigence for taking increasingly bold steps to find out why more had not been done to comply with the law.

In the mid-1970s, as a high school student on Long Island, Rollin Haffer appeared to be the opposite of the catalyst behind the *Hutchins v. MSU Board of Trustees* case, Kathleen DeBoer. A petite five feet six inches tall, Haffer was a self-described shy, quiet tennis player when her tennis coach invited her to try the sport of badminton. The more outspoken, physically bigger and stronger five-foot eleven-inch DeBoer competed in high school tennis, too, but she also embraced the opportunity to compete in almost any sport available. DeBoer's father was a professor, while no one in Haffer's family had attended college. Beneath these differences, the two girls, as high school students growing up in different parts of the country, shared a strong sense of principle and a commitment to social justice grounded in their religious upbringings. Haffer's success in high school badminton, where she was team captain and MVP, became an unexpected route to a college scholarship. In the mid-1970s, along with introducing her to badminton, her high school coach also introduced her to Title IX, a topic about which the coach thought her athletes should at least be aware. Haffer had no way of knowing just how important that law would become in her own life, but the topic interested her enough to choose as a research paper topic in her English class. In her careful way, she surveyed coaches, teachers, and administrators in her school and wrote a paper, not thinking much about the topic again until it confronted her in college.[2]

After high school, while attending a reasonably priced community college because of her family's modest financial resources, Haffer was spotted by a faculty member from Temple University who was impressed by her play in a New Jersey badminton tournament. Following that instructor's advice, she visited Temple to see whether she might be eligible for athletic financial aid. In 1977, when she enrolled in Temple on a full tuition scholarship (worth $3,600 a year), she thought she'd been handed the world on a platter.[3] Put in one perspective, her scholarship was worth triple what DeBoer or any of her female peers received at MSU that year.

With thirty-five thousand students, Temple had run a women's athletics program for fifty-two years, offering twelve women's intercollegiate teams when Haffer enrolled. Housed in the department of physical education, the Temple women's intercollegiate athletics program differed from MSU's program in at least one important respect: it had a Student Athletic Council run entirely by and for women athletes. In other ways, Temple resembled MSU in terms of women's athletics: in 1977–88, women made up 42 percent of the intercollegiate athletes but received only 13 percent of the athletic budget. These differences did not matter to Haffer at first as she completed a successful first year as a student and athlete. Proud of Haffer's success, her hometown paper ran a feature on her, highlighting her 9-1 record at the number two singles spot.[4]

In her sophomore year, Haffer incrementally gained self-confidence. Her athletic success emboldened her to become secretary of the Student Athletic Council as a sophomore. In her junior year, respecting her quiet integrity, her peers elected her president of the council. That election began a process that led to the filing of *Haffer v. Temple University* in 1980, just months after the MSU women's basketball team filed suit in *Hutchins v. MSU Board of Trustees*.[5]

For two years leading up to fall 1978, Haffer had attended monthly council meetings in which student representatives from the twelve women's sports voiced repeated complaints. Like at MSU and across the country, differences in treatment between men's and women's sports were undeniable. The women learned about differences through boy-friends or sympathetic guys on the "minor" men's teams who understood and felt similarly ill-treated. They found that in all the areas covered by Title IX, inequities persisted. Male athletes received $700,000 in schol-arship funds, many of them receiving full room and board along with tuition, while only $188,000 went to women. The women's teams lacked resources to travel to find competitors who could challenge their skills; women often bought their own equipment because what Temple gave them was nearly unusable. Men received tutors and book loans; women did not. Men's teams, especially football and basketball, received priority scheduling and higher per diem rates when traveling. Women slept two to a bed, four to a room while the men had their own beds. The refrain sounds somewhat worn and familiar by now, but the Temple women were outraged at the disparities.[6]

When students such as Haffer at Temple, DeBoer and Mankowski at MSU, and others around the nation began asking questions about Title IX and intercollegiate athletics, they never imagined ending up in court. Of course, for the MSU women's basketball team, moving into the legal realm to pursue their Title IX rights was not inevitable. To get there, as a colleague who read a draft of this book observed, "rhetoric shaped choices and choices shaped their rhetoric." It works that way, as another colleague put it, because "rhetoric massively influences perceptions."[7] That is, in every interaction, the words we choose and the way we frame them influence responses. These responses influence the options avail-able, the options perceived, and finally the choices we make. Students, their supporters, and institutional leaders each could have made other choices, which would have led to a different result.

In August 1978, rather than turning to a legal representative, the MSU women's basketball team could have continued to direct their own ongoing rhetorical efforts, perhaps requesting a meeting with university leaders. Those leaders could have met face-to-face with them. The students could have asked the director of women's athletics, Nell Jackson, to represent them in speaking with the MSU athletics director and other administrators. Alternatively, team members could have simply waited for the federal Office of Civil Rights to respond to their June 1978 Title IX complaint.

The dynamics leading the team to enter the realm of legal rhetoric were created through small, everyday rhetorical choices by team members, supporters, and university administrators, along with one momentous, catalytic event described in the chapters to follow. Likewise, the team's decision to obtain legal representation immediately heightened distrust between the students and institutional leaders. All along the way, one rhetorical choice affected another, often in small, seemingly inconsequential ways; none were made in a vacuum. Perceptions—and sometimes misperceptions—shaped responses.

Yet rhetoricians well know that language choices are also subject to the constraints and possibilities of existing rhetorical situations. At colleges and universities across the country, both students and institutional leaders addressed each other at a particular historical moment, employing *standpoint rhetorics*, discourses emerging from a set of circumstances or positions that may be hard to understand outside of their contexts. Therefore, although events could have played out differently, contextual factors often mitigated against other possibilities. In the 1970s, outspoken students were seen as "rabble-rousers," not individuals—and certainly not as "customers" as they are often viewed today, with every right to ask questions and even make demands upon the adults responsible for running the institution. College students were not viewed as equals with their parents or with adult institutional leaders who were charged with protecting young people's educational best interests. Turbulent anti–Vietnam War protests on some campuses in the 1960s and early 1970s generated trepidation on college campuses when student protest came to mind. Outspoken or complaining students were more likely viewed as insubordinate voices to be quieted rather than young adults who could be expected to participate with campus leaders in a mutually respectful conversation.

Moreover, as we have seen, women athletes who spoke out strongly also violated the norms of apologetic rhetoric and gentle persuasion favored by their own physical education leaders and scholars. For example, the highly visible pro–Title IX rhetoric of women athletes put athletic administrators and AIAW members such as Nell Jackson on the spot. Guiding change gradually behind the scenes from their in-the-middle positions became increasingly difficult. They could side openly with their competitive female athletes (and risk being fired) or with the head athletics directors to whom they reported (and risk seeming unsupportive of the female athletes). Either way, AIAW loyalists faced an identity crisis. Especially within athletic department culture, coaches and administrators who couldn't "control" their players' unruly discourse were viewed by supervisors as incompetent or even disloyal.[8]

Notably absent from the conflict at MSU was a mediating figure who might have interjected a discourse of bridge-building and common ground. Without that peacemaking rhetoric, mistrust persisted and the situation escalated. By considering litigation, however, the student athletes turned to what constitutional historian Michael Klarmen has characterized as a form of American protest rhetoric. Whether or not a precedent-setting legal decision results from a lawsuit, Klarmen contended, the indirect consequences of litigation battles in a social movement can matter greatly.[9] They matter, in part, because they matter *rhetorically*. The discourse of one social change movement is echoed in the next, which means advocates for change and supporters of the status quo alike can look to the past and find a reservoir of available rhetoric from which to draw.

12 See You in Court

Started the Chronology.
　　　　　　　—Mark Pittman, June 18, 1978[1]

In the spring and summer of 1978, Mark Pittman's notations in his Title IX "Chronology" became increasingly detailed. No longer writing from memory and informal jottings, he kept his typewriter close at hand, writing nearly every day. That level of detail provides a finely textured account of how politics, processes, and documents of organizational communication can be channels for both social change and status quo rhetoric. In speeches, memos, and reports—combined with news articles and Pittman's "Chronology"—the behind-the-scenes trench warfare that often characterizes local Title IX struggles comes into view. In the 1970s at MSU, upper-level administrators sometimes underestimated the resolve of change agents to persist with moral appeals to principles of justice when confronted with status quo arguments. Meanwhile, students, who were inclined to trust the adults in charge of the institution, sometimes underestimated how they could be subtly directed to act against their own interests. Repeatedly, moral appeals to justice and equality confronted appeals to pragmatism and economic realities.

Today, these same appeals to equality and economics, and their corresponding worldviews, continue to animate competing Title IX rhetorics. One means for moving beyond the stalemate these opposing discourses create is to examine the finer texture of rhetoric in documents that make up an institution's everyday professional communication. In day-to-day institutional documents, meetings, and informal conversations, agenda-driven discourse shapes action and actions shape subsequent discourse.

239

Scrutinizing these textual and verbal encounters reveals what longtime MSU athletics and academic administrator Kathy Lindahl referred to as "defining moments."[2] In those moments, whether an individual speaks up or not, whether someone shares key information, whether communication is clear and respectful, and whether people genuinely seek common ground can make the kind of difference that defines an organization for years to come.

Pitfalls of Comparing and Contrasting

In mid-May 1978, Kathy DeBoer worked on a writing task that seemed more important and urgent than any homework assigned for her MSU classes: a handout on Title IX and a speech for the board of trustees. In crafting the statement, she worked closely with Cookie Mankowski and consulted with her friends Mark Pittman, Bruce Alexander, and Mary Jo Hardy. According to Pittman's "Chronology," Mary Pollock assisted them by giving Mankowski and DeBoer her "background paper," likely the opening statement she wrote to introduce her Title IX questionnaire. As DeBoer composed her speech, she met Kay White, MSU's assistant vice president for student affairs, an administrator reputed to support women's issues and programs. Pittman summarized DeBoer's description of the meeting: "Again, internal procedures are recommended . . . don't pursue Mary Pollock's line of attack." This advice once more puzzled Pittman—by going through Pollock, they *were* following internal procedures. He concluded that White's advice must have been "an attempted cool out tactic."[3]

As they hunkered down, the tide of campus opinion seemed to shift against them ever so slightly. The basketball team's plea for unity circulated at the Women's Sports Banquet had not mentioned the men's basketball team specifically; however, in response to that plea, James Madaleno's open letter published in the *State News* had honed in on a difficulty the women faced in the court of public opinion. "Your only problem," he wrote, "is that you are trying to make known your problem by using the men's program (basketball in particular)."[4] His charge was not entirely accurate, but it warned of a huge rhetorical pitfall that they and Pollock had started to slip into.

In their two written public statements, DeBoer and Mankowski focused on what Title IX required rather than using the men's basketball team as a measuring stick. However, in players' comments to the press and in Pollock's discourse with administrators (especially after other women athletes did not join the women's basketball team in making a Title IX complaint), they had begun to highlight inequalities by making contrasts with the men's basketball team. Sometimes they did so with loaded language such as DeBoer's "they make things so convenient for the men" comment regarding jockstraps.

The strategy of making any comparisons at all fell especially flat during MSU's "magical seasons." As Deb Traxinger recalled, "I loved being on campus during the [Earvin Johnson] years because that was history in the making as well. Magic Johnson was part of changing the face of basketball. And he's a great guy! So we had nothing against the men's basketball team, and I don't think they really had anything against us." But administrators and the public easily interpreted any comparisons that the women made as attacks on the men. "So in a way it was unfortunate that Magic Johnson was there when we were there," Traxinger concluded.[5]

Of course, even without a "magical season" to contend with, women's athletics administrators generally viewed emphasizing contrasts with men's teams as a rhetorical misstep. Not a part of that professional discourse community, DeBoer, Mankowski, and Pollock continued to make comparisons and contrasts. In doing so, they freely used terms such as "discrimination" and "sex equity," diction that women's athletics director Donna Lopiano carefully censored from her rhetoric of fair play at Texas. Even more problematically, no one at MSU assured the men—as Lopiano did at Texas—that the women's program genuinely wanted to contribute to revenue production. Pollock herself used the power of dollar signs to persuade when, in her first months at MSU, she convinced the Varsity Alumni Club chair to accept women athletes as members by pointing out how much the club's income from dues would increase. As a result of her efforts, on March 29, 1978, MSU's athletic council meeting minutes documented that "the Varsity Alumni Club Board of Directors voted to accept women Varsity athletes into the club." At that meeting, the chairman of the council requested that the athletic council formally recognize the ten varsity women's sports. The council then made and passed the motion.[6]

Despite this example of success, Pollock, DeBoer, and Mankowski usually seemed to perceive pragmatic arguments about potential economic benefits of equality as beside the point. Their arguments for equality relied instead on feminist principles and federal law. In any case, only Nell Jackson was well positioned to speak for the women's sports program's philosophy when it came to commercialization, and she was ideologically opposed to doing so. A physical educator at heart, Jackson was less willing than Lopiano to part from her physical education roots and embrace the commercialized character of the men's model of sport. At times, her public statements had even (somewhat hypocritically) implied a willingness to let revenue from men's commercialized sports help support a more "pure" women's program. Together, their discursive choices, generally driven by principled idealism, stoked growing negative feelings toward the women's basketball team.

Coverage of the controversy in the MSU *State News* also subtly undermined women athletes' pursuit of equality, even in the most supportive articles. On May 17, 1978, a student columnist argued that MSU made itself "very susceptible to a lawsuit by taking its time making women's opportunities equal to men's." Tom Shanahan's piece, "MSU Asking for Trouble," supported the women's basketball team; however, it perpetuated the inaccurate idea that the revenue produced by men's and women's teams was a legitimate factor to consider when assessing sex discrimination. Both the US Department of Health, Education, and Welfare and Congress had rejected this argument. The column also perpetuated the idea that revenue producing was synonymous with "profitable." But with women's teams so poorly funded (and bringing in so little revenue), arguments like Shanahan's that women deserved more crumbs, if not the full measure of equity required by law, were compellingly modest and therefore likely to be well received by many readers. Also, information about athletic budgets and accounting practices to determine revenue and profit was hard to obtain and analyze. Shanahan, to his credit, cited men's and women's team operating budgets for the 1977–78 school year. He contended that women's basketball could become revenue-producing if its budget was not "just barely above a nonrevenue spring sport." But he still argued for crumbs: "Women's teams don't expect to receive the money that revenue-producing sports like football, basketball, and hockey get, but they do expect better facilities than locker rooms that have no lockers, [and] one toilet and four showerheads in a shower room that is for MSU and its opponent."[7]

On May 19, 1978, an article in the *State News* demonstrated even more strongly the ways in which framing by the media could give an article a negative slant concerning positive developments for women athletes. The headline read "Women Athletes to Gain Lockers" in large print followed by a second-level heading, "Men's Facilities to Be Reduced." Although the second-level headline seemed to invite controversy, the first article emphasized positive progress in building common ground between individuals representing women's athletics and the institution's leadership. The article quoted MSU executive vice president Jack Breslin as saying, "The project should go a long way toward providing greater equality for women students, and it will help the University meet its obligations under Title IX."[8] In the men's intramural building (somewhat of a misnomer since women's varsity teams competed there regularly), the university added new lockers for women and divided locker space previously devoted entirely to men between male and female students. Jackson used the opportunity to add that "she would also like to see improvements in financial aid, salaries, and team budgets." Pollock praised the institution while also reminding people of the outstanding issues. She noted that the $97,000 renovations "will solve some of the problems the women's varsity teams have been complaining about."[9]

Communication Channels and Politics

The absence of Joe Kearney's voice, usually included in similar articles, may reflect a developing dynamic that the athletics director did not appreciate. In Pittman's view, Kearney sometimes felt betrayed by Jackson for going over his head, as Kearney perceived it. Specifically, Jackson discussed issues related to her program with Breslin, who was also her friend and racquetball partner, and with MSU president Wharton before he left the university in 1977. According to Pittman, the trustees also respected Jackson and were impressed with her always dignified, articulate communications with them. Despite Jackson's title of "assistant" director, because of the separate, hybrid nature of the athletics department structure, she likely took advantage of opportunities to lobby for women's programs with upper administrators. In Pittman's words at the time, she had "an open communication channel to Pres. By-passing Kearney."[10] As a result, some other administrators, mainly Kearney, came to distrust her. In a 1987 statement, Jackson observed that "her superiors in the university believed she was behind" the women's basketball team's actions and that "as a result they didn't talk to her about it very much." Certainly, they must have wondered why she had failed to prevent it.[11]

Behind the scenes, several members of the men's athletic power structure took notice of the women's basketball team's struggle. In an interview with Lansing sportswriter Tim Staudt, DeBoer learned that MSU football coach Daryl Rogers, men's basketball coach Jud Heathcote, and athletics director Joe Kearney harbored "ill feelings" toward the women's basketball team's complaints.[12] Any significantly oppositional feelings from Heathcote, however, were unapparent to women's basketball coach Karen Langeland, who recalled Heathcote as a supportive colleague during the time their coaching careers at MSU overlapped. She remembered him, on occasion, bringing her a cake to console her for a tough loss and commiserating about the difficulties of the coaching profession. In a 2011 interview, Heathcote remembered the Title IX controversy as something that he "never got involved in." "The way I looked at it," he said, "that was an administrative problem, not a basketball problem."[13] As he viewed it, men in nonrevenue college sports such as baseball faced similar resource problems. Whenever someone asked him at the time to comment on the women's situation, he called attention to the similarly disadvantaged situation of men's low (or no) revenue-producing sports. In a February 1979 interview with a newspaper reporter, he acknowledged that the MSU women's actions could "have definite effects on athletics across the country" and that "there [were] some inequities involved," but he didn't think MSU's athletics program would change.[14] Reiterating the dominant perspective, he framed the issue as a revenue versus nonrevenue sport issue rather than a sex discrimination issue. At the time, he didn't perceive discrimination against female athletes as a legitimate social justice problem—at least not one that he felt compelled to help address.[15]

Athletics director Joe Kearney seemed to share Heathcote's sentiments regarding sex discrimination in athletics. Whatever his personal or professional feelings about Jackson, Pollock, or the women's basketball team, his opposition took the form of inaction. Pittman recorded in his "Chronology" that Pollock told him President Harden was "kicking Kearney in the ass" because "Kearney had no plan to respond to the complaint." Arguably, Kearney had responded by delegating the matter to assistant athletics director Clarence Underwood, head of the athletic council's affirmative action committee. But with only a few months before the compliance deadline, delegation amounted to inaction. Underwood himself told the *State News* that the affirmative action committee was "not designed to deal with compliance complaints." Rather, he explained, "We just file reports and make recommendations."[16] Certainly Pollock viewed Kearney as the primary audience for the written questionnaire she had composed at Underwood's request. To investigate the team's Title IX complaint, she needed his cooperation. From Underwood's perspective, Pollock intended for the questionnaire to determine whether the complaints were legitimate and, if so, to gather more information that could be useful in addressing them. However, the lack of cooperation increasingly frustrated Pollock. In response, she developed her own manifesto of sorts: a nineteen-page single-spaced document with multiple appendices entitled "A Plan to Attain Sex Equity in Intercollegiate Athletics at MSU." She waited to deliver it until after DeBoer and Mankowski made their presentation to the board.

Escalation and Impasse

On May 22, 1978, three days before the team's scheduled appearance before the board and less than a week after DeBoer's comment to the *State News* that the team might pursue legal action if they continued to "run into roadblocks," DeBoer received an unexpected phone call from MSU president Harden. He informed her that the university was conducting a "legal audit" of intercollegiate athletics regarding Title IX. As recalled by DeBoer (and recorded in Pittman's "Chronology"), Harden assured her that whatever happened from that point on was "nothing personal." But, he told her in no uncertain terms, "We'll see you in court!"[17]

Those five words came across as a challenge and a threat from the university's chief executive. Like the students' "fighting words," they escalated a tense situation further. Had the president attended more carefully to the rhetorical situation, known the individuals he was dealing with, and considered the psychology of persuasion, he might have avoided this scare tactic. Instead, university administrators seemed unaware that their own resistant responses to initial complaints had sparked a reciprocal wave of resistance and distrust from the students and their supporters—and a vicious circle ensued. The situation was fueled by what social psychologists term "reactance": a resistant state of mind that results when someone's freedom of choice is threatened. Title IX itself had already sparked reactance on a national level from both the men's and women's sports establishments. Initially, they each saw its regulations as a threat to their autonomy, values, and (for men's athletics) budgets. At the local level, students' threatening discourse citing intent to "coerce"—along with administrators' apparent expectations that students would accept more passively whatever the university offered them—must have exacerbated this unreceptive state of mind.

The day after Harden's phone call to DeBoer, Pollock concluded that she had reached an impasse in her efforts to investigate the complaints. In his "Chronology," Pittman quoted directly from Pollock's memo addressed to the Anti-Discrimination Judicial Board (ADJB). He had a personal copy, as did DeBoer and Mankowski, because Pollock had copied all the complainants on her memo, along with President Harden, Pollock's supervisors (Vice President Perrin and Assistant Vice President Bonner), Athletics Director Kearney, Assistant Athletics Director Jackson, and Assistant Athletics Director Underwood. The subject line read "Intercollegiate Athletics."[18] Pollock wrote that the athletics department was unresponsive to her "direct informal approach," and that her supervisors would not authorize her "with the kind of powers needed to look at personnel records and the deeper aspects of intercollegiate athletics expenditures." In a 2011 interview, Pollock recalled that, to her surprise, her supervisors considered it highly inappropriate for her to have copied the complaining parties on these communications. She recalled that no investigative guidelines were in place, so she saw her inclusive communications merely as a means of being fair and transparent to all parties.[19] Even so, she had copied the administrators she described as uncooperative on her memos, and they would not have appreciated being "called out" in that way—in front of the students, no less—by this junior administrator from women's programs.

Pollock's memo to the Anti-Discrimination Judicial Board also pointed out that the discrimination cited by the women's basketball team was not isolated. She mentioned that players from women's gymnastics, softball, track, and volleyball either had provided or planned to provide her office with information about sex discrimination. A group of assistant coaches, she wrote, was considering a group complaint. After noting that she could not "prove or disprove" allegations of discrimination, she noted that if the athletics department decided to investigate on its own, "someone will need to audit their assertions so that our complainants and the public will be assured that we are taking care of our problems in a professional, thorough and proper way."[20] In her conclusion, she offered to work with any committee investigating the complaint and offered one last opinion: "At a later time, I think we should also review the role of the affirmative action officer, the Title Nine Coordinator, and the 504 regulations compliance officer in regard to their *perceived* and *real* compliance authority at MSU."[21] On the last page of Pollock's handwritten "Complaint Investigation Record," she noted, "Gave K [Kathy DeBoer] document and informed handing over to ADJB [Anti-Discrimination Judicial Board]."[22]

On May 24, 1978, the day after Pollock sent her memo to the ADJB, she sent a memo to Kearney, again with a long list of parties copied, including the ADJB; Harden, president; Perrin, vice president; Bonner, assistant vice president and affirmative action officer; Jackson, assistant director; and complainants. She cited two enclosures: her proposed Title IX and sex equity study (with information forms to be filled out) and her ADJB transmittal letter.[23] Pollock's memo appears to have had a dual purpose. The first was to clear up a miscommunication (one that may have been genuine or perhaps constructed to cast her in a negative light). She clarified that she had not "refused to cooperate" with the affirmative action committee but had simply declined to be a member. She had agreed to serve as a consultant and sent over information, including the technical assistance manual on Title IX put together in 1976 by Margaret Dunkle for HEW.[24] The second purpose of her letter was persuasive. She attempted to convince Kearney to exercise his "clear choice to work cooperatively, openly and in good faith" with her to gather information needed to assess Title IX compliance if federal investigators should ever request it.[25]

Pollock, however, based her request on two faulty assumptions, each of which reflected the chasm separating her and Kearney when it came to common values and priorities. Her first assumption was that "since the first Self-Evaluation in 1976 exclud[ed] revenue-producing sports and was not thorough in other aspects," they still needed "to do a satisfactory Self-Evaluation of [MSU's compliance with] the letter *and* spirit of the Title Nine Regulation." Kearney, however, still insisted that the highest "revenue producing" sports could be excluded. Pollock warned that not updating the self-evaluation "may, in future years, come back to haunt us."[26] Her warning of unspecified consequences underscored the difficulty of using the "stick" to persuade a resistant athletics director to assess his program. Pollock also tried a more idealistic appeal: "It is true that there is a risk in being very open about our programs, especially if we are guilty of something or can't explain disparities in treatment with logical rationales. I am assuming that in higher education we should have the courage to examine all dogma, orthodoxies, and assumptions without fear of truth."[27]

Here, Pollock failed to address the root concern of athletic administrators when it came to addressing sex discrimination: money. Her high-minded discourse—grounded in abstract terms such as *truth* and *courage* that are often potent rhetorical tools—sounds hopelessly idealistic and out of step with the fundamental concerns of the athletic power structure.[28]

DeBoer's Speech for the Trustees

DeBoer used a more strategic approach when framing the purpose of her presentation delivered to the MSU Board of Trustees. After the presentation, in comments for the MSU student newspaper printed on May 25, 1978, she diplomatically framed the issue as a "discrepancy in the way Title IX is being interpreted by the University and the athletic teams."[29] And, in a rhetorical move that suggested a common purpose with the trustees, her handout for the trustees began by referencing the board's own policy resolution, adopted in 1970, in which they committed MSU to a "no discrimination" policy. Next, the handout, which Marian Mankowski distributed at the meeting, described Title IX as a law that likewise banned discrimination. Along with noting that the compliance deadline was sixty-one days away, the handout stated that "no distinction is made in H.E.W. regulations between 'revenue' and 'non-revenue' sports or activities." Below that statement, the handout listed ten factors (the so-called "Laundry List") that were "enumerated for determining equality of athletic opportunity under Title IX." The handout then stated: "We charge the University with discrimination in all the items mentioned in 2d above"; that is, the entire list of possibilities under the Title IX "Laundry List." The text ended by referring back to its beginning, reiterating the trustees' own values: "We request that the Board of Trustees reaffirm its commitment to its resolution of February 28, 1970, by pledging the cooperation of all administrators and staff involved in athletics at M.S.U. in this matter." The handout made a logical argument, bookended with the trustees' own policy. In short, DeBoer said, "The women's basketball team is only asking you to follow your own policy."[30] The simple but pointed logic of her statement presented a strong, clear message without the charged language of her earlier discourse.

The brief verbal statement that DeBoer read, however, took a more confrontational stance. In recounting the team's actions to date, DeBoer resurrected earlier references to "blatant discrimination" and "direct violation of Title IX." She stated that the team filed its complaint "in the office of Mary Pollock, the Title Nine coordinator for this university," a point that seemed aimed at establishing that they followed proper procedures. She offered a version of the "Laundry List" to indicate the forms of discrimination they had identified. For emphasis, she preceded each item with the word "unequal":

- unequal budgets
- unequal practice and game facilities and access to them

- unequal coaches' salaries
- unequal number of coaches
- unequal scholarship compensation
- unequal locker facilities
- unequal modes of travel and per diem allowances
- unequal publicity
- unequal lengths of season
- unequal room and board arrangements during vacations
- unequal scheduling of games
- unequal recruiting opportunities
- unequal enforcement of University policies[31]

Like Pollock, DeBoer pushed for openness. She alleged that the university had "so far consistently excluded the men's revenue producing sports, or ha[d] hidden the real scope of discriminations by a failure to break down the men's and women's programs into comparable categories."[32]

DeBoer also reminded the board that it would be in their best interest to remember several facets of Title IX. She said, "First is that, contrary to the wishes of the NCAA and the practice of this University, as of this point there is no indication that revenue producing sports will be exempted from HEW's consideration of a University's Title IX compliance." Then she reminded the board of the July compliance deadline and, this time, stated a consequence of noncompliance more tactfully, using a grammatically passive voice. Rather than the overtly threatening language deployed previously (e.g., "we will coerce you"), she described possible consequences as risks: "After that day any institution not in full compliance risks not only losing its federal funding but having suit brought against it."[33] This statement, more warning than threat, adeptly situated the MSU administrators as decision makers free to exercise options rather than subjects of coercion by students.

In her closing lines, DeBoer requested, rather than demanded, that the trustees become the students' allies, joining them in urging the university to comply with the law. By treating the institution and its trustees as separate entities, she offered the trustees a chance to see themselves as wise counsels of the institution rather than potential adversaries. Conversely, DeBoer identified herself as representing a larger group than in the past—not only of the women's basketball team but of "all other women athletes in similar situations." Finally, as in the handout, she reminded the trustees of their own stated "commitment to nondiscriminatory practices and equal opportunity." She lastly appealed to transparency, asking for a "full and open investigation of MSU's entire athletic program."[34]

A May 30, 1978, *State News* article, "MSU Interpreting Title IX," recounted how President Harden and the trustees received DeBoer's appeals. President Harden embraced a potentially face-saving frame—the idea that the conflict stemmed from differences in interpretations of Title IX. However, Harden had not turned to the institution's designated Title IX coordinator, Pollock, to assist with interpretations. After all, the institution had provided Pollock with a budget to use, in part, to educate herself and the campus about how to interpret and apply the Title IX regulations. Pollock had even traveled to meet the HEW staff member who had worked on the regulations themselves. Pollock recalled, "I had gone to conferences about Title IX, and I took this stuff very seriously. I mean I visited in Washington D.C. the office of the woman who was identified as writing the regulations. And she was in this government office with grey desks and papers stacked up, this messy place. But to me she was an idol. . . . At any rate, I found an instrument that we could use to survey [what the men's and women's teams received]."[35]

Instead of talking with Pollock, Harden apparently turned to his peers, other Big Ten university presidents. He cited collective confusion: "At a recent meeting of the Big Ten presidents, I found no one really knew what Title IX really meant," he said.[36] So, nearly three years into the federally prescribed adjustment period for complying with Title IX, the MSU president's message to the women's basketball team was that "before the University could take steps to equalize opportunity for women athletes, Title IX must be evaluated and understood."[37] The major question— the same question raised by the failed Tower Amendment years before and afterward clarified in a widely distributed HEW memo—remained whether the so-called "big three money-making sports" must be included and "whether they will suffer as women's athletics are upgraded." Quotations from DeBoer show that she addressed questions confidently and succinctly. She explained, "There is no indication that revenue sports are exempt," and "Title IX is a federal law which supersedes both the AIAW and NCAA" (when asked by a trustee whether the AIAW's different standards affect compliance).[38]

Despite the MSU power structure's continued denial of the fact that Title IX covered revenue sports, the meeting with the trustees opened up a potentially productive channel of face-to-face communication between DeBoer and President Harden. Harden's message at the end of the meeting, as quoted in the *State News*, was, "Let our legal beagles go to work." The article concluded, "You have initiated something. You will get answers."[39] To find those answers, Harden had charged a university attorney, Byron Higgins, to conduct the "legal audit" that he had mentioned in his phone call to DeBoer.

Pollock's Plan

By May 31, 1978, MSU had initiated its legal audit, the women's basketball team's complaint was in the hands of the Anti-Discrimination Judicial Board, and Pollock's "Plan to Attain Sex Equity at MSU"—including a survey instrument modeled after Dunkle's technical assistance manual—was being distributed internally. By early June, Pollock's supervisors, athletics director Kearney, assistant athletics director Jackson, and other MSU administrators had copies of her plan. Pollock's report was in no small part a manifesto. As she acknowledged later, "I was pretty full of myself at the time, but I really believed in the principles involved."[40]

Pollock's report did not invite face-saving on the part of the institution or sanction the idea that they needed time to interpret the law. Rather, she directly confronted institutional power holders, decision makers, and ideologies that conflicted with values of equality, the rule of law, openness, and sex fairness. In short, she did not behave like the untenured, pink-suited woman her supervisors thought they hired. Nor did she write in a language that her target audience could identify with or respond to positively on either emotional or logical levels. From word choices to basic assumptions, the gender lens through which she viewed social reality fundamentally differed from the world her intended readers inhabited.

Quite likely, they never read her statement at all. Many academic administrators would recoil at reading what they would likely view as a nineteen-page tome. And Pollock's main target audience was Joe Kearney, the head athletics director, who likely wondered why this woman continued to bother him. In response to her phone calls, he had already informed her that he had a full schedule through the end of March. Mark Pittman, however, read the report word for word, highlighting and annotating the copy he likely received from DeBoer. In fact, he kept a copy of Pollock's report for more than thirty-five years. Among his materials is a mislabeled folder at the top of which Pittman had scribbled: "Pollock's Plan to Attack Sex Equity at MSU." Although Pollock had used the term "attain" rather than "attack," Pittman's probably inadvertent choice of words captured the tone of the document—and his own conviction that an assault on the status quo was necessary.

Just as Pittman was not a typical 1970s women's track or cross-country coach (in part because few men coached women's sports at the time), Pollock was an anomaly as a Title IX coordinator. Typically, young activist women inclined to agitate for change did not work their way up into such positions of internal authority.[41] As a result, young, untenured women such as Pollock were typically not charged with preparing reports for higher administrators regarding sensitive issues such as gender equality. More often, such tasks fell to trusted insiders, including a class of women sometimes referred to as "queen bees."[42] These women had paid their dues and achieved their status not by activism or agitation, but in part by conduct viewed as acceptable to powerful men with authority over them. Looking back on her time at MSU, Pollock wondered whether some of the women she suspected of playing the queen bee role undermined her efforts more than she realized at the time.[43] But in May 1978, she thought little of such matters. She hoped that the report would achieve one of its primary aims—an affirmation that she was the proper individual to coordinate a Title IX compliance effort at MSU.

Pollock's plan included five sections typical of the technical report genre: a history of the issue, assumptions, options for action, an assessment of those options, and recommendations for action. However, Pollock's report was anything but typical. The document was an explicitly feminist piece of professional communication, a text intended to catalyze institutional change. Pollock pointedly made explicit important tacit assumptions about gender or other power relations that supported and perpetuated inequities. Prior to writing the report, Pollock could identify with athletes and coaches whom she viewed as lacking institutional power because she found herself blocked from obtaining information from more powerful administrators. Therefore, in the copy of the report that she submitted to her boss, Assistant Vice President Bonner, and to his supervisor, Vice President Perrin, Pollock included a paper trail that documented her unsuccessful attempts to access information.

Following a table of contents, the document began with an "Opening Statement" that introduced the report with a section called "Background on Title IX and Sports." This section included the words of the Title IX statute, followed by a background section in which she first identified the two tools available for intercollegiate athletic programs when interpreting Title IX: the 1975 final Title IX regulation and a subsequent 1975 "Sports Memorandum," in which HEW provided additional guidance for athletics.[44] She then listed twenty different rulings provided by the Office of Civil Rights or HEW that provided for sex-separate teams, "equal opportunity and not equal aggregate expenditures," criteria for setting coaches' salaries, adjustment periods, scholarships, definition of a contact sport, and a technical assistance document. Her list concluded with the 1978 reaffirmation by the HEW general counsel that revenue-producing intercollegiate athletic teams were subject to Title IX.[45]

The sections that followed included "History of Compliance Efforts at Michigan State University," "Developments Between 1975 and 1977," "Recent Concerns—1977–78," "Recommendations for Action," and "Conclusion." Addenda to the report included a "Proposed Title IX Sex Equity Study [for] Intercollegiate Athletics," which listed twenty-five questions that Pollock estimated to "represent approximately half of the items necessary for obtaining the information which will provide a complete picture of the corrective and remedial actions still needed (if any) to bring the MSU intercollegiate athletic program into compliance with Title Nine." A final note suggested her growing frustration: "Unless these twenty-five items are approved for a review tool, it does not seem worthwhile to invest more time in completing the instrument." The report included a second addenda: a copy of MSU's 1976–77 affirmative action report to HEW and MSU's July 21, 1976, "Self Evaluation as Required by Title IX of the Education Amendments of 1972."[46]

The report's opening statement was in effect a plea to Pollock's superiors, including interim President Harden, to confer upon her that which she initially assumed came with her position title: legitimacy. Through her discourse, Pollock needed to instill in others a belief that she was the legitimate authority on Title IX at MSU. The stakes were higher for Pollock than she realized. In her first year at MSU, she was considered a "probationary employee," which meant that if her supervisors decided not to renew her contract because she pushed too hard or they disagreed with her methods, she would have little recourse. The two women who had turned down Pollock's job before her had done so because they refused to take the position without the security of tenure.

Recklessly, Pollock didn't pull many punches. She took a feminist stance in her plan by commenting on society's gendered perceptions of athletes. For Pollock, as she explained in her plan, an important purpose of the document, including the twenty-five-item questionnaire, was educational and activist: "to teach those who are filling [the questionnaire out] how subtle discrimination can be."[47] In her plan, Pollock openly acknowledged that to address and overcome widespread "resistance to both the letter and the spirit of Title Nine" presented a challenge for administrators in her position. She noted that "both active and passive opposition ha[d] caused the compliance authority, the Office of Civil Rights in HEW, to hesitate in enforcement, waffle on rulings, and generally fail to provide a calm, rational, secure atmosphere in which to reason together."[48]

These observations, in theory, would have helped put resistant readers at ease: she was acknowledging, and to some extent legitimizing, their resistance. In fact, in creating her plan, Pollock faced the rhetorical challenge of establishing the rational, reasoned, secure atmosphere that she considered necessary to discuss the highly sensitive topic of sex equity in athletics. However, Pollock did not have an adequate insider's knowledge of men's or women's athletic department culture to inform her idea of what this reasonable, secure atmosphere for discussion should be. Her rhetoric reflected her lack of personal experience with the circumscribed, apologetic discourse inculcated into many female athletes, coaches, and administrators responsible for women's program development in the Title IX era. She had not been socialized into the traditional values of physical education. And while she could describe physical educators' perspectives, she was not one of them. She was, in a word, brash.

A Critique of MSU's Self-Evaluation

In her "Plan to Attain Sex Equity in Intercollegiate Athletics at MSU," Pollock made it clear that she considered MSU's 1976 self-evaluation, written under Jackson's watch, a highly problematic document. As Pollock noticed when she first joined MSU as director of women's programs and Title IX coordinator, the authors of the 1976 Title IX self-evaluation chose for the institution an interpretation of Title IX that compared women's sports to only men's nonrevenue sports, excluding men's basketball, hockey, and football from their analysis. In 1978, athletics administrators still excluded those sports from their compliance calculations. To a great extent, Pollock's plan responded to the earlier document and its premise that those three men's sports programs need not be included in MSU's program comparisons. Her written plan was, in essence, a social movement document written by a radical institutional change agent. She sought to make her readers aware that the view of social reality assumed in the 1976 self-evaluation was, quite simply, false.

In this task, she faced seemingly insurmountable challenges. To begin with, Vice President for University Relations Perrin and his staff, including his assistant Sally Reardon (a woman Pollock later described as a "queen bee–type"), had authored the 1976 self-evaluation.[49] Perrin supervised Pollock's immediate supervisor, Ralph Bonner, which meant he had the authority to hire and fire within that unit. Although Bonner, a black man who held a doctorate in sociology, sympathized with Pollock's vision of advancing the interests of marginalized groups, Pollock recalled his reminders that "you have to go along to get along."[50] As for Perrin, Pittman noted in his "Chronology" that he had close ties with a Michigan

Congressman, Representative O'Hara, who had introduced legislation to protect and exclude men's high-revenue sports from Title IX compliance requirements (Perrin had been an employee of O'Hara's at one time). On top of that, an MSU trustee was a member of the same law firm as the congressman. "SUCH COLLUSION!" was Pittman's exclamation.[51]

As Pollock sought institutional legitimacy for herself, she critiqued her supervisors and leaders of the athletic department while simultaneously pleading for them to support her leadership in a more rigorous compliance process. She needed to access information that only the athletic department could provide, so in writing her document, she faced the rhetorical challenge of overcoming their resistance. But Pollock did not subscribe to Lopiano's tradition of tact. In a subsection entitled "History of Compliance Efforts at MSU," Pollock used a variety of red-flag-waving adjectives to describe the 1976 self-evaluation conducted by Perrin's staff: "stale," "hurriedly" written, uninformed by "institution-wide faculty and staff training," and "looked upon by many as another pesky administrative chore." The result, she noted, was "many frivolous marks on the administrative forms returned," that responded in part to "hostility" created when the forms were distributed.[52]

As a result of this flawed process, Pollock claimed, the findings of the self-evaluation were also highly problematic. As she put it, "The only inequity identified that needed further action, according to the study, was in scholarships."[53] She attributed the decision to exclude "revenue sports" in part to "the ambiguity of HEW in ruling on revenue sports coverage" but also to MSU's own choice. As she put it, "We could continue to defy the HEW opinion" regarding revenue-producing sports, as did both MSU's 1976 self-assessment and its 1977 affirmative action report.[54] In both of these reports to HEW, MSU cited "common sense" as the reason for not including the three "revenue-producing sports" in their comparisons of athletic opportunities for men and women.[55] Even though the affirmative action report acknowledged that "these three revenue-producing sports also consume the largest share of the budget expenditures—in coaching staff, equipment, travel, athletic scholarships, etc.," it offered no evidence of profitability (not for any individual sport or for the three sports combined). The claim is simply made: the decision to exclude these sports was based on "the reality of popular interest" that leads to "revenues that support these sports as well as the non-revenue-producing sports." The authors of the 1976 self-evaluation never mentioned the law as a factor to consider in decision making, prompting a note from Pittman in the margins of a draft Pollock provided him: "What of the law?"

Pollock characterized the decision to exclude three men's sports from the Title IX self-evaluation in neutral terms, calling it "MSU's evaluation strategy." On page six, in a gesture intended to save face for the institution, she suggested a change in strategy in light of new, clearer information. She wrote: "Recently, Secretary of HEW, Joseph Califano, released their legal counsel's opinion reaffirming the inclusion of revenue sports in assessment of equal opportunity at institutions covered by Title Nine. This would suggest that we need to modify our original evaluation strategy and review our entire intercollegiate athletics program again."[56]

Continuing her face-saving efforts, Pollock added that new technical assistance materials not yet published in 1975–76 "indicate that we should really be looking at our entire array of athletic opportunities," including club and intramural sports. However, such potential olive branches were sporadically eclipsed in the document by direct attacks on the very individuals whose cooperation Pollock needed most. She characterized protectors of men's revenue sports as "extremists." In her conclusion, she highlighted shortcomings of the athletics director, citing Kearney by name: "An internal review conducted by the Intercollegiate Athletics Department is not enough. Dr. Kearney has had two chances in 1976 and again in 1977 to do internal reviews and neither was thorough or solved the big problems." As a solution, she offered her own expertise and ability: "There is not the expertise in Title Nine and identifying sex discrimination within the department to conduct a fair and impartial review alone. And there is no way for me to conduct a fair investigation of the women's basketball complaint unless I am fully authorized to conduct a review of intercollegiate athletics at MSU."[57]

Pollock pointed to her job description as backing for her appeal: "I seek presidential reaffirmation of my responsibility to, as my job description states, 'coordinate university efforts to comply with Title Nine' in regard to athletics." She concluded with a warning: "To disallow my involvement or to fail to support my evaluation and monitoring role is to severely undermine for the future the usefulness, authority or influence of our affirmative action efforts at MSU."[58]

In her "Plan to Attain Sex Equity in Intercollegiate Athletics at MSU," Pollock frequently assumed a tone that reflected the authority she sought but did not actually enjoy. She issued warnings; she made recommendations. Sometimes she presented alternatives in a series of "straw man" proposals, which in her view clearly were not acceptable options. She laid out a series of alternative responses to "major areas of disagreement, ambiguity, or resistance," but her loaded language revealed her own sentiments. MSU, she wrote, "could very well choose to continue to defy the HEW opinion."[59] Clearly, though, she did not think MSU should do so. Another option she offered was to "stall" and "perhaps get away with one or more seasons of protecting the men's revenue-producing sports from comparison with the men's and women's non-revenue sports."[60] After these two options, clearly framed as unethical choices, Pollock offered her recommendation: "The third alternative, and the one I favor, is moving quickly ahead to re-evaluation and attempt[ing] to have a new program in place for the academic year 1978–1979 when we open in the fall." She acknowledged the complications involved considering different rules and regulations of the NCAA for men and the AIAW for women, counseling that "we will have to use our common sense and best judgment in regard to what is fair, just, and in the spirit of the law."[61] Clearly, though, one person's common sense was another person's extremist thinking, particularly with so much money and so much principle at stake.

In identifying challenges associated with different philosophies of sports held by men's and women's governing bodies, Pollock engaged in a detailed discussion on philosophical questions related to whether men's and women's intercollegiate athletics should merge. Assuming a didactic tone at times, she offered lessons by analogy to "race relations history": "The major problem with that particular simplistic solution [having complete separation of men's and women's athletics] is that we know from race relations history another lesson: separate is inherently unequal. If we allow separate administrative structure, there is a good possibility, indeed probability, that the men and men's sports will "get more" than the women and women's sports."[62]

At one point, she compared "extremist elements of the male sports establishment" to racial segregationists in the South, for whom integration meant "control by whites."[63] Midway through the plan, she offered a radical vision for achieving "integration without dominance by men." She asserted the need for "shared leadership and shared authority" and bluntly critiqued the status quo: "What has been the MSU resolution of the question, if indeed it has been posed? We have elected to have an athletic director, with several assistant directors, one of whom is in charge of women's sports. The assistant director of women's athletics reports to a male director who, in addition to his general administrative duties, is the associate director (untitled and undesignated, of course) for men's sports."[64]

In a tone that began to sound insolent, Pollock went on to describe a situation common to athletic departments across the country: "The Athletic Director does not meet in a staff meeting with coaches of the women's teams and the men's teams, he meets and supervises only the coaches of the men's teams. Has our women's sports program become the ladies auxiliary to the men's program and could that be one of the sources of any of the inequalities which the students may feel?"[65]

Considering Pollock's status as an outsider to the athletics department, anyone still reading her plan would have considered her vision for a more equitable structure as strikingly bold and probably would have dismissed it as ludicrous. In fact, however, her vision for shared leadership was similar to the plan implemented by the University of Iowa (where women's athletics director Christine Grant observed that she was blessed with a remarkably supportive university president), as well as the University of Texas (where the considerable rhetorical skills of women's athletics director Donna Lopiano came into play). But those structures had not been proposed by an outsider to intercollegiate athletics—and certainly not by a feminist director of women's programs who sprinkled her discourse with terms such as "male privilege," "discrimination," and "sex-role stereotyping."

To say the least, athletic departments did not frequently hear Pollock's type of diction, but she either didn't know this or didn't care. She sounded increasingly enthusiastic about her utopian vision as she elaborated on it. The picture she painted on later pages of her plan was especially audacious in its specificity when it came to individual roles. Pollock mused:

> If Drs. Kearney and Jackson were co-athletic directors and the general administrative responsibilities divided between them (Jackson handling the publicity and facilities, Kearney taking the business office, etc.) in addition to their supervision of the women's and men's sports respectively, we would perhaps have a more gender equitable administration and management of athletics. Both could report to the President and work with the Athletic Council.[66]

Then she seemed to warm to her subject, and her approach shifted from suggestion to prescription:

> To carry the idea further, perhaps Drs. Kearney and Jackson in the following year should be assigned not just the teams of their own sex to supervise, but some of the other sex teams as well? Knowing a little of Dr. Jackson's background in track, I think the men's track team might benefit from her supervision. Dr. Kearney's background in many of the "women's sports" which parallel men's make him highly qualified to supervise some women's teams. In the parallel men's and women's sports we will have a greater likelihood of achieving parity if both coaches report to one person and both have similar per capita budgets.[67]

Pollock continued in this vein until she shifted to more general sociological commentary:

> You can see that this issue of integrating the professional ranks of sport will require all of us to rethink our assumptions about the appropriate role of men and women in society. Most of us were subjected to being taught traditional notions about the limited capabilities of women. Many people are re-examining these notions in calm deliberation and finding that they are not reasonable beliefs to hold![68]

She elaborated:

> There are a good many people—athletes, coaches, physical education
> and recreation specialists, parents, educators, administrators, or both
> sections among them—who are unsure whether is it really right for girls
> and women to run, jump, throw a ball, get sweaty, slide into home plate
> or kick a field goal. Competitive sport has been uniformly seen as a
> *masculinity* training even though we know that athletics is also a source
> of education in cooperation, nurturance, emotional expression, depen-
> dence on others, etc., which are usually seen as "feminine."[69]

Further explicating the lack of social support for equality in athletics, Pollock continued her sociological commentary:

> The image of athletics as masculine has served to discourage females
> from participation and the public is probably realistically afraid, given
> the assumption of sports as masculine, that giving women more sports
> opportunity will de-feminize females and encourage a "unisex" society.[70]

Only briefly did she address the other side of the coin: economics.
"Others are more concerned with pragmatic than moral issues," she wrote,
"[such as] what will it cost, and who will pay for it?"[71]

The Money Factor

When Pollock so quickly moved past the critical question of money, she
failed to fully address the root of the resistance faced by women's sports
advocates. In part because she did not yet have access to all the financial
information she needed, her plan spent little time on the most critical
issue for her audience. Decades later, MSU quarterback Kirk Cousins
(2008–11) addressed the extent to which institutional decisions about
athletics are really and finally almost all about money. In a 2011 interview about the escalating quandary of big-time college sports in trying to
maintain any semblance of real amateur status, he said, "It [corruption in
college sports] becomes a complicated issue, because so many decisions

being made are about money. Yet the whole concept [college athletics] is not about money. It's sort of a two-sided issue where you're talking out of two sides of your mouth. You're trying to make it about money, but you're not trying to make it about money."[72]

Despite Pollock's misstep in focusing on morals instead of money, her idealistic plan was probably doomed either way. Even in 1978, before the value of television contracts and corporate sponsorships entered the stratosphere, the athletic power structure did not want people like Pollock asking too many questions. She was probably the last person the athletic department wanted to have coordinate the series of workshops and administer the evaluation instruments she proposed at the end of her plan.

By early June, rumors began circulating that Pollock would be fired. DeBoer got wind of it and told Pittman and Alexander. On June 7, all head coaches of women's sports received a memo from Jackson stating that her budget for 1978–79 was to be $100,000 less than she requested and that coaches should meet with her to discuss "necessary cuts."[73] Then DeBoer was told that the Anti-Discrimination Judicial Board needed to see a "bottom-line complaint" with all the details. However, the board's executive secretary, attorney Sallie Bright, instructed DeBoer to include only women's basketball in the complaint, not the entire women's athletic program.[74] This instruction, and the team's dutiful compliance with it, would prove to be pivotal. Limiting the complaint to one sport rather than the whole women's program made the team's complaint more difficult to view through the still little-understood programmatic emphasis of Title IX.

You're Fired!

Distressed about the situation, the "cabal" members met to brainstorm. DeBoer, Pittman, Alexander, and Hardy began working on a detailed complaint for the ADJB. DeBoer visited Pollock's office and learned that the rumors were accurate—Perrin urged Pollock to resign so that the university would not have to fire her (that is, not renew her contract). Pittman recorded the following in his notes: "He, Perrin, has offered her, if she resigns, 7 more weeks of pay, if she doesn't resign, immediate termination of pay. If she resigns, 10 days of paid vacation."[75] Pollock told Pittman that VP Perrin had delivered this ultimatum on June 8.

Just the day before, on June 7, Pollock had complied with her supervisor's request that she submit materials that described the role of the Title IX coordinator. She sent the job description that she had responded to when initially applying for her position. Under "Function of Job," it said, "Serves as the focal point on campus for the initiation, consideration, reference and redress of matters of concern to women as faculty, staff, or students; and is the person responsible to coordinate University efforts to comply with and carry out responsibilities under Title IX of the Education Amendments of 1972."[76] Based on this description, Pollock was doing her job. However, decades later, one individual familiar with the situation remembered Pollock this way: "She [the Title IX coordinator] was really kind of rough and got in folks' faces. She didn't stay too long. They were soon able to ease her out of here. I forgot her name. I need to look at old records. She was one to pull people to the fire." This former administrator (who asked not to be identified) explained that Pollock "wanted to move too fast" when "resources were not adequate to respond to all of the needs immediately." Instead of being patient with "a gradual implementation process," Pollock's approach resulted in people "going around the AD [athletics director] and going to her to complain about issues." Her primary misstep was, as this former colleague put it, "using the law as a standard to show they weren't complying with the law." As the former administrator recalled, "I think it made people very nervous."[77]

On June 10, 1978, DeBoer and Mankowski expressed their feelings about Pollock losing her job in this letter to Harden:

Dear President Harden,

We would like to express both the deep concern and rage we felt over the termination of Mary Pollock's appointment. She has been of tremendous assistance to us as complaintants [sic] and as women seeking our rights.

We were convinced that those in administration here at Michigan State University, although possibly not agreeing with us on every specific, were generally committed with us to the development of equitable athletic programs for men and women. This vindictive maneuver on your part has seriously challenged that conviction. We cannot help but wonder how an administration which fires anyone attempting to examine its program for possible discriminatory practices can dare claim that it is committed to parity.

We feel the University is losing one of its most competent and committed people. We are disappointed in Michigan State; we are hurt by your attitude.

Sincerely,
Kathleen J. DeBoer
Mariann Mankowski
Representatives, Women's Basketball Team[78]

As the letter implied, the administration's response to the team's presentation to the board of trustees had reestablished a tenuous trust that was soon undermined by Pollock's firing.

As Pollock herself digested the turn of events, she prepared for a meeting with President Harden. The meeting had been arranged by a supporter, economics professor Charles P. Larrowe, who wrote satirical columns for the *State News* between 1971 and 1989 under the pen name "Lash Larrowe" and served as a faculty grievance officer. Representatives from several campus groups attended, including women's studies professor Marilyn Frye. Pollock recalled that President Harden was friendly and respectful to her in the meeting, but he would not overturn Perrin's decision.[79] She vowed to fight back, determined not to quietly go away in shame as she supposed they might have expected.

More Complaints and a Media Blitz

Spurred by the shocking turn of events, DeBoer focused intently on the team's written complaint for the ADJB. Working night and day, the "cabal" members generated pages of drafts on yellow ledger paper. More than twenty pages of notes in the handwriting of DeBoer, Pittman, and Alexander demonstrated the effort, research, and extensive revising that went into preparing the written complaint. They submitted the eleven-page, single-spaced final version on June 12, 1978. The document's concluding paragraph recommended that the board's investigation of the complaint "be broad enough in scope to cover the larger question of whether the [athletic] Department's definition of 'revenue-producing sports' is actually gender neutral in application or whether it is a neutral-sounding justification for the continuation of a pattern of discrimination." Their concluding sentences urged the board to consult the university's financial reports for the years 1971 to 1976, noting that "the men's basketball program has cost the University approximately three hundred five thousand dollars ($305,201) more than it generated in revenue." They contended that this fact "holds up to question the characterization of men's basketball as a sport that pays its own way and should, therefore, be exempted from examination for the purposes of Title IX compliance."[80]

In their letter to the ADJB, DeBoer and Mankowski listed seven people, including themselves, whom they recommended ADJB contact over the summer if needed (i.e., Carol Hutchins, Mary Kay Itnyre, Diane Spoelstra, Ann Sober, and coach Karen Langeland). They also quoted a section from MSU's *Student Handbook* that indicated the ADJB's executive secretary had twenty working days to resolve the matter through mediation. They noted that only DeBoer and Mankowski could make a binding decision, and asked that the executive secretary and a witnessing party sign a statement indicating she had read, understood, and assented to their request.[81] They weren't taking any chances.

Also on June 12, after DeBoer and Mankowski submitted the complaint to the ADJB, DeBoer typed a two-page, single-spaced letter addressed, "Dear Local Rats." In it, she updated seven individuals about the complaint and a "plan of attack for the summer" (she referred to them by their nicknames: Stra, Kaybird, Annie, Nina, Hutchann, Lily). Pollock was going to lose her job, she said, and the complaint had been turned over to the Anti-Discrimination Judicial Board. (DeBoer added, "Don't get excited yet, it sounds impressive but it's not.") Alerting them that she had given their names to the ADJB executive secretary, she warned, "She is a lawyer for the university; if this thing goes to court, she will argue their side." DeBoer suggested that they help out if asked but make it clear that they could not speak for the rest of the team, "not as a power play on our part but simply as a measure to keep us from pimping each other by making contradictory agreements." DeBoer emphasized the need to have a plan: "I don't know if this thing is going to break over the summer. It might or it might not. If and when it does things may get very nasty. In order to protect all of us from being played off against each other, and those of you who will be playing next year from possible harassment, let me request that, at least for the summer, you refer all media people to Cookie or myself."[82]

Finally, after providing them with her summer schedule, she mentioned that she would be in touch with Pittman and Alexander throughout the summer. At the end of the letter she added, "I think you all should know that Mark and Bruce spent hours with me preparing these reports. There is no way they would have gotten done without their help—you might just want to thank them the next time you see them. Also, Tuna [Laurie Kuna]—our English major friend—proofread it and Joann helped write parts (this is starting to sound like acknowledgements at the beginning of a book). Anyway, have a great summer!"[83]

A few tasks remained, however, before the group disbanded for the summer. In the following days and nights, strategy sessions commenced. "A very late night," Pittman noted on June 13. "Another very late night," he wrote on June 14. That same day, he noted, "We deviously get Mary Pollock to come to meet us in the Administration Building. Have a long talk about report and about her status."[84] That night, or shortly thereafter, Pollock passed along to them a discrimination complaint form from HEW and an article entitled "How to Benefit from the Freedom of Information Act," presumably in case the group wanted to access the budget and salary information she had been denied.

By June 15, the "cabal" members had filled another manila folder with drafts and notes in preparation for sending their Title IX complaint to the federal government. Pittman noted, "KDB and MHP [DeBoer and Pittman] visit Mary Pollock at home, she gives us more material." Finally, he noted, "OCR complaint is mailed."[85] But they still had more letters to write. They wanted to notify the media and key individuals that the team had filed a Title IX complaint with the federal government (the sample complaint form Pollock had given them from OCR noted at the bottom, "If you are sending copies of your complaint to other persons list them below"). Examples cited included senators, state legislators, national organizations, the governor, and newspapers.[86] Rather than simply copying all the groups or individuals on their complaint, the MSU group tailored individual letters to these different audiences. Each letter at some point expressed gratitude for past support, asked for continued support, and mentioned that Pollock had been fired.

On one brainstorming sheet, they listed targeted audiences for their media campaign in three categories, often with names of specific individuals noted. Under "press," they wrote *Detroit News*—Bev, *State Journal*—Lynn Henning and Kim Heron, *State News*—Anne Biondo. Under "magazines," they listed *Ms., Chronicle of Higher Education, U.S. News and World Report, Women's Sports,* and *Time* (with a question mark). Under "women's organizations," they listed NOW, SPRINT, AIAW Legal Counsel Margot Polivy, Center for Women and Sport—Dorothy Harris, PEER [Project on Equal Education Rights], and Project on Status and Education of Women. In very large print at the bottom of the page, they jotted "60 Minutes (?)," with the name Mike Wallace written underneath. Attached to the brainstorming sheet, other lists included names, addresses, and phone numbers of even more individuals, including "political people" (Bob Carr, Martha Griffiths, Donald Riegle Jr., Robert Griffin). At the very top of yet another list was "President Jimmy Carter, The White House, Washington, DC."[87]

Even before the letters went out, an article covering Pollock's firing appeared in the June 15, 1978, issue of the *State Journal*, written by Kim Heron, one of the reporters who would soon receive a letter. The article, "Ouster by MSU Brings Affirmative Action Doubts," represented opposing viewpoints on Pollock's approach to her work. Her supporters claimed she was "a victim of doing her job too well"; some of them citing "her concern with sex equality in athletics, including revenue-producing sports" as "the straw that broke the camel's back."[88] Her supervisors refused to cite reasons for the firing, but the assistant vice president of student affairs, Kay White, noted, "I think she has a record of using the media, and I don't want to go on record as supporting that." Pollock herself commented, "My philosophical bent is different from the institution's. And with no job security, either you reflect the institution or you can't survive there." She also blamed Title IX itself, describing herself as a "victim of the vagueness" she saw reflected in HEW's guidelines "that seem to change from week to week."[89] The article concluded by noting that the students headed by DeBoer planned to take their complaint to HEW and that they viewed Pollock's firing as another example supporting a pattern of discrimination.

The day after the "Ouster" article appeared, DeBoer left for a summer of teaching in volleyball clinics around the country. Alexander and Hardy left to visit family in Indiana. Of the "cabal" members, only Pittman stayed in town. His notes at the time don't indicate that he had begun to feel any concern about possibly being fired himself—those fears surfaced later on. At that point, he still operated somewhat under the radar as the coach of a relatively invisible women's team, not in a high profile position such as Pollock's. Unlike Pollock, he worked directly for a supervisor, the director of women's athletics Nell Jackson, who sympathized with his goals and shared many of them herself.[90]

Exhausted from the all-night writing sessions but not yet fearful of losing his job, Pittman paused at least long enough to note, "MHP [Pittman] takes it easy." But he was back at it the next day, meeting with Jackson and calling Pollock for more information. Jackson suggested calling AIAW attorney Margot Polivy. She also suggested that the team get its own attorney. Based on a meeting with the ADJB and MSU attorney Higgins, Jackson predicted "it is going to get tougher."[91]

With Pollock, Pittman discussed strategy for a June 22 board of trustees meeting, when campus groups would go before the board on Pollock's behalf. According to Pittman's notes, Pollock suggested that someone from the team refute the idea that she "stirred up this entire matter." Pittman recorded his own assessment in a short notation: "Pollock didn't cause the discrimination." He further noted that Pollock was merely informing athletes of rights and procedures, until her supervisors began meeting about the basketball team's complaint without her present. They presumed it was in those meetings that MSU administrators began "making decisions about the complaint which [were] in the opposite direction as the Coordinator was going."[92] That is, they focused on narrowing the scope of the complaint to the basketball team rather than addressing complaints about lack of comparable opportunity in the whole women's program.

The issue of scope related to an interpretive dilemma being debated at the national level that had athletics directors, coaches, and attorneys alike parsing the implications of terms and phrases such as "parity," "parallel sports," and "total program opportunity." In talking with Pittman, Pollock emphasized that how these terms and concepts became translated into official policy would affect whether the women's sports movement would be able to gain "women's rights without submerging women and women's programs." If specific sports had to be compared with one another (such as women's basketball to men's basketball), Pollock—along with the AIAW leaders and women's coaches and administrators—feared that women would forego an opportunity to control their own destinies. She supported Jackson's suggestion to get their own attorney since MSU seemed to be channeling the women's basketball team into a narrow complaint that focused merely on comparing similar sports rather than whole men's and women's programs. Pollock even tossed out a few names for Pittman to consider, including an Ann Arbor civil rights attorney whom Pittman, based on how he (mis)spelled the name, must have assumed was a male: "Gene King."[93]

As the campus emptied for the quieter summer semester, Pittman kept moving forward. For June 17, he wrote, "Packets readied to be mailed." The next day, he delivered copies of the packets to team members still in town. Two days later, he noted, "mailed out the packets." He sent one of them, which he signed as MSU women's cross-country head coach and assistant track and field coach, to AIAW attorney Polivy. He asked for any other material that Polivy thought might be helpful. In closing, he wrote, "I'm deeply involved and committed to this effort and trust your suggestions will aid us in this matter."[94] Then, with the packets in the mail, Pittman braced himself for whatever came next.

13 Deadline!

Deadlines have a way of focusing attention, and the July 1978 deadline for higher education athletics departments to comply with Title IX created momentarily attentive audiences. It was hard to dispute claims that the time for continued delays had nearly expired. Presumably, institutions had spent the past three years gradually working toward compliance, but the lack of results looked like they might have spent three minutes. AIAW attorney Margot Polivy highlighted these delaying tactics in her July 16, 1978, opinion piece published in the *New York Times*: "HEW has spent the last three years doing little more than marching in place, obviously hoping against hope that next Friday would never come."[1] Athletics departments, for the most part, had marched in place along with the Department of Health, Education, and Welfare.

In the wake of Mary Pollock losing her job, the institutional discourse at MSU—reports, memos, speeches, and meetings—provides a sampling of the kinds of Title IX–related rhetoric that circulated as the national deadline approached. Remarkably, lines of argument opposing full compliance then closely resemble opposing arguments repeated decades later. Two issues continually resurfaced: (1) whether males and females naturally bring different levels of interest to athletics, and (2) whether revenue production is relevant—or should be—when determining what constitutes discrimination or equality of opportunity. The discourse generated as the 1978 compliance deadline approached shows that, when it comes to Title IX rhetoric, history repeats itself.

271

Noncompliance and Containment

The loss of Pollock as Title IX coordinator had spurred the MSU women's basketball team to take their Title IX complaint beyond campus. With a swelling of campus support for Pollock unleashed, the university was finally prepared to more seriously examine what Title IX compliance required. Like students cramming for an exam in the final hours, the athletics department's Title IX committee planned to submit a report by June 12, 1978. By that time, some institutions had already admitted that they would not be able to comply by the July 21 deadline. In March 1978, Cornell University reported that it would miss the deadline by more than a year. Although a senior vice president said Cornell would address any inequalities it found, he cited the different histories of men's and women's sports as the reason for the university's noncompliance. He pointed out that whereas their men's teams had a 108-year-old history, women's teams had existed for only five or six years. As a result, the Cornell vice president contended, the institution just could not financially afford to make up for the difference so quickly. The women's program, he remarked by way of explanation, "ran before it walked."[2] However, he did not attempt to explain the reasons why women's teams were not allowed to even "walk" during that first century.

Unlike Cornell, MSU was not ready to admit openly to noncompliance, and certainly not before the internal "legal audit" was complete. In the meantime, its leaders held fast to the contention that distinguishing between (so-called) "revenue producing" and "nonrevenue producing" teams was not discriminatory. However, even as MSU struggled with what its attorney Byron Higgins called "troubled Title IX waters," the institution made a significant statement about its support for women as athletic leaders.[3] The university appointed Gwen Norrell as the first female faculty representative to the NCAA, a prestigious position that had been held for decades by MSU's one-time NCAA president Jack Fuzak.[4] With this announcement, it might have seemed more likely that the women's basketball team would consult with Norrell, now widely publicized as a prominent woman on campus who supported athletics.

However, Pittman and others involved with the women's basketball team's complaint reasoned that Norrell represented NCAA, the men's sports governing body, as opposed to the women's AIAW. They did not see her as a potential ally.

Pittman did, however, keep in touch with Pollock. At the June 22 MSU Board of Trustees meeting, fifteen different groups planned to speak to the board on her behalf, but Pollock herself did not plan to attend. In a phone conversation with Pittman, she reiterated her conviction that the spokesperson for the women's basketball team should emphasize that MSU's Anti-Discrimination Judicial Board executive secretary (also an attorney) may have ill-advised team leaders in an effort to protect the university from a more sweeping Title IX complaint and possible lawsuit. Because the Title IX regulations emphasized comparing—or contrasting—the whole women's program with the whole men's program, Pollock viewed advising the team to limit their complaint to just women's basketball as a containment strategy. In his "Chronology," Pittman recorded Pollock's emphatic instruction: "GIVE QUOTE FROM TITLE IX ABOUT PROGRAM TO PROGRAM."[5]

According to the "Chronology," Pollock also urged Pittman to warn the team's spokesperson not to mention filing with HEW; instead, she urged him to emphasize that the university had fired her, the person who wrote the May 15, 1978, "plan of equity questionnaire." She advised him that the team's spokesperson should point out that after her firing, no one acknowledged the existence of the plan she had created. She told Pittman to "read its recommendations to the Board." Pollock was well aware that her plan never specified a single sport, such as women's basketball, as the primary or only problem; it emphasized a programmatic approach to compliance rather than sport-by-sport comparisons. Finally, Pollock advised Pittman how to reserve a place on the agenda for the June 22 MSU board of trustees meeting. Following her suggestion, Pittman called DeBoer and asked her to send a night telegram to the board secretary, Al Ballard.[6]

Just a few days before the board meeting, Alexander and Hardy had returned from Indiana. Pittman and basketball player Diane Spoelstra updated them. Alexander agreed to ask some of his lawyer friends to investigate possible attorneys to represent the team, if needed. Pittman met with women's basketball coach Karen Langland and filled her in, giving her a copy of his "Chronology" (requesting that she not share it with "non-need" people). Spoelstra, too, read the "Chronology." In another meeting—this time in a parking lot with both Langeland and Jackson present—Pittman learned of Title IX problems at the University of Wisconsin. Jackson requested that Pittman give her "a complete listing of discrimination instances since [he's] been with the [Athletics] Department" so she could prepare for a meeting with university attorney Higgins.[7]

The day after Jackson made this request, Higgins submitted a preliminary legal analysis on Title IX and its regulations to President Harden.

Progress Report from MSU's Legal Beagle

In his five-page report to President Harden, Higgins addressed two topics: (1) what Title IX and its regulations required, and (2) whether MSU was in compliance. By way of introduction, he noted that a Title IX committee chaired by Underwood was "meeting on a daily basis" and that the legal office could meet with them or respond to questions. Also, he noted that the women's basketball complaint was being investigated by the ADJB in the university's Department of Human Relations and that conclusions of the legal office would help them "delineate between what is required by law and what is a proper subject for policy."[8] Finally, he quoted from the 1975 HEW regulations and concluded that the key phrases to interpret and apply were "equal opportunity" and "reasonableness." He noted, "There have been very few court decisions as to the significance of this requirement in intercollegiate sports programs." However, he continued, law review writers unanimously agreed that the regulations specified "a unique approach toward equal opportunity which some compare to the 'separate but equal' education programs struck down by the United States Supreme Court in its decision of *Brown v. Board of Education*."[9] Having provided this background information, Higgins launched into his argument.

Revenue, Interest, and Competence

First, Higgins stated that revenue-producing sports, even though they do not receive any direct federal assistance, are covered by Title IX because they are "an integral part of the general education program."[10] Following this accurate statement, he proceeded with a chain of deductive reasoning founded on a false premise and included at least one questionable claim. He wrote, "The statute and the regulations recognize that many athletic programs would not exist unless they had available the revenues produced from these sports programs." The statute itself, of course, makes no specific reference to sports at all, much less to the ways in which intercollegiate sports are funded. Nor do the 1975 regulations for intercollegiate athletics ever specifically mention the subject of revenue. Higgins's statement was completely unfounded, representing the presumption of the men's athletic establishment but misrepresenting Title IX and its regulations. He continued with another statement unsupported by evidence: "It is a basic assumption that winning teams produce more revenue." From this assumption, he concluded that, therefore, "in revenue-producing sports the level of competency expected of student athletes and the level of competition is such that would justify a higher level of support."[11]

The relationship Higgins claimed between winning teams and revenue production had little basis in fact. Many winning men's and women's teams, such as MSU's 1976 national championship softball team, did not (and do not) generate much, if any, revenue for a variety of reasons, most of them tied to the socially constructed, media-driven nature of spectator interest in particular sports. That is, in the United States, we are socialized to value and enjoy men's football as an exciting spectator sport. From tailgating to marching bands, the sport is tied to a series of social rituals and spectacles that enhance the experience of simply watching the game. In Europe or South America (or much of the rest of the world), the spectator sport of choice is soccer. Indeed, for decades in Iowa the spectator sport that drew the largest crowds was six-player girls' high school basketball (half-court basketball). Tradition, marketing, investment, and

cultural values direct our interests in sports as participants and as spectators. Marketing can create fans where few existed, and continued marketing sustains spectator interest.

To accept Higgins's argument means agreeing that the nonrevenue
and Olympic intercollegiate sports for men and women—swimming,
wrestling, gymnastics, tennis, and baseball—involve less competency
and a lower level of competition than men's football or basketball. In his
report, Higgins connected competency, level of competition, and revenue
in a way that even the most adamant opponents of Title IX would not.
On the basis of a deeply flawed argument, he concluded, "Therefore, our
preliminary conclusion is that MSU may continue to provide greater support to its revenue-producing sport teams to maintain and improve its level
of competition."[12] Higgins's report to President Harden demonstrated a
twisted logic unlikely to prevail with HEW or in court. After all, only a
month before the compliance deadline, MSU and what President Harden
termed its "legal beagles" were just beginning to address Title IX.

After his argument about revenue-producing sports, Higgins addressed the issues of assessing and satisfying student interest and providing necessary support and financial assistance under the heading "Equal
opportunity in nonrevenue-producing sports programs." This heading
itself revealed Higgins's bias toward exempting men's football, basketball,
and hockey from scrutiny when it came to student interest or financial
assistance. Once more, he presumed a distinction that, according to the
1975 athletics regulations, Title IX did not make. He acknowledged, however, that "student interest is not static, and therefore a continuing procedure should be established to ascertain whether that interest may alter
at some future date."[13] In effect, he recognized the socially constructed
and fluid nature of interest in particular sports, but he did not acknowledge that similar fluctuations in interest might affect the so-called revenue sports. For instance, the men's basketball team became a far more
legitimate "revenue-producer" after Magic Johnson appeared on the
scene. Recruitment of a star player demonstrates just one variable that
could transform the revenue-producing potential of any sport. Building
fabulous new facilities—as MSU had done with the Munn Ice Arena and

sought to do with a new football complex—could also increase spectator and participant interest.

But MSU allocated budgets for recruiting, coaching, scholarships, marketing, facilities, and other support services at significantly different levels for different categories of sports. As a result of differential support services, it would be difficult for a sport in the nonrevenue category to break into the revenue-producing category. Higgins noted that the "level of individual competency and level of competition" could be considered in funding support services itemized in the Title IX "Laundry List." As examples, he cited seven areas:

1. provision of equipment and supplies
2. scheduling of games and practice times
3. travel and per diem allowances
4. the quality and quantity of coaching and academic tutoring
5. locker room space
6. adequacy of physical facilities
7. the availability of medical and training facilities.[14]

As he also noted, "The regulations do not require that all of these be equal" but simply that they accommodate "the interest of the student athlete" and "allow the student athlete to participate in the program in a meaningful manner." Clearly, "student interest" and participating in a "meaningful manner" are phrases open to wide interpretation. Higgins wisely pointed out that "[t]his part of the task requires expertise in the area of physical education and athletic competition."[15] Even then, the question of whose voices and expertise would be acknowledged in determining level of competency in a sport remained unclear.

Most important, Higgins ignored the reality that level of athletic competency at a given institution reflects an institution's investment in recruiting, coaching, and supporting interested and competent athletes. In men's Division I sports governed by the NCAA, the standard practice was (and is) to recruit student athletes to attend the school, not to discover talented and interested athletes from among already enrolled students. And Title IX had opened the door for schools governed by the AIAW to begin offering scholarships and recruiting players.

Overall, Higgins's analysis implied an essentialist notion of interest and competency—that is, he presumed that, by nature, sports that brought in more money had more competent athletes and a greater level of student interest. Higgins and many others invested in the status quo viewed such essentialist thinking as simply rational and reasonable. Conveniently, then, Higgins concluded, "All that the law requires us to do is to act in a rational and reasonable fashion." However, he added a final important note: "It [the law] requires the University to assess, and if necessary, adjust its financial ability and resources to achieve this state of equal opportunity for student athletes."[16]

Higgins's preliminary analysis did not address the question of how exactly to determine what adjustments needed to be made. He did not cite the extensive guidance on that subject provided by HEW in its published technical assistance manual (which Pollock used as the basis for her "Plan to Attain Sex Equity in Intercollegiate Athletics at MSU"). Nor did he acknowledge the existence of Pollock's report or questionnaire. By emphasizing a far more general guideline—to be "rational" and "reasonable"—Higgins's analysis left university leaders a lot of room to interpret the law in ways that suited their perceived interest in privileging what they termed "revenue-producing" sports.

On June 21, 1978, one day after Higgins sent his progress report to President Harden, Bernice "Bunny" Sandler in Washington, DC, sent a letter to DeBoer on behalf of the Project on the Status and Education of Women, which Sandler directed for the Association of American Colleges. It was the first of many letters that arrived in the following weeks in response to the letters and packets Pittman had sent out. While Sandler noted that her organization could not take a stand on complaints, she attached a pamphlet they had published entitled "Update on Title IX and Sports." The pamphlet addressed the most hotly contested issue surrounding Title IX: the "Applicability of Title IX of the Education Amendments of 1972 to Revenue-Producing Intercollegiate Athletics." Along with reproducing HEW's April 25, 1978, memo that reaffirmed Title IX's coverage of "revenue-producing" intercollegiate sports, the pamphlet identified eight different—and failed—attempts by Congress to exempt revenue-producing sports from Title IX coverage.[17] Despite these seemingly clear messages, universities continued to grasp for ways to protect and privilege certain men's sports. Higgins's progress report to President Harden demonstrated one such attempt by interpreting terms such as "competence" and "level of competition" as code for revenue and, hence, for football and men's basketball.

A Gesture from the MSU President

On June 22, President Harden himself wrote to DeBoer and Mankowski, responding to their letter expressing outrage and disappointment at Pollock's termination. In contrast with his "see you in court" phone call to DeBoer, with this letter Harden appeared to extend an olive branch. By the time he wrote to DeBoer and Mankowski, though, he knew that the women's basketball team members were not the only ones upset about Pollock's firing, a reality that may have tempered his response. He wrote that he "respected [their] willingness to put their concerns relative to the termination of Mary Pollock in a form that came to [his] attention." He assured them the termination was not "a vindictive maneuver" and that he respected their right to disagree. Harden asserted that the institution was "examining Title IX in all its aspects" and that MSU would "make every effort to comply with the letter of the law, not because of the law alone, but because we believe in the purposes for which the law was passed."[18] Of course, therein lay the problem: the purposes of the law, indeed interpretations of the law, were far from commonly understood.

To his credit, Harden invited DeBoer and Mankowski to visit with him for progress reports and to express any concerns. However, by that time, Harden's gesture of conciliation seemed like too little too late. As Mankowski recalled, the team perceived that the university had fired Pollock during the summer, after many students and faculty left campus, to contain any fallout. "They were just so snaky. They fired her the week after we left—everybody was out of school—there's some premeditated stuff about that. . . . I found it to be really disillusioning."[19] With most of the students disbanded for the summer, Pittman, Spoelstra, and Alexander had already spent the past couple of days composing a speech for the MSU board meeting on June 22.[20] That meeting would provide the next opportunity for Mankowski, at least, to talk with Harden. But since Harden's letter was dated the same day as the meeting, Mankowski could not have read it before then, even if she had been in town to receive mail in the weeks after MSU's spring quarter ended.

A Second Speech to the MSU Trustees

A draft of the "Board Statement" prepared by Pittman, Spoelstra, and Alexander began with a clear statement of intent at the top of the hand-written page: "Purpose: To inform Board that Title IX Complaint is now in the hands of ADJB and to comment on this." Above that was a note, "Pollock didn't draw up the complaint." These notes suggest that some, but perhaps not all, of the points Pollock hoped would be communicated would in fact be presented.

When the time for the board meeting arrived, the crowd was so large that the meeting was moved from a small room to an auditorium. Some of the individuals gathered there had likely seen a June 21 *State News* opinion column that quoted Perrin justifying the decision to fire Pollock: "While there is no doubt as to her commitment to quality of opportunity to women, her conception of her authority did not agree with the type of professional staff function assigned to the director of women's programs, and the results were becoming counterproductive."[21] That column was followed on June 22 with a letter to the trustees, from which a *State News* article subsequently published excerpts, in which philosophy and women's studies professor Frye (whom DeBoer and Pitman knew from class) addressed just that point. In "Viewpoint: Perrin's Job, A Conflict of Interests," Frye stated, "It is very disconcerting that the duties of affirmative action officer and Title IX compliance officer have been assigned, at this University, to the same office—the office whose mission includes 'PR.'" She continued, "To place together in a single office the function of promotion and protection of the positive image of the institution and the function of critic and conscience is simply irrational (to the point that it suggests bad faith)." In support of Pollock, she wrote to the trustees, "Nobody could work as an affirmative action officer in such a situation and manage to 'get along.' The only way one could survive is simply by not doing the job."[22]

Pollock's supporters marshaled their arguments, and a large group had assembled in the auditorium. The group representing women's basketball, however, had a problem. This time, DeBoer could not deliver the speech; she had graduated from MSU and had commitments out of town all summer. With the team's primary spokesperson gone, Pittman described this plan: Spoelstra was to deliver the speech "with the rest of us sitting around her (that is, Cookie, Bruce, Kay, Tuna, Mary Jo, and Mark)."[23] However, when the time came, confusion set in. Spoelstra was ready to speak, having rehearsed responses to possible questions. Then Mankowski showed up at the meeting, visibly upset. She had gotten a call from Pollock insisting that she should give the speech because she had coauthored the one that DeBoer had delivered to the board earlier that year. She explained, "I remember going and passing everything out to the administrators . . . I was the behind-the-scenes person. I wasn't the spokesperson. I was the worker bee. Going to the meetings, making sure everything was ready, following up, getting the paperwork—writing probably—but not any outward role. That's just my personality."[24] Because Mankowski felt more comfortable in a background role, this intervention by Pollock threw a wrench into their plans. Spoelstra decided not to speak after all, and, Pittman noted, "Cookie left." So it turned out that Pittman himself delivered the following speech:

On March 7, 1978, the women's basketball team filed a Title IX complaint in the Office of the Title IX Coordinator against the Department of Intercollegiate Athletics. On May 25, 1978, we appeared before this Board to inform you as to the reasons for the filing of our complaint. Since that time several matters have arisen which we feel the Board should also be informed.

1 — Our complaint is now before the Anti-Discrimination Judicial Board. Initially, we filed with Mary Pollock, the University's Title IX Coordinator, and she began an effort to mediate the complaint within the University. She was subsequently blocked from pursuing the matter and recommended to us that we try to find administrative relief by

filing with ADJB. This we have now done and await the results of their fact-finding.

2 — While it is true that the University's legal audit is being conducted at this time, it appears this is the sole constructive action undertaken by the Administration. We remind the Board that the date for full compliance with Title IX is now less than a month away. Even though the University has known of this compliance date for more than 3 years, we doubt that the University will find itself in compliance on July 21, 1978. While we welcome the legal audit, we wonder first, why the University waited for so long before even beginning such a review, and second, why the Title IX Coordinator was blocked from doing essentially the identical review (document 15, May, 1978 --- "A Plan to attain sex equity in intercollegiate athletics at MSU") at an earlier date?

3 — Finally, we feel it necessary to convey to the Board our alarm at the firing of Mary Pollock. Rather than not doing her job (as alleged in the press) it appears to us in our workings with her that she was doing her job only too well and that she was fired for trying to save this university the embarrassment and expense associated with a continuing policy which results in gender based discrimination in its athletic operations.

We conclude by asking the Board to ensure that no one else in the Department of Human Relations be fired for attempting to resolve our complaint. Thank you![25]

Although the speech did not follow up on Pollock's concern that the ADJB had instructed DeBoer and Mankowski to narrow their complaint to just women's basketball, it did focus on the importance of overall programmatic compliance with Title IX for intercollegiate athletics (not just pressing for the women's basketball team's specific complaints to be addressed). Afterward, Pittman described the meeting as "very exciting" but noted that "the true power lines showed" when, in the discussion period, assistant vice president Kay White came out as "anti-Mary [Pollock]."[26]

In a June 29 satirical editorial, economics professor "Lash" Larrowe— who also happened to be head of the faculty grievance office—corroborated Pittman's note. In "Let's Not Be Beastly to ol' Bob Perrin," Larrowe created a dialogue in which he told a fictitious young instructor picketing in support of Pollock that White, "one of our top administrators," told the board that "Mary turned people off when she went to talk with them about affirmative action, she was too aggressive. She said some of the people Mary hadn't been able to get along with were women, too." Larrowe continued, "Even worse, Dr. White said Mary openly criticized the 'U's administrators. You certainly wouldn't expect a no-nonsense boss like Perrin to keep somebody like that around do you?" The instructor responded by making the main point of Larrowe's editorial: "It's worse than I thought. It ought to be obvious, even to you, Lash, that your friend Kay White was put up there to spout the administration line."[27]

After the Board Meeting

Following the board meeting, Pittman, Alexander, Spoelstra, and Laurie Kuna ("Tuna," the team's English major friend), adjourned to Sir Pizza, a local restaurant, to talk things over. Pittman noted that Itnyre was "too tired" and had opted out. The ongoing conflict was beginning to take a toll on their energy and emotions. According to Pittman, a "rather heated argument" emerged as he and Alexander debated how to best convey information as they proceeded. Pittman wrote, "My position was elitist (and practical, in terms of efficiency)" and "Bruce's position was participatory (and practical, in terms of down the road considerations)."[28]

At that point, the two men had become de facto leaders of the women's basketball team's activism, filling the leadership void left by DeBoer's graduation and Pollock's firing. Looking back on this time years later, Mankowski recalled feeling frustrated that the process had begun to emphasize efficiency over "cooperative dialogue," the kind of discourse that could "empower the young women in their struggle and not take over or dominate it."[29] She had come to MSU from an all-girls' school and well-supported state championship basketball teams to find a surprising lack of support at MSU. Only in her second year did she begin to imagine that she could help make change, a realization sparked when DeBoer "shared her growing feminist ideology on those long car rides to games, jammed into sedans and station wagons." She explained, "It was like a light bulb went off, and I was eager to participate in any way I could. I chose take the back seat to KBD [DeBoer] et al., (or I was placed there and accepted it) because I saw them as older, smarter, and more articulate than I. However, as I gained more confidence intellectually, and became more conscious, I recall I also felt Mark [Pittman] in particular more unwilling to relinquish control of our process." In recalling the board meeting from which she left unexpectedly, Mankowski speculated that she may have shared some of her frustration with Pollock. That conversation likely led to Pollock's call urging her to go ahead and deliver the speech instead of standing back feeling upset as Pittman delegated the task to someone else.[30]

Looking back, Mankowski could see her own internal conflict, torn between her desire to participate fully by stretching into new leadership roles and her support for simply "getting the job done," even if that meant giving up control of the process to men. She observed that "since most of us were younger and a lot less educated than Mark and Bruce, and we were of course women, we needed [their] access and experience, so we did not refuse them or their efforts."

Likely unaware of how deeply conflicted some of the women not present felt about issues they were discussing (concerns about process, roles, and control), Pittman and Alexander concluded their own debate by agreeing that Itnyre, Spoelstra, and Kuna would become more involved. According to Pittman's note, all present at the gathering over pizza after the Board meeting agreed that they needed to meet with the "local rats" (Itnyre, Spoelstra, Ann Sober, and Carol Hutchins) and that, as a next step, they should write a letter to update everyone and request money for a lawyer. Pittman—probably to no one's surprise—"emphasized the need for taking notes and keeping precise records." He cautioned, "We need to keep a central file."[31]

When DeBoer called the next day, Pittman relayed the latest news. He described the meeting and mentioned that he had tried to reach AIAW attorney Polivy as Jackson had suggested. On the back of a handwritten draft of his "Chronology" entry for June 23, 1978, he scribbled the following reminder: "Ask Margot—if another complaint should be filed that deals with the entire program—should we wait or should it be done now?" Clearly, it troubled Pittman that what began as a comprehensive, program-level Title IX complaint had, in one conversation with the ADJB executive secretary, been narrowed to cover just the women's basketball team. He told DeBoer about the flurry of articles coming out about Pollock's termination. The most recent *State News* piece had described an informal press conference she held with journalism students. When they asked Pollock "why she and her superiors did not see eye-to-eye on the Title IX issue," she didn't pull any punches: "Well, I guess it's just because my main priority is stopping discrimination, while their main priority is winning football games."[32]

As Pollock continued efforts to represent her side of the story in the court of public opinion, neither she nor anyone else involved with the women's basketball complaint seemed to consider possible repercussions against Pittman for delivering the team's statement to the board. However, at least one friend on the sociology faculty worried about Pittman's welfare. On June 24, 1978, sociology professor Barrie Thorne wrote,

> Dear Mark,
> I typed up a list of all who testified at the trustees' meeting. Your statement was excellent (hope there won't be repercussions for your athletic position, but let them try, and that can be added to the grievance). Do you think an independent study of aff. Action (as mentioned in today's State Journal) could encompass women's athletics? We should certainly press for it to cover Title IX, one of the biggest can of worms.
> Barrie[33]

Pittman, however, focused on his own report: a fourteen-page, single-spaced, typed document prepared in response to Jackson's request that he record instances of discrimination affecting women's athletics.

As Pittman prepared this report, the MSU Board of Trustees responded to the women's groups who had questioned the firing of Pollock, described in one article as "the university's chief female affirmative action officer." By a vote of three to two, the trustees decided not to review Pollock's dismissal, but they responded to the more than one hundred attendees at the board's comment session by requesting that MSU hire an outside agency to review the institution's affirmative action policies and practices.[34] The trustee who led the push for a review, Jack Stack (a Republican from Alma), emphasized that the investigation should include examining the university's compliance with Title IX.[35] Meanwhile, Michigan Representative George Cushingberry Jr. (a Democrat from Detroit) charged that MSU had fallen behind in its commitment to hire more women and minorities.[36] Pointedly, he asked, "I see that MSU has dismissed its affirmative action officer who assumedly has been doing a good job—any comments?" Pollock's former direct supervisor, Ralph Bonner, clarified that Pollock was director of women's programs, not the institution's affirmative action officer. He also washed his hands of responsibility for her dismissal, claiming that it was "out of his control."[37]

As news accounts of the recent board of trustees meeting circulated, another student complaint initially filed with Pollock's office earlier that year made a headline: "Male Files Sex Bias Charge: Student Complaint Focuses on Union Women's Lounge." The account of this complaint, unrelated to athletics, gives further insight into the range of issues surrounding sex equity that emerged on campuses in the 1970s. It also reveals how Pollock handled a different kind of discrimination complaint while she was still held her Title IX coordinator position. The student charged that having a lounge in the Union exclusively for women violated Title IX. He suggested it be open to males and renamed a "study lounge." (Several years earlier, the men's lounge had been opened to everyone as a game room.) The complainant cited "oppressive counter-forces of hostility and guilt by men who try to use the lounge that amounted to harassment."[38] The executive secretary of the Anti-Discrimination Judicial Board had given the complaint to Pollock to investigate, and Pollock had concluded that "the lounge should not continue as a segregated facility. . . . The clear intent of Title IX is that all programs and activities of an institution must be available to all students except where integration would violate the physical privacy of [the] individual." Pollock was quoted as stating, "While one may agree with the feminist philosophy of segregation based on the need for female self-determination in a male-dominated world, a public institution cannot sponsor sex-segregated programs or facilities on its campus by law under Title IX."[39] This quotation—and perhaps her full statement also—did not mention the most controversial exception: the allowance for sex-segregated athletic teams under Title IX. Under HEW's regulations, eliminating sex discrimination from intercollegiate athletics required much more than simply opening up a lounge to both sexes and changing its name.

Pollock's own "Plan for Sex Equity in Intercollegiate Athletics" highlighted the many complications; Higgins's preliminary legal analysis began to examine them; and Pittman decided to address the subject in his report for Jackson. Rather than simply listing examples of discrimination, he took on the larger issues. Unlike Pollock, he honed in on the root of the matter—the role of money in decision making related to Title IX compliance.

Pittman's Title IX Report

Pittman titled his report "Recollections of Discrimination towards the Women's Athletic Program at Michigan State by the Department of Intercollegiate Athletics" and submitted it to Jackson on June 2, 1978. He noted that he had been associated with the women's athletic program since the fall of 1974 and listed two areas of discrimination: academic provisions and financial aid. He covered academic provisions in three brief sentences, citing a lack of tutoring, no book rental allowance for women, and (until the fall of 1974) preferential treatment for scheduling classes around practices times. Financial aid took up the remainder of the report, which like Pollock's plan, presented a series of arguments. Pittman's claims emerged from his standpoint as a coach and supporter of women's athletics. Along with his personal experience, his studies in sociology informed his standpoint and discourse, which allowed him to occasionally employ a set of critical terms unlikely to have been in the lexicon of most coaches. Also, he had access to internal information because of how closely he worked with DeBoer and Pollock (and how freely Pollock had shared information with complainants).

Pittman's thesis appeared on page one: "From the following sources, I think an argument can be clearly made concerning the policies and practices of the Department of Intercollegiate Athletics concerning the difference between their public image pertaining to women's athletics (in the form of financial aid) and the 'real' workings or effects of their discrimination toward women." In good graduate student form, he cited evidence to support his claims, including: (1) MSU's 1976 affirmative action plan, (2) Title IX budget information that athletics director Joe Kearney presented to the board's affirmative action committee on February 3, 1978, and (3) the Roger Wilkinson's February 14, 1978, memo to Mary Pollock. Pittman's writing revealed strong emotions: he explained that before 1976, women received no scholarship money, and after received only fifteen thousand dollars to cover ten sports. He wrote, "Needless to say, this was given in a paternalistic manner and, no doubt, thought enough to placate those of us in the women's program. It wasn't."[40]

Then Pittman made a series of forceful points. He first tackled the fact that the athletics department based its 1976 self-evaluation and subsequent affirmative action report on "a fallacious interpretation of Title IX" and what he called a "lame duck common sense approach." He asserted that the phrase "we just don't know what to do!" summed up that approach. Claiming the need to rely on "common sense," the university elected to exempt from Title IX what Pittman termed its "largest, most important, most costly, most prestigious, and most protected" sports.[41] He charged the Department of Intercollegiate Athletics with selectively choosing sentences from the 1975 HEW Sports Memorandum to support its members' preferred interpretation, ignoring additional sentences that, in Pittman's words, "more than nullify their lame duck approach which is based on the exclusion of part of the men's athletic program." He contended that the athletic department's "highly questionable interpretation of Title IX (and its cloak of self-interested 'ir' rationality)" was "a bit too thin even for the Vice President in Charge of Federal Relations, the author of the AAR [Affirmative Action Report]."[42] That vice president, of course, was Robert Perrin, the individual responsible for Pollock's termination.

In his second point, Pittman challenged the claim that MSU's three major revenue-producing sports merited special status. Quoting from the women's basketball team's complaint to the Office for Civil Rights (OCR), he promised to unmask the revenue-producing claim for what he believed it really was: "a neutral sounding justification for the continuation of a pattern of sex discrimination (OCR Complaint, 13 June, 1978, 11)." To support this point, Pittman provided a table entitled "Direct Revenues and Expenditures Attributable to 'Revenue' Producing Sports at MSU." For the period 1972 through 1977, this table drew upon data in the memo from vice president of finance Roger Wilkinson to show revenue and expenditures for football, hockey, and men's basketball each year.[43] Again, Pittman quoted from the women's basketball OCR complaint, noting that the debt on the $3,600,000 facility for men's ice hockey would not be retired until 1994, until which time student football tickets would pay for the arena. Once more, he reiterated that "the figures in [Wilkinson's] table 3 clearly indicate that the Department of Intercollegiate Athletics' claim concerning football, ice hockey, and men's basketball is nothing more than a neutral-sounding justification for the continuation of a pattern of gender based discrimination." To support this claim, he wrote:

> One finds that football is the only revenue producing sport, producing revenues of $2,574,783 over the 1972–1976 period. Men's basketball has resulted in a loss of $305,861 over this time period. Ice hockey appears to be a revenue producer to the tune of $68,913. But since students are forced to pay a hidden athletic department tax in the form of football tickets to retire the debt on Munn Ice Arena, this apparent surplus in the hockey team's budget, is not such at all. If the hockey team's revenue was applied to debt retirement, they as the men's basketball team would not be producing revenues in excess of expenditures. They would not be paying their own way![44]

To sum up the points made using Wilkinson's data, Pittman continued, "The issue of what is and what is not 'revenue producing' is (embarrassingly) open to debate. Two of the three protected sports lose more." In other words, he contended, "The University's own reasoning based on its own figures totally collapses."[45]

Then, having dissected the university's argument regarding revenue production, Pittman concluded that the athletics department could, "by the consistent application of their use of revenue producing criteria, classify any sport (men's or women's) revenue producing." He cited the example of what might happen if women's volleyball or basketball were "actively promoted and marketed" and if a new arena were "constructed to increase interest and to accommodate spectator demands, while being paid for from other than its own operating budgets." Asking this hypothetical question, he noted, contested the university's practice of presuming the issue of "popular interest" to be a fixed variable, automatically tied to particular sports independent of investments, marketing, and facilities. And for a third time, Pittman repeated his mantra: "By now, hopefully, such rhetoric is recognized for what it is . . . a neutral-sounding justification."[46]

Pittman also addressed the university's contention that the different philosophies of sports embraced by the NCAA and the AIAW accounted for differences in how men's and women's teams were treated. Until the 1973 *Kellmeyer v. National Education Association* lawsuit filed by tennis player Fern Lee "Peachy" Kellmeyer and others, the AIAW had prohibited athletic scholarships for women athletes in member institutions. Yet even though Kellmeyer's Title IX lawsuit had forced a change in the AIAW policy, in 1976 when MSU conducted its self-evaluation, MSU was still behind on providing equitable scholarship aid to female athletes. In 1978, MSU still compared women's scholarships to those for men's nonrevenue sports, excluding the three sports in which men received full-ride scholarships.

Pittman questioned why MSU had not gone before the AIAW to ask about policies and philosophies that MSU leaders believed prevented them from complying with Title IX. He pointed out that the institution would go to great lengths to fight for its men's programs, even when fighting required questioning the NCAA's actions. Specifically, he cited the example of MSU's former President Wharton going before Congress to claim that the NCAA had denied MSU due process under its constitutional rights when it placed the football program on a three-year probation for NCAA violations. "Juxtapose this concern for Constitutional rights when it comes to women's athletics," Pittman wrote. With women's sports, Pittman pointed out, the university was only too satisfied to discount section 86.6 (c) of the Title IX regulations, a section stating that the obligation to comply with Title IX "is not obviated or alleviated by any rule or regulation of any organization, club, athletic or other league, or association."[47]

Pittman summed up, "The conclusion is very clear, when the men's protected sports are in violation of national regulations . . . [MSU] will protest publically and attempt to have the abridged Constitutional rights incorporated into its men's governing organization policies and practices." Yet, he continued, when the university violated the law by following the women's governing organization policies "which permit[ed] the University to cleverly conceal its abrogation of the provision of equal opportunity, it [didn't] attempt to publically call 'foul' or use its influence to change the women's organization."[48] In fact, Pittman pointed out, MSU did not even take the internal actions toward Title IX compliance promised in MSU's 1976 Title IX self-evaluation—specifically, seeking a means to determine student athletic interests. He charged that the university initiated action only after the women's basketball team filed its ADJB complaint.[49]

Pittman, of course, could not leave the issue of Pollock's termination unaddressed. He pointed out that the internal audit that MSU had finally begun was "essentially gathering the same data as found in an earlier developed questionnaire by the Coordinator of Title IX." He charged that the university never used the questionnaire because "it asked very embarrassing questions." More colorfully, he editorialized, "She [Pollock] traversed into the sacred territory of big-time college athletics, a male only (by sex or ideology) arena. She was not a 'team' member and was appropriately sent to the showers . . . permanently!"[50]

With Pollock "sent to the showers" and her questionnaire ignored, Pittman offered his own perspective on the subject of how to measure the interests and abilities of MSU's women athletes. He pointed out that MSU attracted interested and highly skilled female athletes despite their experiences of "gross discrimination" once they joined MSU teams. He argued that the core of Title IX was to provide the opportunity for women, as well as men, to realize their full athletic potential. The success experienced by some women athletes at MSU could be attributed to those women being sufficiently motivated and skilled to overcome handicaps of discrimination, or it could be interpreted to mean that women had received all the necessary support for achieving their full potential.[51]

As other women's sports advocates often did, Pittman made his ultimate point through an analogy to the civil rights struggle for black Americans. He wrote, "Looking at the success record of women athletes is analogous to the same erroneous reasoning and examples used by anti civil rights advocates when they pointed to well placed (occupationally, monetarily, and status wise) blacks." Specifically, he argued, "Looking at the few achievers fails to account for the many many nonachievers and for the systematic blockages to the path to success." Furthermore, he wrote, "Looking at the success fails to take into account the 'extra' efforts and fortuitous circumstances not necessary for the protected privileged class to succeed." For Pittman, the most significant extra effort required of female athletes at MSU stemmed from the unequal approach to providing athletic scholarships. He contended that women were placed in a "double bind" because they, contrasted with male athletes, bore a "disproportionate burden" in financing their educations.[52]

To conclude his report, Pittman elaborated:

> Not only do [women athletes] spend time in practices and competitions, but they must (in order to afford going to school) rely [on] other than athletic financial aid to pay for their education. This places women athletes at MSU in a double bind situation. First, they must secure funds from some source, be it through their own work during their off season (if, in fact an off season exists at this level of competition), from their family, or from some form of a loan, which eventually takes time and energy from both their educational pursuits (the main reason for college, I presume) and from time available for ability and conditioning improvement. Women athletes, then, face a double binding situation. The discrimination they encounter in the form of financial aid burdens them not only in the areas of athletic pursuit, but also in the area of educational achievement.[53]

The connection Pittman made between athletic aid and educational achievement would have been particularly important for the report's target audience: Nell Jackson. Because Jackson's ambivalence about scholarships and loyalty to the AIAW educational model of athletics ran deep, these arguments seem well-tailored for her consideration. If they influenced her thinking at all, the record leaves little sign that she ever embraced athletic scholarships as a focus for her sex equity advocacy efforts.

Yet even as Pittman wrote these words, at least one women's basketball player confronted the dilemma he outlined. Mankowski was deciding whether she could afford to play basketball for MSU the following year, or whether she needed to devote the hours she spent on athletics to a paying job to cover the cost of her tuition, room, and board. In fact, her small athletic scholarship of approximately six hundred dollars was deducted from her total financial aid package. Meanwhile, men's basketball, football, and hockey players continued to enjoy full scholarships and the opportunity to realize their athletic potential over four (sometimes five) years of financial support. Granted, men in the nonrevenue sports did not get offered full scholarships, and many of them faced the same problem as Mankowski and other women. But in 1978–79, not even one MSU woman had the opportunity to experience competition as a fully supported student athlete. That season, even as talented a basketball and volleyball player as DeBoer—considered one of the top players in the nation in both sports—received only about thirteen hundred dollars in athletic scholarship funds.[54]

One Month Left

With a month left before the July 21 Title IX compliance deadline, the MSU intercollegiate athletics program still waited for direction from its affirmative action committee and the university's legal audit. Behind the scenes, Pittman's notes indicate that Jackson informed him she had met with the ADJB executive secretary and Higgins to discuss coaching salaries. According to Pittman's notes, Jackson shared with him that the two attorneys had deemed comparing men's and women's salaries irrelevant for three reasons: (1) the women's coach was viewed as not doing enough work to be paid equally with the men's coach, (2) the men's coach's jobs were more "on the line," and (3) coaching constituted a full-time position for the men's team but was only part of the women's coach's full position, which also include teaching.[55] Pittman asked Jackson to obtain the most detailed file that she could with information on coaches' salaries.[56]

Title IX and Football Parking Fees

An indication of the mood surrounding Title IX in the athletics department at this time can be found in the phrasing of a letter to MSU donors (to athletics and the overall university) regarding VIP parking fees for football games. The letter, from athletics director Joe Kearney and Terry Braverman, the director of the Ralph Young Fund (an account for inter-collegiate athletics donations), directly linked such fees to Title IX: "Dear Spartan: Due to the impact of inflation and the Federal Government's implementation of Title IX regarding required funding for women's ath-letics, we will be charging for V.I.P. football parking in 1978."[57] The note generated a response from assistant vice president for student affairs Kay White. She might not have supported Pollock but nonetheless objected to this statement.

On June 29, 1978, White addressed a note to "Joe and Terry," identify-ing herself as a generous donor to MSU's athletic program who supported a fee for VIP parking but objected to their blaming Title IX for it. She expressed disappointment that "people of [their] caliber could not be more tactful and supportive of the women's intercollegiate program at M.S.U." The new law, she reminded them, did not require that women's funding come "at the expense of their male counterparts," and she suggested that such an attitude may have led to the legal audit targeting MSU's athletic department.[58]

White copied only two individuals, MSU president Harden and Gwen Norrell. That she did not copy Jackson, the assistant director of women's athletics, may well reflect some of the power lines and groups within the institution. Jackson apparently did not move in the circle of powerful women that included Norrell, White, and Lou Anna Simon—the group that DeBoer, Mankowski, and Pittman had neglected to con-sult and cultivate.

Publicity, Support, and Advice

Just two days before White wrote her letter, an article appeared in the *Detroit News* written by Mary Rouleau, one of the sportswriters who in early June had received a letter and information packet compiled by DeBoer, Mankowski, Pittman, and Alexander. Rouleau reported that the team had filed a twelve-page Title IX complaint with the HEW's Office for Civil Rights in Chicago, charging that MSU had "engaged in illegal discrimination on the basis of sex since 1972." The article cited ten areas of alleged discrimination, reflecting the "Laundry List" provided in the Title IX regulations for athletics: academic services, financial aid, coaching, recruiting, facilities and equipment, practice time, travel allowances, athletic training, support services, and publicity. It concluded with a quote from Jackson, whose comment reflected her sympathies for the women's basketball team, despite her own in-between position in relation to the team and her MSU administrator colleagues. "I don't see it as an adversary situation," Jackson commented. "I know there are discrimination problems and we are working on other remedies."[59] No other MSU administrators commented for the article, likely because the reporter had called Pittman prior to writing it. She asked for an explanation of the Title IX regulations related to sports governing organizations, and Pittman noted that he "read her the rule and explained." Also he jotted down, "Gave her Nell [Jackson]'s number."[60] To some extent, the women's basketball team and their advocates had successfully influenced the framing of press accounts.

The *Detroit News* article also mentioned that the women's basketball team considered Pollock's termination an especially "poignant area" in a pattern of discrimination. The article did not report, however, that by the end of June, Pollock had been denied a grievance process because she was in only her first year at MSU and was therefore a probationary employee. In a 2011 interview, Pollock remarked that had she known that her status as a probationary employee made her position so vulnerable, she might have proceeded more cautiously in that first year. Despite regrets about not being more strategic when it came to self-preservation, she fought on by preparing to file her own sex bias complaint. She was still without a job. Faced with mortgage payments and other bills, she soon looked into selling diamonds she had inherited from her mother.

Toward the end of June, DeBoer and Pittman began receiving notes of support for the women's basketball team from groups and individuals who had received letters and packets about the OCR complaint and Pollock's termination. US Senator Donald Riegle Jr. sent a note saying he had asked the OCR to keep him informed with regard to the MSU women's basketball team's complaint and to let his staff know if he could be of assistance.[61] A more detailed letter came from SPRINT of the Women's Equity Action League. In response to DeBoer's inquiry about complaints at other institutions, Marguerite Beck-Rex, SPRINT's project director, wrote that numerous complaints resembled the MSU players' issues, but she had not yet seen anyone raise the issue of revenue-producing sports. She noted the April 1978 reaffirmation by HEW that revenue-producing sports were not exempted from Title IX and enclosed the relevant press release. She suggested that DeBoer contact the Women's Law Fund in Cleveland, Ohio, for possible monetary support and advice for a legal battle. Finally, she recommended that DeBoer contact Marcia Federbush from Ann Arbor, who spearheaded complaints filed against the University of Michigan. She provided Federbush's name and phone number as well as information for Carol Grossman, a contact in Pontiac, Michigan.[62]

As responses trickled in, Pittman needed a break. "Incredible sleepless night," he recorded in his "Chronology." The next day, to get away, he took his motorcycle on a ride to Flint, where a friend of DeBoer's lived. DeBoer came down from Saginaw, and the three of them traveled back to East Lansing together. By June 29, Pittman was back to work on Title IX. Pittman, Alexander, Hardy, Itnyre, and Kuna, whose mother had a connection with MSU trustee Jack Stack, arranged a meeting with Stack at his home in Alma. During their one-and-a-half-hour meeting, Stack explained that he and the rest of the board felt that they lacked understanding of both Title IX and women's athletics. He told the group of a big change in the works: the next individual responsible for Title IX would report directly to the university president. He also advised that the women's basketball team pressure Jackson to "force intra-organizational movement on Title IX." He assured Pittman that Jackson was in an "invulnerable" position concerning Title IX, indicating that the board was impressed with her.[63]

The meeting with Stack suggested that the women's basketball complaint and fallout from Pollock's termination had an impact. Possibly as a reminder of what was at stake for the university, Pittman clipped and saved a news article reporting that MSU had received a final installment of a $1.2 million National Science Foundation grant to "complete the world's first superconducting cyclotron." This important grant was an example of one kind of federal funding tied to Title IX compliance—the penalty for failure to comply was withdrawal of federal funding for the entire university.[64]

On June 30, DeBoer was still in East Lansing, and she joined Alexander and Pittman for a meeting at Jackson's home. Pittman wrote: "Mainly informed Nell of meeting with Stack. Asked Nell what she is doing to aid us. Discovered she has an open communication channel to Pres. By-passing Kearney. We'll keep each other informed. Nell volunteered information in great fashion. Well-pleased with meeting."[65]

Despite Pittman's satisfaction with the meeting, it seems that he and Jackson never seriously discussed Stack's advice that Jackson take advantage of her good standing with the trustees and the MSU president to become the primary spokesperson at MSU for gender equity in athletics.

As June turned into July, faculty and students continued to voice their displeasure at Pollock's termination, and the group involved with the women's basketball complaint turned their attention to the legal aspects of the complaint. Joyce Ladenson, an MSU professor of American thought and language, applauded Pollock's support for students and faculty during her short time at MSU. She concluded that "for the first time in its history, the Office of Women's Programs has become an effective, critical voice on women's issues."[66] A student in MSU's James Madison College, Bruce Guthrie, offered a brief feminist analysis of patriarchy: "In Mary Pollock's case, sexism preserves the position of males in society. Automatically, half of the population is inferior to the other half which maintains this system through its control over the entire structure of power in society. When an individual rises to push for equality, the structure simply eliminates the individual."[67]

To determine how the law might facilitate—even accelerate—a continued push for equality, DeBoer, Spoelstra, Pittman, and Alexander met on July 3 with Tracy Dobron, a law student interested in Title IX. According to Pittman's notes, Dobron reminded the group that the law required them to exhaust administrative remedies before they could take a case to court. She also suggested that the group refile their OCR complaint with Itnyre as the primary complainant since DeBoer had graduated, and the compliance deadline had passed. She may have been concerned about

OCR's stipulation that a complaint needed to be filed within 180 days of when discrimination occurred. However, refiling under a current student's name was unnecessary since being directly affiliated with an institution is not a requirement to file a Title IX complaint. Dobron suggested they were generally on the right track but reminded them to give the Office for Civil Rights a reasonable amount of time to act on the complaint. She pointed out that suing the US federal government's OCR may be necessary to get that office to take action. Finally, she offered to look into attorneys to represent the women's basketball team if its leaders needed further legal expertise and support.

Backlogged and Second Tier

In a letter dated July 3, the same day DeBoer and the others met with the law student, DeBoer received a letter from OCR. The office had received her complaint, determined that it fell within its jurisdiction, and "placed it on a backlog of complaints for future investigation."[68] The latter statement was not at all what the group hoped to hear; it only intensified their search for a legal advocate to guide them. As they contemplated their next step, DeBoer received a call from the executive secretary of MSU's ADJB, Sallie Bright (the legal counsel for MSU's Department of Human Relations, headed by Perrin). Her news also disappointed DeBoer. Bright had completed her fact finding, and, according to Pittman's notes, she supported increasing support for the women in "small items, not $$" and found that "the division between 'revenue/profit-producing sports' and other sports should be maintained." Title IX compliance would focus on the "levels of competition" and "athletic competency" of males and females.[69] Her findings seemed to echo the interpretation of Title IX suggested in Higgins's progress report and seemed to relegate all women's sports to a permanent second-tier status.

On July 7, Pittman talked with AIAW attorney Polivy. His notes indicate that Polivy thought they were "doing a good job" and that she was "concerned with the AIAW shortcomings" they had pointed out (presumably Pittman referred to AIAW policies and philosophies that complicated the process of equalizing support for male and female intercollegiate athletes). Polivy told Pittman that she had forwarded the team's complaint to Marcia Greenberger at the Center for Law and Social Policy in Washington, DC, where she directed the National Women's Rights Project (the precursor to the National Women's Law Center, founded in 1981). Polivy also advised Pittman that the group need not refile their complaint. Rather than considering a lawsuit against HEW's Office for Civil Rights if they failed to act on their complaint, she thought it better to consider suing the university if necessary. She recommended calling Ken Mines, the OCR director in Chicago, if MSU was "not really attempting to solve [their] complaint."[70] Finally, Polivy advised that the women's basketball team did not "need to be ready with a complete program complaint," because their existing complaint—focused on the women's basketball team contrasted with the men's team—was sufficient.[71] This advice, of course, contradicted Pollock's understanding that the Title IX regulations required focusing on comparing whole men's and women's programs, not only specific teams.

That same day, DeBoer followed up with a call to Greenberger, who had reviewed the MSU complaint forwarded by Polivy and found it "terrific." According to Pittman's notes, Greenberger indicated that the Center for Law and Social Policy was "looking at [their] complaint as a possible test case." If the MSU complaint turned out to be the Title IX test case they sought, she told DeBoer, there would be no attorney fees, only expenses for travel back and forth between Michigan and Washington, DC. She warned that the MSU team should not expect HEW to do much and assured DeBoer that they would decide on their test case in a few weeks. Pittman assessed Greenberger's tone in two words: "Very supportive."[72]

Commerce and Education

As DeBoer and Pittman anticipated further word from Greenberger, Pollock contacted Pittman to urge the team to file an additional complaint under the Michigan Civil Rights Act 453. Pollock had filed under that law herself, charging MSU with sex discrimination and retaliation against her for assisting the women's basketball team. Pittman noted that Pollock suggested that the team's filing would help them and her. DeBoer, however, could not act on this request because she was leaving town again to work at volleyball camps. Pittman drove her to Grand Rapids.

As they drove, neither of them knew that DeBoer was being considered for a historic new professional basketball league for women, the Women's Basketball League (WBL). A twelve-game season was slated to begin on December 17, 1978. The league announced in late June that it would use a basketball one inch smaller in circumference and slightly lighter than the standard NBA ball. Until the mid-1980s, women's college basketball teams played with the same size ball as the men's teams; a shift was made to a smaller size ball at the college level in 1984.[73] The decision to use a smaller ball reflected the challenge of "trying to sell the public [a women's] version of a sport already standardized by taller and stronger male athletes." A reporter for the *Lansing State Journal* offered this perspective on making adaptations to sell women's professional sports: "Women have been slow to discover that altering the dimensions of the game is not a sign of inherent weakness. Quite the contrary, it is the first evidence of the economic intelligence. If women athletes are compared unfavorably to their male counterparts by the ticket-buying public, it is obvious that turnstiles will soon rust shut."[74]

In college athletics, by contrast, the commercial imperative faced by professional teams was not supposed to exist. However, by 1978 it was common knowledge that men's college athletics was regarded as a business, and decisions about equality under Title IX continually confronted the money factor.

On July 16, a *New York Times* article by AIAW attorney Polivy identified money as the root of opposition to Title IX compliance. The three-year adjustment period since the 1975 regulations, she contended, had provided an "emotional adjustment period" during which "all the old arguments about the preference of 'normal' girls for passive pursuits have come to be universally recognized for the foolishness that they are."[75] While her statement that such views were universally recognized as foolish overstated her point—the idea that females are less competitive and physically active than males persists to some extent today—Polivy honed in on the primary reason why almost no major university athletic program would likely comply with the law by the July 21 deadline. She argued, as critics of big-time college athletics have increasingly pointed out, that "men's inter-collegiate athletic programs are labeled educational to preserve their tax-exempt, tax deductible status and their eligibility for funds and facilities, but they are in fact business enterprises operated solely for the economic aggrandizement of educational institutions."[76] Without using the term, she essentially characterized big-time men's college sports as a fraud. She contended that young male athletes were routinely exploited as "hired hands" working for little more than minimum wage, whose academic achievements received only incidental regard. But she reserved her harshest criticism for HEW. She argued that the government's "studied ignorance of the real conflicts underlying Title IX could make July 21 the funeral of women's athletics rather than the birthday of equal opportunity."[77]

While DeBoer was in Grand Rapids, she and Mankowski received a note from Michigan Congressman Bob Carr. He thanked them for the letter they sent in June, describing himself as "a leader in the fight for Title IX in the Congress of the United States" and "deeply committed to the program." He indicated that he had written to the Chicago OCR to express his interest in "a speedy resolution of the complaint" but that to intervene further would be "inappropriate."[78] Although it might indeed have been inappropriate for an elected representative to intervene on behalf of some of his constituents, lobbyists representing men's commercialized higher education athletics kept the pressure on HEW. Just a few days before the July 21 headline, HEW officials undermined their own earlier messages meant to provide clarity and finality. On July 21, the *State News* reported that HEW secretary Joseph Califano ordered an accelerated handling of complaints but that he also was undecided about "whether to count football scholarships when comparing a college's athletic programs for men and women."[79] This statement seemed to contradict HEW's legal counsel's widely distributed April 27 press release stating that "revenue sports" could not be excluded from Title IX comparisons. Whether because of big-time college sports lobbyists or their own ambivalence, HEW spokespersons were stuttering, sputtering, and contradicting themselves. As a result, they rendered their own deadline almost meaningless.

MSU at the Deadline

A *State News* article published just a day before the HEW deadline described a "rift" between Kearney and Jackson on Title IX compliance. Kearney suggested that out of a total budget of $4.2 million, the women's athletics budget would likely be $500,000 for 1978–79, to match the women's budget at UCLA, which he claimed was "known as the epitome of what is happening in women's athletics." For supportive services, MSU women were slated to receive $240,000 out of a total budget of $1.4 million.[80] Notably, the law required comparing the men's and women's programs within a single institution, whereas Kearney was comparing the MSU women's program to the women's program at another institution— one likely not in compliance even though it was a leader in women's athletics funding. Kearney may have identified UCLA as a leader in part because it was widely known to have offered the first full athletic scholarship to a woman, basketball standout Ann Meyers. In fact, within MSU's own Big Ten Conference, Ohio State University's director of women's athletics, Phyllis Bailey, informed the Associated Press that OSU allocated $700,000 for women's intercollegiate athletics in 1978–79. However, their men's budget, like many other prominent schools with prominent football programs, was much higher at $7 million, according to Bailey.[81]

In the past, Jackson focused her public comments on how much support for women's sports had improved, even if men's finances dwarfed what women received. However, for the news article published close to the HEW deadline, she spoke more assertively, stating that financial aid and coaches' salaries for women's teams needed increased funding. She noted that a $500,000 budget was "certainly an improvement," but she claimed that women's athletics needed at least $800,000 for minimum compliance with Title IX.[82]

Even as Jackson spoke out, a movement was afoot to question her effectiveness as an administrator. In a July 21 letter to President Harden, MSU attorney Higgins identified a problem with the athletic department's administrative structure and dissatisfaction with Jackson's "administration and philosophy." Notably, Higgins did not copy Jackson on the letter. Higgins explained that because coaches in the men's program met regularly with athletics director Kearney and women's coaches with assistant athletics director Jackson, "this creates a self-image among some of the latter group that they are 'second class' and the men's program has priority."[83]

In his letter to Harden, Higgins described the hybrid nature of the MSU structure as "straddling the fence." He noted, "Though technically they are part of the same program, the women's program is treated as a separate and autonomous subunit."[84] A better structure, he recommended, would be either to establish completely separate programs or separate but equal programs within the same administrative unit. A complicating factor was the close ties of the women's program to academics, with many coaches also hired as instructors or professors. Increasingly, the same individual could not fulfill both roles, as coaching was becoming its own career path, one filled by people without credentials for an academic appointment. Higgins also cited criticisms of Jackson by women's coaches who felt she favored track over other sports (when the AIAW philosophy was to treat all sports equally). Similarly, Phyllis Bailey at Ohio State recalled being criticized for favoring basketball, which she had coached.[85] Such allegations may have been inevitable when an athletic administrator was also coaching. However, Jackson was apparently not given an opportunity to respond to critiques that surfaced during Title IX–related inquiries. Such crosscurrents within the women's program did not help the women present a unified front; rather, they undermined Jackson's credibility and authority to advocate on their behalf.

On July 20, the eve of the compliance deadline, Higgins submitted an eighteen-page "Legal Audit of Title IX and the MSU Intercollegiate Athletic Program." To write the report, Higgins and Bright had interviewed coaches of women's sports, men's so-called nonrevenue sports, men's and women's athletics administrators, directors of men's and women's intramurals, the head trainer, the chair of the Physical Education Department, a student, and the assistant controller of the university.[86] The report stated that neither HEW's final regulations for Title IX nor its subsequent communications resolved the issue of how Title IX applied to "the so-called 'revenue-producing' sports." The evidence Higgins offered to support this statement made explicit the self-serving translational process employed by the men's athletic establishment. Higgins explained, "In the popular verbiage, level of competition has sometimes been translated into 'revenue' and 'nonrevenue' programs." He continued, "HEW has tacitly recognized that the level of competition in spectator-oriented sports which produce revenue for the entire intercollegiate athletics program should not necessarily be jeopardized by Title IX." Finally, he concluded that if the level of competition was higher in spectator sports, "they may be funded at a higher level and the total program would still be in compliance with Title IX."[87]

Although this reasoning was biased toward the administration's interest in maintaining funding for their existing hierarchy of sports at status quo levels, Higgins had adjusted his argument somewhat. He employed the arguably more accurate term "spectator sport" for "revenue-producer" and no longer connected level of revenue with level of competition. Although he stretched considerably for an interpretation of the law that would exempt the three sports that MSU wanted to exclude from measures of Title IX compliance, he opened the door for alternative viewpoints by comparing scholarships for men and women in two different ways—once with football, basketball and hockey included and again with those three sports excluded.[88]

In all, Higgins's report acknowledged a variety of compliance problems and cited progress. He pointed out that "the Athletic Department had not done its self-evaluations . . . in a proper manner" and that the primary steps "were not completed in a timely fashion."[89] He defined progress questionably at times—for example, he cited as a positive development that the university contemplated building a new training facility for football and transferring the old facilities to the women.[90] Yet he acknowledged the problem of women's teams not being able to practice in the location where they competed for their home competitions and noted that "the Athletic Department should reassess these priorities and adjust them."[91] He termed the women's locker room in Jenison Fieldhouse "totally inadequate." As an example, he explained that when competing there, visiting women's teams either shared the women's locker room with MSU women or used the men's locker room with a sign on it declaring it "temporarily off limits." However, he noted, "this sign is regularly ignored by men who barge into the visiting team's locker facility, to the embarrassment of all."[92] This sort of graphic anecdote seemed to rally support for improvements from all decision makers.

The scholarship issue, though, remained complicated—and far more expensive to address. Higgins noted that disparities in scholarships existed whether the women's program was compared with the whole men's program or only the "non-spectator" part of it. However, Higgins acknowledged that, either way, MSU continued to be out of compliance regarding scholarships. Still, he argued that MSU's efforts must be assessed in the context of peer institutions. He pointed out that "if total and immediate equality of financial support were required by law," it would curtail the men's program and "severely impact on 'big-time' revenue programs, whose spectator and alumni appeal provides essential financial support to the entire athletic program." Higgins cited the failure of many institutions to achieve "absolute equal opportunity" in the three-year adjustment period, vacillation by HEW when implementing and clarifying its regulations, and ongoing "judicial attacks by groups who feel the regulations are inadequate." He concluded that any confusion or shortcomings on the part of MSU were completely justified. He also determined that until the Title IX committee appointed by Kearney completed its reports, his office was "not in a position to substitute its judgments for the forthcoming analysis of [the] committee."[93]

Ultimately, then, the MSU legal audit put the ball back in Kearney's court. Neither Jackson nor the women's basketball team received a copy of Higgins's report to President Harden, so they were all in waiting mode. As the Title IX compliance deadline came and went, the university had made unmistakable progress. Even so, women's sports advocates found little reason to celebrate. Birthday parties for equal opportunity did not sweep the country—but neither was there cause just yet for a funeral.

14 Can You Play with Magic?

> We practiced in different places. We lived in parallel universes, but they weren't really very parallel. . . . Women's sports were very, very separate.
> —Kathleen DeBoer[1]

The attempt by federal policymakers to be flexible and reasonable in defining "sex equity" and "equal opportunity" in athletics had not created a smooth transition toward compliance with Title IX. Nearly a hundred complaints piled up as the deadline passed on July 21, 1978, and the US Department of Health, Education, and Welfare fielded complaints from institutions confused and frustrated by, or simply resistant to, the Title IX regulations. At that point, anyone who followed media coverage of the subject knew that the men's athletic establishment perceived the law as a threat to "revenue-producing" sports. But they would have heard almost nothing about another controversy that had faded into the background: the debate between feminists and physical educators about whether female athletes could achieve equality by competing apart from men in sex-segregated teams.

After a long silence on this issue, the debate about whether sex-separate can ever be equal reemerged in 2010. In their book *Playing with the Boys: Why Separate Is Not Equal in Sports*, Eileen McDonagh and Laura Pappano questioned whether the intractable hierarchy that "separate but equal" inherently supports women was a good idea to begin with and whether it serves women well today.[2] Their liberal feminist argument for greater integration of men's and women's teams sparked a response from legal scholar Deborah Brake. Brake's book *Getting in the Game: Title IX*

306

and the Women's Sports Revolution took a closer look at the feminist theories underlying Title IX, acknowledging the tradeoffs and limitations of each. Brake noted that the law "leaves intact a structure in which women's sports are too often marginalized as secondary to the men's games, a poor stepsister to the 'real' varsity programs."[3] Yet she maintained that, on the whole, Title IX pragmatically, even creatively, "navigates the tricky terrain of gender separation and assimilation in sports."[4]

No evidence suggests that college student athletes in the 1970s sought integrated teams. Nor did college women focus on or question the stipulation in Title IX's 1975 regulations that women could not integrate men's teams in contact sports such as football or basketball (females did have integration rights under Title IX for sports designated "noncontact" if no team existed for girls or women and if overall playing opportunities for females were insufficient). Some college women sought to compete on men's noncontact sport teams such as swimming or tennis when no teams existed for women. But, unlike school-aged girls, college women seemed largely unconcerned about seeking legal support for integrating men's college football, basketball, or baseball teams. Rather, they assumed that those sports were entitled to separation rights (sex-separate teams were, after all, the status quo). Certainly in 1978, the MSU women's basketball team never discussed the practical or philosophical implications of integrating men's intercollegiate athletic teams. The women's basketball players, a number of whom played multiple sports, appreciated the wide variety and respectable quantity of teams MSU offered for women. Their concern was how to gain needed resources within the existing sex-separate but obviously unequal model.[5]

The Activists: A Mixed-Sex Team

The local struggle at MSU faced a critical turning point late in summer 1978 after Pollock was fired. By July, members of the women's basketball team that had filed the sex discrimination complaints had dispersed. Some players, like DeBoer, worked at summer jobs; others moved back home for a few months; a few competed in summer softball leagues. Two of the team's starting guards—Diane Spoelstra and Karen Santoni—had graduated, along with starting forwards Kathy DeBoer and Jill Prudden. Lori Hyman was still gaining strength after her knee injury, and two players had decided not to return the following season (one left school, and Mankowski was not returning to the team).[6] It was a rebuilding year for the women's team, and with their Title IX complaint still unsettled, it remained to be seen whether a newly configured team would continue the struggle.

With DeBoer graduated and Pollock fired, the MSU group needed a new leader or leaders. Unlike the women's basketball team, the group of activists was, so to speak, a mixed-sex "team." Its most dedicated members included not only the women basketball players but the two male graduate students as well, Mark Pittman and Bruce Alexander. In summer 1978, Pittman was the only member of the group who remained on campus most of the time, so it fell to him to guide a transition to the next step. Yet the place of male allies and co-organizers in the women's movement could be complicated. As Pittman wrote in a letter to his parents a few months later, he didn't think of himself as a "guide" or a "leader," but he could see—as a friend pointed out to him—that he was becoming the "glue" that, over time, held the effort together.[7] Still, even when the struggle was left primarily in his hands during that summer, he never completely took the ball and ran with it. Like Alexander and Hardy, he viewed himself as helping his good friends in a cause he cared deeply about himself. But he understood that while his role was vital, it was complicated by the very nature of the struggle itself. One reason Title IX supported separation rights for women's sports, after all, was to prevent men from taking over and thereby diminishing women's opportunities to contribute, lead, and develop skills.

In some ways, Pittman's role in the MSU struggle recalls the ways in which supportive men could play an important part in feminist causes. For instance, Billie Jean King credited her husband Larry King, also a tennis player, with initially calling her attention to inequities in sports. Likewise, the husband of activist and policymaker Bernice "Bunny" Sandler demonstrated the power of language when he labeled the inequities she experienced as "sex discrimination," plain and simple. And Senator Birch Bayh of Indiana was motivated to take a leading role in the process of enacting Title IX when he experienced women as partners on the family farm and when he saw his (first) wife rejected for admission to the

University of Virginia specifically because she was a woman.[8] In Pittman's case, he played a consciousness-raising role at times, especially in communicating with Nell Jackson regarding scholarships, and he had fully "thrown himself into the situation" (as Mary Jo Hardy put it years later). Looking back, the MSU women generally seemed grateful for his support and did not recall him dominating the group or pushing his own agenda.[9] He was working with strong-willed individuals, and if anything, his notes suggest that on occasion he felt unexpectedly excluded or a little taken for granted. Yet he persevered. That summer, his continuing behind-the-scenes efforts kept the women's basketball team's cause alive when it could easily have lost momentum.

The contrast between what the women's basketball team received and the whole-hearted institutional support for MSU men continued to be obvious to anyone paying attention. As the women's team scattered for summer work and other pursuits, the Spartan men's team looked forward to a two-week trip to Brazil in September. Actually, Coach Heathcote wrote in his memoir that he regretted scheduling that trip late in the summer because Magic Johnson was exhausted from competing in an all-star tour of the Soviet Union; he regretted not just allowing his star to stay home and rest. But he had not considered that a real option, so the whole team enjoyed the cross-cultural experience of a preseason trip to South America, where they represented MSU by competing in two tournaments.[10] When they defeated Brazil, thought to be one of the world's premiere amateur teams, senior forward Gregory Kelser started to imagine the team as "good enough to win it all."[11] Clearly, the MSU men's team had been afforded the resources needed to make the most of their opportunity to do just that. And certainly the women's team would have welcomed the opportunity to make the kind of trip that the men's coach—at least in that particular season—did not fully appreciate.

Pittman Perseveres

As the MSU men's basketball team began to visualize a national championship and the women's team disbanded for the summer, Pittman's immediate attention turned to ongoing efforts to address the issue of Pollock's firing as well as affirmative action in general at MSU. A few days after the July 21 Title IX compliance deadline passed, Pittman got a call from his sociology professor friend, Barrie Thorne. She wanted him to attend another board of trustees meeting in which women's groups hoped to keep the Pollock issue alive. They intended to keep up pressure for an extended, outside review of affirmative action at MSU. At the meeting, Pittman found that his good deed—showing yet another sign of support for Pollock at no small risk to his own job—would not go unpunished. He vented his feelings in his "Chronology": "Went to the Board meeting . . . [after the meeting] got ass chewed out by Mary [Pollock] about not filing with State [of] Michigan. Marilyn Frye there with her group . . . very uncomfortable feeling. . . . Like I'm to blame. *MEN ARE ALWAYS RESPONSIBLE AND TO [BLAME]*."[12]

Although Pittman did not describe what specifically made him so uncomfortable, his feelings echoed a sense of exclusion he had also felt as one of only two males in Frye's women's studies class. DeBoer recalled that "Pitt was one of only two guys in the class and clearly smarter than the other guy, an undergraduate who would try to debate Dr. Frye, an avowed lesbian separatist, on topics of male dominance and patriarchy." In her recollection, "It was not a pleasant scene, although indicative of the hostile tone of the debate over women's rights at the time, as Dr. Frye would just verbally eviscerate this student, who—to his credit or fault—routinely acted out every stereotype of the male culture that had spawned feminism."[13] Pittman, observing this dynamic early on, decided to keep quiet in the class, especially since he was only auditing. Nevertheless, DeBoer recalled that "Pitt," as she and her friends called him, did the bulk of the work for group assignments in the class, assignments which DeBoer herself "hated."[14] To some extent, a similar dynamic applied to the women's basketball team's Title IX struggle: DeBoer provided the initial spark, but after graduation shifted to offering encouragement from afar as Pittman and others completed the project.

Pittman seemed not to mind (or even remember) doing most of the group's work in Frye's class, but the experience of feeling unwelcome at times there stayed with him. Pittman remembered Frye—a supporter of the women's basketball team and of Pollock—as a "separatist" feminist. As such, she advocated that women needed their own space apart from men to experience real empowerment and meaningful equality. In Pittman's recollection, she went even further, acting out her ideology by acknowledging men only in "the most condescending and humiliating way," whether in class or "if one saw her around campus."[15] Pollock recalled that a radical feminist practice in the 1970s involved some women setting a goal not to see or speak with a male except when absolutely necessary for work or professional obligations.[16] In 2010, Pittman reflected that Frye's approach amounted to "evening the score."[17] Of course, even in 1978, Pittman was well aware that Title IX allowed separatism by permitting single-sex teams, yet as a male coach of a women's team, he represented an element of integration. As a pro-feminist male and coach of a women's team, he must have felt at times like an individual without his own country. But he was also among a growing number of males who had benefited from an opportunity to coach in women's programs as teams for females expanded under Title IX. Of course, the benefits in 1978 were dubious—low pay and, especially for males coaching women, even lower status.

After Pittman attended the board meeting, Pollock wanted him to take immediate action by getting someone on the women's basketball team down to the state of Michigan civil rights department to file their complaint there. When Pittman hesitated, Pollock called Hardy's place— where Mary Kay Itnyre was staying—a few days later to request that Itnyre file the team's complaint with the Civil Rights Office. Pollock herself had already filed a retaliation complaint on her own behalf with that office and with OCR. After talking with Pollock, Hardy and Itnyre made an appointment for August 10.

In the meantime, Pollock accepted a new job. She had been offered a consultant position with the staff of Representative George Cushingberry Jr. to work with the state of Michigan Joint House-Senate Committee on Affirmative Action. According to Representative Cushingberry's assistant, she was hired because of "her experience and aggressiveness in pursuing affirmative action programs."[18] Although it was only a six-month job, Pollock commented in a news article at the time that the job went "along with [her] wildest dreams." She added, "At least I'll be able to ask some questions."[19]

As Pollock prepared to get involved with affirmative action at the state and national levels, Pittman scribbled a "note to self" that read "see back for ERA" on a news clipping about Pollock's new position. His note called attention to the national context for the tumult over sex discrimination at MSU: the struggle for an Equal Rights Amendment to the Constitution. President Jimmy Carter's administration sought to extend the ratification deadline, citing the amendment as a continuing priority.[20] Pittman's attention, however, was fully engrossed in the more immediate, local struggle of the MSU women's basketball team.

Just as Pittman learned of Pollock's new position, a letter arrived from a friend familiar with the legal community in Michigan. Pittman had told him the MSU women's basketball team was considering legal action, and he asked for advice. The friend sent names of three attorneys with contact information: Jean L. King, Philip Green, and Marilyn Mosier. After noting that he didn't have any direct knowledge of any of the three, Pittman's friend added, "But my guess is that Jean King might be your best bet." He also counseled, "My only suggestion—stay out of court at all costs—and remember that lawyers can be *expensive*. Good luck."[21]

None of the MSU women's basketball players or their supporters had funds for a legal battle. Mankowski had taken a paying job with a Peace Studies Center at an East Lansing church after a talk with Coach Langeland during fall basketball tryouts. She recalled meeting over lunch to discuss her prospects for earning a starting position because she had contributed as one of the first players to come in off the bench the past season. She had worked hard in the off season to improve her game, alone and with help from Pittman and Alexander, but when she perceived little encouragement from her coach, or even an assurance that she would make the team in light of the talented younger players trying out, she decided not to play that year after all. She was living with Hutchins and Hyman at the time and had been keeping them updated about the Title IX complaint process. When she decided to leave the team, she asked Hutchins to take over her role as the "face" of the Title IX complaint. She assured her friends and former teammates that she would still help with behind-the-scenes work, but she needed to earn money in her new job to pay for school.[22]

For the fall, DeBoer planned to accept a graduate research assistant-ship in sociology at MSU, with the goal of attending law school the fol-lowing year. This goal emerged from the struggle at MSU, which the principle-driven DeBoer defined primarily as an effort "to get an inter-pretation on Title IX." Responding at the time to the critics of the team's actions, she explained, "We're not trying to destroy anybody's program or anything. But just being involved with that showed me there's a definite need for women lawyers to defend women's interests." Referring to her own economic situation, she explained, "I got a pretty decent research assistantship, which means I was hurting for money."[23] She also earned money working all summer at volleyball camps across the country, includ-ing Wake Forest, North Carolina; Auburn, Alabama; St. Paul, Minnesota; Portland, Oregon; and Seattle, Washington. While working a camp in St. Paul, though, she received some surprising news: she had been drafted in the fourth round of the free agent phase by the Milwaukee Does of the new professional Women's Basketball League. So she faced a big deci-sion: whether to take her research assistantship and apply to law school or attend tryouts and take a risk with the new league (a previous attempt to start a similar league had failed before the first game). Of the two choices, law school was the more stable, predictable path.

A Letter from WEAL

As the outgoing and incoming MSU women's basketball players made plans for the fall, athletics director Joe Kearney received a letter he prob-ably did not expect or welcome. On July 25, 1978, the Women's Equity Action League and Legal Defense Fund wrote to express concern over "the discrimination practiced against female athletes at Michigan State University." The executive director, Carol Parr, was following up on the request for help sent to her organization in June by the women's basketball team (the director copied the team on the letter to Kearney). Specifically, Parr informed Kearney that she was "aware that M.S.U. [had] attempted to draw a distinction between revenue-producing sports and non rev-enue-producing sports." She explained that such a distinction for Title

IX compliance purposes was "not only unacceptable, it [was] unlawful." She reminded him that "Congress [had] repeatedly refused to adopt an amendment that would exempt revenue-producing sports from Title IX." Finally, she raised the issue of intent: "If you were previously unaware of the invidious discrimination practiced within your department, I am sure the complaint filed by the women's varsity basketball team has brought it to your attention."[24]

Title IX, Parr continued, requires equality of opportunity, yet MSU continued to withhold funds from the women's basketball team while providing "first class treatment" for the men. She acknowledged that "bottom line expenditure figures for men and women varsity teams do not have to be identical; an overnight equalization of athletic funding—however desirable of a goal that may be—is not required under Title IX." By law, she concluded, MSU must provide "the support and funding necessary to provide a varsity level of intercollegiate competition commensurate with the ability and interests of women athletes."[25] Her letter probably added to the growing store of ill feelings by Kearney toward anyone involved with the women's basketball complaint. But it also achieved at least one rhetorical purpose: in a court of law, MSU would have trouble claiming unintentional discrimination, or even confusion, after this forthright letter.

The week after Kearney received this letter, Pittman received his contract renewal for the following academic year, with a salary of $10,500. Jackson reappointed him as assistant coach for women's track and field, including additional duties coordinating the weight training program for women's athletics and assisting with coordinating facility needs for the women's program. The latter responsibility may have reflected the ongoing discussions surrounding facility use sparked by the Title IX complaint.[26]

The women's basketball complaint, combined with the compliance deadline, had at least prompted key decision makers at MSU to discuss the institution's Title IX obligations for athletics. The quantity of discourse on the subject had increased exponentially. Inquiries from individuals and groups outside the institution also exerted mild pressure on MSU and perhaps OCR. On August 8, 1978, DeBoer received a copy of a letter to Senator Griffin from the OCR director, confirming that they had received his memo on behalf of the MSU women's basketball team and also the team's complaint. The OCR director assured the senator that an investigation would begin within the next three months, so this nudge from a politician seemed to expedite attention to the complaint.[27] Meanwhile, Itnyre and Hardy kept their appointment for August 10 with the Michigan Department of Civil Rights. There, Itnyre signed a sworn statement and the department informed her that in the next six months, they would talk to witnesses, and if they found cause, would try to facilitate conciliation.

Itnyre's statement alleged discrimination under Michigan Act 453 regarding scholarships, practice facilities, locker rooms, and coaching, a list that highlighted areas that she may have found most troubling as a player. She returned to the office the following day to sign a typed version of the statement that read in part, "I and other women similarly situated are denied an equal opportunity based upon our sex. I am a woman. We feel this is a part of a pattern of discrimination by the athletic department." Pollock's complaint of retaliation, too, was filed in the same department.[28]

A Deal with the Devil?

As the MSU women's basketball players pursued their complaints, they never considered whether they might be making a Faustian bargain. But that is just what they pursued according to an August 6, 1978, *New York Times* editorial written by the associate director of alumni affairs for Long Island University, Edward Jaworski. In his commentary, written in response to AIAW attorney Margot Polivy's "Deadline or Deadend?" editorial on the Title IX compliance deadline, he argued that Polivy's concern about an impending "Title IX funeral" was unfounded. On the contrary, he claimed that women's sports were doing very well indeed. He contended that—spurred by Title IX to invest in the men's commercial approach to college sports—women's sports were increasingly a "hot idea at the ticket office." As evidence, he cited twelve thousand fans at a Madison Square Garden women's basketball contest. But he also pointed to "ethical consequences."[29] He alleged that, along with experiencing increased scholarship money, larger budgets for recruiting and cross-country travel, and possible big television contracts, women's athletics grew amid "an atmosphere of hearsay violations." He agreed with Polivy that the answers to all questions could be found by focusing on money. "Money is the reason why there has been no Title IX funeral," he claimed.[30] Thus, by the end of the article, the headline, "Women's Sports Are Doing Just Fine," took on a double meaning. In terms of growing support and spectators, the headline meant just what it said. But the phrase "just fine" also meant that women's sports were doing a fine job of becoming just as ethically compromised as men's sports.

At MSU, Joe Kearney's eventual solution to the Spartan's problems surrounding Title IX supported the claim that Title IX was driving women's sports into the same commercialized, ethically questionable paradigm as men's sports. As he realized that he could not avoid Title IX altogether, Kearney floated the idea of building one or two women's teams into revenue-producing sports (according to Pittman's notes, he specifically mentioned women's basketball and gymnastics). This line of thought demonstrated that the initial fears of AIAW leaders were being realized. Not only were schools failing to comply with Title IX, but even when they were trying, the law had not spurred a serious dialogue around possible models of sports for both sexes. The law was simply pushing women into the men's commercialized model. Records of communication at MSU show that, with revenue production so highly valued, discourse never for a minute focused on the possible advantages of adopting some aspects of the women's model for all sports. Instead, the philosophy of the women's program—that is, to treat all sports and athletes as equally as possible—provided a handy justification for not providing women additional resources. The reasoning went as follows: since providing all the women's teams top-tier treatment was out of the question, then to keep treatment relatively equal, none of the women's teams would be treated like top-tier men's sports. And treating teams equally within the men's program would have been considered ludicrous. By 1978, pursuing sports revenue had become a nearly unquestioned good within the NCAA and college athletics, even before ESPN and March Madness had entered the picture.

In August 1978, however, Kearney was not yet likely to have been thinking about supporting "a deal with the devil" for selected women's sports. Gwen Norrell, the new MSU faculty representative to the NCAA, was not even acknowledging that discrimination against women athletes existed at MSU. When asked about sex discrimination pointedly in an August 20, 1978, interview, she dodged the question. Even though she was a member of the athletic department's affirmative action committee charged with addressing Title IX, she claimed not to have seen the women's basketball team's complaint and was "really not certain how much substance there [was] to it."[31] She implied that "discrimination" *per se* was not the issue when she stated, "I don't know how you support everything as well as everyone always wants." Ultimately, she concluded that the courts would need to decide what Title IX required, and they would "just have to wait and see."[32]

Norrell's noncommittal, unsupportive stance may have reflected her own new rhetorical situation as a female pioneer among the men of the NCAA. Years later, she wrote that when she became the faculty representative, she expected that some of her male peers would likely accept her, while others would "adopt a 'wait and see' attitude." Especially in her first year, taking a strong position supporting women athletes and their rights under Title IX would not have endeared her to the male coaches who needed to "feel comfortable about coming to her" to make rule interpretations.[33] As Bruce Alexander observed, for women administrators in particular, "Many of them were in situations where any advocacy—anything other than 'I'm doing my job based on what I've been told to do right now'—would've been difficult, perhaps personally and professionally."[34] For Alexander, that realization made it critical that individuals in the group supporting the women's basketball complaint "weren't asking people to have to step over a line that they weren't comfortable [with]." Alexander explained that the team's supporters wanted to allow Coach Langeland and Assistant Director of Women's Athletics Jackson to focus on their roles as coach and administrator, respectively. Then, they would not be in a position of "saying one thing publically and doing something else privately."[35] In part because of this protective impulse, as the women's basketball team contemplated legal action, they still did not consider turning to either Norrell or Lou Anna

Simon for assistance. In a 2011 interview, Alexander said he did not imagine that these influential women leaders "would have felt terribly badly about the fact that they weren't being asked to be involved."[36] In making that assumption, he miscalculated both gender and university politics.

Waiting and Weighing Alternatives

Pittman clipped, noted, and filed the article in which Norrell commented on the women's basketball team's complaint. Her comments could not have encouraged him or the players to place further trust in a system they felt had already betrayed them with Pollock's termination. After consulting with DeBoer (who was in Portland, Oregon, at the time), Pittman had a follow-up phone conversation with attorney Marcia Greenberger regarding the women's basketball team's complaint and next steps. Greenberger said her colleagues would look over the complaint and get back in touch, but she thought "an independent suit might be best for immediate action."[37]

With this advice to weigh, a few days later, DeBoer and Mankowski received a letter from MSU's Sallie Bright with the ADJB. Her letter, like Norrell's comments, inspired little faith in the system at MSU. Bright's first sentence conveyed tentativeness, vagueness, and lack of direction. She noted technicalities that could be problematic and may need to be considered in a review.[38] The passive voice, nominalizations, and jargon in the letter's second paragraph created a tone that communicated a lack of will to move forward with a focused investigation. These language choices reflect a bureaucratic style that obscures meaning and must have conveyed to DeBoer and Mankowski a sense of inertia."[39]

Buried in a long third paragraph, Bright did inform them (again in the passive voice) that efforts were being made to address problems with lockers and practice facilities.[40] However, this assurance of progress was sandwiched between two discouraging statements. The first informed them that recent opinions from HEW indicated that matching funds would likely not be required; the second stated that it would be impossible to determine what actions the university needed to take. Bright's concluding sentence was no more promising. She wrote that her office would continue to work on understanding the problem and keep them informed.[41] Bright's cumbersome, noncommittal discourse contrasted sharply with what the team experienced with Pollock. Still, Bright's letter mentioned that the MSU ADJB might review the situation at its September meeting, so the women's basketball team and its supporters had another month to wait for further news.

Welcome Week 1978

Pittman retained four copies of the August 21, 1978, letter from Bright in his files, suggesting it held some importance as he and the others digested its content and tone. If the group also looked to other sources for signs of the athletic department's attitude toward gender equality at the time, they could find a not-too-subtle hint in a fall 1978 Welcome Week statement by athletics director Joe Kearney. Kearney's column, "Spartan Sports Scene," applauded the MSU football and basketball coaches for earning Coach of the Year recognition in the Big Ten (the award went to the MSU football coach even though the team was still on probation for NCAA rules violations). In fact, being on probation for cheating was, apparently, nothing to be ashamed of or downplayed. (Kearney wrote, with enthusiasm, that "coming up is the final football season in which the Spartans will be on probation. Fan interest is on the rise and decided upswing in season ticket sales is anticipated.") In contrast, Title IX apparently posed a real problem. Echoing his earlier words to VIP parking pass recipients, Kearney wrote, "We need your support, both in terms of season ticket purchases and donations to the Ralph Young Fund. Inflation and increased costs for the women's program due to the so-called 'Title Nine' have put the total varsity sports program in an economic bind."[42]

MSU's Welcome Week edition of the *State News* described prospects for the Spartans' two basketball teams. An article describing the incredible turnaround of the men's program quoted "Magic" stating his goals: "My goal is to just win games, the Big Ten and national title. These are my goals for next year and they are the same for every season."[43] For the women's team, the big news was that they would be playing "in a permanent home." A press release touted the fact that "[a]ll Spartan home contests will be in the Men's IM Sports Arena."[44] While having a permanent location for home games marked an improvement, it was a bittersweet sign of progress considering that permanent location was an intramural building with a floor prone to warping in some weather conditions. But the university did paint a large "S" on the middle of the court that nevertheless remained a smaller, less impressive space than many high school gymnasiums.

In the fall, a press release from the MSU athletic department referenced another challenge for women's athletics at the time. The release mentioned a "mythical Big Ten Championship" to be held at the end of the season and hosted by the University of Minnesota. As Hardy recalled, because women's teams competed under the AIAW, they weren't actually part of the Big Ten, hence the term "mythical." When the MSU volleyball team that she and DeBoer played on won the 1975 "mythical" Big Ten championship, they were awarded a University of Minnesota keychain for their accomplishment. The token award provided a not too subtle, though probably unintentional, reminder that the championship was insignificant to anyone not closely associated with the team.[45] Readers of the MSU press guide unfamiliar with the different governing bodies for men's and women's sports must have puzzled over the term "mythical." The reference marked yet another way in which invisibility and confusion plagued the progress of women's athletics programs.

Just as puzzling, the women's basketball three-fold brochure for 1978–79 featured a picture of DeBoer grabbing a rebound in an empty Jenison Fieldhouse. DeBoer, of course, had graduated, so the decision to use her image seems strange. Nevertheless, by doing so, the brochure inadvertently highlighted the primary spokesperson for the women's basketball team's continuing, off-court battle over sex equality (another kind of "mythical" championship, perhaps). The men's program for 1977–78 had also broken with tradition by featuring a photo of the senior co-captains that included for the first time a freshman player, "Magic" Johnson. In 1978–79, Johnson appeared on the brochure again, this time with senior Gregory Kelser, with both of them seated beneath the iconic statue of "Sparty" on the MSU campus.[46] The contrast between the two brochures signified which team the college sports-following community viewed as the real Spartans.

As both MSU basketball teams anticipated their new seasons, DeBoer unexpectedly returned for a few days to East Lansing. On September 15, Pittman had spent the day at a conference held at MSU's Kellogg Center on "The Status of Title IX Compliance in State Universities and Colleges." When he returned home after a day full of presentations, Pittman found "a great surprise: KDB [DeBoer] sat reading in the front room." After recapping her summer of volleyball, DeBoer shared her big news. She had decided to try out for professional basketball in Milwaukee. With excitement, Pittman wrote, "She's going to tryouts next weekend. We start training immediately—running, strengthening, and basketball."[47]

As they made plans, Pittman caught DeBoer up on "all the Title IX stuff."[48] Just that afternoon he had met one of the attorneys who had been recommended, by then twice, to the women's basketball team: Jean Ledwith King. At the time, female attorneys—much less feminist civil rights attorneys—were rare. Finding a civil rights advocate who was making a name for herself right there in Michigan must have made the idea of taking legal action begin to seem like a real possibility.

Jean Ledwith King at MSU

On the printed schedule for the Title IX conference, King was scheduled to speak in the afternoon from two o'clock to four o'clock, and Pollock's name appeared on the program in the morning for a talk entitled "Employment and Affirmative Action." Although Pittman knew nothing of King's past involvement as an advisor to Vicki Nyberg and the Alliance to End Sexual Discrimination at MSU, he certainly recognized her name. It had, after all, topped his friend's list of recommended attorneys for the MSU women's basketball team. After her talk, Pittman recorded his impression of King in two words: "very impressive." His next step was to talk with Pollock for a few minutes, catching her up on what was going on and explaining their "lull of activity." Pollock told him that she thought she could arrange a meeting for the team with King.[49]

With her talk on "The Developing Law of Sex Discrimination in Athletics," King provided a two-page handout that identified a range of legal tools for addressing sex discrimination, including state legislation (the Michigan Civil Rights Act and the Public Accommodations Act of 1972), federal legislation (Title IX of the Education Act of 1972 and Title VI of the Civil Rights Act of 1964, by analogy), and the Constitution (the equal protection clause, the due process clause, and the proposed Equal Rights Amendment). According to the outline provided on the handout, King discussed state ERAs and equal protection clauses as legal tools to fight sex discrimination. And she covered a range of issues surrounding lawsuits—from attorney fees, to individual liability of school officials, to the psychology of appealing to judges in sex discrimination cases. Pittman wrote down that, according to King, judges (invariably males) could often "identify with sports cases in their gut." He recorded King's observation that a judge's gut feelings were extremely important for an attorney to consider in crafting a case.[50] These jottings suggest that Pittman was impressed with King's rhetorical abilities in audience analysis.

Pittman's notes further portray King's understanding of the rhetorical principal of identification, thought by rhetorician Kenneth Burke to be the key to successful persuasion.[51] Pittman recorded that, according to King, male attorneys could often identify with girls' desire to participate in sports, especially if they had daughters or had coached girls. Such identification, on the part of both judges and attorneys, could be critical for a successful case. King used the example of Ann Arbor attorney Lawrence Sperling to suggest that attorneys with daughters themselves could most easily identify with a sports discrimination case; it was Sperling, after all, who had first suggested to King that athletics could be an important arena for feminist legal action.

Finally, King's handout noted that discrimination in athletics limited career training opportunities, and it identified "athletics as a vehicle for caste distinctions in American society."[52] Her choice of the term "caste" is an example of the provocative metaphors with which she often peppered her discourse, lending shock value to her rhetorical style. Though hyperbole, King emphasized that skills and networking opportunities obtained through athletics can provide a means for upward social mobility, but this avenue for advancement is unavailable to individuals who are unfairly excluded from athletic opportunities.

Based on his copious notes, Pittman listened as attentively to other speakers as he did to King. He took notes on King's talk on the back of an order form for the SPRINT publication on Title IX and athletics, *In the Running*. On that form were more of Pittman's notes, these taken from the talk preceding King's by SPRINT project director Marguerite Beck-Rex, who spoke on "Athletics: Current Status and Future Perspectives." On the form, SPRINT requested that people submit their comments on a variety of topics: scholarships, recruitment, athletic association rules (including basketball), assessing equality of opportunity, contact sports (next to which Pittman wrote "cover-up for discrimination"), comparable facilities, interests and abilities (Pittman's comment was "athletics socialization"), scope of remedy, physical education department mergers ("not seriously considered yet" was Pittman's note), coaches' pay, and officials' pay. The list suggested the topics HEW wrestled with at the time (the note above the list stated that an HEW committee was "currently debating Title IX policy on the following issues").[53] The range of items reflected uncertainties still circulating around Title IX in 1978. It was a law with yet-unpublished policy interpretations, a law untested in the courts—a law without teeth. Its status, in short, was uncertain. Thus, as King pointed out, a whole gamut of legal tools were available and necessary to combat sex discrimination, not just Title IX.

We Need More Help

In the month after Pittman met King, neither he nor DeBoer followed up on Pollock's offer to help put them in touch with the attorney. They were waiting to hear news from MSU, and Pittman was working out with DeBoer as she prepared to fly to Milwaukee for her tryout. He also attended a Division of Girls and Women's Sports clinic in Pennsylvania and visited friends at West Point, learning about their weight training program. By the time Pittman returned to East Lansing, DeBoer had been to Milwaukee and back. She had good news: she made the team. Always one of her biggest fans, Pittman wasn't surprised. He wrote, "What's new? Talent is talent pure and simple."[54]

On October 11, DeBoer's hometown newspaper, the *Grand Rapids Press*, ran an article in which she reflected on her decision to sign a modest contract with the Does (just enough to live on for the five-month season, according to DeBoer). She observed, "Attitudes about women in athletics are finally starting to change in this country. People are beginning to find out that it's okay for us to sweat. It doesn't detract from our femininity."[55] At the same time, she acknowledged that as a professional, she had an added responsibility to help sell women's basketball. It was a new idea, she said, to think of herself as a commodity, but she offered her ideas about how to make a case for women's sports with the public. After acknowledging that she couldn't jump as high and wasn't as strong as a man, she contended, "That doesn't mean I'm not the best I can be." She offered an analogy to weight classes in boxing or wrestling, arguing that just because a 125-pound man can't compete with a heavyweight, people don't say, "The lighter man isn't any good." People realize that "they compete in their own weight class."[56]

DeBoer also observed that as women's sports continued to improve, as a five-foot-ten-inch forward, she was "becoming obsolete"; as more women played the game, the height of players available to play each position increased.[57] The coaching that women received was improving, although most of the first professional WBL players never received the same level of skill instruction and performance expectations experienced by men's high school and college players.[58] Even though many women coaches were just adapting to more competitive play, DeBoer was pleased that her WBL coach was a woman. She felt that a woman would better understand what it meant to continually get the message that sports were not (and shouldn't be) important for girls and women. DeBoer believed that her new coach, as the only female coach in the new league, would be able to relate to the experiences of players unused to the "external rewards . . . that aren't there yet for women."[59] In the new league, at least, DeBoer would finally compete in the same facility as her male counterparts. She noted that the Does would play in the same arena as the Milwaukee

Bucks, the men's NBA team. The women's first game on December 9, 1978, would be the first professional women's basketball game ever played in the United States. Organizers of the WBL's first game made plans with an eye to history, well aware that between 1869 and 1896, the city had also hosted the United States' first professional baseball, football, and men's basketball games.[60]

Despite her possibly historic new career in professional basketball, DeBoer's mind was still mostly on her primary sporting interest: volleyball. Referring to the place where some of the MSU players lived in East Lansing, Pittman called it "volleyball mania at the Oasis."[61] DeBoer also felt deeply concerned about the status of the MSU team's sex discrimination complaint. In mid-October, just as the baseball World Series was underway (duly noted in Pittman's "Chronology"), Pittman, Alexander, DeBoer, and Mankowski met at Cookie's place. They felt frustrated by "internal delays" by the university, which they viewed as "a tactic of waiting us out so we'll disappear." But, Pittman wrote, "Little do those fools know." He had no intention of giving up.[62]

Mankowski had been in touch with Pollock, and Pittman heard from Jackson that President Harden had the athletics department's affirmative action report. However, Jackson wouldn't give Pittman a copy of the report. Stymied by a lack of information and little action, Pittman concluded, "We need more help." They agreed that Mankowski would write to Sallie Bright at the MSU ADJB and to President Harden. On October 23, Pittman noted, "MM [Mankowski] completes letters, I make copies and she sends them to there [sic] designated places."[63]

Mankowski's letters simply referenced the last correspondence and reminded Bright and Harden of their promises to keep her and the team updated. Soon after Mankowski sent the letters, Pollock called. On October 24, after they spoke, Pittman noted, "We are to have a meeting with Jean King at her home in ANN ARBOR. This is to be tomorrow night." So the next evening, DeBoer, Mankowski, Carol Hutchins, Pollock, Alexander, and Pittman drove to Ann Arbor together. The meeting, in Pittman's words, was "very low key." They gave King copies of the complaints, described their backgrounds, and answered some questions. Pittman concluded that "all were impressed," adding that "Hutchie finally [got] her feet wet with the political nature of the struggle." He noted with emphasis, "No money issues were discussed!"[64]

Playing with the Boys?

For DeBoer, the tone of the meeting may have been low key, but King's questions troubled her. Over the years, she carried with her one enduring memory of the first time she met Jean Ledwith King. She recalled that King had pointedly asked the women, "Can you play with Magic Johnson?" Then, DeBoer continued, "She started asking lots of questions about boys playing on girls' teams and just having one competition—having competition that's open to everyone." She talked about "just having one team and all the girls and boys try out for the same team." DeBoer explained that King "wasn't a sports person so much as she was a civil rights activist and attorney." For her, "it was like, this is a great idea— we'll just have one team, and everybody gets to play on it." Making a sad, horrified face, DeBoer remembered her first thought: "Well, it'll only be boys." And Pittman interjected, "Yeah, just Magic Johnson and his guys." To sum up her assessment of the interchange with King, DeBoer concluded, "So she was giving us credit for being that good, and we were like—Naaah."[65]

King's questions about sex-integrated teams may have reflected her reservations from a liberal feminist perspective about Title IX's separate but equal approach. Or she was simply trying to understand her potential clients' goals. Possibly, they reflected her standpoint as a woman who, as an adolescent, was "younger, smaller, and shorter than [her] classmates," both males and females. According to King, because of her smaller physical stature, she "wasn't competitive in sports."[66] Of course, metaphorically speaking, the law is a highly adversarial "sport." And when King attended law school, she was among a minority of female attorneys (in 1965, she was one of just ten women in her University of Michigan law school class). In that situation, she gained experience competing verbally and academically with and against men.[67] Still, physiological sex differences in weight, strength, and height matter when boxing out for a rebound in basketball. And while bodily rhetoric plays a role in courtroom and classroom discourse, physical sex differences have a less clear and obvious impact than they would in an intercollegiate basketball game. King, like many feminists of her day, had not personally experienced high-level competition in a contact sport with men or other women. Without that personal experience, mixed-sex teams could have seemed more feasible to her than they did to the MSU women's basketball players. After all, King felt that she couldn't compete with larger and taller women in athletics any more than she could with men. In the same way, few males in the United States could actually hold their own on a basketball court with Magic Johnson or with other Spartan men's basketball players.[68]

For her part, Hutchins recalled that King asked a lot of questions about "what the men got and what the women got."[69] Although nearly forty years later, Hutchins could not recall specifics, like DeBoer, she found some of King's questions puzzling. They made her wonder whether the attorney knew anything about basketball. But Hutchins figured it probably didn't matter whether she really knew the sport.[70] Still the question remained: if they filed suit, what exactly did they want to see happen? The MSU women already had a team and the opportunity to play college ball— something none of them took for granted. For Hutchins, only occasional playdays had been available in basketball until her senior year at Lansing Everett High School. Then, for the first time, she had the opportunity to play a full season of interscholastic competition. In Hutchins's senior year of high school, she and freshman student Earvin Johnson (not yet known as "Magic") were the top male and female athletes at the school. However, the opportunities provided for them to develop as athletes were worlds apart. Most strikingly, the school offered no softball team, so the future national championship college coach could not compete in her best sport in high school. There was no team for the entire four years.[71] At MSU, by contrast, Hutchins and her teammates found an impressive quantity of participation opportunities, but equal treatment lagged behind. As King recalled, "The total amount of money available for athletics per school tended to stay the same even though female teams had been added. This slowed progress."[72]

In 1978, King had limited experience with sex discrimination in sport cases, as did most attorneys at the time. In the experience she did have, she had focused on the rights of school-aged girls rather than college women. In high school situations, usually girls either wanted an opportunity to play on boys' teams, or they sought to have a girls' team created. In fact, King's colleague Lawrence Sperling had filed a groundbreaking Fourteenth Amendment lawsuit in 1972 on behalf of a girl who wanted to join the Ann Arbor Union High School tennis team, a team restricted by a Michigan High School Athletic Association rule to boys only. The district judge invalidated the rule and ordered a preliminary injunction. The case, which broadened to a class action including all girls in the state, influenced the Michigan legislature to pass a statute effective in the spring of 1973. The law, Public Act No. 138, states that female students must be allowed to participate in all noncontact interscholastic activities, including vying for a position on a boys' team if no team exists for girls. A year later, in 1974, King became involved in her first case involving sex discrimination in sport law.[73]

In the 1974 case, King claimed Title IX as a cause of action when representing Julie Alexander, who wanted to join the track team at Mona Shores High School. By that time, cases involving school-aged girls seeking to compete on boys' teams had been filed around the country. Most of these cases filed after 1972 claimed both the Fourteenth Amendment and Title IX as causes of action. Public awareness of a new "sports law" called Title IX often mobilized female athletes—and their fathers—to make inquiries. In King's experience, fathers (more than mothers) helped girls pursue their sports aspirations and sex discrimination claims; often these were men with no sons with whom they could share their enthusiasm for athletics.[74]

Repeatedly, however, Title IX was ruled powerless. Even though it motivated lawsuits, the public bestowed on Title IX "mythic power" it did not possess.[75] Sports historian Sarah Fields pointed out in *Female Gladiators* that judges routinely dismissed the Title IX cause of action, ruling that "the language of Title IX did not provide individuals with a clear right to sue and that even if individuals did have that right, they must have first exhausted administrative remedies."[76] Therefore, the Constitution's Fourteenth Amendment filled the gaps in Title IX law that the public did not even know existed.[77]

But factors apart from the law itself also came into play. In the absence of legal precedents, cases turned on judges' instincts, their close reading of particular cases, and their own "personal beliefs and attitudes about sports and women." Some court opinions supported separation rights for girls; others denounced them.[78] For contact sports such as basketball and especially football, the challenge of overcoming stereotypes and prejudices was particularly great. As Fields observed, sports deemed the most "manly" generated the most lawsuits because "protecting the masculine integrity of these games has been important to protecting the masculine integrity of America."[79]

These challenges did not deter King from taking further sports cases, especially after her first case was settled out of court to her client's satisfaction. In a subsequent 1975 case, she represented the daughter of a wrestling coach who wanted to compete in the Eastern Amateur Athletic Union meet, an all-boys event. In that case, because the AAU did not receive federal funds, Title IX did not apply, so King filed under the Fourteenth Amendment. In addition, a new legal tool in 1976, the Elliot-Larsen Civil Rights Act, which prohibited sex discrimination in education and public accommodations, supported King's and other attorneys' efforts. So by the time King met with the MSU women's basketball team in 1978, she was building a name for herself in sports discrimination law. But the country had not yet seen a court decision under Title IX, and cases at the college level were virtually nonexistent.[80]

Davidina versus Goliath

College sports posed an arguably even greater challenge than cases involving school-aged girls. With revenue sports and the money they generated in the picture, American masculinity was not the only or even the most important thing at stake. As Lopiano put it, each time women athletes took on large institutions, it was "Davidina versus Goliath." Compared with high schools or junior highs, universities had deep pockets and prized their autonomy. Therefore, as Lopiano recalled, the women's legal community began organizing, working out a strategy to advance the overall goals of the movement for girls' and women's sports.[81] Part of that strategy involved identifying test cases, as Pittman and DeBoer had learned from speaking with Marcia Greenberger at the Center for Law and Social Policy.

In 1978, feminist attorneys needed collective strategies for the nearly impossible situation in which they and their clients found themselves. Without question, taking on a large university like MSU was a tall order, especially for a small law office with just a single attorney. Still, King presented a possible source of help for the MSU women Spartans. She had heard their story, and she had not brought up the matter of money. So the group that met her in Ann Arbor felt hopeful.[82]

Orienting the New Team

Before DeBoer traveled back to join her new teammates in Milwaukee, Bruce Alexander suggested that someone needed to explain the complaint to the newly constituted MSU women's basketball team. They had made final cuts and in the process of holding tryouts had added two new players: Nanette "Net" Gibson, a forward from Saginaw, Michigan, and Deb Traxinger, a point guard from Wyoming, Michigan.

The additions of Gibson and Traxinger to the 1978–79 MSU women's basketball team reflected the workings of what the AIAW policies termed "talent assessment" in an era during which the AIAW forbade formalized recruiting for women. Coaches formed their college teams primarily from in-state students (most of them would have attended the university as students even if they hadn't played an intercollegiate sport). Traxinger recalled that Gibson had not come to MSU planning to play basketball. After enrolling as a student, she tried out for the team. In her, the Spartans gained a player, Traxinger said, who "didn't back down from anything and knew how to win."[83] The last thing either of them expected, of course, was that before they even played a game or finished their first quarter of classes, they would be asked to join a sex equality struggle.

Although Mankowski was not on the 1978–79 women's basketball team, she and Pollock had stayed in touch, exchanging ideas about the ongoing situation.[84] Mankowski also waited for a response to the letter she had written to President Harden and to the ADJB. In East Lansing, as she prepared to leave town, DeBoer visited for a few days with her parents, who had traveled to MSU for a football game and picnic (ironically not a women's basketball or volleyball game). Until just before she left, she continued her close involvement with the women's basketball complaint; in fact, she participated in an interview about it for the University of Michigan student newspaper. When she and Pittman made a quick trip to Ann Arbor so she could referee a volleyball match, they picked up a copy of the paper. In it, they learned a bit of what was going on at MSU. They read that Sallie Bright was waiting for the university's legal audit to be completed and that she had "a very secure feeling for the women's basketball team."[85]

According to the article, Bright felt that "all [the team's] problems will be taken care of."[86] She was also reportedly waiting for HEW to send her a copy of the complaint filed there. The article quoted Underwood explaining that the MSU athletic department was studying Title IX requirements in general but not the women's basketball complaint specifically. And DeBoer expressed the team's frustration with the process: "It seems to us that the University is hoping that since this is a new year, everyone will have just forgotten about the whole issue. There is an obvious hierarchy of importance, and we are at the bottom." She concluded bluntly, "Not only is that unfair, it is illegal." Yet she insisted that the team was being realistic, just looking for signs of "a commitment from someone at the university towards women's basketball, and women's athletics in general." She framed the scope of the problem and solution broadly, lamenting, "No one seems committed to change, and there is so much that could be done to help MSU athletics." The headline on the second page of the article inaccurately declared "Women Cagers Sue," reflecting how easily misinformation could spread. Contradictorily, the article also stated that the team awaited word from "several lawyers" with whom they had spoken.[87] They were, in fact, still waiting to hear from Marcia Greenberger about whether they might have a suitable test case for Title IX. And, of course, they had just met with Jean Ledwith King.

A few days after the trip to Ann Arbor, after a farewell dinner with friends, DeBoer departed. In her absence, Alexander talked with Lori Hyman—co-captain of the 1978–79 team, along with Hutchins—to "give her an idea of what's been going on with the complaint." Pittman noted, "She's enthusiastic." Then Mankowski spoke with the entire 1978–79 women's basketball team about the sex discrimination complaint. She obtained copies of the ADJB and OCR complaints from Pittman and gave them to the team to "read and study."[88] As the team was brought up to speed, the individuals who had met face-to-face with King looked forward to hearing from her—and wondered whether she would want to take their case.

Due to conflicting schedules, a full month passed before team members met with King a second time. During that month, Mankowski had a phone conversation with Bright from MSU's ADJB, and Pittman was "forcefully buttonholed" by Bright for forty-five minutes at a Women's Booster Club wine and cheese party. She accused Pittman of writing the ADJB complaint, to which he replied "NOT ME!!" as he "set her straight in a hurry." According to Pittman's notes, she asked him to help "her figure out a way to get 'the institution' and 'her' off the hook." In response to that request, he jotted in parentheses "GOOD LUCK," but he agreed to meet. The following week, keeping in mind a warning from Jackson that Bright was shrewd and after consulting with DeBoer by phone, Pittman and Alexander met with Bright.[89]

On November 22, in Bright's office, they learned that the athletic department's affirmative action report and the legal audit were complete and being circulated. Having been warned about her possible ulterior motives, Pittman doubted Bright's sincerity when she asked for his assistance "doing interpretive work on the two reports" in order to make her own report to Lou Anna Simon. A little more than a week earlier, the *MSU Bulletin* had announced that Simon had been tapped to fill a new position that included Pollock's former responsibilities for affirmative action and Title IX. In the article, Simon distinguished herself from Pollock, describing herself as "not a sign carrier" or "protester." As the author of the *Bulletin* article put it, Simon was "an unlikely sort to be in the center of a storm of controversy." In fact, Simon saw herself as a problem-solver who would apply "research, study and communication" to the position. She observed that "the strong advocacy role of particular groups serves to identify problems very well, but it doesn't necessarily serve to get them solved."[90] Pittman noted that Bright described Simon as "'the star,' or at least the person who is trying to be the 'star,' in this whole matter."[91]

As for herself, Bright claimed not to know enough about intercollegiate athletics to interpret the reports, neither of which specifically addressed problems in the complaint. She told them that "she was responsible for new changes for women's athletics" and "wanted very much for the women's basketball team to receive equal treatment." However, warned ahead of time about Bright's sincerity, Pittman left the meeting skeptical of her motives, especially when she would not let them have copies of the two reports. Instead, she asked them to return the following week to work with her and her assistant. Of course, they would have liked nothing more than to have had those reports to take with them as they traveled with Hardy to Kokomo, Indiana, where they spent Thanksgiving at Alexander's family home.

Legal Audit and Title IX Committee Report

As it turned out, Pittman and Alexander never returned to Bright's office. When they called her after the break, she apologetically told them that Bryon Higgins advised her not to let them see the reports. So they never saw them. Today, however, a report to the MSU Board of Trustees based on the legal audit and affirmative action report from the athletics department's Title IX committee report can be found in the MSU institutional archives.[92] As Bright indicated, the women's basketball team's complaints were not mentioned specifically in either the legal audit or Title IX committee report. In his summary report for the board, MSU attorney Higgins criticized the vagueness of HEW's guidelines in espousing "a 'reasonable approach' to equality." He highlighted conflicting rules between the AIAW and NCAA that "permit different treatment between male and female athletes under Title IX." Most notably, he continued to insist that the men's revenue-producing sports must be emphasized. This time he offered a new reason: he claimed that although "the level of competition of the women's program is equal to the entire men's program," the men's program must be self-supporting. Therefore, he concluded once again that the men's "revenue-producing" sports must continue to receive special treatment.[93]

It was unclear from the report whether anyone within the institution questioned that premise. Unlike at the University of Texas-Austin, where women's athletics director Lopiano responded to a similar rhetorical situation by insisting that women's sports must share responsibility for generating needed funds, MSU women's athletics director Jackson did not. Perhaps Jackson felt more invested in the AIAW model of equality among sports than Lopiano, or she was simply unable to marshal the rhetorical resources to make the seemingly contradictory argument that an educational model of sport could include increased revenue production efforts. Jackson may also have been more concerned with a need to belong and be accepted in the culture of the MSU athletic department. With her past experiences of exclusion and discrimination as a racial minority, fitting in—belonging—was likely an even greater concern for her than it would have been for a nonminority woman in her position. And, as she told colleagues years later, throughout her career, she never knew for certain when she herself was facing subtle discrimination based on her race, sex, or both.[94]

With no one individual who represented women's athletics gaining a forum for advocacy, Higgins faced little contestation when he offered his (partial) interpretation of Title IX, with the gravitas conferred by the term "legal audit" authorizing his discourse. He continued to assume that a meaningful goal was for the women's sports program to achieve equality with the nonrevenue men's program, despite instructions from HEW that all sports were to be included in Title IX. Despite ignoring HEW's policy regarding revenue sports, the recommendations Higgins forwarded to the board from the Title IX committee included some movement toward more equitable treatment. He reported that the Title IX committee recommended an eighty thousand dollar budget increase for women's sports for 1978–79, along with five scholarships added each year for five years beginning in 1980–81.[95] The committee recommended reviewing scheduling of practice and event facilities and allocated fifty thousand dollars to improve "facilities for the women's program in the area of field hockey, lockers in Jenison, equipment area for women in Jenison, and to construct a softball fence and backstop."[96] It also advised establishing a standing committee to monitor Title IX. Among these investments in women's sports, the Title IX committee made one major recommendation: an administrative reorganization of the athletics department to create more centralization to ensure equitable treatment for both programs. The proposed change was framed positively: to support the goal of "equal opportunity for the women's program to communicate and participate in department decisions." However, the reorganization sounded a lot like the "submerger" of women's sports under men's sports that was a frequent response to Title IX and feared by many women's athletics directors. It did not appear to be good news for Nell Jackson.

As the MSU Board digested the latest reports regarding Title IX and treatment of women's sports, the growing excitement surrounding men's basketball may have discouraged a serious examination of the continuing assumption that men's basketball, football, and hockey could somehow be exempted from Title IX. In November 1978, *Sports Illustrated*, the most-read sports publication in the country, featured Earvin "Magic" Johnson on its cover. The cover exclaimed, "The Super Sophs" with the subtitle, "Michigan State's Classy Earvin Johnson." Meanwhile, the women's basketball team continued to feel that their complaints went unaddressed. On October 27, Mankowski had received a letter from President Harden in response to her inquiry and request to talk with him. He told her to meet with the university attorney, Higgins. Feeling once again put off, the team members wanted badly to see some sign of being heard. By that point, they were more interested in hearing from their potential advocate, attorney King, than in meeting with the university attorney. The MSU administrators seemed to be endlessly passing the buck—or promising yet another report.

King Will Run the Show

Looking back in 2011, DeBoer observed that the situation would not have continued to escalate if only the MSU administration had brought some of the women's basketball players into their self-evaluation and interpretive process. If, for example, Mankowski, DeBoer, Hutchins, or even Pittman as a coach had been invited to serve on the Title IX committee, they would have felt a part of the process. An administrator at the time (who asked not to be named) added another perspective: Because President Harden was an interim president, he would not need to live with the results of the controversy. His interim status probably contributed to the lack of genuine attempts to engage in a relationship-building process with the student athletes who filed complaints. By excluding all the complainants from the process, each side could assume the worst about the other. Gradually, the team moved toward court. Hutchins recalled later that, even when they first traveled to meet King, she had no idea that the team would actually file a lawsuit. Although the team had not yet made the decision to sue, a second face-to-face meeting with King moved them a step closer to court.

On November 29, King met Pollock, Alexander, Hutchins, Hyman, Traxinger, and Mary Vielbig in Pittman's office at MSU. (Vielbig was a center on the basketball team who was becoming more involved in the process.) In his notes, Pittman wrote that the meeting was "straight to the point and very good."[97] King warned the team that their coach would probably be fired and offered a lesson in power plays. Pittman summed up King's message, perhaps filtered through some of his own philosophy as well: "The institution looks to all possible sources outside (this could be internal) of itself to point the blame. It is a tactic to keep the 'weak' in place. Divide and rule, as it were."[98] This sort of discourse demonized the university, as social movement rhetoric often does to the establishment; it constructed MSU administrators as the enemy, a foil to the team's own collective identity as change agents, not as a partner they would need to work with in a longer-term relationship. As rhetorician Richard Gregg noted, foils "serve as rallying points" and "reference points" for shared notions of group identity, "painting the enemy in dark hued imagery."[99] Simultaneously, rhetoric of attack can serve an ego-building function, instilling self-confidence in relatively powerless groups asserting their rights. These negative characterizations of the opposition can become— for whichever side that chooses to adopt them—a form of self-persuasion, providing confirmation that they are morally superior and justified in their own actions.[100]

Since the players had already lost faith in MSU's administration, they were receptive to negative representatives of a university that they found unresponsive. They also felt drawn to King, a confident, clear-spoken woman, as a potential advocate. However, as Pittman put it, those present were "woken up" a bit by King's warning. If her perspective assumed an adversarial relationship, that was perhaps to be expected from an attorney. Yet there was no talk about how a legal battle might affect the women's basketball team or its coach in future years, even if she was protected from losing her job in the short run. No one expressed concern about the women's basketball program's future relationship to the institution's decision makers; sizing up the immediate threats was the focus. As the meeting concluded, King instructed those present to check with other team members and decide if they wanted to hire her as their attorney, with one condition: Pollock needed to understand that she, Jean Ledwith King, would run the show.[101]

The next day, the team met and agreed to hire King. They still did not talk of fees, their ability to pay, or even what exactly they wanted her to do. When Pittman called King to give her the news, she requested another meeting as soon as possible. With a few phone calls, they set the meeting for final exam week, December 3, at Hutch's place. Pittman and Alexander began scouring the MSU library's records for information on the athletic department budgets. Pittman also sent King copies of his report on scholarships, which he still considered the most critical area of inequality, but he decided that it would be better for him not to join the others at Hutch's. Although Alexander and Mankowski both planned to attend, Pittman wrote, "It is the team's meeting."[102] Pollock too had stepped aside, and the team placed their struggle in the hands of Jean Ledwith King.

15 Fast-Forward

As the MSU women's basketball team turned their struggle over to attorney Jean Ledwith King, a second part of their story was just beginning. Of course, neither the story of the MSU women's basketball team nor the impact of Title IX and its associated rhetoric ended there. The behind-the-scenes social and institutional change rhetoric that shaped college sports lawsuits deserves its own fine-grained rhetorical analysis—one that falls beyond the scope of this book. But a quick fast-forward through subsequent events provides a broad sketch of how the *Hutchins* case came to be filed and a glimpse into how its extended denouement played out during a formative period for higher education sports law. The 1980s— often dismissed as the "dark ages" of Title IX's history—is nevertheless a period that included the groundbreaking *Haffer v. Temple University* case, the demise of the AIAW, the *Grove City College v. Bell* Supreme Court decision that exempted athletics from the purview of Title IX, the 1986 Civil Rights Equalization Act (which precluded universities from arguing Eleventh Amendment Immunity in Title IX cases, thereby opening the door for monetary damages), and the Civil Rights Restoration Act (which reinstated athletics within the statute's scope).[1]

By summing up the localized story of the *Hutchins* case alongside this larger history, I offer a context for further study of how discourse employed in Title IX's first decades fundamentally shaped activism and advocacy into the twenty-first century. "The rest of the story" is also an important bridge to the present and future. A sense of this history is necessary to really understand what it took in the 1970s and 1980s, and what is still required, to achieve the full promise of Title IX and to understand more deeply that passing a law only begins a rhetorical process. That process requires hundreds—even thousands—of individuals to interpret, implement, and communicate the requirements of a statute. A primary message of this book has been that the sometimes complicated narratives of ordinary people's courage too easily disappear behind simpler narratives that credit government initiatives—such as the passage of a law or a court decision—for creating change. As Congresswoman Edith Green, an influential, early advocate for Title IX, was known to remark, "The trouble with every generation is that they haven't read the minutes of the last meeting."[2]

A Legal Strategy

In the summer of 1978, when all the MSU women's basketball team members indicated their willingness to persist in their struggle, attorney King began devising a legal strategy. No Title IX precedent existed for King to consult; to her knowledge, no one had yet taken a Title IX violation related to college athletics to court. No one knew how the courts would view Title IX cases and clients with no funds to pay legal fees. Critical questions loomed. Do individuals actually have a right to legal action under Title IX? Could universities be held liable for damages? Would a case comparing two teams—rather than the entire men's and women's programs—be successful under Title IX? Would the law be found to apply to all educational programs, or would athletics be exempted because they receive federal funds indirectly? And, not incidentally, how long could a small law firm with clients who couldn't pay fees sustain a case against a major university's legal team?

Before rushing into court, King worked closely with team members and Pittman to write and send to OCR a revised Title IX complaint, this one narrowing the list of complaints to just twelve. MSU addressed several of the issues, but not all. In the meantime, a memo from an MSU administrator led the players to believe that further action would be delayed indefinitely. With levels of mistrust high, the possibility for miscommunication was also great. King also sent a note to athletics director Joe Kearney to make certain he had been personally informed about the team's complaints. In December 1978, a draft of the long-awaited policy interpretation for Title IX was published.[3] By February 1979, the team and King had given up on the university taking what they considered serious action, and they saw legal action as the necessary next step.

Leary of a long, drawn-out case that her clients might not be able to afford or win, King used a number of legal tools when she filed suit; these included both Title IX and the Fourteenth Amendment to the Constitution. As opposed to focusing their suit on Title IX, which would have required an examination of MSU's entire athletics department, focusing their suit on the Fourteenth Amendment seemed a more direct, less expensive way for the team to get results. This strategy only required a comparison of the resources allocated to men's and women's basketball. King's approach to the case was unique and her arguments compelling in their simplicity. She decided to use a "reductionist strategy"—styled after Ruth Bader Ginsberg's tactics as ACLU counsel—and argue the case against Michigan State primarily as a violation of the Fourteenth Amendment to the US Constitution. King also advised the players to reduce their complaint to only two areas: equal money for food and for accommodations when traveling to away games. King hoped this straightforward strategy would expedite a favorable ruling, though no one had any idea whether the team would prevail in the lawsuit. Still, King's public words at the time displayed an unshakable confidence that earned the trust of her clients. "In order to get rid of this thing," King told reporters who inquired about the players' lawsuit, "they're going to have to get rid of the Constitution."[4] For weeks King prepared the players for their court appearance; the athletes were more accustomed to physical than verbal performance, and King became their teacher.

By the time the case was scheduled to be heard in court, Kathy De-Boer and Cookie Mankowski had graduated. Because they needed someone still on the team to serve as named plaintiff, Carol Hutchins agreed to do her part for the cause by allowing her name to appear on the official complaint. King filed the complaint with the federal court in Grand Rapids, where the case was given to Judge Noel Fox, a Kennedy appointee whom a colleague described as "an old liberal" with working-class sympathies, who may have appreciated the nerve of these young women taking on their powerful university. On the bench, Fox had his own style, "frequently interjecting with questions of witnesses and lawyers. He [did] not attempt to cloak his feelings about a case."[5]

On February 5, 1979, the team traveled to Grand Rapids for their hearing. "That was another education," Mankowski reflected. "It was a federal court . . . the big seal and the whole nine yards."[6] Michigan State University's lawyers, assuming Title IX would be the primary basis for King's case, had planned to show that it was not only the women athletes who suffered from lack of funds; "non-revenue-producing" men's sports faced many of the same problems. MSU's baseball coach was ready to testify that he often made ham sandwiches for his team when they traveled to away games. University leaders, like many of their counterparts across the country, could not conceive of why it should be illegal to treat participants in non-revenue-generating sports, whether they were male or female, differently from the football and men's basketball players, who filled stadiums and gymnasiums with paying spectators. Even the MSU men's basketball coach, Jud Heathcote, whom Coach Langeland believed to be supportive of the women's team, begrudged having to take time away from his "magical season" to give a deposition. He felt that men's basketball received less than its due with so many university resources going to football.

However, to the dismay of MSU lead attorney Byron Higgins, the opportunity to put the baseball coach on the stand never came. King's legal strategy of focusing on the Fourteenth Amendment took MSU by surprise. Repeatedly, Higgins implored Judge Fox to make a ruling on Title IX because, as he put it, "the whole country is confused about this law and we need the courts—and that is you, sir—to tell us what this means. We intend to follow this law, we just don't know what it is trying to tell us to do."[7] Higgins argued that MSU was not discriminating against women per se; out of financial necessity, they were discriminating against athletes in all the "minor" sports. King, in turn, objected that this case was about only the women's basketball team and men's basketball team, not about any of the other sports.[8]

Watching King in court inspired the MSU women's basketball players. Deb Traxinger recalled that King and Judge Fox seemed to connect with each other. King's assertive yet grandmotherly persona, combined with her straightforward arguments, seemed appealing to the elderly judge in contrast with the younger, three-piece-suited Higgins. When several of the women's basketball players, including Hutchins, Lori Hyman, and Mary Kay Itnyre, testified before Judge Fox in the February 1979 hearing, they described the lack of resources provided them by the university. They testified that eating fast food—all that they could afford with their per diem—upset their stomachs. Some players even skipped meals because they could not afford decent food. Players also testified that having two tall people sleeping in the same bed the night before a game was uncomfortable and did not allow them to sleep restfully. In addition, having four people in one small room was chaotic, and it was often difficult to keep up with their homework. Under Jean Ledwith King's reductionist strategy, the players did not mention that, excluding coaching salaries, the men's basketball budget ($116,000) was more than eight times higher than the women's budget ($13,500). Arguing the right to equal protection, they did not mention that, under Title IX, women had the same right as men to cheerleaders and a band at their home games. They did not mention that Title IX required them equal access to athletic scholarships. In fact, the women did not mention Title IX at all. Nor did they argue for treatment equal to that of the "magical" men's team—they only argued that they deserved adequate funds for food and shelter.

Players who attended the hearing can still recall memorable moments of the proceedings. Judge Fox, for example, seemed particularly taken by the testimony of Hyman, who was badgered relentlessly by Higgins about whether she was squandering her per diem money by ordering a diet soda instead of a higher calorie beverage. Higgins interrogated her about whether or not she had ordered cheese on her hamburger. Traxinger remembers that Higgins used the phrase, "What's good for the goose is good for the gander." In response, Fox interjected: "Well, that's the reason we are all here today, isn't it?"[9]

After testimony from the players and rebuttals by attorney Higgins, Judge Fox agreed with Jean Ledwith King and the women's team, and he issued a temporary restraining order against Michigan State. The order required immediate allocation of funds for equal lodging and meal money. In his words, "If these girls are going to play a rough game, they do need sleep and rest and proper nutrition."[10] News of Fox's ruling was reported by the Associated Press and published in major newspapers across the United States, including the *New York Times* and *Los Angeles Times*. In Michigan, the *Detroit News, Detroit Free Press, Michigan Daily, State Journal, Ann Arbor News,* and others ran stories featuring the ruling. Athletic departments at other universities took notice too. Overlooking that fact that Judge Fox's ruling was limited to food and lodging, University of Michigan athletics director Don Canham told Associated Press reporters that equal funding "would end a lot of things for both men and women athletes." He warned that "track and field would be one of the first to go," and argued that football be exempt from Title IX coverage.[11] But a full-page column in *Sports Illustrated* entitled "Spartan No Longer" warned readers that the MSU case should alert college administrators that "Title IX may not be their only concern," and that using the Constitution's Fourteenth Amendment, the MSU team had demonstrated that their travel conditions "were unacceptable even for Spartans."[12]

Consequences of Winning

After the initial win in the court of law, the women's team returned their attention to the basketball court. The effects of the lawsuit were felt immediately—each player was given sixteen dollars per day for meals, and two players shared each hotel room instead of four. Attorney Jean Ledwith King, however, remained hard at work on their case for another six years with no certainty of ever being paid.

Judge Fox's temporary restraining order was upheld upon appeal by MSU, a preliminary injunction was ordered, and a trial date set for summer 1985. As the case stretched on, MSU athletics director Joe Kearney directed coach Karen Langeland to tell her players to withdraw their lawsuit. Kearney's action became public record in court testimony, which may have factored into his decision to leave the university at the end of the year, with fans of the Magical Spartans wondering why he left MSU at the apex of his men's basketball program's glory.

Because the trial date would extend the case until long after the current team members would have graduated, King consulted the players about making the suit into a class action. By this point, only one of the

1978–79 team members, Deb Traxinger, was still a student at MSU. She had been the lone first-year player on the team. It was up to her to decide whether the case would continue or whether the university would prevail in its strategy of delaying until all the original plaintiffs graduated. Traxinger's strong loyalty to the team, and by this time her admiration and loyalty to King, compelled her to lend her name to the class action. Still, the university continued to fight, arguing unsuccessfully that Traxinger was not eligible to represent the class. The contentious case generated page after page of arguments, even though university leaders continued to claim they intended all along to create a uniform per diem policy for all students and employees. Administrators fully intended to comply with Title IX—if only they could understand it.

While MSU's stance may seem inexplicably defiant, the institution's response reflected the times. As Carpenter and Acosta explained in their 2005 book on the legal history of Title IX, across America there was "a climate of fear and wildly divergent rumors about the havoc or positive changes that Title IX and its regulations would bring. Would coed locker rooms be required? Would all teams be integrated? Would sports for males cease to exist so that females could have access? Are females anatomically and physiologically able to participate in sports without ending their child-bearing potential?"[13] Within this context, the university did provide what the restraining order dictated, creating a new policy on travel money that provided all MSU athletes with the same per diem. In addition, shortly after the court-ordered injunction in 1979, MSU surprised Coach Langeland by offering her enough full scholarships to bring in a well-supported new recruiting class in 1980 and to offer a full ride to at least one of the players who had been involved in the team's initial Title IX complaints: Deb Traxinger.

By 1982, when I enrolled in MSU, the women's basketball team had twelve full athletic scholarships, although we still competed in an intramural building until two years later when Jenison Fieldhouse became our home court.

Over the years, as arguments for the case continued, the players and their supporters realized that "winning" had consequences. By the time the women's basketball players took the stand in the federal court hearing in 1979, MSU administrators had become convinced that a group of young college students must have had adult help to make a federal case out of their Title IX complaints. They saw a level of writing, thinking, and research into budgets and legal matters that made them that suspect that the team's coach, Karen Langeland, or perhaps Mary Pollock after she was fired had secretly assisted them. When DeBoer took the stand under oath, MSU's attorney Higgins interrogated her:

Q: With reference to the complaint filed with the ADJB and the complaint filed with HEW, did you actually compose those complaints yourself?

A: Yes, I did.

Q: With no help?

A: Could you clarify what you mean by "help"?

Q: Did you consult with anyone with respect to the writing of those complaints? They're very elaborate and very long. . . .

Q: I am showing you now Exhibit Number 5, which is the complaint filed with HEW, and I am asking if you composed by yourself that complaint.

A: I had help.

Q: And who gave you that assistance?

A: I had assistance from Bruce Alexander in some of the writing. I also had assistance from Mark Pittman in some of the writing. I had assistance in the typing from Joanne Hardy.

Q: And did you consult with anyone else with respect to the details of that prior to filing?

A: No.[14]

Years later, Pittman described his "internal shaking and trembling" when DeBoer spoke his name, a reaction he noted was "certainly not fitting for a former Marine officer with Viet Nam combat experience." In that moment, he saw he would be part of the suit's collateral damage. He was right. When his contract expired at the end of the 1979 academic year, it was not renewed. No longer employed by MSU, he felt "chopped up by the legendary MSU mascot 'Sparty.'" The next fall, as he gathered with friends, including some players involved in the lawsuit, he felt isolated, taking little comfort from their general consensus: "you should have known you would be fired."[15]

The consequences for Nell Jackson were more subtle but no less disturbing. Her position as women's athletics director was redefined after the ruling, placing her position and the women's program under the male athletics director. Viewing this change as a demotion because she had not "kept her coaches in check," she left the university. Even though Karen Langeland had distanced herself from the complaint and trial, she was regarded by some as surreptitious until she retired as head coach in 2000, when she took on the position of associate athletics director. Although her teams benefited from the lawsuit and Title IX complaints, the university also found it difficult to fully embrace and celebrate the team and coach under the shadow of a lawsuit. For years, the intangible support that can mean so much more than money did not flow readily from MSU administrators to the women's basketball team, or to other women's teams for that matter.

The demotion of Nell Jackson reflected a national trend as formerly separate athletics programs for men and women merged in many schools, with notable exceptions such as Tennessee and Texas. The effects were often devastating for women's careers:

> Female head coaches became assistant coaches. Female department chairs with doctorates became deputy chairs of merged departments headed by males possessing only master's degrees. Many of the fears of women professionals about the continuation of a patronizing mind-set were realized. On the other hand, it is difficult to find fears held by their male counterparts that became reality. Locker rooms remained single sex; facilities were either shared or remained male dominated. Sports opportunities for males on every level continued to grow. . . . Even today the massive increase in participation by females has still brought them to a position less than that enjoyed by males when Title IX was enacted [decades ago].[16]

Although *Hutchins v. MSU Board of Trustees*, *Blair v. Washington State University*, and *Haffer v. Temple University* all displayed the effectiveness of coupling Title IX suits with Fourteenth Amendment complaints as a legal tool for addressing sex discrimination, between 1984 and 1988, one legal precedent froze most Title IX cases. That precedent, *Grove City College v. Bell* (1984), effectively exempted athletics from Title IX. Because of the court-issued injunction in the *Hutchins* 1979 case, MSU players in the 1980s received adequate funding for basic necessities, but other efforts to achieve equity faltered. Anticipating the Grove City ruling and wanting the *Hutchins* case to continue under Constitutional claims that she had always continued primary, King withdrew the Title IX claim from the ongoing lawsuit. Likewise, attorneys representing the athletes at Temple University withdrew their Title IX claim and altered their case to focus on the Fourteenth Amendment, as King had done from the outset.

During those years when Title IX did not apply to athletics and the MSU case remained unsettled, Joanne P. McCallie, Langeland's successor as MSU basketball coach (and later head coach at Duke), remembered playing against MSU as an athlete at Northwestern from 1983 to 1987: "What I remember about MSU is that I don't think [they were] progressive. . . . I thought it was odd that we played in the intramural building."[17]

In 1984, the *Hutchins* case was turned over to Judge Benjamin Gibson when Judge Fox was forced to retire for health reasons. Gibson issued a controversial ruling that dismissed claims for monetary damages, agreeing with MSU that the institution should be considered immune under the Constitution's Eleventh Amendment because damages would be paid out of state funds. A few years later, Congress acted to exclude Title IX claims from Eleventh Amendment Immunity, a ruling that came too late for the *Hutchins* case and others that initially included Title IX claims but ended up as Fourteenth Amendment lawsuits in the wake of the *Grove City* decision.[18]

Yet the *Hutchins* case continued as King sought declaratory relief—a ruling that the university had violated the law. Finally, in 1986, the case was settled out of court, with King arguing successfully that she be awarded attorney's fees as the party likely to have prevailed if the case had gone to trial. The university signed an agreement to continue following the uniform per diem policy they had adopted after the 1979 temporary restraining order. The players agreed to the settlement, and a year later the players at Temple also reached a settlement. While these out-of-court settlements have no value as legal precedents, as Carpenter and Acosta contend, they set the stage for future cases and illustrate "the fortitude required to pursue a Title IX claim in the courts during the years when Title IX was young."[19]

In 1988 the *Grove City* decision was overturned by the Civil Rights Restoration Act, and equity in athletics was again the law. At this point, the doors were opened for new cases to go forward. These cases would build on the foundation created by the first generation of teams who struggled on and off the court for respect and equity under Title IX and the US Constitution. The stands taken by these young women at MSU and elsewhere marked the beginning of systematic institutional changes that paved the way for what women's basketball has become today. Their actions changed and strengthened them as context for their future positions as coaches, teachers, and business people.

After her brief employment at MSU, Mary Pollock continued to advocate for women and unrepresented groups as affirmative action director for the Michigan Department of Social Services and the Michigan Department of Mental Health, and as the affirmative action coordinator for the state government affirmative action program at the Michigan Department of Civil Service. After Governor John Engler abolished the state's affirmative action program, she became the manager of the Employment Relations Board for the Michigan Department of Civil Service; in retirement she continues to be active in NOW and state politics. Kathy DeBoer and Carol Hutchins remained in the world of college athletics: DeBoer became head coach of women's volleyball and the first woman senior associate athletics director at the University of Kentucky; city manager for Lexington, Kentucky; and head of the American Volleyball Coaches' Association. Hutchins, as head softball coach at the University of Michigan and the winningest coach in Wolverine history, led her teams to eighteen Big Ten championships. Her 2005 team won the NCAA National Softball Championship title, and she considers college athletics an integral part of her players' college education. In recent years, she has asked her teams to write essays on what they know about Title IX, and a few have asked her about the *Hutchins* case after hearing about it in one of their college courses.

After earning a master's degree in physiology, Deb Traxinger became a high school physiology teacher, union president, and coach at a Lansing-area high school. Mary Kay Itnyre worked as a police officer and firefighter in Los Angeles, California, before joining the FBI. After graduation, Cookie Mankowski coached basketball at the University of Illinois; she later earned a doctoral degree and is now an assistant professor of social work at the University of West Virginia. Mary Jo Hardy and Bruce Alexander, now married, continue to live in East Lansing, where Hardy retired from teaching fitness at Lansing Community College and Alexander retired from his job as director of information technology at MSU (their two children are MSU graduates). Mark Pittman, married to Kathy DeBoer, works on university-related grant and research projects. Mary Pollock's replacement as Title IX coordinator in the 1970s, Lou Anna Simon, became the twentieth president of Michigan State University.

The Invisible Tradition

For the most part, the "invisible season" of 1978–79 has long since disappeared from newspaper editorials and courtrooms, and fans of MSU women's basketball know few of the details. When the MSU women's basketball team reached the 2004–5 Final Four, Nancy Lieberman-Cline, former women's basketball star and an ESPN announcer, lamented "the lack of tradition" in women's basketball at Michigan State, prompting a flurry of emails from members of the 1978–79 team. If "tradition" is defined simply by wins and losses, then she was correct. The Michigan State women's basketball story represents another kind of tradition—the tradition of struggle. The team's success in the 2000s and the institution's pride in being a "poster program" for gender equity stand upon a tradition of hard work and commitment to principle initiated by the efforts of Pollock, Pittman, DeBoer, Mankowski, and King. To carry on the legacy of the 1978–79 team, however, this struggle must inform the present as well as the future. To be certain, their efforts ensured much-needed equitable funding for food and accommodations. Even more important, these individuals, along with the actions of others across the country, set a series of events in motion that increased opportunities for future female athletes across America and around the globe.

As Alexandra Allred, former member of the US Olympic bobsled team, wrote, "As the popularity and worldwide acceptance of women in sport grows, cultures that have typically kept their women under close patriarchal control are realizing they need to reevaluate their social structures . . . and more females from more nations are entering the Olympic Games than ever before."[20]

Recognizing and honoring this tradition of struggle for equity will not only help ensure that future women's basketball games take place in full view, under the bright lights of television cameras, before packed stands in large arenas. Honoring past struggles will also enable young women who now have opportunities to compete with full support at the highest levels to see themselves as both athletes and citizens. They will see the role of verbal as well as athletic skills in social change. They will see their place in a larger history of American sportswomen whose struggles have contributed to a changing, more inclusive democracy. They may even invent future athletic programs that combine the values of equity and high-level competition with the spirit of play, educational values, and financial restraint that could reform athletics in American higher education.

16 Conclusion

Defining Moments

> Rhetoric is a way of "altering reality." Its aim is to "produce action or change" in response to a perceived "defect, an obstacle, something waiting to be done, a thing which is other than it should be."
> —Lloyd Bitzer, "The Rhetorical Situation"[1]

One aim of this book has been to discover how the past holds insights and raises critical questions that can guide our decision making in the present and future. Some of the most revealing clues about the past are hidden deep within institutional memories—retrievable in long-forgotten written documents: memos, reports, speeches, and notes from conversations. To really understand what it took in the 1970s, and what it will still require, to achieve the full promise of Title IX, we need to read—and study—the rhetorical discourse that got us to where we are today. The core promise of Title IX is rarely controversial: to create an educational environment in which both males and females can function unhampered by discriminatory treatment and attitudes. In theory, under those conditions, girls and women would have the opportunity to be as productive and accomplished as boys and men. But what would it mean to take seriously the idea that women in college sports have the potential to be breadwinners as much as their male peers? Do women as a group even aspire to play that role? And how do these questions, and the assumptions behind them, change when considering how the law applies to transgender students? These are the kinds of questions that make Title IX rhetoric so compelling, confounding, and complex. The debates about equality in sports reflect larger anxieties about changing gender roles in society. These anxieties make questions around gender equality in sports as fundamentally destabilizing for some as they are empowering for others.

Throughout the Title IX stories told in these chapters, I have highlighted rhetoric as a tool for strategic communication and influence. Early opponents of Title IX, then often the NCAA, used rhetorical strategies to maintain the status quo, ensuring that women athletes did not get so many new resources that they were running, as some of them put it, before they could actually walk. In turn, women athletes, women's sports administrators and physical educators, feminist activists, and attorneys have all used the power of language to make certain that girls and women have a fair share of opportunities in school-sponsored sports. Sometimes that meant adopting an apologetic or diplomatic tone instead of giving in to the urge to stridently demand rights. Often it meant compromise, accepting less than even the law clearly allowed in order to be viewed as reasonable and maintain goodwill with male colleagues who benefited from the status quo. Although even these cautious strategies brought backlash and conflict within women's sports communities, they ensured incremental progress as American social values and gender roles gradually changed.

Because Title IX's regulations and policy interpretations for athletics reflect the time period in which they were written, every so often it makes sense to ask whether the law has kept up with the times. Is Title IX fulfilling its promise of making certain that sex discrimination is no longer accepted in taxpayer-supported education in the United States? A white paper published in response to the 2012 conference "Progress and Promise: Title IX at 40," sponsored by the Women's Sports Foundation and University of Michigan's SHARP Center for Women and Girls, says that when it comes to school-sponsored athletics, the answer is "no." The authors argue much progress has been made, but our public, private, and even professional conversations concerning Title IX are as clouded by misinformation, myths, and unwarranted assumptions as they were in the 1970s and 1980s when the law was first being interpreted and implemented.[2]

As a rhetorician, part of my role in society is to help remedy misunderstandings, guide deliberation on public issues, and facilitate clear, effective communication for a variety of audiences. Toward that end, I offer here a rhetorician's perspective on where we need to go next to achieve two goals for the women's sports movement as articulated by the SHARP Center: (1) to create a culture of respect and compliance regarding Title IX, and (2) to create messaging around the law that breaks down myths and misrepresentations.

First, we need to acknowledge that most Americans—including many coaches, administrators, and even Title IX coordinators—would be hard pressed to accurately and clearly explain what the athletics regulations for Title IX actually require. The first step toward deliberating over policy is to understand and seek agreement as to the relevant facts, in this case beginning with the law itself. When I talk with students about Title IX, I begin by asking them to imagine that they worked for the Office of Civil Rights in the 1970s. Pretend, I tell them, that it is your job to determine how to translate the thirty-nine words of the Title IX statute into concrete applications for college sports. Their initial response is often what I call the 50-50 plan. To them, the most commonsense solution is typically to split everything in halves—give the women's program and men's program equal budgets to spend as each program sees fit. It seems a simple solution that gives men's and women's programs self-determination to include the smorgasbord of sports that meet students' interests and abilities. It surprises them, therefore, when I tell them that having separate programs for males and females was not a foregone conclusion for the actual OCR staff members who formulated Title IX policy. Even more surprising is the fact that Title IX does not simply divide resources in half, even though equal per capita expenditures for male and female athletes was proposed in a draft of what became the 1979 Title IX policy interpretation for intercollegiate athletics.

While some students have heard of the three-part test, a key component of the 1979 Title IX policy interpretation for intercollegiate athletics,[3] they are surprised to learn that one part of the "test" allows institutions to comply with Title IX even today by showing that the institution is simply making progress toward equality. They are also surprised to learn that instead of measuring equal treatment for male and female athletes by comparing similar teams or by ensuring equal amounts of money are allocated for men's and women's programs, a complicated system of "offsetting benefits" is used to determine compliance. I show them the 309-page self-evaluation workbook published in 2004 by Valerie Bonnette, a Title IX consultant and former OCR compliance reviewer. I also show a video clip extracted from an interview I conducted with civil rights attorney Arthur Bryant in which he explains how Title IX works in regard to the areas of equal treatment in the 1975 Title IX regulation. As an attorney in the *Haffer* case and later in a precedent-setting decision involving Brown University, Bryant discovered that litigating full Title IX compliance in the these areas is virtually impossible because of the complexities and ambiguities involved. In the *Hutchins* case, foreseeing the complications and expense of analyzing an entire athletics program budget, attorney Jean Ledwith King determined that reducing her clients' complaint to a few items that she could clearly connect with basic needs of health and safety was the only viable strategy. In an interview, Bryant explained that in settlement negotiations for the *Cohen v. Brown University* case (1996), both sides eventually threw up their hands and admitted it was nearly impossible to sort out.

But Bryant also pointed out a detailed analysis is hardly necessary because the reality is, as he put it, that "separate is never equal." From that perspective, he offered this assessment of the current Title IX compliance situation:

> What is happening in almost every school around the country is that there are some men—usually the football team and the basketball team—who, right, are being treated royally. There are some women—usually the women's basketball team—who are being treated royally. And everybody else is not being treated so well. And so when you do the numbers, well, wait a minute, there are a whole lot more men being treated way better, than a whole lot of women, and on average, the women are being treated way worse than the men are being treated, and that's not equal, and that's not right. And it's not legal.[4]

Despite this damning assessment, the dominant national narrative about Title IX is one of great progress, which is accurate, and the presumption of widespread full compliance, which is not. Getting beyond a plausible, comfortable narrative to address less pleasant actual facts is a tall order. Attempts by various parties to do just that have been largely ineffective except for in convincing the already convinced.

In a list entitled "Title IX Work Not Done," data gathered by the Women's Sports Foundation and the National Coalition for Girls and Women in Education, published during the year of Title IX's thirtieth anniversary, illustrate the inadequate state of compliance in 2002:

- Women make up 54 percent of college students and only 43 percent of college athletes.
- Title IX compliance has been driven by lawsuits and threats of lawsuits.
- Although the law states that schools that violate Title IX will lose their federal funding, in thirty years no school has ever lost federal funding for not complying with Title IX.
- Male college athletes receive 36 percent more scholarship dollars than female college athletes at NCAA institutions.
- Men's college athletics receives more money than women's in scholarships, recruiting, head coach salaries, and operating expenses.
- Men have substantially more employment opportunities than women in college sports. Women are 16.9 percent of the athletic directors, 44 percent of the head coaches of women's teams, 2 percent of the head coaches of men's teams, and 27.8 percent of the full-time athletic trainers.[5]

Ten years later, on Title IX's fortieth birthday, little had changed. Although I could cite here a raft of statistics to support that statement, doing so would simply perpetuate an ongoing dual of competing numbers that has already played out in public discourses. Realistically, these numbers just don't matter all that much to anyone except members of the public who already identify with the values of the feminist, educational, and women's sports advocacy groups who put them together.

As a rhetorician, I know that productive, conflict-solving discourse requires a first step of seeking agreement on what are the facts and what are *relevant* facts. With Title IX, we could probably agree that the facts show lack of compliance. However, we must also address what is sometimes called the question of "quality." That is, how serious is the problem being articulated?

In the case of Title IX, even if everyone were to agree that widespread noncompliance is still a fact in 2016, is it really a significant societal problem that fewer women are receiving sports opportunities and funds than the law technically requires? The answer to this question still divides Americans. It divides us because in addressing this question, the logic of unregulated capitalism collides with the logic of regulation and civil rights. Beyond educating more Americans about the facts of what Title IX actually requires, this core conflict of logics must be examined more deeply if conflicting Title IX discourses are to progress beyond their current deadlock.

The statistics demonstrating continued noncompliance with the law are deemed irrelevant by a huge cross-section of the American public that accepts the idea that building ever larger and more expensive sports programs is justified by arguments that college sports bring in revenue, successful teams and popular coaches attract students, and big-time sports generate spending by fans on games days, which supports local economies. As we have seen, the same kinds of arguments for keeping "the golden goose" well-fed also circulated in the first decades after Title IX was enacted. Then, as now, they serve as justifications for turning a blind eye to ways in which schools are not fully complying with the law.

When I talk with college students, they rarely consider important counterarguments. Like university administrators in the 1970s, they initially fail to distinguish revenue from profits, and they offer false analogies between the operations of nonprofit college athletic departments and for-profit professional sports teams. At first, students whom I talk with about college sports and Title IX rhetoric don't fully understand why a federal antidiscrimination law such as Title IX would need to apply to college sports. Shouldn't the teams that bring in the most money be provided more funds and more participation opportunities, even if those resources and opportunities fall disproportionately (or only) to men? This is the logic of completely unregulated capitalism, a logic that ignores the nonprofit status and university affiliation to which big-time college sports teams owe much of their appeal and affordability (if, in fact, they still are affordable).

Even for-profit corporations in the United States cannot and do not operate on such a simplistic formula when they make decisions about how to invest in and diversify their products or programs for sustainable, successful growth.

Most of the college students whom I have talked with initially found it easy to imagine ways in which successful teams and popular coaches can benefit a school (and Knight Commission–sponsored reports acknowledge these benefits, along with pointing out ways in which they are frequently overstated or emphasized). Upon reflection, however, the students began to see how without the "college" part of college athletics, their favorite big-time football team would be just another professional team.

But in the many analyses of the college sports "business," even the harshest critics rarely point out the multitude of ways in which athletics departments—even so-called "self-supporting" ones—depend for their very existence, credibility, and popular appeal on the taxpayer-supported universities of which they are just one part. To make fully visible all of the ways in which even the most successful and profitable college football programs (and there are but a few of them) depend upon "overhead" from the universities that house them would require an insider's knowledge of the intricacies of university budgets and access to information available only through Freedom of Information Act requests. This sort of information is what Mary Pollock sought as Title IX coordinator at MSU in the 1970s. How many Title IX coordinators today even seek out, study, or have the financial literacies to scrutinize such data even if it were available?

The NCAA's Gender Equity Reports have gone a long way toward mandating some transparency, and in those reports, seemingly obvious violations of Title IX emerge, such as male practice players counting as part of female participation numbers. Also, scholarship percentages for numerous schools have not consistently shown compliance.[6] But no one is systematically scrutinizing this data or holding institutions accountable. Doing so would require the kind of arduous, painful process that lost Pollock and Pittman their jobs at MSU, and toward what end? One fear holding back anyone with the inclination to conduct such inquiries is the possibility that things would be even worse if the status quo were disrupted. What if it is true that the quasi-professional men's sports programs fielded by our nation's universities really are the cash cows for the entire university that so many Americans believe them to be? Where is the line between perception and reality?

The invisibility of the inner workings of athletics programs and university budgets shields the men's athletic establishment and power structure—the status quo—from serious scrutiny. To the public at large and to gender equality advocates, the inscrutable nature of athletic department budgets and the (we are told) complicated ways in which money flows to and through our taxpayer-supported institutions of higher education can be obstacles to change. The most effective social change agents must also be sophisticated rhetoricians, able to ask questions and obtain information that allow them to expose what rhetorician Wayne Booth called " rhetrickery."[7] What Booth referred to was the kind of language use meant to cover up and deceive, or simply distract our attention from narratives that we are not meant to consider too carefully, if at all.

Sports are all about storytelling, as a CBS sports commercial for the Golf Channel that I once came across reminded viewers, pointing out the fundamentally rhetorical basis for our nation's obsession with athletics. That is, the appeal of sports is created through the rhetoric of narratives. So it stands to reason that the most powerful leaders of the big-time college sports establishment—including the NCAA and sports media corporations—are among America's most gifted storytellers. Perhaps the biggest tall tale of all that the NCAA and the sport-entertainment complex continues to perpetuate is the amateur myth. That mythology is worth millions to big-time coaches and athletics directors. It is supported by university presidents and boards of trustees.[8] And while the amateur myth has proven remarkably persuasive, proposals to pay male big-time college athletes as employees of the university have gained traction. The controversy concerning pay for college athletes has prompted the public at large to begin questioning some of the contradictory presumptions behind the business of big-time college sports. Still, in debates about whether male big-time college athletes should be paid like the professionals rather than treated as true student athletes, the matter of how Title IX and gender equality come into play is often ignored.

For coaches such as Carol Hutchins at the University of Michigan, the disparities in coaching compensation and opportunities that persisted when I interviewed her in 2012 have generated as much or more deep-seated emotion—both pain and anger—as the inequalities she and her MSU teammates combated in the 1970s. She attributed these ongoing inequalities in part to opportunities provided by Title IX for better-paying positions in women's sports, positions that have proven attractive to men.[9] Certainly, a federal law cannot regulate who applies for open positions, the role that men's still-stronger sports networks play in providing opportunities, and societal conventions that support the assumption that men are fully capable of coaching women but not the reverse. But huge discrepancies in pay that still exist for coaching college men and coaching college women reflect a dismissal of Title IX's requirement for overall equal access to quality coaching in men's and women's programs. Or these differences reflect inflated salaries for coaches of high-profile men's teams, where salaries in the millions do not really add up to a higher quality of coaching. If these men are not better coaches than their female counterparts, then what are educational institutions paying for? One higher education administrator whom I interviewed cited inflated salaries as essentially "I love you money"—that is, extra hundreds of thousands that bolster a coach's status in a self-interested ego contest among big-time college coaches nationwide. (These funds supposedly prevent successful college coaches from leaving the college ranks to coach professionals, a point that underscores the extent to which big-time college sports has become a business, not an educational enterprise.)

Many inequalities at numerous institutions—some of them reflecting outright violations of Title IX's equal treatment requirements—may not be apparent or of much concern to today's generation of women athletes. These realities are simply familiar givens to many players. Likewise, college sports fans as a whole continue to uncritically view as normal and natural the significant advantages that continue to accrue to male college athletes, coaches, and athletics directors as a collective group. For example, at the May 2012 conference "Progress and Promise: Title IX at 40," a woman employee at ESPN felt "nauseous" when she heard in one presentation what a minuscule percentage of her influential company's programming covered women's sports. Although she lived with this, to me, seemingly obvious reality every day, she never even saw it.

Young women athletes and even coaches can also be unknowingly complicit in their own unequal treatment. Mary Jo Hardy recalled that her daughter told her how the girls' basketball players at her high school had complained to their coach about having to practice on Fridays when they would rather be socializing during that time. When their coach agreed to call off practice, Hardy asked whether the boys still practiced on Fridays, even though they wanted the additional free time as much as the girls did. As Hardy saw it, the girls were contributing to lower standards and expectations being applied to them, standards that the boys' coaches would never accept regardless of how often their players grumbled.[10]

This anecdote brings me back to my original question inspired by the remarks of former Michigan football coach Bo Schembechler to President Gerald Ford: Do women really want the Rose Bowl? That is, do girls and women today seek the fully equal programs envisioned by student athlete activists and their supporters in Title IX's first decade? Then and now, implementing fully equal college athletics programs would seriously challenge the highly lucrative business as usual of big-time men's college sports. With these countervailing perspectives often left unarticulated or unaddressed, informed, productive dialogue about equality in college sports can be hard to come by. Even many women athletes accept dominant societal norms that continue to presume that college athletics are about entertainment more than education and that men's sports are, by nature, always more entertaining and profitable. Given that these social realities have not changed all that much since 1978, the rhetorical challenges that faced the MSU women's basketball team, and subsequently their feminist attorney, look remarkably familiar today.

For present-day female athletes and even college sports alums, Title IX is increasingly a part of history, a law perhaps to be celebrated but not used to redress existing inequalities. Even celebrations of progress are sometimes muted—or unfairly labeled reverse discrimination—when athletics directors choose, unfortunately, to comply with the law by cutting men's sports that they regard as lower priority than the high-revenue, high-cost sports of football and men's basketball.

I found a representative sampling of contemporary perspectives on Title IX in a 2012 MSU Varsity Alumni Association newsletter that acknowledged the fortieth anniversary of the law. Perhaps predictably, former MSU male athletes celebrated the sports opportunities enjoyed by their daughters, and a few blamed Title IX for cuts made to MSU's lower-revenue men's teams over the years. The Title IX discourses represented in the newsletter, whether celebratory or critical, all ignored the fact that countless institutions even today still fail to fully comply with the law's regulations.[11] In fact, if today's athletes understood the extent to which equality remains an elusive goal, they might confront an identity crisis similar to that faced by AIAW members in the 1970s. Or at least they might recognize themselves being confronted with a defining moment when they have to decide whether or not they want to do something—or remain on the sidelines and watch what happens next.

For some coaches, changes that embrace a commercial model of sport may not even be desired. In a 2012 interview, Dennis Wolfe, then women's basketball coach at Virginia Tech, recalled being perplexed by a women's basketball coach (with whom he worked at another institution) who became extremely upset when she was offered some of the perks often provided for men's college coaches (i.e., a university vehicle, corporate accounts for purchasing sporting apparel, a higher salary, and the like). From his point of view, she was being offered all that she had fought for during years of marginalization. From her point of view, these "over the top" benefits put her at risk for being fired if her teams did not consistently win. She wanted to coach more than she sought the status symbols that have become increasingly expected as part of a package for major college coaches of both men and women.[12]

Examples such as these suggest that sometimes, for some people, "equal enough" is quite simply good enough. Alternatively, they could suggest that if given an opportunity to operate within a genuinely separate women's program, women might choose a different model of sport. And given equal representation in a more democratic decision-making process, male students might choose likewise. Certainly, men at the bottom of the male sports hierarchy—especially those at risk for being cut—have an incentive to consider how a more educationally oriented model might serve their interests better than a hyper-commercialized paradigm. Perhaps if more decision-making power within athletics were returned to students, they might prove wiser than adult administrators tempted by the possibilities of becoming millionaires through running students' nonprofit, taxpayer-supported college sports programs. Students might recognize that with a presumed need for our public universities to spend ever more public funds, along with private donations, to maintain nationally competitive athletics programs, equality appears—and will continue to appear—unaffordable.

A study conducted by the Delta Cost Project at the American Institutes for Research (distributed by the Knight Commission on Intercollegiate Athletics) even shows that spending on college athletics is escalating at a pace that exceeds spending on academics.[13] A Title IX policy revision that would reverse this outrageous trend is to return college athletics to control by students, with guidance from administrators and advisors paid as faculty, not as Wall Street executives. Under this model, elected students representing existing sports and the student body at large could manage separate but equal budgets for the men's and women's programs (the 50-50 plan). Student athletics directors for each program could work hand-in-hand with a men's and women's athletics director, Title IX coordinator, and other advisors. Women's programs would no longer be colonized under a head athletics director whose first priority is men's athletics, and participants in nonrevenue men's sports could more easily understand that it is up to men themselves to negotiate with each other for the kind of program that meets their collective interests and abilities. Such a program might or might not include 120 football scholarships and no wrestling team. For women, such a program might or might not include competitive cheerleading or sand volleyball along with more traditional sports. For student leaders, managing their athletics programs would be an experiential civics lesson in democratic rhetorical processes, much as it was when athletics in years past were run out of physical education departments. Unfortunately, that kind of vision—or some version of it—will never be seriously considered without a social change movement comparable to what women's sports advocates launched in the 1970s. Quite simply, too many people have too much of their personal financial fortunes and celebrity at stake for change to happen any other way.

Still, we cannot afford to abandon the goal of achieving a more informed citizenry on policy concerning gender equality and college sports. A more educated public will require a strategic program of consciousness-raising. For today's athletes, and most of the taxpaying public at large, the details of what Title IX actually requires and important information about how athletic department budgets operate are simply not readily available. Women's sports advocates hold back from imagining or proposing significant policy changes to Title IX out of fear that change would mean losing hard-won gains in moving toward the ever-elusive goal of equality. Know-your-rights meetings such as those offered by Title IX coordinators and women's athletic administrators in the 1970s rarely take place today. So misperceptions about what Title IX actually requires continue to abound. And with the improvements we have seen in women's programs since the 1970s, few students or coaches may have the incentive to educate themselves.

The question then becomes whether the women's sports movement has come so far that we can safely assume continued strides will come without sacrifices and conflict. Certainly questions of costs, benefits, and principle face change agents everywhere. "Rocking the boat" means risking hard-earned gains and a comfortable equilibrium. For female athletes and coaches today, asking hard questions could mean risking some incredible privileges provided in the name of equity (if not equality) and compromising remarkable opportunities, even if those opportunities still don't quite add up to the Rose Bowl.

If my contention is true—that most players today, and even many coaches, lack the basic understanding of how Title IX's regulations actually work and can't even imagine what full compliance with the law might mean—then more historical knowledge and rhetorical education is needed. More people need to hear Title IX stories that highlight the role of discourse in shaping perceptions, policies, and actions. These stories prompt us to imagine what equality might look like in school-sponsored, taxpayer-supported sports, and they show us how college student activists of the past used persuasive language to seek it. With this largely invisible era of Title IX's past brought to light, future generations can draw upon the strategies and eloquence of our sporting pioneers—and also learn from their missteps—to craft new rhetorics of reform.

Appendixes

Notes

Bibliography

Index

Appendix A

Guide to People in the Book

This guide categorizes people according to the general roles they played in the time period covered by the microhistory of Michigan State University (MSU) women's basketball Title IX struggle.

Bruce Alexander	Graduate student in sociology at MSU; volunteer statistician and timekeeper, MSU women's basketball
Ralph Bonner	Assistant Vice President for University and Federal Relations at MSU
Sallie Bright	Attorney and Executive Secretary of Anti-Discrimination Judicial Board at MSU
Donald Canham	Athletics director at the University of Michigan
Kathleen DeBoer	Undergraduate student and athlete at MSU; women's basketball team spokesperson and co-captain (1977–78); Women's Professional Basketball League player
Noel Fox	Federal judge
Rollin Haffer	Named plaintiff in a lawsuit against Temple University
Edward Harden	Interim President of Michigan State University beginning in 1978
Mary Jo Hardy	Volleyball and track student athlete at MSU (1973–77); assisted with MSU women's basketball team's struggle against sex discrimination
George Heathcote	Men's basketball coach at MSU; known as "Jud"
Byron Higgins	Attorney for MSU
Carol Hutchins	Undergraduate student and softball and basketball athlete at MSU; named plaintiff in lawsuit

368 · Appendix A

368   ·   Appendix A

Lorraine Hyman	Undergraduate student at MSU, co-captain of women's basketball team (1978–79)
Mary Kay Itnyre	Undergraduate student and women's basketball player at MSU
Nell Jackson	Assistant Director of Women's Athletics, Associate Professor of Physical Education, Women's Track and Field Coach, MSU
Earvin Johnson	Undergraduate student and men's basketball player at MSU; known as "Magic"
Joseph Kearney	Athletics Director at MSU (1977–79); Director of the Western Athletic Conference
Jean Ledwith King	Civil rights attorney and activist based in Ann Arbor, Michigan
Karen Langeland	Women's basketball coach at MSU (1977–2000)
Mariann Mankowski	Undergraduate student and athlete at MSU; women's basketball team spokesperson and co-captain (1977–78); known as "Cookie"
Gwen Norrell	Faculty member in counseling at MSU; faculty representative to the NCAA
Vicki Nyberg	Activist, cofounder of the Alliance to End Sex Discrimination at MSU
Robert Perrin	Vice President for University Relations at MSU
Mark Pittman	Graduate student in sociology; MSU women's cross-country coach and assistant women's track coach
Margot Polivy	Attorney for the Association for Intercollegiate Athletics for Women
Mary Pollock	Residence Hall Director and Assistant Dean of Students, University of Illinois; Director of Women's Programs and Title IX Coordinator, MSU
Lou Anna Simon	Faculty member at MSU, Assistant to President for Institutional Assessment; Affirmative Action Officer (including Title IX Coordinator)

Deborah Traxinger   Undergraduate student and women's basketball team
                           member at MSU

Clarence Underwood   Assistant Athletics Director of Academics and
                           Eligibility, MSU

Clifton Wharton   President of MSU (1970–78)

Kay White   Assistant Vice President for Student Affairs and
                           Services, MSU

Appendix B

Timeline of Title IX's First Decades, 1972–1992

The following timeline tracks events connected with this book's microhistory. It offers a synopsis of the threads that the narrative weaves together, beginning with the genesis of Title IX (1972–75) and culminating with a landmark legal decision in 1992.

Interested readers can find out more about Title IX milestones after 1992, including the history of Title IX at Michigan State, through exploring the extensive body of published sources.[1]

July 9, 1868: The Fourteenth Amendment is adopted to the US Constitution and ratified as one of the Reconstruction Amendments after the Civil War. The equal protection clause, meant to protect the rights of freed slaves, guarantees all persons equal protection under the law. The clause states that "the laws of a state must treat an individual in the same manner as others in similar conditions and circumstances."[2] In the 1970s, Ruth Bader Ginsburg will argue that the Fourteenth Amendment protects against discrimination based on sex as well as race.

May 18, 1896: In *Plessy v. Ferguson*, the US Supreme Court decides that "separate" facilities for blacks and whites are constitutional as long as they are "equal." The case is sparked by Homer Plessy's refusal to sit in the "blacks only" railway car in Louisiana during a time in which nearly all public facilities are separated for blacks and whites. In the 1975 Title IX regulations approved by Congress, the US Department of Health, Education and Welfare (HEW) mandated a "separate but equal" approach to athletics, despite the fact that *Plessy* is later overturned.)[3]

May 17, 1954: In *Brown v. Board of Education*, the US Supreme Court decides that the "separate but equal" ruling in *Plessy v. Ferguson* is a violation of

Fourteenth Amendment rights and that separate facilities are inherently unequal.

July 2, 1964: President Johnson signs the Civil Rights Act of 1964 into law. The law, considered the benchmark civil rights law in the United States, prohibits discrimination based on race, color, religion, sex, or national origin. The language used to describe the prohibition of sex discrimination would become the basis for Title IX.

May 1970: Jean Ledwith King coauthors and files with the US Department of Health, Education, and Welfare (HEW) a landmark complaint against the University of Michigan, which results in the federal government withholding fifteen million dollars in funds from the university. The complaint leads the University of Michigan to double the salaries of one hundred women faculty and address sex discrimination in other areas at the university.

1970–72: "The Alliance to End Sexual Discrimination at MSU" forms. Its founders bring public awareness to sex discrimination at Michigan State University (MSU) and push higher-ups to end discriminatory practices. As a result (before Title IX is even enacted), the university creates more positions in women's athletics and makes administrators increasingly accountable for prohibiting discrimination in all programs.

April 27, 1972: In one of the first sports discrimination cases in the United States, *Morris v. Michigan State Board of Education*, two girls want to play tennis on their high school team, but the Michigan High School Athletic Association forbids girls from playing on boys' varsity teams. In federal court, the judge rules in the girls' favor. The case is argued under the Fourteenth Amendment, which many attorneys will later use with, and sometimes instead of, Title IX in sex discrimination cases.[4]

June 23, 1972: Congress passes Title IX of the Education Amendments Act of 1972.[5]

1973: Mary Pollock cofounds the "Concerned Women Athletes" (CWA) group at the University of Illinois.

1973: MSU hires Nell Jackson as the assistant director of women's athletics responsible for administering the women's sports program.

January 17, 1973: In *Kellmeyer, et al. v. National Education Association, et al.*, Fern "Peachy" Kellmeyer, a women's athletics director and star tennis player, sues eight organizations, including the National Education Association (NEA) and the Association for Intercollegiate Athletics for Women (AIAW) to challenge the AIAW's anti-athletic scholarship policy for women athletes. Rather than engage in a legal battle, the AIAW decides to allow scholarships for women athletes (and tightly regulate the process).

September 3, 1973: Pollock and the CWA at Illinois file a complaint with HEW and take out an advertisement in the *Chicago Tribune* to appeal for public support against the university's sex discrimination.

September 20, 1973: Billie Jean King accepts an invitation from (1939 Wimbledon champion) Bobby Riggs to a tennis match. The media terms the game the "Battle of the Sexes."[6]

1974 (–77): The Women's Equity Action League (WEAL) files a complaint against HEW, claiming that Title IX and other anti–sex discrimination laws are not being enforced. The National Organization for Women (NOW), the National Education Association, the Federation of Organizations of Professional Women, the Association of Women in Science, and four individual plaintiffs join WEAL in the complaint. In 1977, the suit results in "the WEAL order," which requires that HEW respond to complaints in a "timely manner" (though even after this date, individuals and organizations continue to file complaints charging the government with noncompliance).[7]

1974: Jean Ledwith King files a complaint under Title IX against Houghton Mifflin of Boston on behalf of a group of parents in Kalamazoo, Michigan, who object to gender bias in the publisher's textbooks. The publisher issues a revised version of the textbooks and eliminates sexism in subsequent books, setting a precedent for other publishers to do the same (although textbooks would later be excluded from Title IX).

1974: Jean Ledwith King takes her first athletics case; she files suit on behalf of Julie Alexander, an eighth-grade student who is told she is not allowed to run track at Mona Shores High School. Alexander is the only plaintiff, but the suit garners attention from the press, which leads the school to settle out of court (and forty girls join the team).

1974: The AIAW hires feminist attorney Margot Polivy as a response to the National Collegiate Athletic Association (NCAA) opposition to Title IX.

April 1974: Pollock and the CWA at Illinois achieve some success: the university increases the women's budget, organizes women's sports under the athletic association, and hires a new administrator for women's athletics.

May 16, 1974 (–1978): The first female president of the student government at the University of Minnesota hears a speech about Title IX. She leads the student government to investigate sex discrimination at the university and finds the athletics department as the most noncompliant. The student government as an organization files a lawsuit against the university. By 1978, the students' campaign and lawsuit produce significant change: the university ends up having a much higher enrollment rate for women, and their women's athletics department leads the Big Ten Conference with its budget. The Minnesota case demonstrates the power of students acting as an organization.[8]

May 20, 1974: Senator John Tower (R-TX) proposes the "Tower Amendment," which would exclude revenue-producing sports (men's football, basketball, and hockey) from Title IX compliance. The amendment is rejected.[9]

June 20, 1974: HEW publishes a draft of the Title IX regulations for public comment and receives over ten thousand comments.

July 1, 1974: The Javits Amendment is enacted. The amendment requires HEW to issue regulations for Title IX compliance that include "reasonable provisions considering the nature of particular sports."[10] Women's sports advocates consider the amendment a loophole in Title IX. Its vague language allows for universities to use a loophole argument—that differences based on *type of sport* instead of sex constitute differential treatment of men's and women's teams. The amendment also exemplifies the kind of vague language in legislation that often leads to contention ("reasonable provision").

May 27, 1975: HEW issues Title IX regulations to President Ford, who signs them.[11]

June–July 1975: Six resolutions attempting to disapprove HEW's Title IX regulations or exclude revenue-producing sports are introduced in Congress (including the O'Hara Resolution and a second Tower Amendment, "Tower II"). None are passed.

July 14, 1975: Bo Schembechler writes a letter to President Ford arguing that Title IX poses a serious threat to men's college sports.[12]

July 21, 1975: HEW's 1975 Title IX regulations become law. The regulations require "reasonable opportunity" for women athletes to earn scholarships, introduce the "Title IX Laundry List" of ten factors for which schools must maintain equal opportunity, and require all federally funded high schools and colleges to comply with Title IX by a July 21, 1978, deadline. Though the regulations make no mention of revenue-producing sports, many universities continue to attempt to exclude men's football, basketball, and hockey from their Title IX compliance efforts.

September 1975: Amid a growing number of complaints from athletic departments across the country, HEW issues a press release with a memo addressed to leaders of all federally funded schools entitled "Elimination of Sex Discrimination in Athletics Programs."[13]

1976: MSU completes a self-evaluation of its sports programs for Title IX compliance under Nell Jackson's watch, excluding men's football, basketball, and hockey.

1976: MSU hires George "Jud" Heathcote to coach the men's basketball team during their efforts to recruit Earvin "Magic" Johnson to the team.

February 17, 1976: The NCAA files a lawsuit in an attempt to challenge the legality of Title IX, claiming that college athletic programs do not use federal funds. The lawsuit is dismissed.[14]

March 3, 1976: Yale women's crew team members, led by Chris Ernst, write "Title IX" on their naked backs and read a statement protesting inequalities between their program and the men's program to Yale's director of physical education, Joni Barnett.[15] Looking back in 2002, Ernst summed up the spirit behind her team's actions: "I don't care who you think I am. I don't care what picture you want to present of me. This is who I am. You can't make up a story about us. And we won't be invisible."[16]

August 1, 1977: MSU hires Mary Pollock as the director of women's programs and Title IX coordinator.

August 1977: Earvin "Magic" Johnson arrives as an undergraduate and men's basketball player at MSU, bringing national attention to the MSU men's basketball program.

September 1977: Rollin Haffer enrolls as a physical education student and women's badminton athlete on a tuition-only scholarship at Temple University, where she becomes secretary and then president of Temple's Student Athletic Council.

October 1977: Mary Pollock attends a meeting for MSU women's athletic coaches, where she informs them about Title IX. Mark Pittman attends the meeting, which inspires him to begin collecting detailed notes and papers regarding Title IX compliance at MSU: "Title IX: Chronology and Comments and Complaints."

1978: HEW awards grant funds to WEAL, in part to create a Sports Referral and Information Network (SPRINT). SPRINT, a clearinghouse for news and information related to women's sports, creates a much-needed communication medium for women athletes and administrators.[17]

September 1978: At Temple University, women's student athletics director Rollin Haffer hears repeated complaints to the Student Athletic Council about inequalities from athletes representing twelve different women's sports.

February 1, 1978: Mary Pollock sends a memo to the MSU Vice President for Business and Finance, Roger Wilkinson, requesting all financial information from 1976–77 for both men's and women's athletics so that she can do a comparison.[18]

February 3, 1978: Mark Pittman, Kathleen DeBoer, and Bruce Alexander attend an MSU Board of Trustees affirmative action committee meeting focused on Title IX and athletics. Mary Pollock requested the meeting and intended to discern whether MSU administrators were ready to make changes in order to bring the university into Title IX compliance.

February 14, 1978: Roger Wilkinson sends Mary Pollock a memo with financial information showing that while men's football, basketball, and hockey are revenue-producing sports, they are not self-sufficient (from each other or the university) profit producers. The three sports absolutely rely on general university funding to operate.[19]

March 1978: The MSU women's basketball team deals with a series of "mini-crisis incidents," including "having to sell decals for funds in order to attend the Queens Tournament in New York, having early season games cancelled due to strict enforcement of university policy while the men's teams still played, not receiving the full per diem allowance permitted by the university, *ad infinitum*."[20] The incidents lead Kathleen DeBoer to approach Mary Pollock about filing a complaint, and Pollock suggests that DeBoer should ask the entire team to sign the complaint in order for the university to take them seriously.

March 1978: The MSU women's basketball team meet after practice and unanimously decide to file a complaint with Mary Pollock's office.[21] Mariann Mankowski and Kathleen DeBoer meet with Pollock to file the team's complaint.

March 1978: With the Title IX compliance deadline fast approaching, Mary Pollock appeals to student organizations for support in asking the university to survey students' needs and interests regarding opportunities in sports. The Associated Students of MSU, the Council of Graduate Students, and the Student Council come together to write a resolution asking administrators to support Pollock's survey.[22]

March 28, 1978: Mary Pollock sends a letter to Joe Kearney and Nell Jackson (copied to Kathleen DeBoer and Mark Pittman) informing the administrators of complaints. Pollock states that she will "attempt to research" the complaints and "find amenable solutions," but that if she's prevented from doing so, she'll refer the complaints to the Anti-Discrimination Judicial Board (ADJB).[23]

March 29, 1978: As a result of Mary Pollock's efforts, the MSU Varsity Alumni Club votes to accept women's varsity athletics into the club.[24]

April 6, 1978: Clarence Underwood, Mary Pollock, and Nell Jackson meet to discuss Title IX at MSU.[25] Underwood sends a memo to Joe Kearney about the meeting and communicates that Pollock's concerns were her own (instead of the university's), representing her as hostile to men and unreasonable, weakening her credibility.[26]

April 19, 1978: Kathleen DeBoer sends an open letter to the *State News*, making the MSU women's basketball team's complaint public.[27] She also states that the team plans to send their complaint to the Office of Civil Rights (OCR) and request a federal investigation.

April 25, 1978: The MSU women's basketball team members sign a one-page memo to Mary Pollock officially charging the university with sex discrimination.

April 25, 1978: The *State News* publishes a reader's response to Kathleen DeBoer's April 19 open letter about sex discrimination at MSU. The author of the letter claims that because women's sports attract fewer spectators than men's sports and therefore earn less revenue, then men's sports are entitled to more resources.[28] (This often-repeated argument fails to acknowledge the fact that women's sports are often never given the resources and opportunities needed to *become* revenue-producing sports.)

April 27, 1978: HEW publishes a memo from secretary Joseph Califano in which he requests in writing that HEW's general legal counsel clarify its stance on the relationship between revenue-producing college sports and Title IX. The secretary explicitly states the impending compliance deadline of July 21, 1978, and instructs the OCR to "arrange for a review of the implementation of Title IX with respect to athletics with particular attention to revenue-producing sports." Califano includes a list of previously failed congressional attempts to exempt revenue-producing sports from Title IX.[29] Along with the memo, HEW publishes a statement from its attorney reaffirming that revenue-producing sports are not exempt from Title IX compliance.[30]

April 27, 1978: The MSU women's basketball team members attend the annual Women's Sports Banquet, where they hand out a petition that implores other women athletes to join their complaint.

May 9, 1978: Mary Pollock sends a memo to Joe Kearney that outlines her plan of action regarding the women's basketball team's complaint; she requests that the university redo its 1976 self-evaluation since revenue sports were excluded from it. She includes a list of fifteen areas in which the university practices sex discrimination.[31]

May 16, 1978: Kathleen DeBoer, Mariann Mankowski, and Mark Pittman appear on WELM TV, Channel 11 to discuss the team's Title IX complaint against MSU.

May 22, 1978: MSU President Edgar Harden informs Kathleen DeBoer that the university is conducting a legal audit of athletics at MSU in regard to their Title IX compliance. Harden assures DeBoer that whatever happens is "nothing personal," but tells her, "We'll see you in court!"[32]

May 23, 1978: Mary Pollock sends a memo to the Anti-Discrimination Judicial Board. She writes that the athletics department is not responding to her requests for budgetary information, brings attention to the fact that players from other women's teams have also filed complaints with her, and asks for a meeting to go over with administrators the responsibilities of her position.[33]

May 24, 1978: Mary Pollock sends a memo to Joe Kearney (copied to the ADJB, Edgar Harden, Robert Perrin, Ralph Bonner, Nell Jackson, and complainants) with two enclosures: her proposed Title IX sex equity study and her ADJB transmittal letter.[34]

May 25, 1978: Kathleen DeBoer and Mariann Mankowski present to the MSU Board of Trustees and distribute a handout at the meeting. Their handout notes that the Title IX compliance deadline is only sixty-one days away and that HEW has repeatedly stated that revenue-producing sports are not exempt from Title IX compliance. The handout also states that the women's basketball team charges the university with discrimination based on the entire list of possibilities under the Title IX "Laundry List" and requests that the board reaffirm its commitment to cooperate with Mary Pollock and the team in bringing the university into compliance.[35]

May 31, 1978: MSU initiates its legal audit of sports programs, the ADJB receives the women's basketball team's complaint, and Mary Pollock distributes her "Plan to Attain Sex Equity at MSU." By early June, higher-ups in university and sports administration have a copy of Pollock's plan.

June 2, 1978: Mark Pittman submits a complete list of discrimination instances he's witnessed since working with the athletics department so that Jackson can prepare for a meeting with university attorney Byron Higgins.[36]

June 7, 1978: Nell Jackson sends a memo to all head coaches of women's sports at MSU. The memo states that her 1978–79 budget will be one hundred thousand dollars less than she requested and that coaches should meet with her to discuss "necessary cuts."[37]

June 7, 1978: Kathleen DeBoer receives instructions from Sallie Bright (an attorney who serves as the ADJB executive secretary) to include *only* women's basketball in their bottom-line complaint, not the entire women's athletic program.[38]

June 7, 1978: Mary Pollock submits materials to her supervisor that describe her job function as Title IX coordinator (at his request). She includes the job description that was provided when she initially applied for the job (which detailed exactly what she was doing).

June 8, 1978: Robert Perrin urges Mary Pollock to resign, telling her that if she does, the university will give her seven weeks of pay, but if not, they will terminate her pay immediately.[39]

June 10, 1978: Kathleen DeBoer and Mariann Mankowski send a letter to Edgar Harden expressing their "deep concern" and "rage" over the university's decision to fire Mary Pollock.[40]

June 12, 1978: The women's basketball team submits an eleven-page written complaint to the ADJB (as the ADJB secretary had requested), detailing the areas in which they believe MSU is in noncompliance with Title IX. They ask that the ADJB resolve their complaint within twenty days (per the MSU *Student Handbook*'s description of the ADJB's duties).[41]

June 12, 1978: The MSU athletic department's Title IX committee plans to submit a last-minute report by this date but is nowhere near fully compliant with Title IX. (Many other universities scrambled to produce paperwork at the last minute before the July 21 deadline, but some, like Cornell, report that they will need an entire extra year to comply.)

June 15, 1978: Mark Pittman mails the MSU women's basketball team's official complaint to the OCR. He and the team also send letters to various media outlets notifying them of the team's complaint.[42]

June 20, 1978: MSU attorney Byron Higgins submits a preliminary legal analysis on Title IX and its regulations to Edgar Harden. The report justifies MSU's exclusion of men's football, basketball, and hockey from Title IX compliance, using a lengthy and faulty argument.

June 21, 1978: Joe Kearney and the director of the Ralph Young Fund at MSU write to MSU donors stating that "due to the impact of inflation and the federal government's implementation of Title IX," the athletics department will have to charge for VIP parking for the 1978 football season.[43]

June 22, 1978: Fifteen different groups speak on behalf of Mary Pollock at an MSU Board of Trustees meeting. Mark Pittman reads the women's basketball team's speech informing the board that the team has officially filed their complaint with the ADJB and that they are distressed over the university having fired Mary Pollock.[44]

June 22, 1978: Edgar Harden writes a letter to Kathleen DeBoer and Mariann Mankowski in response to their June 10 letter to him about Mary Pollock's termination. Harden assures them that Pollock's firing was not a "vindictive maneuver" on the university's part and that the university was "examining Title IX in all its aspects" so that administrators could "make every effort to comply with the letter of the law, not because of the law alone, but because [they] believe in the purposes for which the law was passed." Harden also invites the women to visit with him for progress reports and to express any concerns.[45]

June 24, 1978: Mark Pittman receives a letter from Barrie Thorne (a professor at MSU), who expresses concern that Pittman may face "repercussions" from the university for speaking out about Title IX at the board meeting.[46]

June 29, 1978: The women's basketball team members, Mark Pittman, and Bruce Alexander meet with an MSU trustee, who explains that he and the board do not understand Title IX or women's athletics, but that (on the positive side) the next Title IX coordinator hired will report directly to the university president. The board member also advises the team to pressure Nell Jackson to force compliance from within athletics, and that the board considers her "invulnerable."[47]

June 30, 1978: Kathleen DeBoer, Bruce Alexander, and Mark Pittman meet Nell Jackson at her home, where they discuss the team's meeting with the board member and the fact that Jackson has an open line of communication with Edgar Harden. They agree to keep each other informed.[48]

July 3, 1978: Kathleen DeBoer receives a letter from the OCR stating that they have received her complaint, determined that it fell within their jurisdiction, and "placed it on a backlog of complaints for further investigation."[49]

July 3, 1978: Kathleen DeBoer receives a call from Sallie Bright, who (according to Mark Pittman's notes) tells her that the ADJB supports increasing support for the women's basketball team with "small items, not $$" and that "the division between 'revenue/profit-producing sports' and other sports should be maintained." Bright also informs DeBoer that the university's Title IX compliance will focus on "levels of competition" and "athletic competency" of males and females.[50]

July 7, 1978: Mark Pittman receives a call from AIAW attorney Margot Polivy, who tells him that the team is doing a "good job" and that she's "concerned with the AIAW's shortcomings." Polivy also tells Pittman that she's forwarded the team's complaint to Marcia Greenberger at the Center for Law and Social Policy in Washington, DC. She advises Pittman to consider a lawsuit against the university if the team's complaint is not addressed. She also advises Pittman that the team does not need to refile their complaint as coming from the entire women's athletics department (instead of just the women's basketball team).[51]

July 16, 1978: In an opinion editorial in the *New York Times*, Margot Polivy identifies money as the root of opposition to Title IX compliance.[52]

July 20, 1978: Joe Kearney informs Nell Jackson that the women's athletic department will likely receive a $500,000 budget for 1978–79 (out of $4.2 million). Kearney claims that this budget will match the women's budget at UCLA, known for their progressiveness with women's athletics (in spite of the fact that Title IX compliance requires comparing the women's athletic department *at MSU to the men's department at MSU*, not to the women's department at another institution).[53]

July 20, 1978: Byron Higgins submits an eighteen-page "Legal Audit of Title IX and the MSU Intercollegiate Athletic Program." In his report, Higgins claims that neither HEW's final regulations for Title IX or its subsequent communications resolve the issue of how Title IX applies to revenue-producing sports. He (wrongly) claims that MSU's men's revenue-producing teams must also be self-supporting, and that the university can continue to exclude them from Title IX compliance.[54]

July 21, 1978: Byron Higgins writes Edgar Harden a letter expressing dissatisfaction with Nell Jackson's "administration and philosophy." Higgins explains that because coaches in the men's program meet with Joe Kearney (the athletics director) and coaches in the women's program meet with Jackson (the assistant director), an image of the woman being "second class" is created. Higgins also suggests that MSU have completely separate programs or separate but equal programs with the same administrative unit.[55]

July 21, 1978: The Title IX compliance deadline arrives with many schools having just begun to attempt to bring their institution into compliance.

July 25, 1978: Joe Kearney receives a letter from Carol Parr, the executive director of WEAL, expressing her concern about discriminatory practices at MSU. Parr reminds Kearney that attempting to exclude any specific programs from Title IX compliance is "unacceptable [and] unlawful." Parr's forthright description of MSU's refusal to include men's football, basketball, and hockey from Title IX compliance as unlawful discrimination gives MSU's women's teams an advantage, as MSU will have difficulty claiming ignorance after this letter.[56]

August 8, 1978: Kathleen DeBoer receives a copy of a letter from the OCR to Senator Robert Griffin (R-MI). The OCR director states in the letter that an investigation will begin at MSU within the next three months.[57]

August 10, 1978: MSU women's basketball player Mary Kay Itnyre and former volleyball and track and field athlete Mary Jo Hardy visit the Michigan Department of Civil Rights, where Itnyre signs a sworn statement claiming discrimination under Michigan Act 453 regarding scholarships, practice facilities, locker rooms, and coaching. The department informs her that in the next six months, they will talk to witnesses and, if they find cause, try to facilitate conciliation.[58]

August 20, 1978: When asked in an interview whether she thinks MSU is discriminating against women, Gwen Norrell says that she's "really not certain how much substance there is to [the women's basketball team's complaint]" (even though she is a faculty member of the athletic department's affirmative action committee charged with addressing Title IX).[59]

August 21, 1978: Kathleen DeBoer and Mariann Mankowski receive a letter from Sallie Bright of the ADJB in which she communicates that "certain technicalities" with the women's basketball team's complaint are holding up the investigation.[60]

October 23, 1978: The MSU women's basketball team sends letters to Sallie Bright and Edgar Harden referencing their previous correspondence and reminding both MSU administrators of their promises to keep the women's basketball team informed as to progress with their complaint.[61]

October 25, 1978: Kathleen DeBoer, Mariann Mankowski, Carol Hutchins, Mary Pollock, Bruce Alexander, and Mark Pittman meet Jean Ledwith King at her Ann Arbor home for a "low key" meeting in which the team describes the history of their complaint and need for a lawyer.[62]

October 27, 1978: Mariann Mankowski receives a response to the team's October 23 letter to Edgar Harden. He informs her that if she has questions regarding their complaint, she needs to meet with Byron Higgins (despite his earlier claim that he would be available to discuss the team's questions when they had them).

November 22, 1978: Mark Pittman and Bruce Alexander meet with Sallie Bright in her office, who informs them that the athletic department's affirmative action report and legal audit are complete and being circulated. Bright asks Pittman for his assistance with "doing interpretive work on the two reports," but he's skeptical of her intentions. (Bright later informs Pittman and Alexander that she cannot show them reports anyway per Byron Higgins's advice.)[63]

November 29, 1978: Jean Ledwith King meets with Mary Pollock, Bruce Alexander, Carol Hutchins, Lori Hyman, Deb Traxinger, and Mary Vielbig in Mark Pittman's office at MSU. They agree to hire King as their attorney and, after meeting with the rest of the team, officially let her know. King accepts as long as they agree that she (not Pollock) will take the lead.[64]

December 1978: HEW issues a draft of its policy interpretation entitled "Title IX and Intercollegiate Athletics." They receive approximately seven hundred comments regarding the interpretation.[65]

February 14, 1979: *Hutchins v. Board of Trustees of Michigan State University* is filed in federal court on February 5. On February 14, Judge Noel Fox issues a temporary restraining order requiring the university to provide equal food and lodging funds for the women's basketball team as was already being given to the men's team.

February 22, 1979: In a hearing, attorney King requests the temporary restraining order in *Hutchins* be extended. She also asks that the team's Title IX claim be stricken from the complaint. The unsettled nature of the law, combined with the uncertainty around how the regulations may be interpreted, makes the constitutional Fourteenth Amendment claim seem the stronger one. In fact, an important legal issue has not been established: could an individual sue under Title IX before exhausting all administrative remedies (e.g., internal to an institution, to a state civil rights department, or to the federal Office of Civil Rights)? Moreover, MSU is preparing its defense around Title IX. King's reductionist strategy, by contrast, focuses on comparing two similar teams, men's and women's basketball, in only two areas—food and lodging—rather than taking on a lengthy and expensive comparison of the entire men's and women's athletics programs as Title IX seemed to require.

At the time, including a Title IX claim increasingly seems only to complicate matters for the plaintiffs. But Judge Fox refuses. He declares, "Well, a judge should not be a ball-and-strike referee. In the Federal courts we must seek out the justice of the situation and the truth of the situation, and we are mandated by even the Declaration of Independence and the Fourteenth Amendment and we are mandated by the Preamble to the Constitution and these are the vantage points from which I am searching and working . . . what we have to do is search out the intent of Congress."[66]

February 26, 1979: The Michigan Department of Civil Rights notifies player Mary Kay Itnyre, the named complainant for the MSU women's basketball team, that its investigation of MSU athletics is set to proceed.[67] Attorney King suggests that Mark Pittman talk with them about the case because if anything happens with his job at MSU, some of their provisions may offer protection.

May 14, 1979: In *Cannon v. the University of Chicago*, the Supreme Court decides that Title IX complainants have the autonomy to decide what forum is best for their particular cases. If certain requirements are met, individuals may bypass time-consuming administrative avenues and file a lawsuit.

May 1979: Rollin Haffer and students at Temple University meet with an attorney from the National Women's Law Center. The center considers Haffer as a possible Title IX test case to argue that Title IX applies to all university programs and activities, including athletics, not only ones that directly receive federal funds.

March 1979: MSU men's basketball team wins NCAA National Championship; Evelyn Johnson, Magic's sister, signs with South Carolina instead of MSU, her second choice, claiming South Carolina women have everything their men have.[68]

June 1979: Mark Pittman learns that his coaching contract at MSU is not renewed.

October 1979 (–87): Despite the defeat of the two Tower Amendments, Washington State University leaders attempt to exempt their football team from Title IX compliance. Women coaches and athletes file suit, claiming a violation of their rights under the Fourteenth Amendment and Title IX. The court orders Washington State University to increase funding for women's athletics (including scholarships), but maintains that the university can exclude its funding rates for football when calculating how much more women's athletics will receive. In 1987, the case goes to the state appellate court, which determines that the trial court had "'abused its discretion' by excluding football."

The case is a "resounding affirmation that all sports [are] to be considered equal under Title IX, in terms of scholarships and participation."[69]

October 16, 1979: The Michigan Department of Civil Rights holds a conciliation conference to resolve issues in the MSU complaint. Their initial investigation finds the allegations credible.[70]

October 22, 1979: The US Equal Employment Opportunity Commission files suit against Sears, Roebuck and Company under Title VII of the Civil Rights Act of 1964. The commission charges Sears with discriminatory practices against women and minorities (only hiring white men for positions of power). Sears attorneys argue that women are not interested in positions that require competitiveness and authority. The case revolves around two issues: whether women's interests are best served by public policies that treat women and men identically; and whether the public should recognize differences between women and men and seek greater recognition for traditionally female values and behavior (much like the issues the sports world attempted to address).[71]

December 11, 1979: HEW issues its final Title IX Policy Interpretation on Intercollegiate Athletics with detailed instructions as to how institutions should assess for Title IX compliance.[72]

April 8, 1980: Rollin Haffer and seven other named plaintiffs file a class action lawsuit against Temple University under Title IX. They forgo filing a complaint first with HEW, seeking a remedy before the federal government would likely address the growing national backlog of uninvestigated Title IX complaints. The situation at Temple is more dire for women athletes than at MSU, especially considering improvement that followed the Spartans' Title IX struggle: along with all the other inequities at MSU, at Temple, no female athlete has a full scholarship (MSU is offering ten for women's basketball), playing opportunities are severely limited with far fewer sports offered, and sports lack necessary equipment.

July 28, 1980: OCR produces the *Interim Title IX Intercollegiate Athletics Manual* to give investigators instructions (this interim manual was not replaced until 1990 because the ground under Title IX shifted so frequently in the 1980s).

August 1980: Kathleen DeBoer leaves the Women's Basketball League, citing economic reasons and conditions worse than she faced as a college student at MSU. She becomes head volleyball coach (and later assistant athletics director) at Ferris State College.

February 6, 1981: In meeting with Judge Fox and attorneys in the *Hutchins* case (and later in an appellate brief), MSU attorney Higgins contends that the Fourteenth Amendment suggests one standard of equality (similarly situated individuals, such as men's and women's basketball players, must be treated similarly) and the federal Department of Education with Title IX suggests another (equity is required only at the programmatic level, between men's and women's athletics programs, each considered as a whole). He claims that siding with the plaintiffs means declaring Title IX regulations "null and void." He argues that MSU could be "whipsawed between two conflicting standards that have the potential of being imposed upon us. One by this Court, and one by the Department of Education."[73] Attorney Jean Ledwith King, in response, contends "we are maintaining our claim under Title IX, but we would prefer that the Court decide this case under the Constitution, directly under the 14th Amendment." She argues that "Title IX does not extend to the entire reach of the Constitution . . . and if Congress [with Title IX] did not go the full reach of the Constitution, that is not the problem of this Court."[74]

March–April 1981: OCR conducts compliance review of MSU athletics, one of eighty institutions chosen for review. A stay is issued in the *Hutchins* case while OCR investigates MSU's athletics program. The preliminary injunction remains in effect.[75]

May 1981: Nell Jackson announces she is leaving MSU to become the director of intercollegiate athletics at the State University of New York at Binghamton, citing "constraints" at MSU.[76]

1981: The professional Women's Basketball League, unable to pay players' salaries, goes out of business; players charge mismanagement.

February 24, 1982: To continue the suit after the original plaintiffs all graduated, *Hutchins v. MSU Board of Trustees* is certified as a class action that includes the following: (1) future members of the women's varsity team; (2) team members from February 5, 1979, until the date of class certification; and (3) team members from February 5, 1976, through February 5, 1979. Deborah Traxinger serves as the class representative.[77]

March 1982: The Chicago branch of the US Department of Education issues findings of MSU's Title IX investigation. Typically OCR negotiates a plan with institutions to begin moving toward greater compliance. Full compliance is not the standard. OCR congratulates MSU for implementing plans that have or will remedy the non-equivalencies in a reasonable time period.

OCR will review progress reports. MSU has begun a process of remedying issues outlined in the women's basketball team's complaint to the ADJB, OCR, and the Michigan Department of Civil Rights.

June 1982: NBC cancels television contract for AIAW women's championships. The AIAW and the NCAA compete for schools to participate in the women's championships they sponsor and for coveted television contracts. The NCAA wins out, and the AIAW ceases business, except for an ongoing antitrust lawsuit against the NCAA. Women's intercollegiate athletics are fully governed by the NCAA.

September 1982: After graduating from MSU in 1979, Carol Hutchins, who has become assistant softball coach at MSU and Indiana, is hired in 1982 in a one-year, part-time position as softball coach and instructor at Ferris State College. Mariann (Cookie) Mankowski is Assistant Women's Basketball Coach at the University of Illinois, a position she took shortly after graduation. The Big Ten Conference has begun sponsoring women's basketball, and the first Division I NCAA Women's basketball tournament is scheduled for the end of the 1982–83 season.

1984: College women switch to a smaller basketball in an effort to improve the pace and quality of the game for spectators. MSU's summer basketball camps for girls were a test site for the research study that supported the change.[78]

February 28, 1984: The *Grove City College v. Bell* US Supreme Court decision determines that only subunits of an educational institution that directly receive federal funds are subject to Title IX. As a result, intercollegiate athletics programs, which typically do not receive direct federal funds, were exempt from Title IX.[79] This strict definition of the word "program" leads the judge in the *Haffer* case to require they strike their Title IX claim. In light of Grove City, attorney King is now permitted to withdraw the Title IX claim from *Hutchins* as she had sought to do earlier. Both cases move forward with the Constitution's Fourteenth Amendment as the primary basis for their cases (the Title IX claim had been secondary from the beginning in the *Hutchins* case.) However, Rollin Haffer, working after graduation as a physical education teacher for developmentally challenged children, is devastated that her case would not go forward under Title IX, feeling that even if the women athletes prevailed under a "back up strategy," losing Title IX from the case signified a victory for those who opposed her efforts to enforce Title IX at Temple—that is, school administrators, peers, and faculty whom she said "tried to break" her, making life as a student nearly unbearable toward the end of her years there.[80] She and the other plaintiffs lose a symbol as much as a legal tool.

June 22, 1984: In light the Grove City decision, attorney Jean King withdraws the Title IX claim from *Hutchins*.

September 26, 1984: In the *Haffer* case, a motion is granted to add claims to the suit, including a claim under the Fourteenth Amendment. At this point, neither *Haffer* nor *Hutchins* proceeds with a Title IX claim; both focus on the Fourteenth Amendment, which was King's strategy and intention from the beginning. In the minds of the plaintiffs in both cases, however, their court battles remain struggles under the banner of Title IX, the law that motivated their fights for equity.

October 10, 1984: With a different judge presiding over the *Hutchins* case after Judge Noel Fox retired due to poor health, the plaintiffs' claims under the Fourteenth Amendment for monetary damages are dismissed. In so doing, the judge has supported MSU's claims of Eleventh Amendment Immunity. Previously, when Title IX was still part of the case, Judge Fox emphasized his view that "the Eleventh Amendment has no place in this litigation" because the Fourteenth Amendment directs "Congress to enforce by legislation [such as Title IX] the objectives of the Fourteenth Amendment as far as discrimination is concerned." He said, "I hereby declare that it's out, and never again to hear that argument."[81] Even though MSU was able to claim Eleventh Amendment Immunity in the end, in part because Title IX was no longer part of the case, the team's claims seeking equitable relief for food and lodging [as opposed to monetary damages] and declaratory relief [a statement of responsibility for wrongdoing] were not dismissed.[82]

October 16, 1984: A settlement is agreed to in the *Hutchins* case that stipulates ongoing equal per diem for food and lodging for male and female MSU basketball players.

June 14, 1985: Kathleen DeBoer and Mark Pittman marry.

1986: The Civil Rights Equalization Act precludes universities from arguing Eleventh Amendment Immunity in Title IX cases, thereby opening the door for monetary damages.[83]

1987: Rollin Haffer testifies before Congress supporting the Civil Rights Restoration Act, which would redefine the word "program" in Title IX to encompass the entire institution rather than only subunits, thereby reinstating athletics within the Title IX's scope.

1988: Congress passes the Civil Rights Restoration Act.[84]

1988: The *Hutchins* case is officially closed; attorney Jean King is awarded attorney fees in the final settlement (customary for the prevailing party), but MSU is not required to admit any wrongdoing (a kind of compromise).

April 4, 1988: Rollin Haffer's case goes to trial, and Title IX is reinstated as one of the legal claims. By this time, Haffer is a thirty-year-old teacher, and for nearly a decade, she has been working on her case, communicating with generations of student plaintiffs and different attorneys (first Margaret Kohn and Ellen Vargas from the NWLC, then Arthur Bryant from Trial Lawyers for Public Justice for the trial). From early on, the attorneys frame their arguments as a test case, asserting that in violating Title IX, Temple is typical of the majority of college and universities in the nation.[85] Attorney Bryant brings to the case experience with using the Fourteenth Amendment to argue school equality cases in Philadelphia, where he successfully proved that the city's all-girls and all-boys schools were fundamentally separate and unequal.[86]

June 13, 1988: After three weeks of trial and seven weeks of negotiation, the Haffer case settles out of court. As early as 1985, Rollin Haffer believed that the lawsuit had already begun to improve the situation at Temple (they added women's crew and some scholarships, for example), and she stayed in frequent communication with current athletes, most whom "knew little or nothing about the lawsuit." Still, she regretted that the Student Athletic Council no longer existed so that the athletics programs had little student input and speculated that the administration wanted it that way. She finds the decision to settle the most difficult one of her life because she stayed in the fight so long in part because she wanted to keep "pushing for true equality." She hoped that *Haffer* would set the standard and stop discrimination everywhere against college women athletes.[87] Yet the financial costs of seeing a full-blown Title IX case to fruition were mounting and daunting. The young plaintiffs had no money, no prospect of monetary damages existed, and the attorneys affiliated with nonprofit organizations lacked the funds to fully investigate the endless details of a large athletic program budget and for an extended trial.[88] Still, the *Haffer* settlement does set a standard, providing a holistic model for comparing athletic benefits for men's and women's programs and offering techniques for identifying discrimination.[89] The changes Temple is required to make, though not resulting in full equality or even complete Title IX compliance, leads attorney Arthur Bryant to deem it the most equitable large athletics program at the time in the country.[90]

1992: *Franklin v. Gwinnett County Public Schools* marks a leap forward in Title IX enforcement. *Franklin* is a landmark case because the court's decision supports compensatory and punitive damages in cases of intentional sex discrimination. *Franklin* gives Title IX the teeth it lacked throughout its first two decades. Because monetary damages are now possible, it becomes easier for potential plaintiffs to find willing attorneys to represent them. The *Franklin* case involves a student who charged a school employee with sexual harassment, an area covered by Title IX from the beginning that was eclipsed in public discourse by the public, controversial focus on equity in athletics. In 2016, sexual harassment and assault, areas long covered by Title IX, are increasingly the focus of Title IX education and enforcement, with some universities requiring college professors to include Title IX statements on course syllabi and attend required training sessions that now rarely address athletics in much detail.[91]

Defining moments for Title IX continue. See endnote 1 in this appendix for brief list of sources on Title IX's ongoing social and legislative history.

Notes

Preface

1. Title IX, Education Amendments of 1972, 20 U.S.C. §§ 1681–1688 (1972), § 1681a.

2. Judy Cochrane, "A Leader in Pursuit of Fields to Conquer," *East Press*, May 22, 1979.

3. Civil Rights Restoration Act of 1987, 20 U.S.C. § 1687 (1988).

4. Bob Becker, "MSU Women Hurt Cause with Suit," *Grand Rapids Press*, February 14, 1979.

5. Bernice Sandler, support letter to the National Endowment for the Humanities, October 1, 2006.

1. Introduction

1. Mary Jo Festle, *Playing Nice: Politics and Apologies in Women's Sports* (New York: Columbia Univ. Press, 1996), 287.

2. Russlynn Ali, "Dear Colleague," United States Department of Education, Office for Civil Rights, April 4, 2011.

3. Carol Hutchins (undergraduate student and athlete at MSU), interview with the author, Ann Arbor, MI, September 23, 2005.

4. Eileen McDonagh and Laura Pappano, *Playing with the Boys: Why Separate Is Not Equal in Sports* (New York: Oxford Univ. Press, 2008) 249.

5. Deborah Traxinger suggested the phrase "off the ball" to convey the "history from below" nature of this book.

6. Ali, "Dear Colleague."

7. Iris Marion Young, *Inclusion and Democracy* (New York: Oxford Univ. Press, 2000), 120.

8. Wayne Booth, *The Rhetoric of Rhetoric* (Malden, MA: Blackwell Publishing, 2004), xx–xi, quoted in Debra Hawhee, "Rhetorics, Bodies, and Everyday Life," *Rhetoric Society Quarterly* 36, no. 2 (2006): 155–64.

9. As women's sports advocates thus reduced expectations and made compromises, the term "sex" has been conflated with "gender," with no reflection at all about the implications of that shift in terminology. What's more, the term "discrimination" nearly disappeared from the public discourse surrounding Title IX.

10. Charles Joyner, *Shared Traditions: Southern History and Folk Culture* (Champaign: Univ. of Illinois Press, 1999), 1.

11. Fred Stabley Jr. and Tim Staudt, *Tales of the Magical Spartans: A Collection of Stories from the 1979 Michigan State NCAA Basketball Champions* (Champaign, IL: Sports Publishing, 2003).

12. For an account of opposition to interpretations and implementation of Title IX between 2001 to 2008, including the 2002 lawsuit filed by the National Wrestling Coaches Association against the US Department of Education, see Nancy Hogshead-Makar and Andrew Zimbalist, eds., *Equal Play: Title IX and Social Change* (Philadelphia: Temple Univ. Press, 2007), 179–305. For an excellent source that documents the need for financial reforms and greater accountability in college athletics, see *Restoring the Balance: Dollars, Values, and the Future of College Sports* (Miami: Knight Commission on Intercollegiate Athletics, 2010).

13. Katherine Hanson, Vivian Guilfoy, and Sarita Pillai, *More Than Title IX: How Equity in Education Has Shaped the Nation* (Lanham, MD: Rowman and Littlefield, 2009), 61.

14. Bernice Sandler, letter to the National Endowment for the Humanities, October 2006.

15. Karen Offen, *European Feminisms 1700–1950: A Political History* (Stanford: Stanford Univ. Press, 2000), 17.

Part One. Do Women Want the Rose Bowl?

1. Patricia Ann Rosenbrock, "Persistence and Accommodation in a Decade of Struggle and Change: The Case of Women Administrators in Division 1-A Intercollegiate Athletics Programs" (PhD diss., University of Iowa, 1987), 85.

2. The term "gender" began to be used to include "sex" in the 1980s, with "gender equality" or "gender equity" eventually becoming the commonly used terms.

3. Linda Jean Carpenter and R. Vivian Acosta, *Title IX* (Champaign, IL: Human Kinetics, 2005), 5.

4. Ibid.

5. Dorothy Jongeward and Dru Scott, *Affirmative Action for Women: A Practical Guide for Women and Management* (Reading, MA: Addison-Wesley, 1973), 63.

6. Sarah K. Fields, *Female Gladiators: Gender, Law, and Contact Sport in America* (Champaign: Univ. of Illinois Press, 2005), vii.

7. Rosenbrock, "Persistence and Accommodation," 70.

2. Teaming Up

1. Leslie Heywood and Shari L. Dworkin, *Built to Win: The Female Athlete as Cultural Icon*, Sport and Culture 5, ed. Toby Miller, and M. Ann Hall (Minneapolis: Univ. of Minnesota Press, 2003), 53.

2. Billie Jean King, publisher's letter, *womenSports*, August 1976, quoted in Susan Ware, *Game, Set, Match: Billie Jean King and the Women's Sports Revolution* (Chapel Hill: Univ. of North Carolina Press, 2011), 51–52.

3. Billie Jean King, form letter, June 7, 1974, quoted in Ware, *Game, Set, Match*, 57.

4. Donna Lopiano, lunch keynote presentation at the academic and legal conference "Girls and Women Rock: Celebrating 35 Years of Sport & Title IX," Cleveland, OH, March 28–31, 2007.

5. Grace L. Lichtenstein, *A Long Way, Baby: The Inside Story of the Women in Pro Tennis* (New York: William Morrow, 1974), 150, quoted in Ware, *Game, Set, Match*, 153.

6. Ware, *Game, Set, Match*, 151–52.

7. Billie Jean King, lunch keynote presentation at the academic and legal conference "Girls and Women Rock: Celebrating 35 Years of Sport & Title IX," Cleveland, OH, March 28–31, 2007.

8. Ibid.

9. Ibid.

10. Ware, *Game, Set, Match*, 152.

11. Ibid., 150.

12. Michael A. Messner, *Taking the Field: Women, Men, and Sports* (Minneapolis: Univ. of Minnesota Press, 2002), 30.

13. Christine Grant, "Liberty, Equality and Sorority," speech, AIAW, Region 9 Delegate Assembly, 1980, transcript, in Christine Grant Papers, Iowa Women's Archives, University of Iowa Libraries, Iowa City, IA.

14. The use of the "feminine apologetic" to describe how female athletes deal with role conflict was first developed in detail by Jan Felshin in *American Women in Sport*, by Ellen Gerber et al. (Reading, MA: Addison-Wesley, 1974), 203–9. Felshin's discussion originates in an excerpt from an unpublished paper by Dorothy V. Harris, "The Social Self and the Competitive Self in the Female Athlete," August 1971, Dorothy V. Harris Papers, 1951–1991, Pennsylvania State University Libraries, State College, PA. Historians, especially Susan Cahn and Mary Jo Festle, have documented the persistence of what Festle calls "apologetic behavior" among female athletes throughout the twentieth century, suggesting that even with growing acceptance of female athleticism the need to insist on the compatibility between sport and femininity persists. See Festle, *Playing Nice*, 45–52. One continuing form of what I term "apologetic rhetoric" has been identified by sociologist Cynthia Fabrizio Pelak, who examines the practice of marking girls' and women's teams with the term "lady" (e.g., the Lady Bulldogs). See Pelak, "The

Relationship of Sexist Naming Practices and Athletic Opportunities in Colleges and Universities in the Southern United States," *Sociology of Education* 81, no. 2 (2008): 189–210. Related to this vein of rhetorical research into how female athletes represent themselves are studies of media representations, including content analysis of sports broadcasting, newspaper coverage, magazines, and other media. Studies by Mary Jo Kane, a professor of kinesiology and the director of the Tucker Center for Research on Girls and Women in Sports, highlight the agenda-setting power of the media in which "more ladylike sports" such as golf and tennis receive more coverage than contact sports such as basketball or soccer. See Mary Jo Kane, "Media Coverage of the Female Athlete: Before, During, and After Title IX: *Sports Illustrated* Revisited," *Journal of Sport Management* 2 (1988): 87–99.

15. Stephanie Kadel Taras, *Fighting for Fair Play: Stories from the Feminist Legal Career of Jean Ledwith King* (Ann Arbor: Time Pieces Personal Biographies, 2010), 13.

16. Sarah A. Rigg, "Executive Profile: Jean Ledwith King, Attorney, Ann Arbor," *MLive*, August 21, 2008, http://www.mlive.com/businessreview/annarbor/index.ssf/2008 /08/executive_profile_jean_ledwith.html.

17. Alice Kessler-Harris, *Out to Work: A History of Wage-Earning Women in the United States* (New York: Oxford Univ. Press, 2003), 312.

18. Rigg, "Executive Profile."

19. Anonymous attorney colleague of Jean Ledwith King in telephone interview with the author, February 2006.

20. Bernice Sandler, "'Too Strong for a Woman': The Five Words that Created Title IX," *About Women on Campus* 6, no. 2 (1997): 3.

21. Maryanne George, "Lawyer Is Fearless Champ of Equality in Schools, Sports," *Detroit Free Press*, March 15, 1999.

22. Ibid.

23. Ibid.

24. Emily Bazelon, "The Place of Women on the Court," *New York Times*, July 12, 2009.

25. George, "Lawyer Is Fearless Champ."

26. Heather Booth and Day Creamer et al., "Socialist Feminism: A Strategy for the Women's Movement," position paper, Hyde Park Chapter of the Chicago Women's Liberation Union, Chicago, 1972, http://www.cwluherstory.org/socialist-feminism-a-strategy -for-the-womens-movement.html.

27. Deborah Traxinger, interview with the author, Grand Ledge, MI, August 2007. For the complete Douglass quotation, see the 1857 speech "The Significance of Emancipation in the West Indies" in *The Frederick Douglass Papers*, Series One: Speeches, Debates, and Interviews, edited by John W. Blassingame, vol. 3, *1855–63* (New Haven, CT: Yale Univ. Press, 1986), 204.

28. Jean Ledwith King, speech, Washtenaw County Bar Association and the Women Lawyers of Michigan Washtenaw Branch, n.d., transcript, in Jean King Papers, Michigan Historical Collections, Bentley Historical Library, University of Michigan, Ann Arbor.

29. Taras, *Fighting for Fair Play*, 16.

30. George, "Lawyer Is Fearless Champ."

31. Carol J. Pierman, ed., "Women and Sports," *Women Studies Quarterly* 33, nos. 1/2 (Spring-Summer 2005): 8.

32. Ibid., 6.

33. Ware, *Game, Set, Match*, 51–52.

34. Ibid., 161.

35. Bernice Sandler, presentation at the academic and legal conference "Girls and Women Rock: Celebrating 35 Years of Sport & Title IX," Cleveland, OH, March 28–31, 2007.

36. Jay Searcy, "Foe of Men's Myth Braces for Battle," *New York Times*, July 14, 1974.

37. Margaret C. Dunkle and Bernice Sandler, "What Constitutes Equality for Women in Sport? Federal Law Puts Women in the Running," paper, Project on the Status and Education of Women, Association of American Colleges, Washington, DC, 1974.

38. Ibid.

3. Identity Crisis

1. Festle, *Playing Nice*, 114.

2. Baile, Mikki, talk presented at a Michigan State University women's basketball alumna event.

3. Rosenbrock, "Persistence and Accommodation," 88.

4. Ibid., 60–63.

5. Ibid., 80.

6. Margaret Dunkle, quoted in Stephanie L. Twin, *Out of the Bleachers: Writings on Women in Sport* (Old Westbury, NY: Feminist Press, 1979), 176.

7. John A. Lucas and Ronald A. Smith, "Women's Sport: A Trial of Equality," in *Her Story in Sport: A Historical Anthology of Women in Sports*, ed. Reet Howell (West Point, NY: Leisure Press, 1982), 239–65.

8. Ibid., 247–49.

9. Clarence Underwood, *The Student Athlete: Eligibility and Academic Integrity* (East Lansing: Michigan State Univ. Press, 1984), 9.

10. Knight Foundation, "Introduction," in *Reports of the Knight Foundation Commission on Intercollegiate Athletics, 1991–1993* (Miami: Knight Commission on Intercollegiate Athletics, 1991–93), iii.

11. Phyllis Bailey, interview by Judy Fountain, December 8, 2004, transcript, Ohio State University Oral History Program, Ohio State University Archives, Columbus, OH, http://hdl.handle.net/1811/29293.

12. Phyllis Bailey, interview with the author, Columbus, OH, July 22, 2007.

13. Pamela Grundy and Susan Shackelford, *Shattering the Glass: The Remarkable History of Women's Basketball* (New York: New Press, 2005), 41–42, 52.

14. Ibid., 47.

15. Ibid., 77.

16. Bailey, interview with the author, July 2007.

17. Bailey, interview by Fountain, December 2004.

18. Bailey, interview with the author, July 2007.

19. Ibid.

20. Lucas and Smith, "Women's Sport: A Trial of Equality," 257.

21. Gail F. Maloney, "The Impact of Title IX on Women's Intercollegiate Athletics" (PhD diss., State University of New York at Buffalo, 1994), 25.

22. Julie Byrne, *O God of Players: The Story of the Immaculata Mighty Macs* (New York: Columbia Univ. Press, 2003), 16–18.

23. Maloney, "The Impact of Title IX," 25.

24. Murray Sperber, *Onward to Victory: The Crises that Shaped College Sports* (New York: Henry Holt and Company, 1998), 97.

25. Ibid.

26. Ibid., 297–99.

27. Ibid., 312 (quoting Nat Holman in *Sport Magazine*, December 1951).

28. Ibid., 364–65.

29. Ibid.

30. Ibid., 365.

31. Danny Andrews, "Wayland Baptist Celebrates Half a Century of Women's Basketball," *Plainview Daily Herald*, November 7, 1998.

32. Jere Longman, "Before UConn, There Was Wayland," *New York Times*, December 19, 2010.

33. Ibid., 22.

34. Grundy and Shackelford, *Shattering the Glass*, 109–10.

35. Sperber, *Onward to Victory*, 285–93.

36. Maloney, "The Impact of Title IX," 28–29.

37. Sperber, *Onward to Victory*, 500.

38. Underwood, *Student Athlete*, 36.

39. Bailey, interview with the author, July 2007.

40. Tina Sloan Green and Carole A. Oglesby et al., *Black Women in Sport* (Reston, VA: AAHPERD Publications, 1981), 29.

41. Grundy and Shackelford, *Shattering the Glass*, 157.

42. This notion persisted in the women's sports world even in the 1990s. Volleyball star and model Gabrielle Reece attacked this notion in her autobiography, calling the attitude "a Victorian notion retooled for the 90s, an update of Virginia Woolf's 'angel in the house'—the woman who is good, productive, virtuous, lending a genteel civilizing influence to the home. Only the new attitude is 'angel of the court.'" See Gabrielle Reece, *Big Girl in the Middle* (New York: Three Rivers Press, 1998), 98. Other women athletes support the idea that women can change sports culture for the better by emphasizing nurturing (empowerment, encouragement, and support) in competition rather than ruthlessness and aggression. See Mariah Burton Nelson, *Embracing Victory: How Women Can Compete Joyously, Compassionately, and Successfully in the Workplace and on the Playing Field* (New York: Avon Books, 1998).

43. Ying Wushanley, *Playing Nice and Losing: The Struggle for Control of Women's Intercollegiate Athletics, 1960–2000* (Syracuse, NY: Syracuse Univ. Press, 2004), 68–69.

44. Festle, *Playing Nice,* 116.

45. Wushanley, *Playing Nice and Losing,* 63.

46. Ibid., 66.

47. Linda Estes, telephone interview with the author, October 2008.

48. Wushanley, *Playing Nice and Losing,* 80.

49. Ibid., 80–81.

50. Estes, interview, October 2008.

51. Ibid.

52. Ibid.

53. Ellen Gerber, telephone interview with the author, December 4, 2010.

54. Ibid.

55. Ibid.

56. Ibid.

57. Ibid.

58. Ibid.

59. Ibid.

60. Lopiano, lunch keynote presentation at the academic and legal conference "Girls and Women Rock: Celebrating 35 Years of Sport & Title IX," Cleveland, OH, March 28–31, 2007.

61. Grant, "Liberty, Equality and Sorority," 2.

62. Ibid., 1–3.

63. Ibid., 4.

64. See Ying Wushanley, *Playing Nice and Losing* (Syracuse, NY: Syracuse Univ. Press), 72; Ronald A. Smith, "Women's Control of American College Sport: The Good of Those Who Played or an Exploitation by Those Who Controlled?" *Sport History Review* 29 (1998): 103–20.

65. Festle, *Playing Nice*, 113–14.
66. Ibid.

4. Full-Court Press

1. Festle, *Playing Nice*, 113, 318.
2. Ibid., 127.
3. Ibid., 126.
4. Jan Felshin, "The Full Court Press for Women in Athletics," in *Women's Athletics: Coping with Controversy*, ed. Barbara J. Hoepner (Washington, DC: AAHPER Publications, 1974), 92.
5. Welch Suggs, *A Place on the Team: The Triumph and Tragedy of Title IX* (Princeton, NJ: Princeton Univ. Press, 2005), 57.
6. Festle, *Playing Nice*, 129.
7. John R. Thelin, "Good Sports? Historical Perspectives on the Political Economy of Intercollegiate Athletics in the Era of Title IX, 1972–1997," *Journal of Higher Education* 71, no. 4 (2000): 395.
8. Ibid., 393.
9. Ibid.
10. *NCAA News*, January 1, 1974, NCAA News Archives online, accessed January 12, 2011. Site discontinued.
11. "Don't Be Fuelish," video, 0:30, from Super Bowl IX televised by NBC on January 12, 1975, http://adland.tv/commercials/ad-council-dont-be-fuelish-1975-030-usa.
12. "Energy Committee Offers Conservation Suggestions," *NCAA News*, March 1, 1974.
13. For an argument that the AIAW increasingly—and hypocritically—embraced commercialism during the 1970s, see Wushanley, *Playing Nice and Losing*, 158. Wushanley claimed, "From All-Star to All-American, from Hanes Classic to Louisville Slugger, from NBC to ESPN, from airlines to automobile dealers, and from Coca-Cola to alcoholic beverages, the AIAW pursued the commercial model as hard as it could. If there was a significant difference between the AIAW and the NCAA by the turn of the decade, it was not their philosophical commitment but the degrees of success in their commercial endeavors."
14. "NCAA Takes First Steps For Energy Conservation," *NCAA News*, February 1, 1974.
15. Ibid.
16. Kim Golombisky, "Unexcused Absences: Education Discourses in Women's Sports, Student-on-Student Sexual Harassment, and Gender Equity Advocacy," *Microform Publications Bulletin: Health, Physical Education and Recreation* 15, no. 2 (2002): 48.
17. Mabel Lee, *A History of Physical Education and Sports in the U.S.A.* (New York: John Wiley & Sons, 1983) 325, quoted in Golombisky, "Unexcused Absences," 48.

18. *NCAA News*, March 1, 1974.

19. Ibid.

20. Ibid.

21. *NCAA News*, April 15, 1974.

22. Steven Weston, "Title IX Regulations Confuse All but a Very Few People," *Tucson Daily Citizen*, August 15, 1974.

23. "NCAA Council Adopts Resolutions on Senate Bills, Women's Sports," *NCAA News*, May 15, 1974.

24. See Festle, *Playing Nice*, 132–33, for an excellent discussion of the AIAW opposition to the Tower Amendment.

25. Festle, *Playing Nice*, 132–33.

26. N. Peggy Burke, "Power and Power Plays," *Vital Speeches of the Day* 45, no. 7 (1979), 207–12.

27. Ibid., 211.

28. Ibid., 208.

29. Ibid.

30. N. Peggy Burke, "Statement of Peggy Burke, President of the Association for the Intercollegiate Athletics for Women," speech, Subcommittee on Education of the Senate Committee on Labor and Public Welfare, September 18, 1975, transcript, in Iowa Women's Archives, University of Iowa Libraries, Iowa City, IA.

31. Bonnie L. Parkhouse and Jackie Lapin, *Women Who Win: Exercising Your Rights in Sport* (Englewood Cliffs, NJ: Prentice Hall, 1980), 17.

32. "H.E.W. Head Says Title IX Won't 'Bankrupt' Schools: Title IX Explained by Official," *New York Times*, June 26, 1975.

33. "Weinberger Responds to Questions Concerning Title IX," *NCAA News*, August 1, 1974.

34. Ibid.

35. "James Reviews NCAA Position on Title IX," *NCAA News*, August 1, 1974.

36. Ibid.

37. "Logic Lacking in Title IX Guidelines," *NCAA News*, September 15, 1974.

38. Festle, *Playing Nice*, 168.

39. *NCAA News*, November 1, 1974.

40. Festle, *Playing Nice*, 168.

41. "High Schools Denounce Title IX," *NCAA News*, October 1, 1974.

42. "Title IX Letter Shows Effort Needed in Battle," *NCAA News*, August 15, 1974.

43. Carpenter and Acosta, *Title IX*, 64–65.

44. "The Editor's Views: HEW Challenge Unauthorized," *NCAA News*, January 1, 1975.

45. "Assassination or Assimilation," *NCAA News*, February 15, 1975.

46. *NCAA News*, August 15, 1974.

47. Festle, *Playing Nice*, 168.

48. John U. Bacon, "Michigan Creates the BigTime: U-M and the Invention of High Stakes, Big-Money College Sports," *Michigan Today News*, Spring 2006.

49. Bo Schembechler, letter to President Gerald Ford, July 14, 1975, White House Central Files: Name Files, Glenn "Bo" Schembechler Folder, Gerald R. Ford Presidential Library and Museum Archives, Gerald R. Ford Presidential Library and Museum, Ann Arbor, MI.

50. Ibid.

51. Ibid.

52. Ibid.

53. Ibid.

54. Patricia L. Geadelmann, Christine Grant, Yvonne Slatton, and N. Peggy Burke, *Equality in Sport for Women* (Washington, DC: AAHPER Publications, 1977), 152.

55. *NCAA News*, "Ford Recipient of 1975 'Teddy' Award," January 1, 1975.

56. NCAA News, January 1, 1975.

57. Golombisky, "Unexcused Absences."

58. See Candace Lyle Hogan, "NCAA & AIAW: Will Men Score on Women's Athletics?" *womenSports* 4, no. 1 (January 1997): 46–49, and Golombisky, "Unexcused Absences."

59. *NCAA News*, January 1, 1975.

60. *Hearings on H.C.R. 330 (Title IX regulation), First Session, Before the Subcomm. on Equal Opportunities of the Comm. on Education and Labor, House of Representatives*, 94th Cong. 50 (1975), 50.

61. Ibid.

62. Ibid.

63. Ibid.

64. Ibid., 51–54.

65. Ibid., 64.

66. Ibid., 58.

67. Ibid.

68. Ibid., 54.

69. Ibid.

70. Ibid.

71. Ibid.

5. Transition to Equality

1. Christine Grant, "What Does Equality Mean?" in *Equality in Sport for Women*, ed. Patricia L. Geadelmann et al. (AAHPERD, January 1977), 1–25.

2. Carpenter and Acosta, *Title IX*, 210.

3. Ibid., 11.

4. Ibid.

5. Ibid.

6. Nancy Hicks, "Women's Groups and Educators Urge Approval of Sex Bias Rules," *New York Times*, June 26, 1975.

7. Michael J. Klarmen, *From Jim Crow to Civil Rights: The Supreme Court and the Struggle for Racial Equality* (New York: Oxford Univ. Press, 2004), 7.

8. Norma V. Cantu, Assistant Secretary for Civil Rights, Office for Civil Rights, *Clarification of Intercollegiate Athletics Compliance: The Three-Part Test*, January 16, 1996, http://www2.ed.gov/about/offices/list/ocr/docs/clarific.html.

9. Hicks, "Women's Groups and Educators Urge Approval," 19.

Part Two. Grassroots of Change

1. Mariah Burton Nelson, *The Stronger Women Get, the More Men Love Football: Sexism and the American Culture of Sports* (San Diego, CA: Harcourt, 1994).

6. Spartans

1. Charles T. Clotfelter, *Big-Time Sports in American Universities* (New York: Cambridge Univ. Press, 2011), xii.

2. Anonymous former MSU administrator, interview with the author, East Lansing, MI, September 2005.

3. Jud Heathcote and Jack Ebling, *Jud: A Magical Journey* (Urbana, IL: Sagamore Publishing, 1995), 249.

4. Anonymous former MSU administrator, interview, September 2005.

5. See, for example, Forrest J. Berghorn, Norman R. Yetman, and William E. Hanna, "Racial Participation and Integration in Men's and Women's Intercollegiate Basketball: Continuity and Change, 1958–1985," *Sociology of Sport Journal* 5, no. 2 (1988): 107–24.

6. Green and Oglesby et al., *Black Women in Sport*, 29.

7. Anonymous former MSU administrator, interview, September 2005.

8. Green and Oglesby et al., *Black Women in Sport*, 28.

9. Ibid., 29.

10. These budget figures were obtained by Mark Pittman in 1978 from public information available in the Michigan State University Library. The figure of approximately ninety thousand dollars for the total women's sports budget matches those reported in the media in the 1970s. In terms of comparison with other schools, the Big Ten as a point of reference is somewhat problematic because women did not officially participate in the Big Ten until 1982, when women's sports became part of the NCAA.

11. "Lady Gets MSU Job," *Detroit News*, July 25, 1973.

12. "Women's Athletic Director Named at MSU," *Albion Evening Recorder,* July 24, 1974.

13. Nell Jackson, *Sex Differences* (Columbia, SC: National Association for Sport and Physical Education Resource Center on Media in Physical Education, 1970), audiobook on cassette.

14. Ibid.

15. Ibid.

16. Karen Langeland, interview by Jeff Charnley and Fred Honhart, January 17, 2001, transcript, Michigan State University Sesquicentennial Oral History Project, Michigan State University, *On the Banks of the Red Cedar,* Michigan State University Archives and Historical Collections, Michigan State University, East Lansing, online archives, http://onthebanks.msu.edu/sohp/Object/2-D-93/transcript-with-karen-langeland-on-january-17-2001.

17. Ibid.

18. Ibid.

19. Anonymous former MSU administrator, interview, September 2005.

20. "Aquamania—MSU Green Splash," Michigan State University Archives and Historical Collections, accessed March 4, 2016, http://archives.msu.edu/collections/aquamania.php.

21. Javier Pescador and Portia Vescio, "The Floor Was Warped: Women Athletes and MSU Athletics in the Title IX Era," MS PowerPoint, 2010, http://www.docstoc.com/docs/38997059/WOMEN-AND-SPORTS-1960-2000.

22. "Pre–Title IX Athletes Get Overdue Letters," *Coaching Management,* 10, no. 9 (December 2002), http://www.momentummedia.com/articles/cm/cm1009/bboverdue.htm.

23. Heathcote and Ebling, *Jud: A Magical Journey,* 29.

24. Ibid., ix.

25. Ibid., 61.

26. Ibid., 68.

27. Ibid., 70.

28. Ibid., 65.

29. Traxinger, interview, August 2007.

30. Ibid.

31. Hutchins, interview, September 2005.

32. Stabley and Staudt, *Tales of the Magical Spartans,* 78–79.

33. Ibid., 51.

7. An Activist's Story

1. Mary Pollock, interview with the author, East Lansing, MI, August 2, 2011.

2. Ibid.

3. Ibid.

4. Mary Pollock Papers, 1972–1977, University of Illinois Archives, University of Illinois at Urbana-Champaign, Urbana, IL.

5. Robin Morgan, ed., *Sisterhood Is Powerful: An Anthology of Writings from the Women's Liberation Movement* (New York: Vintage Books, 1970).

6. Vivian Gornick and Barbara K. Moran, eds., *Women in a Sexist Society: Studies in Power and Powerlessness* (New York: Signet, 1970).

7. Pollock, interview, August 2011.

8. Ibid.

9. *Greater Champaign Area NOW Newsletter* 1, no. 8 (April 1974): 3, in Mary Pollock Papers, University of Illinois Archives. Joyce Glenn was cosponsor of the task force.

10. *Chicago Tribune*, October 30, 1973.

11. Rollin G. Wright, Head of University of Illinois Department of Physical Education, "Illini Notes," *University of Illinois Mothers' Association* 11, no. 1 (November 1973).

12. Marcia Federbush to Mary Pollock, note attached to copy of Title IX Complaint against the University of Michigan, November 13, 1972, in Mary Pollock Papers, University of Illinois Archives. Federbush's first sentence was "Nope, U of M was worse—$0 for Women's Intercollegiates."

13. Fred Eisenhammer, "Money Key Word for Indebted AA," *Daily Illini*, November 30, 1973.

14. Joan Huber, letter to the chancellor's committee on the status of women's athletic programs' funding at the University of Illinois, January 16, 1974, in Mary Pollock Papers, University of Illinois Archives.

15. Mary Pollock, "Dear Sisters in the Struggle for More Money for Women Athletes, otherwise known as Concerned Women Athletes at the University of Illinois-Urbana," letter, February 2, 1974, in Mary Pollock Papers, University of Illinois Archives. In this letter, Pollock conveyed her sense that Illinois students' actions could contribute to a larger social change movement: "I think some of the stories I heard—the horror stories—would strengthen our case considerably. We need these written down in your own words as they happened to you. Some of you are tired of talking about it, but sit down and write your experience for the sake of all women athletes who will follow you. . . . I intend to print up a lot of copies of our complaint and distribute them to the media and other colleges. Please understand that the more furor we can create, the more pressure the University feels. It also helps the women in other colleges to feel like there are others in the same boat and they can get out of theirs, too."

16. Students' notes to Pollock, in Mary Pollock Papers, University of Illinois Archives.

17. Ibid.

18. Booth and Creamer et al., "Socialist Feminism."

19. Ibid., 9.

20. Suzanne Guy, *Greater Champaign Area NOW Newsletter* (July 1973): 1, in Mary Pollock Papers, University of Illinois Archives.

21. Booth and Creamer et al., "Socialist Feminism," 9–10.

22. Mary Pollock Papers, University of Illinois Archives.

23. "Group Probes Women's Athletics: Task Force Studies Financing," *Courier-News*, November 11, 1973.

24. Handwritten notes from interview with John G. Pace, Director of Alumni Projects, in Mary Pollock Papers, University of Illinois Archives.

25. Ibid.

26. Polly Anderson, "Illinois' Women Athletes Demand Equal Rights," *Daily Illini*, February 1974.

27. Mary Pollock, "A Documentary History of Demands for Sex Equality in Intercollegiate Sports at the University of Illinois," in Mary Pollock Papers, University of Illinois Archives.

28. John Husar, "Illini Women's Athletics Death Near?" *Chicago Tribune*, October 30, 1973, in Mary Pollock Papers, University of Illinois Archives.

29. Ibid., 1–2.

30. Ibid.

31. Fred Eisenhammer, "AA Grows to Complex Organization," *Daily Illini*, November 28, 1973.

32. Bil Gilbert and Nancy Williamson, "Sport Is Unfair to Women," *Sports Illustrated*, May 28, 1973, http://sportsillustrated.cnn.com/vault/article/magazine/MAG1087396/.

33. Marjorie Blaufarb, "Solomon's Judgment on Women's Sports," presentation, First Delegate Assembly of AIAW, November 4, 1973, in Mary Pollock Papers, University of Illinois Archives.

34. All quotations in this paragraph are from Joan Huber, memo to Bernice Sandler, November 7, 1973, in Mary Pollock Papers, University of Illinois Archives.

35. Margaret Dunkle, "Equal Opportunity for Women in Sports," speech, Association for Health, Physical Education and Recreation Annual Convention, April 13, 1973, transcript, in Mary Pollock Papers, University of Illinois Archives.

36. Susan Sternberg, "Women Athletes May Sue University," *Daily Illini*, November 6, 1973.

37. Jeff Metcalfe, "WISA Rates Over New Turf," *Daily Illini*, November 7, 1973.

38. Charles Tilly, *Social Movements, 1768–2004* (Boulder, CO: Paradigm Publishers, 2004), 53.

39. Sternberg, "Women Athletes May Sue."

40. Huber, letter to the chancellor's committee, in Mary Pollock Papers, University of Illinois Archives.

41. Arlene Mennenga, "Women's Sports Issue Is Debated: House Subcommittee Holds Hearing at UI," *Champaign-Urbana Courier*, March 6, 1974.

42. Susan Sternberg, "Equality for Women Athletes Is Long Overdue," *Daily Illini*, April 26, 1974.

43. Mary Pollock, "Problem Areas with the Task Force on Women's Athletics Report," presentation to Chancellor Peterson, University of Illinois, May 1974, in Mary Pollock Papers, University of Illinois Archives.

44. Pollock, interview, August 2011.

45. Ibid.

8. Catalysts

1. Kathleen DeBoer, *Gender and Competition: How Men and Women Approach Work and Play Differently* (Monterey: Coaches Choice Books, 2004), 11.

2. Christine Grant, "The Meaning of the Existence of the AIAW," speech, AIAW Region 1 Delegate Assembly, 1980, transcript, in Christine Grant Papers, Iowa Women's Archives, University of Iowa Libraries, Iowa City, IA.

3. Quoted from a profile of Kathleen DeBoer in Mark Pittman's personal files, 1978. This document appears to be a draft of a news article or press release written when DeBoer was twenty-one years old and had just transferred to Michigan State.

4. Ibid.

5. DeBoer, *Gender and Competition*, 12.

6. Kathleen DeBoer, interview with the author, Lexington, KY, February 18, 2011.

7. Wushanley, *Playing Nice and Losing*, 12.

8. *Wolverine*, Michigan Agricultural College Yearbook, 1920, 160.

9. Ibid.

10. "Spartanettes Drub U-M, 73–35," *State Journal*, January 25, 1974.

11. All quotes in this paragraph are from Pollock, interview, August 2011.

12. Mary Pollock, interview by Maria Finitzo and Peter Gilbert, conducted for the author, East Lansing, MI, June 10, 2010.

13. Ibid.

14. Ibid.

15. Mary Jo Hardy and Bruce Alexander, interviews with the author, Okemos, MI, February 19, 2011.

16. Mark Pittman, interview with the author, Lexington, KY, February 12, 2011.

17. Kathleen DeBoer, email to the author, June 14, 2010.

18. Susie Thomas, "Grand Rapids Volleyball Connection," *Grand Rapids Press*, October 26, 1976.

19. DeBoer, email, June 14, 2010.

20. Ibid.

21. Ibid.

22. DeBoer, interview, February 2011.

23. Mark Pittman, "Title IX: Chronology and Comments and Complaints," Mark Pittman Personal Files, 1.

24. Pittman, interview, February 2011.

25. DeBoer, email, June 14, 2010.

26. DeBoer, interview, February 2011.

27. Ibid.

28. Gayle Jacobson, "Women Cagers Reach for National Prominence," *State News*, November 30, 1977.

29. Lynn Henning, "MSU Women Cagers Seek Tougher Foes," *Lansing State Journal*, December 20, 1977.

30. Mel Greenberg, *Philadelphia Inquirer*, December 1977, photocopy in Pittman's "Chronology." The six-page article previewed the 1977–78 season and featured the top ten preseason teams for that year: Wayland Baptist, Delta State, Montclair State, North Carolina State, Maryland, Old Dominion, Tennessee, Louisiana State, St. Joseph's, and UCLA.

31. Although university-level fundraising efforts likely never focused on women's athletics in the 1970s, it is a common practice for university development professionals to approach potential donors themselves rather than allowing individual faculty or coaches to solicit funds ad hoc.

32. Mel Greenberg, "Some 'Name' Boosters: Benefits for Women's Game," *Philadelphia Inquirer*, n.d., photocopy in Pittman's "Chronology."

33. Greenberg, *Philadelphia Inquirer*, December 1977.

34. Ibid.

35. Suggs, *A Place on the Team*, 76–77, 267. The lawsuit was filed as *National Collegiate Athletic Association v. Califano*, 444 F. Supp. 425 (D. Kans., 1978), affirmed, 622 F. 2d 1382 (10th Cir. 1980).

36. Alexander, interview, February 2011.

37. "MSU Official Says: Contact Sports Good for Women Too," *Coldwater Daily Reporter*, December 21, 1977.

38. Jon Roe, "Lady Statesmen? That Stops Betty Friedan," *Minneapolis Tribune*, March 23, 1977.

39. Mark Pittman, email to the author, August 17, 2010.

40. DeBoer, interview, February 2011.

41. Alexander, interview, February 2011.

42. Pittman, "Chronology," 1.

43. Pittman, interview, February 2011.

44. Alexander, interview, February 2011.

45. Pittman, "Chronology."

46. Alexander, interview, February 2011.

47. Pittman, email, August 17, 2010.

48. DeBoer, interview, February 2011.

49. Ibid.

50. Ibid.

Part Three. Students Take Action

1. Vicki Nyberg, interview with the author, East Lansing, MI, November 2005.

2. Ibid.

3. Ibid.

4. Ibid.

5. Ibid.

6. Ibid.

7. Ibid.

8. Ibid.

9. Ibid.

10. Ibid.

11. Ibid.

9. Consciousness-Raising

1. Pittman, "Chronology," 3.

2. In 1971, Jean King helped form the Alliance to End Sexual Discrimination at MSU with twenty women.

3. Nyberg, interview, November 2005.

4. Ibid.

5. Pollock, interview, August 2011.

6. Margaret Roach, "Mich. State Easy Victor in Women's Basketball," *New York Times*, December 28, 1977.

7. Pittman, "Chronology," 2.

8. Ibid.

9. Mary Pollock, "A Plan to Attain Sex Equity in Intercollegiate Athletics at MSU," June 15, 1978, 16, in Mary Pollock Papers, University of Illinois Archives.

10. Ibid.

11. Anne S. Crowley and Anne Marie Biondo, "U May Lose Funds if Sports Renovation Demands Unheeded," *State News*, February 6, 1978.

12. Ibid.

13. Ibid.

14. Pittman, interview, February 2011.

15. "Women's Sports Club Not Varsity," *University of Washington Daily*, May 18, 1972.

16. "Women Athletes Ask for Bigger Bankroll," *Seattle Post-Intelligencer*, February 17, 1974. See also Aaron Adsit, "The Rise of the Modern Athletic Department at the

University of Washington: A Study of the Athletic Scholarship from 1955 to 1975," n.d., accessed August 9, 2016, iBrarian.net.

17. Pittman, "Chronology," 2.

18. Ibid.

19. Lorraine Hyman, interview with the author, East Lansing, MI, November 24, 2011.

20. Hutchins, interview, September 2005.

21. Doralice McEuen Graff and Kathleen M. Meyers et al., "Making State ERA's a Potent Remedy for Sex Discrimination in Athletics," *Journal of College and University Law* 14, no. 4 (1988): 576.

22. Ibid.

23. Pittman, interview, February 2011.

24. Alexander, interview, February 2011.

25. Ibid.

26. Mary Flannery, "Women's Review," *Basketball Weekly*, January 5, 1978.

27. Hardy, interview, February 2011.

28. Ibid.

29. Ibid.

30. Ibid.

31. Ibid.

32. Mary Pollock, memo to Bob Perrin, February 1, 1978. Original in Pittman's "Chronology."

33. Roger Wilkinson, memo to Mary Pollock, February 14, 1978 (including reports completed by MSU's financial analysis staff and other memos containing information regarding MSU's financing). Original in Pittman's "Chronology."

34. Ibid.

35. Ibid.

36. Presumably Pittman was referring to the university policy concerning cancellations related to weather conditions or other factors that required administrative judgment calls about whether a game could be played as scheduled.

37. Pittman, "Chronology," 3.

38. Ibid., 4.

39. Alexander, interview, February 2011.

40. DeBoer, interview, February 2011.

41. Hardy, interview, February 2011.

10. Fighting Words

1. Roscoe Brown Jr. in panel discussion with Nell Jackson and Vivian Stringer, "Minority Women in Administration," American Alliance for Health, Physical Education,

Recreation and Dance 101st Convention, Cincinnati, OH, April 9–13, 1986, cassette recording (Crofton, MD: Recorded Resources).

2. "Spartan's Star Injured," *Lansing State Journal*, January 31, 1978.

3. "'U' Cagers Honored by State Legislature," *State News*, April 27, 1978.

4. DeBoer, interview, February 2011.

5. Beverly Eckman, "Co-ed Cagers Play an Exciting Game—But Where Are the Fans?" *Detroit News*, Spring 1978.

6. "Spartan Women Thwarted," n.d. Photocopy in Pittman's "Chronology."

7. Karen Langeland, interview with the author, East Lansing, MI, July 7, 2005.

8. Parkhouse and Lapin, *Women Who Win*, 1–2.

9. Ibid., xiii.

10. Deb Traxinger, interview by Maria Finitzo and Peter Gilbert, conducted for the author, Grand Ledge, MI, June 2010.

11. Steve Wulf, "Title Waves," *ESPN The Magazine*, June 14, 2012, para. 8. A copy of the full memo by the Yale women's crew team to Joni Barnett, March 3, 1976, can be found in the Records of the Athletic Director, 1970–94, Manuscripts and Archives, Yale University Library, Yale University, New Haven, CT.

12. Ibid.

13. Parkhouse and Lapin, *Women Who Win*, xi.

14. Ibid., 6.

15. Ibid., 6.

16. Bonnie L. Parkhouse and Jackie Lapin, *The Woman in Athletic Administration: Innovative Management Techniques for Universities, Colleges, Junior Colleges, High Schools, and State High School Associations* (Santa Monica: Goodyear Publishing, 1980), 2.

17. Kenneth Burke, "Boring from Within," *New Republic* 65, no. 844 (1931): 326.

18. Parkhouse and Lapin, *Women Who Win*, 5.

19. Ibid., 6.

20. Ibid.

21. Stephanie L. Twin, *Out of the Bleachers: Writings on Women in Sport* (Old Westbury, NY: The Feminist Press, 1979), 182.

22. Ibid.

23. Ibid.

24. Geadelmann et al., *Equality in Sport for Women*, quoted in Parkhouse and Lapin, *Women Who Win*, 8.

25. Roscoe Brown Jr. in panel discussion with Nell Jackson and Vivian Stringer, "Minority Women in Administration," American Alliance for Health, Physical Education, Recreation and Dance 101st Convention, Cincinnati, OH, April 9–13, 1986, cassette recording (Crofton, MD: Recorded Resources).

26. Deborah Correa-Gonzalez, "For the Welfare of the Participant: Women's Intercollegiate Athletic Administration at California State University, Long Beach, 1950–1975" (PhD diss., California State University, Long Beach, 1988), 110.

27. Maloney, "The Impact of Title IX," 106.

28. Bailey, interview with the author, July 2007.

29. Ibid.

30. Ibid.

31. Ibid.

32. Parkhouse and Lapin, *The Woman in Athletic Administration*, 4.

33. Ibid., 9.

34. Bailey, interview with the author, July 2007.

35. Ibid.

36. Meredith Bagley, "Playing Fair: The Rhetorical Limits of Liberalism on Women's Sport at the University of Texas, 1927–1992" (PhD diss., University of Texas, Austin, 2011), 171.

37. Ibid.

38. Ibid., 182–83.

39. Maloney, "The Impact of Title IX," 80.

40. Bagley, "Playing Fair," 182–83.

41. Ibid., 171–72.

42. Ibid., 172.

43. Ibid., 196–97.

44. Ibid., 196.

45. Charles J. Stewart, Craig Allen Smith, and Robert E. Denton, *Persuasion and Social Movements*, 5th ed. (Long Grove, IL: Waveland Press, 2006), 63.

46. For a discussion of contrasting yet potentially complementary approaches that social psychologists term "alpha" and "omega" strategies, see also Roy F. Baumeister and Brad J. Bushman, *Social Psychology and Human Nature: Brief Version*, 2nd ed. (Belmont, CA: Wadsworth Publishing, 2010), 465–67.

47. Maloney, "The Impact of Title IX," 81.

48. Ibid.

49. Donna Lopiano, "Recommendations for Implementation of Philosophy and Objectives." Internal document, University of Texas, Austin. Quoted in Maloney, "The Impact of Title IX," 81.

50. Maloney, "The Impact of Title IX," 82–83.

51. Nell Jackson and Christine Grant et al., "AIAW: A Retrospective on a Brief Existence," panel discussion, American Alliance for Health, Physical Education, Recreation and Dance Centennial Convention, April 18, 1985, cassette recording (Crofton, MD: Recorded Resources).

52. Ibid.

53. Cyndi Meagher, "MSU Administrator Predicts Women's Sports Will Grow," *Detroit News*, September 16, 1975.

54. Ibid., 30.

55. "The Old Days: 'It Wasn't Nice for Girls,'" *Macomb Daily*, February 28, 1975.

56. Meagher, "MSU Administrator Predicts."

57. Ibid.

58. Nell Jackson, "Past Olympic Reflections," in *Women's Athletics: Coping with Controversy*, ed. Barbara J. Hoepner (Washington, DC: American Association for Health Physical Education and Recreation Publications, 1974), 74–75.

59. Olga Connally, "Looking Forward to Montreal," in *Women's Athletics: Coping with Controversy*, ed. Barbara J. Hoepner (Washington, DC: American Association for Health Physical Education and Recreation Publications, 1974), 78–80.

60. Jackson, *Sex Differences*.

61. See Nell Jackson and Barbara Forker et al., "Women [in the] Political Structure of Sport," panel discussion, American Alliance for Health, Physical Education, Recreation and Dance Centennial Convention, Atlanta, GA, April 20, 1985, cassette recording (Crofton, MD: Recorded Resources).

62. Roscoe Brown Jr. in panel discussion with Nell Jackson and Vivian Stringer, "Minority Women in Administration," American Alliance for Health, Physical Education, Recreation and Dance 101st Convention, Cincinnati, OH, April 9–13, 1986, cassette recording (Crofton, MD: Recorded Resources).

63. All quotes in this paragraph are from Nell Jackson, Vivian Stringer, and Roscoe Brown Jr., "Minority Women in Administration," panel discussion, American Alliance for Health, Physical Education, Recreation and Dance 101st Convention, Cincinnati, OH, April 9–13, 1986, cassette recording (Crofton, MD: Recorded Resources).

64. See George H. Hanford, *An Inquiry into the Need for and Feasibility of a National Study of Intercollegiate Athletics: A Report to the American Council on Education* (ERIC Document Reproduction Service No. ED. 132942, March 22, 1974). Also, in a 1974 *State News* article that Pittman saved with no title, date, or author visible, Jackson described her work for the report. She attributed low participation rates for minority women in college sports to their lack of skills coming out of high school. However, she never explicitly connected the women's lack of skills to their unlikeliness to experience qualified coaching and equitable resources (including equipment and uniforms) that make participation in sports appealing to the most athletically talented girls.

65. Nell Jackson, Vivian Stringer, and Roscoe Brown Jr., "Minority Women in Administration," American Alliance for Health, Physical Education, Recreation and Dance 101st Convention, Cincinnati, OH, April 9–13, 1986, cassette recording (Crofton, MD: Recorded Resources).

66. Maloney, "The Impact of Title IX," 117.

67. Ibid.

68. Ibid., 116.

69. Pittman, "Chronology," 4. Pollock's attendance at these events is also documented in a March 28, 1978, letter that she wrote to Joseph Kearney and Nell Jackson.

70. Anne Marie Biondo, "Student Organizations Join to Encourage Poll to Comply with Title IX," *State News*, March 7, 1978.

71. Mary Pollock, letter to Joseph Kearney and Nell Jackson, March 28, 1978. Original in Pittman's "Chronology."

72. In an interview with the author, Pittman could not recall whether he had actually filed a complaint, and, in fact, he was never identified by name in any correspondence as the complainant. Seemingly, after this initial step, he focused on helping the women's basketball team pursue their complaint.

73. Pittman, "Chronology," June 1978. This meeting is also documented in a memo from Clarence Underwood to Joseph Kearney.

74. Clarence Underwood, memo to Joseph Kearney, Office of the President, Edgar L. Harden Papers, Michigan State University Archives and Historical Collections, Michigan State University, East Lansing, MI, April 6, 1978.

75. Ibid.

76. Ibid.

77. Carla Freed, "Nell Jackson Assesses Women's Athletics," *MSU News-Bulletin*, April 12, 1978.

78. Ibid.

79. Ibid.

80. Ibid.

81. Kathleen DeBoer, "Letter to the Editor of the *State News*," unpublished original document, Mark Pittman Personal Files. See also "Probe MSU on Title IX," *State News*, April 19, 1978.

11. A Plea for Unity

1. Parkhouse and Lapin, *Women Who Win*, 186.

2. DeBoer, *Gender and Competition*, 66.

3. Pollock, interview, August 2011.

4. Ibid.

5. Ibid.

6. Ibid.

7. Mariann Mankowski, interview with the author, Ann Arbor, MI, September 20, 2005.

8. Parkhouse and Lapin, *Women Who Win*, 185.

9. Char Mollison, "More than a Sliver, Less than a Slice: Cutting Up the Big Ten Pie," *In the Running* (Fall 1978): 4.

10. Parkhouse and Lapin, *Women Who Win*, 187.

11. Ibid.

12. Ibid., 187–91.

13. Ibid., 192.

14. Ibid., 189.

15. Ibid., 189–95.

16. Peggy Layne, interview with the author, Blacksburg, VA, April 15, 2009.

17. Ibid.

18. Ibid.

19. Ibid.

20. Parkhouse and Lapin, *Women Who Win*, 186.

21. John Markoff, *Waves of Democracy: Social Movements and Political Change* (Thousand Oaks, CA: Pine Forge Press, 1996), 45.

22. Women's Equity Action League Records, 1967–1990, Radcliffe Institute for Advanced Study, Schlesinger Library, Harvard University, Cambridge, MA. Sports Project Referral and Information Network (SPRINT), 1970–1983, Series XIX.

23. Women's Equity Action League Records, Harvard University. Legal: WEAL Order, 1970–1989, Series XIV.

24. Women's Equity Action League Records, Harvard University.

Sports Project Referral and Information Network (SPRINT).

25. Women's Equity Action League Records, Harvard University.

WEAL documents subpoenaed, correspondence, and notes related to *Equal Employment Opportunity Commission v. Sears, Roebuck and Company.*

26. Ruth Milkman, "Women's History and the Sears Case," *Feminist Studies* 12, no. 2 (Summer 1986): 375.

27. Ibid., 382.

28. Ibid., 384–85.

29. Ibid., 386.

30. Phyllis A. Wallace, ed., *Equal Employment Opportunity and the AT&T Case* (Cambridge: Massachusetts Institute of Technology Press, 1975).

31. "Women's Basketball Team Files Title IX Complaint," *State News*, April 20, 1978.

32. Anne Marie Biondo and Gayle Jacobson, "Women Athletes Outline Violations of Title IX Rules," *State News*, April 24, 1978.

33. Ibid.

34. Ibid.

35. Ibid.

36. "Voices in the Wilderness," *State News*, April 26, 1978.

37. James Califano, memo to Peter Libassi (General Counsel), David Tatel (Director, US Department of Health, Education, and Welfare, Office for Civil Rights), and Cynthia Brown (Deputy Director, Office for Civil Rights), April 25, 1978. Copy in Pittman's "Chronology."

38. John Hoekje, open letter to Kathleen DeBoer, *State News*, April 25, 1978.

39. Bill Christie, editorial in response to Hoekje's letter, *State News*, April 25, 1978.

40. Eckman, "Co-ed Cagers."

41. Robin Herman, "Women's Basketball Arrives," *New York Times*, March 20, 1978.

42. Ibid.

43. "Voices in the Wilderness."

44. Ibid.

45. Peter Libassi and Colleen O'Connor, press release, US Department of Health, Education, and Welfare, April 27, 1978. Copy in Pittman's "Chronology."

46. Ibid.

47. Ibid.

48. *State News*, May 11, 1978.

49. Kathleen DeBoer and Mariann Mankowski, petition to women athletes at the Fourth Annual MSU Women's Sports Banquet, May 9, 1978. Original in Pittman's "Chronology."

50. Ibid.

51. Mankowski, interview, September 2005.

52. Ibid.

53. Norma Haan, M. Brewester Smith, and Jeanne Block, "Moral Reasoning of Young Adults: Political-Social Behavior, Family Background, and Personality Correlates," *Journal of Personality and Social Psychology* 10, no. 3 (1968): 183–201, quoted in Elton B. McNeil, *The Psychology of Being Human* (San Francisco: Canfield Press, 1974), 162.

54. Testimony of Mariann Mankowski, *Hutchins v. Board of Trustees of Michigan State Univ.*, 595 F. Supp. 862 (W.D. Michigan, S.D. 1984).

55. The lack of support from other women athletes was disappointing and somewhat ironic given the motivational keynote address at the sports banquet by Patty Berg, a champion golfer and the first president of the Ladies Professional Golf Association (LPGA). Berg chose not to focus on the lack of opportunity she experienced as a college athlete, a frustrating situation that years earlier led her to voice her opinions as a student delegate to a national convention for women's athletics at the University of Minnesota. Instead, her talk in East Lansing exhorted women to never give up when it came to turning their dreams into reality: "You have to have a will to win. You have to have a will that can turn that dream into a reality . . . that will to win, the will to conquer. . . . Champions never give up. They refuse to give up no matter what the circumstances." She presented this message as a formula for sports greatness, but her words, of course, could be applied

beyond sports. Certainly, the MSU women's basketball players and their leaders, Kathleen DeBoer and Mariann Mankowski, had their Title IX manifesto at the forefront of their minds, so it would have made sense for them to apply her message to their off-court struggle. However, with the opposition being their own university and its administrators, most women athletes at MSU were reluctant to join the contest.

56. Mary Pollock, letter to Edgar L. Harden, May 12, 1987, Office of the President, Edgar L. Harden Papers, Michigan State University Archives and Historical Collections, Michigan State University, East Lansing, MI.

57. Mary Pollock, letter to Joseph Kearney, May 9, 1978. Original in Pittman's "Chronology."

58. Ibid.

59. Ibid. The technical document that Pollock refers to is likely Margaret Dunkle's "Competitive Athletics: In Search of Equal Opportunity" (Washington, DC: US Department of Health, Education, and Welfare, 1976).

60. Ibid.

61. "Football Facility Resolution OK'd," *State News*, April 27, 1978.

62. Pollock, interview, August 2011.

63. "Women Cagers Address Board," *State News*, May 17, 1978.

64. Ibid.

65. James Madaleno, open letter to Kathleen DeBoer and Mariann Mankowski, *State News*, May 17, 1978.

66. Ibid.

67. Pittman, "Chronology."

68. Madaleno, open letter to DeBoer and Mankowski.

69. Pittman, "Chronology."

70. Ibid.

71. Anonymous former MSU administrator, interview with the author, 2005.

72. Gwen Norrell, interview by Jeff Charnley, November 22, 2000, mp3 recording, Michigan State University Sesquicentennial Oral History Project, Michigan State University, *On the Banks of the Red Cedar*, Michigan State University Archives and Historical Collections, Michigan State University, East Lansing, MI, online archives, http://onthebanks.msu.edu/sohp/Object/2-D-1C/interview-with-gwen-norrell-on-november-22-2000-part-34/.

73. Pittman, "Chronology."

74. Mankowski, interview, September 2005.

Part Four. Escalation

1. The students' discourse was essentially what rhetorician Gerald Hauser calls "vernacular rhetoric," by which he means everyday, nonexpert uses of language. I am

calling this language use simply "everyday rhetoric." By contrast, MSU's legal audit was a response to students' everyday rhetoric of protest with an institutionally authorized specialized rhetoric of a legal expert.

2. Rollin Haffer, interview with the author, Port Jefferson, NY, September 18, 2012.
3. Ibid.
4. Ibid.
5. Ibid.
6. Ibid.
7. These observations came from Kathleen Jones and Steve Mooney, respectively.
8. Haffer, interview, September 2012.
9. Klarmen, *From Jim Crow to Civil Rights*, 463.

12. See You in Court

1. Pittman, "Chronology," 12.
2. Kathy Lindahl, interview with the author, East Lansing, MI, December 2012.
3. Pittman, "Chronology," 8.
4. Madaleno, open letter to DeBoer and Mankowski.
5. Traxinger, interview, August 2007.
6. Athletic Council Meeting Minutes, March 29, 1978, Michigami Room, Kellogg Center, Office of the President, Edgar L. Harden Papers, Michigan State University Archives and Historical Collections, Michigan State University, East Lansing, MI.
7. Tom Shanahan, "MSU Asking for Trouble," *State News*, May 17, 1978.
8. Nancy Rogier, "Women Athletes to Gain Lockers, Men's Facilities to Be Reduced," *State News*, May 19, 1978.
9. Ibid.
10. Pittman, "Chronology," 18.
11. Nell Cecilia Jackson, deposition, April 14, 1987. Copy in Pittman's "Chronology." This deposition taken by the MSU's attorney as part of the *Hutchins v. Board of Trustees of Michigan State University* lawsuit.
12. Pittman, "Chronology," 6.
13. George "Jud" Heathcote, telephone interview with the author, August 24, 2011.
14. Jud Heathcote, quoted in a news article clipped and saved in Pittman's "Chronology."
15. Ibid.
16. "Women's Basketball Team Files Title IX Complaint," *State News*, April 20, 1978.
17. Pittman, "Chronology," 8. The note reads: "President Harden calls KDB [Kathy DeBoer]. Informs her of legal audit . . . says we see you in court, but nothing personal is involved!!!!"

18. Ibid. The note reads: "Memorandum (23 May 1978) concerning Intercollegiate Athletics, Pollock to ADJB memorandum," and is followed by a four-point summary of the memo's contents.

19. Pollock, interview, August 2011.

20. Mary Pollock, memo to the Anti-Discrimination Judicial Review Board, May 23, 1978. Copy in Pittman's "Chronology."

21. Ibid.

22. Mary Pollock, "Complaint Investigation Record." Original in Pittman's "Chronology."

23. Mary Pollock, memo to Joseph Kearney, May 24, 1978. Original in Pittman's "Chronology."

24. Margaret Dunkle, "Competitive Athletics: In Search of Equal Opportunity" (Washington, DC: US Department of Health, Education, and Welfare, 1976).

25. Pollock, memo to Kearney, May 24, 1978.

26. Ibid.

27. Ibid.

28. See Michael McGee, "The 'Ideograph': A Link Between Rhetoric and Ideology," *Quarterly Journal of Speech* 66, no. 1 (1980): 1–16.

29. "Women Cagers Confront Board," *State News*, May 25, 1978.

30. Kathleen DeBoer, handout distributed to the Michigan State University Board of Trustees, May 25, 1978. Original in Pittman's "Chronology."

31. DeBoer, statement read aloud to the MSU Board of Trustees, May 25, 1978. Original in Pittman's "Chronology."

32. Ibid.

33. Ibid.

34. Ibid.

35. Mary Pollock, interview by Maria Finitzo and Peter Gilbert, conducted for the author, East Lansing, MI, June 2010.

36. Anne Marie Biondo, "MSU Interpreting Title IX," *State News*, May 30, 1978.

37. Ibid.

38. Ibid.

39. Ibid.

40. Pollock, interview, August 2011.

41. See the chapter by Kay Klotzburger, "Political Action by Academic Women," in *Academic Women on the Move*, ed. Alice S. Rossi and Ann Calderwood (New York: Russell Sage Foundation, 1973), 359–91.

42. Correa-Gonzalez, "For the Welfare of the Participant," 89–90.

43. Pollock, interview, August 2011.

44. Peter E. Holmes, memo to Chief State School Officers, Superintendents of Local Education Agencies and College and University Presidents on Elimination of Sex

Discrimination in Athletic Programs, US Department of Education, September 1975. http://www2.ed.gov/about/offices/list/ocr/docs/holmes.html.

45. Pollock, "A Plan to Attain Sex Equity," 2.

46. Ibid.

47. Ibid., 17.

48. Ibid., 5.

49. Pollock, interview, August 2011.

50. Ibid.

51. Pittman, "Chronology," 10–11.

52. Pollock, "A Plan to Attain Sex Equity," 6.

53. Ibid.

54. Ibid., 7.

55. "Affirmative Action at Michigan State University 1976–1977," Addenda III, in Pollock, "A Plan to Attain Sex Equity."

56. Pollock, "A Plan to Attain Sex Equity," 6.

57. Ibid., 19.

58. Ibid.

59. Ibid., 8.

60. Ibid.

61. Ibid., 10.

62. Ibid., 11.

63. Ibid., 10.

64. Ibid.

65. Ibid.

66. Ibid., 11.

67. Ibid.

68. Ibid., 12.

69. Ibid., 5.

70. Ibid.

71. Ibid.

72. Pete Thamel, "College Football's Ugly Season, Facing Scandals of Every Stripe," *New York Times*, August 20, 2011.

73. Nell Jackson, "1978–79 Budget and Odds and Ends," memo to all head coaches of women's sports, June 7, 1978, Office of the President, Edgar L. Harden Papers, Michigan State University Archives and Historical Collections, Michigan State University, East Lansing, MI. This development was also noted in Pittman's "Chronology," 9.

74. Pittman, "Chronology," 9. The note reads: "KDB [Kathy DeBoer] sees Sallie Bright. Learns, (1) Bright has a secretary and intern taking notes of meeting. (2) Bright specifically requests a bottom line complaint in full detail of specifics, and (3) Bright

specifically limits the complaint to the women's basketball team—not to include the entire women's athletic program."

75. Pittman, "Chronology," 10.

76. Mary Pollock, "Title IX Coordinator Role Description," memo to the Women's Advisory Committee to the Vice President for Student Affairs, June 7, 1978, copy in Pittman's "Chronology."

77. Interview with anonymous former MSU administrator, September 2005.

78. Kathleen DeBoer and Mariann Mankowski, letter to Edgar J. Harden, June 10, 1978. Copy in Pittman's "Chronology."

79. Pollock, interview, August 2011.

80. Kathleen DeBoer and Mariann Mankowski, letter to Sallie Bright (executive secretary, Anti-Discrimination Review Board, Michigan State University), June 12, 1978. Copy in Pittman's "Chronology."

81. Ibid.

82. Kathleen DeBoer, letter to women's basketball team members, June 12, 1978. Original in Pittman's "Chronology."

83. Ibid.

84. Pittman, "Chronology," 10.

85. Ibid.

86. "Sample Letter for Filing a Title IX Complaint," United States Office of Civil Rights. Original in Pittman's "Chronology."

87. Pittman, "Chronology."

88. W. Kim Heron, "Ouster by MSU Brings Affirmative Action Doubts," *State Journal*, June 15, 1978.

89. Ibid.

90. In *Jackson v. Birmingham Board of Education*, the United States Supreme Court (No. 02.1672) decided on March 29, 2005, that "when a funding recipient retaliates against a person because he complains of sex discrimination, this constitutes intentional discrimination 'on the basis of sex' in violation of Title IX." See October Term, 2004, Bench Decision, Syllabus. The case originated when a high school girls' basketball coach received poor job evaluations and lost his position after complaining to his supervisor that the girls' team was not receiving funding and equipment equal to the boys' team. Had this ruling been in effect in the 1970s, individuals such as Pollock, Pittman, and others would have been protected from retaliation for speaking up about Title IX violations. It took more than thirty years after Title IX's enactment for such protection to be ensured by the courts.

91. Pittman, "Chronology," 12.

92. Ibid., 11.

93. Ibid., 12.

94. Mark Pittman, letter to Margot Polivy (attorney for the AIAW), June 17, 1978. Original in Pittman's "Chronology."

13. Deadline!

1. Margot Polivy, "July 21: Deadline or Deadend?" *New York Times*, July 16, 1978, S2.

2. "Cornell Unable to Meet Sports Parity Deadline," *New York Times*, March 4, 1975.

3. Byron Higgins, report to Edgar J. Harden, Office of the President, Edgar L. Harden Papers, Michigan State University Archives and Historical Collections, Michigan State University, East Lansing, MI.

4. Bob Gross, "NCC, Big Ten, Stint Near End for Jack Fuzak," *State Journal*, June 21, 1978.

5. Pittman, "Chronology," 13.

6. Ibid.

7. Ibid.

8. Higgins, report to Harden.

9. Ibid., 3.

10. Ibid.

11. Ibid.

12. Ibid., 3.

13. Ibid.

14. Ibid.

15. Ibid.

16. Ibid.

17. This memo was issue in a press release on April 27, 1978, by Peter Libassi and Colleen O'Connor.

18. Edgar L. Harden, letter to Kathleen DeBoer and Mariann Mankowski, June 22, 1978. Original in Pittman's "Chronology."

19. Mankowski, interview, September 2005.

20. Pittman, "Chronology."

21. "Perrin's Purge of Pollock a Setback to AA and MSU," *State News*, June 21, 1978.

22. Marilyn Frye, "Viewpoint: Perrin's Job, a Conflict of Interests," *State News*, June 22, 1978. Original in Pittman's "Chronology." A note at the end of the article indicates that "the above viewpoint . . . is part of the text from a letter sent to the MSU Board of Trustees on June 22."

23. Ibid.

24. Mankowski, interview, September 2005.

25. Pittman, "Chronology."

26. Pittman, "Chronology," 15.

27. "Lash" Larrowe, "Let's Not Be Beastly to Ol' Bob Perrin," *State News*, June 29, 1978.

28. Pittman, "Chronology," 16.

29. Mariann Mankowski, email to author, February 14, 2016.

30. Ibid.

31. Pittman, "Chronology," 16.

32. Daniel Hilbert, "Board Orders Probe in Wake of Dismissal," *State News*, June 26, 1978.

33. Barrie Thorne, letter to Mark Pittman, June 24, 1978. Original in Pittman's "Chronology."

34. W. Kim Heron, "MSU Seeks Outsider to Review Affirmative Action Policy," *State Journal*, June 24, 1978.

35. Hilbert, "Board Orders Probe."

36. Daniel Hilbert, "'U' Officials Respond to Hiring Accusations," *State News*, June 26, 1978.

37. Anne Marie Biondo, "Legislators Scold 'U' for Hiring Practices," *State News*, June 23, 1978.

38. Mary Lucille Hoard, "Male Files Sex Bias Charge: Student Complaint Focuses on Union Women's Lounge," *State News*, June 26, 1978.

39. Ibid.

40. Mark Pittman, "Recollections of Discrimination towards the Women's Athletic Program at Michigan State by the Department of Intercollegiate Athletics," report to Nell Jackson, June 2, 1978, 1, in Pittman's "Chronology."

41. Ibid., 4.

42. Ibid.

43. Ibid., 6–7.

44. Ibid., 10.

45. Ibid., 10.

46. Ibid.

47. Ibid., 8.

48. Ibid., 9. In making his analogy, Pittman inaccurately referred to rights under Title IX as constitutional rights. This error made his analogy seem clearer; it also speaks to the lack of some legal literacies even among highly educated citizens who are extremely motivated to understand the law as it applies to situations of immediate concern to them.

49. Ibid., 11.

50. Ibid., 12.

51. Ibid.

52. Ibid.

53. Ibid.

54. DeBoer, interview, February 2011.

55. Pittman, "Chronology," 17. Pittman also recorded notes from this conversation on a June 23, 1978, memo on Women's Intercollegiate Athletics stationary (a "note to self").

56. Pittman, "Chronology," 18.

57. Joseph Kearney and Terry Braverman (Ralph Young Fund Director), letter to MSU donors and the university, 1978, Office of the President, Edgar L. Harden Papers, Michigan State University Archives and Historical Collections, Michigan State University, East Lansing, MI.

58. Kay E. White, letter to Joseph Kearney and Terry Braverman, June 29, 1987, Office of the President, Edgar L. Harden Papers, Michigan State University Archives and Historical Collections, Michigan State University, East Lansing, MI.

59. Mary Rouleau, "Women Cagers Say MSU Discriminates, File Bias Complaint," *Detroit News*, June 27, 1978.

60. Pittman, "Chronology," 17.

61. Senator Donald W. Riegle Jr. (R-MI), letter to Kathleen DeBoer and Mariann Mankowski, June 27, 1978. Original in Pittman's "Chronology."

62. Marguerite Beck-Rex, letter to Kathleen DeBoer, June 27, 1978. Original in Pittman's "Chronology."

63. Pittman, "Chronology," 18.

64. Paul Cox, "'U' Cyclotron Project Gets Research Grant," *State News*, June 26, 1978.

65. Pittman, "Chronology," 18.

66. Joyce Ladenson, "Viewpoint: Pollock in Perspective, Equity for the Status Quo," *State News*, July 3, 1978.

67. Bruce Guthrie, "Viewpoint: Societal Trends, Is the Right to Property Wrong?" *State News*, July 3, 1978.

68. Michael F. Kruley (equal opportunity specialist, Office of Civil Rights), letter to Kathleen DeBoer, July 3, 1978, original in Pittman's "Chronology."

69. Pittman, "Chronology," 19.

70. Ibid.

71. Ibid., 20.

72. Ibid.

73. Joan Ryan, "Different Is Better—Women's League Makes Changes," *State Journal*, June 28, 1978. The change to the smaller ball is discussed in Karra Porter, *Mad Seasons: The Story of the First Women's Professional Basketball League, 1978–1981* (Lincoln, NE: Bison Books, 2006), 113.

74. Ryan, "Different Is Better."

75. Polivy, "July 21: Deadline or Deadend?"

76. Ibid.

77. Ibid.

78. Congressman Bob Carr (D-MI), letter to Kathleen DeBoer and Mariann Mankowski, July 14, 1975. Original in Pittman's "Chronology."

79. Chris Connell, "Title IX 'Grace Period' Ends Today," *State News*, July 21, 1978.

80. Mike Klocke, "Title IX: Uncertainty Prevails," *State News*, July 20, 1978.

81. Connell, "Title IX 'Grace Period' Ends Today."

82. Klocke, "Title IX: Uncertainty Prevails."

83. Byron Higgins, letter to Edgar L. Harden, July 21, 1978, Office of the President, Edgar L. Harden Papers, Michigan State University Archives and Historical Collections, Michigan State University, East Lansing, MI.

84. Ibid.

85. Bailey, interview with the author, July 2007.

86. Byron Higgins, "Legal Audit of Title IX and the MSU Intercollegiate Athletic Program," report, July 20, 1978, 2, Office of the President, Edgar L. Harden Papers, Michigan State University Archives and Historical Collections, Michigan State University, East Lansing, MI.

87. Ibid.

88. Ibid., 12.

89. Ibid., 10.

90. Ibid., 15.

91. Ibid., 16.

92. Ibid., 14.

93. Ibid., 11.

14. Can You Play with Magic?

1. DeBoer, interview, February 2011.

2. See McDonagh and Pappano, *Playing with the Boys: Why Separate Is Not Equal in Sports* (New York: Oxford Univ. Press, 2007) and Brake, *Getting in the Game: Title IX and the Women's Sports Revolution* (New York: New York Univ. Press, 2010). Brake contended that McDonagh and Pappano raised important concerns but that to address them requires recognizing that Title IX's application to athletics incorporates "many feminisms" and that the "formal equality" of straightforward, gender-blind liberal feminism has "pitfalls" (8). Title IX, as Brake put it, provides a creative feminist strategy that combines separation rights with limited integration rights. She pointed out that by combining both separation and integration rights (albeit limited ones), the law is more progressive and creative than a straightforward liberal feminist, gender-blind approach that treats males and females equally and as individuals. Therefore, it addresses some of the problems inherent in a separate but equal framework. Brake explained that Title IX's regulations go beyond the formal equality of liberal feminism by taking at times both an

antisubordination and cultural feminist bent. Sex-separate teams reflect a cultural feminist (or difference feminist) perspective, whereas the regulations take an antisubordination stance by recognizing that males and females are situated differently when it comes to athletics because of both physiological differences and a history of "power disparities that have left girls and women with fewer opportunities than men have to play competitive sports" (43). She argued that "a gender-blind approach often further entrenches inequality rather than eradicates it" (38).

3. Brake, *Getting in the Game*, 15.

4. Ibid., 17.

5. Ware, *Game, Set, Match*, 162, 170. In truth, Title IX has never been a "separate but equal law"; rather, it affords women a "separate but equitable" opportunity to compete. If the proposed ERA had been ratified (either in 1923 when first proposed or in the 1970s), college women's sports would have been shaped by a different philosophical stance toward the dilemma of difference, which may have led to more (or only) mixed-sex teams, as Ware pointed out.

6. Mike Klocke, "Women Cagers Hurt by Key Graduation Losses," *State News*, Welcome Week edition, 1978.

7. Mark Pittman, letter to Riley and Janet Pittman, Summer 1978, in his "Chronology."

8. Ware, *Game, Set, Match*, 152. Also see Ware's note 12 on page 252 for her original sources on Billie Jean King crediting her husband for her developing feminist consciousness. Sandler also credited her former husband's influence in her essay "Too Strong for a Woman," a story she also told in her presentation at the academic and legal conference "Girls and Women Rock: Celebrating 35 Years of Sport & Title IX," March 28–31, 2007. At his presentation at that conference, Birch Bayh also shared anecdotes about how women in his life influenced his support for Title IX.

9. Hardy, interview, February 2011.

10. Heathcote and Ebling, *Jud: A Magical Journey*, 2.

11. Stabley and Staudt, *Tales of the Magical Spartans*, 47–48.

12. Pittman, "Chronology," 20.

13. Kathleen DeBoer, email to the author, July 15, 2010.

14. Ibid.

15. Pittman, email, August 17, 2010.

16. Pollock, interview, August 2011.

17. Pittman, email, August 17, 2010.

18. Daniel Hilbert, "Pollock to Join Staff of Rep as Affirmative Action Advisor," *State News*, July 24, 1978.

19. Daniel Hilbert, "State Rep in Kansas City: Pollock to Aid Anti-Bias Plan," *State News*, July 26, 1978.

20. United Press International, Washington, "White House Helps: ERA Efforts Supported," *State News*, July 26, 1978.

21. Russ [no last name given], letter to Mark Pittman, July 1978. Original in Pittman's "Chronology."

22. Mankowski, email, February 14, 2016.

23. DeBoer, interview, February 2011.

24. Carol Parr (executive director, Women's Equity Action League Educational and Legal Defense Fund), letter to Joseph Kearney, July 25, 1978, Office of the President, Edgar L. Harden Papers, Michigan State University Archives and Historical Collections, Michigan State University, East Lansing, MI.

25. Ibid.

26. Nell Jackson, "Appointment for 1978–79 Academic Year," memo to Mark Pittman, August 8, 1978. Original in Pittman's "Chronology."

27. Cynthia Brown (for David S. Tatel, director, Office of Civil Rights), letter to Senator Robert P. Griffin (R-MI), August 8, 1978. Copy in Pittman's "Chronology."

28. Pittman, "Chronology," 21.

29. Edward Jaworski, "Women's Sports Are Doing Just Fine," *New York Times*, August 6, 1978.

30. Ibid.

31. "First Woman in Major College Role: Norrell Adjusts as MSU Faculty Rep," *State Journal*, August 20, 1978.

32. Ibid.

33. Mike Klocke, "Gwen Norrell Faces a Unique Challenge as the First Woman Faculty Representative," *State News*, Welcome Week edition, 1978.

34. Alexander, interview, February 2011.

35. Ibid.

36. Ibid.

37. Pittman, "Chronology," 22.

38. Sallie Bright (department counsel, Human Relations), letter to Kathleen DeBoer and Mariann Mankowski, August 21, 1978. Original in Pittman's "Chronology."

39. Ibid.

40. Ibid.

41. Ibid.

42. Joe Kearney, "The Spartan Sports Scene," Fall 1978. This text was obtained from the Michigan State University Archives and Historical Collections. The larger document in which this column was published was not cited.

43. Jerry Braude, "MSU Cage Scene Turned Around Like 'Magic,'" *State News*, Welcome Week edition, 1978.

44. "Pre-Season Outlook," Michigan State University press release, 1978. Copy in Pittman's "Chronology."

45. Hardy, interview, February 2011.

46. Stabley and Staudt, *Tales of the Magical Spartans*, 37.

47. Pittman, "Chronology," 22.

48. Ibid.

49. Ibid.

50. Jean Ledwith King, "The Developing Law of Sex Discrimination in Athletics," presentation at The Status of Title IX Compliance in State Universities and Colleges event, Kellogg Center, Michigan State University, September 15, 1978, copy in Pittman's Personal Files.

51. See Kenneth Burke, *A Rhetoric of Motives* (Berkeley: Univ. of California Press, 1950), 3–46.

52. Pittman, handwritten notes on handout from King's presentation on "The Developing Law of Sex Discrimination," September 1978.

53. Pittman, "Chronology."

54. Ibid., 23.

55. Ruth Butler, "Kathy Was a Surprised Draftee," *Grand Rapids Press*, October 11, 1978.

56. Ibid.

57. Ibid.

58. Porter, *Mad Seasons*, 39.

59. Ibid.

60. Ibid., 14.

61. Pittman, "Chronology," 58.

62. Ibid.

63. Ibid., 23.

64. Ibid.

65. Pittman, interview, February 2011; DeBoer, interview, February 2011.

66. Taras, *Fighting for Fair Play*, 3–4.

67. Ibid., 13.

68. Collette Dowling argued in *The Frailty Myth: Redefining the Physical Potential of Girls and Women* (New York: Random House, 2001) that we have yet to know the boundaries of physical development for women in sport because of the history of restrictions, exclusion, and social abrogation. Full gender equality in sport may remain elusive until sex-integrated athletics become more commonplace, at least as an option.

69. Hutchins, interview, September 2005.

70. Ibid.

71. Ibid.

72. Taras, *Fighting for Fair Play*, 21.

73. M.C.L.A. 340.379(2), Pub. Act No. 138 (Mich. May 22, 1972).

74. Taras, *Fighting for Fair Play*, 19–20.

75. Fields, *Female Gladiators*, 15.

76. Ibid., 61.

77. Ibid., 15.

78. Geadelmann et al., *Equality in Sport for Women*, 87. See also Fields, *Female Gladiators*, 66–82.

79. Fields, *Female Gladiators*, 82.

80. Geadelmann et al., *Equality in Sport for Women*, 87.

81. Lopiano, lunch keynote presentation at the academic and legal conference "Girls and Women Rock: Celebrating 35 Years of Sport & Title IX," Cleveland, OH, March 29, 2007.

82. Pittman, "Chronology," 24.

83. Deborah Traxinger, email to the author, October 19, 2011.

84. Pittman, "Chronology," 25.

85. Paula Lashinsky, "MSU Women Cagers File Bias Action," *Michigan Daily*, October 31, 1978.

86. Ibid.

87. Ibid.

88. Pittman, "Chronology," 25.

89. Ibid.

90. "Simon Tackles Job with 'Faculty Bent,'" *MSU News-Bulletin*, November 9, 1978.

91. Pittman, "Chronology," 26.

92. Higgins, "Legal Audit of Title IX."

93. Ibid.

94. Jackson and Stringer et al., "Minority Women in Administration."

95. Higgins, "Legal Audit of Title IX," 3.

96. Ibid.

97. Pittman, "Chronology," 27.

98. Ibid.

99. Richard B. Gregg, "The Ego-Function of the Rhetoric of Protest," *Philosophy and Rhetoric* 4 (1971): 71–91.

100. Gregg, "Ego-Function of the Rhetoric," 80–82.

101. Pittman, "Chronology," 27.

102. Ibid.

15. Fast-Forward

1. For details on each of these events or cases, see this book's Appendix B.

2. Blumenthal, Karen, *Let Me Play: The Story of Title IX, the Law That Changed the Future of Girls in America* (New York: Atheneum Books, 2005) 129.

3. "Policy Interpretation: Title IX and Intercollegiate Athletics."

4. See for example "Lawyer Says Title IX Covered by Constitution," *State News*, February 21, 1979.

5. Quotations are from a profile of Judge Fox in the *Grand Rapids Press*, clipped from the paper and provided to the author by Deborah Traxinger. No title or date available.

6. Mankowski, interview, September 2005.

7. *Hutchins v. Michigan State University Board of Trustees, et al.*, Civil Action #G79-87-CA. United States District Court Western District of Michigan Southern Division. Excerpts from *Proceedings*, Wednesday, February 21, 1979.

8. Ibid.

9. Traxinger, interview, August 2007.

10. "MSU Women Cagers Win Sex-Bias Ruling: Judge Says Meal Money, Lodging Must Be Equal," *Detroit Free Press*, February 7, 1979.

11. "College Athletics' Future in Trouble—Canham," *State Journal*, February 7, 1979; "Canham Raps Title IX," *Detroit Free Press*, February 7, 1979.

12. Jerry Kirshenbaum, ed., "Spartan No Longer," Scorecard, *Sports Illustrated*, February 19, 1979.

13. Carpenter and Acosta, *Title IX*, 108.

14. Transcript of hearing, United States District Court for the Western District of Michigan, Southern Division, February 21 and 22, 1979, 45.

15. Mark Pittman, "The Spartan Way," Personal reflection paper written for a graduate course called Pastoral Care and Counseling, September 17, 2009. A copy was provided to the author.

16. Carpenter and Acosta, *Title IX*, 108–9.

17. Joanne P. McCallie, interview with the author, East Lansing, MI, September 2005.

18. For an explanation of the Eleventh Amendment and how it applies to Title IX cases, see Justia, *Title IX Legal Manual*: D. Lack of States Eleventh Amendment Immunity at https://www.justia.com/education/docs/title-ix-legal-manual/private-right-of-action.html; and Carpenter and Acosta, *Title IX*, 183–84. In the *Hutchins* case, part of Michigan State's defense focused on Eleventh Amendment Immunity, a doctrine that prohibits citizens from suing a state, or an actor of the state, if monetary damages would come from state funds. Carpenter and Acosta explain that the amendment originated with concerns in the early days of the United States about the relationship between individual states, the new federal government, and citizens who might want to sue when states violated federal law (184). As MSU's attorney argued, a public, tax-supported university could be considered a state actor. Significantly, though, Congress holds the power to limit how the Eleventh Amendment Immunity doctrine is applied. When the *Hutchins* case was filed in 1979, no limitations to the doctrine cited Title IX or Fourteenth Amendment claims, so this doctrine presumably shielded MSU from lawsuits filed under either Title IX or the Fourteenth Amendment. However, in 1986—as the *Hutchins* case was winding down and when attorney King had withdrawn the team's Title IX claim—Congress acted to prohibit Eleventh Amendment Immunity as a legitimate defense against a Title IX claim.

Specifically, "in 1986, Congress enacted 42 U.S.C. 2000d-7 as part of the Rehabilitation Act Amendments of 1986 . . . to abrogate States' immunity from suit for violations of Title IX, Section 504, Title VI, the Age Discrimination Act, and similar nondiscrimination statutes" (Justia, *Title IX Legal Manual*). But institutions considered state actors could still claim Eleventh Amendment Immunity to defend themselves against lawsuits based on the Constitution (in particular, the Fourteenth Amendment in the case of *Hutchins*). Judge Gibson could therefore justifiably dismiss the women's basketball team's constitutional claims for monetary damages based on MSU's claim of Eleventh Amendment Immunity.

19. Carpenter and Acosta, *Title IX*, 127.

20. Alexandra Powe-Allred and Michelle Powe, *The Quiet Storm: A Celebration of Women in Sport* (Indianapolis, IN: Masters Press, 1997).

16. Conclusion

1. Lloyd F. Bitzer, "The Rhetorical Situation," *Philosophy and Rhetoric* (Winter 1968): 3–6.

2. Don Sabo and Marj Snyder, "Progress and Promise: Title IX at 40," white Paper (Ann Arbor, MI: SHARP Center for Women and Girls, 2013).

3. "A Policy Interpretation: Title IX and Intercollegiate Athletics," published by the US Office for Civil Rights in 1979, first delineated what came to be termed the three-part test. In 1996, assistant secretary for civil rights Norma Cantu issued a subsequent "Dear Colleague" letter to clarify how to use the test for determining whether opportunities to participate in athletics supported by federal funds (whether directly or not) are offered to both males and females without discrimination.

4. Arthur Bryant, interview with the author, Ann Arbor, MI, May 10, 2012.

5. Feminist Majority Foundation, "Interesting Facts about Athletics, Sports, and Title IX," *Gender Equity in Athletics and Sports*, Fact sheet (Arlington: Feminist Majority Foundation, 2013), http://www.feminist.org/sports/titleIXfactsheet.asp.

6. The NCAA Gender Equity Reports are published every other year based on information provided by institutions as required under the Equity in Athletics Disclosure Act (EADA), enacted in 1994. This act requires coeducational institutions receiving federal funding to provide data to be used by the US Department of Education in its required reports to Congress on equity in college athletics. Data are available for searches and research at the "Equity in Athletics Data Analysis" website (http://ope.ed.gov/athletics). The act was intended "to make prospective students aware of a school's commitment to providing equitable athletic opportunities for its men and women students" not specifically to determine compliance with Title IX.

For information on the NCAA reports, see the "Gender-Equity Research" website (http://www.ncaa.org/about/resources/research/gender-equity-research). As this site notes, data are self-reported by institutions, and it "may be used to track gender-equity issues." That is to say, data are reported and made public but not necessarily used by the NCAA or any other entity to track compliance with Title IX.

Scholars have used the publically available EADA data to analyze Title IX compliance. For example, in 2006, Charles L. Kennedy found that only 48 out of the 103 institutions included in his study satisfied the Title IX scholarship requirements, while only 12 met the participation requirements ("College Sports and Title IX #3," *Gender Issues* 23, no. 27: 70–79.). Other studies used regression analysis to examine participation and scholarships and concluded that institutions with larger undergraduate enrollments and lower proportions of female undergraduates are more likely to be in compliance: see Sarah L. Stafford ("Progress Toward Title IX Compliance: The Effect of Formal and Informal Enforcement Mechanisms," *Social Science Quarterly* 85, no. 5 [2004]: 1469–86) and Deborah J. Anderson, John J. Cheslock, and Ronald G. Ehrenberg ("Gender Equity in Intercollegiate Athletics: Determinates of Title IX Compliance," *Journal of Higher Education* 72, no. 2 [2006]: 225–50). A 2007 study used statistical evidence to demonstrate that the overall majority of higher education institutions would not meet the participation and scholarship requirements of Title IX (see John J. Cheslock, "Who's Playing College Sports? Trends in Participation," East Meadow, NY: Women's Sports Foundation). Donald E. Agthe and R. Bruce Billings ("The Role of Football Profits in Meeting Title IX Gender Equity Regulations and Policy," *Journal of Sport Management* 14, no. 1 [2000]: 28–40) and Stafford (2004) also suggest that schools with football programs are less likely to comply with Title IX's requirements. A 1999 study by Lee Sigelman and Paul J. Wahlbeck concluded that schools with football teams were "nowhere near compliance" ("Gender and Proportionality in Intercollegiate Athletics: The Mathematics of Title IX Compliance," *Social Science Quarterly* 80, no. 3: 518).

These quantitative studies on Title IX compliance were initially compiled as background for a study that uses Data Envelopment Analysis (DEA) to develop a model for efficiently managing athletic department resources in light of gender equity compliance requirements. See Gary Fetter, Mauro Falasca, and Kelly Belanger, "Gender Equity and College Athletics: An Efficiency Analysis of Title IX Compliance," Columbia, SC: Southeast Decision Sciences Institute, 2012, proceedings published at http://www.sedsi.org/2012_Conference/proc/start.htm.

7. Booth, *The Rhetoric of Rhetoric*, xx–xi.

8. Alan L. Sack and Ellen J. Staurowsky, *College Athletes for Hire: The Evolution and Legacy of the NCAA's Amateur Myth* (Westport, CT: Praeger Publishers, 1998).

9. Carol Hutchins, interview with the author, Ann Arbor, MI, May 8, 2012.

10. Hardy, interview, February 2011.

11. Michigan State University Varsity Alumni Letter, Fall 2012.

12. Dennis Wolfe, interview with the author, Blacksburg, VA, November 2012.

13. Donna M. Desrochers, *Academic Spending Versus Athletic Spending: Who Wins?* (Washington, DC: Delta Cost Project at the American Institutes for Research, January 2013), http://www.air.org/files/DeltaCostAIR_AthleticAcademic_Spending_Issue Brief.pdf.

Appendix B: Timeline of Title IX's First Decades

1. For more reading on Title IX and compliance at Michigan State, see "Title IX: Twenty-Five Years Later; College Sports for Women Still Given Unequal Play," *Detroit Free Press*, March 28, 1997. For more recent history of MSU women's basketball, see Brian Colloway, "MSU Women's Basketball at 40 Years," Lansingstatejournal.com, March 19, 2005. For a national perspective on contemporary enforcement challenges, see Katie Thomas, "Long Fights for Sports Equity, Even with a Law," *New York Times*, July 28, 2011, http://www.nytimes.com/2011/07/29/sports/review-shows-title-ix-is-not-significantly -enforced.html; see also Done Sabo and Marjorie Snyder, *Progress and Promise: Title IX at 40*, White paper, Ann Arbor, MI: SHARP Center for Women and Girls, 2013, http://www .rackham.umich.edu/downloads/michigan-meetings-title-ix-at-forty-white-paper.pdf. For up-to-date analysis of past gender equity cases and ongoing issues nationwide, in addition to books and articles cited in the bibliography, see current issues of legal journals that focus on sports law. For the time period emphasized in this book, among the many useful law articles include those written by individuals active in the court and policy arenas, including one of the *Haffer* attorneys, Ellen Vargas, and the principal author of the Title IX regulations issued in 1974, Jeffrey Orleans. Their articles explain what Title IX's regulations require and discuss compliance challenges at particular points in time; see Ellen J. Vargas, "Gender Equity and Athletics: Governing Legal Standards and Practical Considerations," *Journal of Legal Aspects of Sport* 2, no. 1 (1992), 74–79; and Jeffrey H. Orleans, "An End to the Odyssey: Equal Athletics Opportunities for Women," in "Gender and Sports: Setting a Course for College Athletics," special issue, *Duke Journal of Gender Law and Policy*, Spring 1996: 131–62. Diane Heckman's work is especially thorough on the 1972–92 time period: see "Women and Athletics: A Twenty Year Retrospective on Title IX," *University of Miami Entertainment and Sports Law Review*, 1992, 1–64.

2. "Equal Protection: An Overview," Legal Information Institute, Cornell University Law School, accessed August 11, 2016, http://www.law.cornell.edu/wex/equal_protection.

3. "Plessy v. Ferguson (1896)," The Rise and Fall of Jim Crow, Public Broadcasting Service, accessed August 11, 2016., http://www.pbs.org/wnet/jimcrow/stories_events _plessy.html.

4. Gene Sperling, "The Battle for Title IX and the Opportunities It Created," *White House Blog*, June 23, 2012, http://www.whitehouse.gov/blog/2012/06/23/battle-title -ix-and-opportunities-it-created.

5. Title IX, Education Amendments of 1972. 20 U.S.C. §§ 1681–1688 (1972), §1681a.

6. Larry Schwartz, "Billie Jean Won for All Women," ESPN.com, n.d., http://espn.go.com/sportscentury/features/00016060.html.

7. WEAL Order, 1970–1989, Series XIV, Women's Equity Action League Records, 1967–1990, Radcliffe Institute for Advanced Study, Schlesinger Library, Harvard University, Cambridge, MA.

8. Parkhouse and Lapin, *Women Who Win*, 185.

9. "A Title IX Timeline," *Seattle Times*, June 16, 2012, http://seattletimes.com/html/localnews/2018453670_titleninetimeline17.html.

10. "The Living Law," *Title IX*, TitleIX.info, accessed August 11, 2016, http://www.titleix.info/history/the-living-law.aspx.

11. Ibid.

12. Schembechler, letter to President Gerald Ford, July 14, 1975.

13. "The Living Law."

14. Sarah Kwak, "Title IX Timeline: How the Law Has Evolved through 40 Years of Legal Challenges," *Sports Illustrated*, May 7, 2012.

15. Steve Wulf, "Title Waves," *ESPN Magazine*, June 14, 2012.

16. Johnette Howard, "Rocking the Boat: Yale Rowers Reflect on the Day They Made Waves," *News Day*, June 23, 2002.

17. Sports Project Referral and Information Network (SPRINT), Women's Equity Action League Records, Harvard University.

18. Pollock, memo to Bob Perrin, February 1, 1978.

19. Roger Wilkinson, memo to Mary Pollock, February 14, 1978 (including reports completed by MSU's financial analysis staff and other memos containing information regarding MSU's financing), original in Pittman's "Chronology."

20. Pittman, "Chronology," 3.

21. Ibid., 4.

22. Biondo, "Student Organizations Join."

23. Pollock, letter to Kearney and Jackson, March 28, 1978. Original in Pittman's "Chronology."

24. Athletic Council Meeting Minutes, March 29, 1978.

25. Pittman, "Chronology," June 1978. This meeting is also documented in a memo from Clarence Underwood to Joseph Kearney.

26. Clarence Underwood, memo to Joseph Kearney, MSU Archives and Historical Collections.

27. "Probe MSU on Title IX," *State News*, April 19, 1978.

28. Hoekje, open letter to DeBoer, April 25, 1978.

29. Califano, memo to Libassi, Tatel, and Brown, April 25, 1978.

30. Libassi and O'Connor, press release, April 1978.

31. Pollock, letter to Kearney, May 9, 1978.

32. Pittman, "Chronology," 8. The note reads: "President Harden calls KDB [Kathy DeBoer]. Informs her of legal audit . . . says we see you in court, but nothing personal is involved!!!!"

33. Ibid.

34. Pollock, memo to Kearney, May 24, 1978.

35. DeBoer, statement to the MSU Board of Trustees, May 25, 1978.

36. Pittman, "Recollections of Discrimination."

37. Jackson, "1978–79 Budget and Odds and Ends."

38. Pittman, "Chronology," 9. The note reads: "KDB [Kathy DeBoer] sees Sallie Bright. Learns, (1) Bright has a secretary and intern taking notes of meeting. (2) Bright specifically requests a bottom line complaint in full detail of specifics, and (3) Bright specifically limits the complaint to the women's basketball team—not to include the entire women's athletic program."

39. Pittman, "Chronology," 10.

40. DeBoer and Mankowski, letter to Harden, June 10, 1978.

41. DeBoer and Mankowski, letter to Bright, June 12, 1978.

42. Pittman, "Chronology," 10.

43. Kearney and Braverman, letter to MSU donors and the university, June 21, 1978.

44. Pittman, "Chronology."

45. Harden, letter to DeBoer and Mankowski, June 22, 1978.

46. Thorne, letter to Pittman, June 24, 1978.

47. Pittman, "Chronology," 18.

48. Ibid.

49. Kruley, letter to DeBoer, July 3, 1978.

50. Pittman, "Chronology," 19.

51. Ibid.

52. Polivy, "July 21: Deadline or Deadend?"

53. Klocke, "Title IX: Uncertainty Prevails."

54. Higgins, "Legal Audit of Title IX."

55. Higgins, letter to Harden, July 21, 1978.

56. Parr, letter to Kearney, July 25, 1978.

57. Brown, letter to Senator Griffin (R-MI), August 8, 1978.

58. Pittman, "Chronology," 21.

59. "First Woman in Major College Role: Norrell Adjusts as MSU Faculty Rep," *Lansing State Journal*, August 20, 1978.

60. Bright, letter to DeBoer and Mankowski, August 21, 1978.

61. Pittman, "Chronology," 23.

62. Ibid.

63. Ibid., 26.

64. Ibid., 27.

65. "The Living Law."

66. Judge Noel P. Fox, transcript of hearing, United States District Court for the Western District of Michigan, Southern Division, February 21 and 22, 1979, 311.

67. Barbara E. Miatech, Field Representative, Enforcement Bureau, letter to Mary K. [sic] Intyre, February 26, 1979.

68. Karen Langeland, interview with the author, East Lansing, MI, August 2005.

69. Nicole Mitchell, *Encyclopedia of Title Nine and Sports* (Westport, CT: Greenwood Publishing Group, 2007).

70. Remona Green, Director Conciliators Division, Michigan Department of Civil Rights, letter to Sallie Bright, Legal Counsel, MSU, October 3, 1979. Copy in Pittman, personal files.

71. Milkman, "Women's History and the Sears Case."

72. "The Living Law." See *Federal Register* 44, no. 239, Tuesday, December 11, 1979.

73. Byron H. Higgins, transcript of hearing, Grand Rapids, MI, before Noel P. Fox, Federal Judge, United States District Court, No. G 79–87 CA 5, February 6, 1981, 9–10; Higgins, Appeal from the United States District Court for the Western District of Michigan (Southern Division), Sixth Circuit, No. 81–1227, September 11, 1981, 4.

74. Jean L. King, transcript of hearing, Grand Rapids, MI, before Noel P. Fox, Federal Judge, United States District Court, No. G 79–87 CA 5, February 6, 1981, 24.

75. "Title IX Test Awaits MSU," *Lansing State Journal*, January 24, 1981.

76. Deb Pozega Pierce, "Jackson Leaving MSU Post," *Lansing State Journal*, May 13, 1981.

77. Jim Harger, "MSU Women Seek Class Action Suit," *Grand Rapids Press*, January 20, 1982.

78. Larry Glen Owens, "Smaller Basketball Will Mean a Better Women's Game," *Grand Rapids Press*, November 9, 1984.

79. Carpenter and Acosta, *Title IX*, 119–20.

80. Rollin Haffer, letter to attorney Margaret Kohn, April 8, 1984. Haffer, personal files.

81. Judge Noel P. Fox, transcript of hearing, United States District Court for the Western District of Michigan, Southern Division, February 21 and 22, 1979, 311–12.

82. Even if Title IX had remained part of the case, Congress had not yet enacted the Civil Rights Equalization Act, which made clear Congress's intention that defendants against discrimination complaints who were actors of the state could not claim immunity under the Eleventh Amendment.

83. Civil Rights Remedies Equalization Act, 42 U.S.C. §2000d-7 (provisions of the act effective after October 21, 1986).

84. Civil Rights Restoration Act of 1987, 20 U.S.C. §1687 (1988).

85. "After Long Delay, Temple Sex Bias Suit Ready for Trial," *Philadelphia Inquirer*, April 4, 1988.

86. Arthur Bryant, interview with the author, Ann Arbor, MI, May 2012.

87. Rollin Haffer, "Honor Award Speech," 1988, and interview with the author, September 2012.

88. Bryant, interview with the author.

89. Carpenter and Acosta, 127.

90. Bryant, interview with the author.

91. Carpenter and Acosta, 115, 124–25.

Bibliography

Archives and Collections

Burke, N. Peggy, Papers. Iowa Women's Archives, University of Iowa Libraries, Iowa City, IA.

Grant, Christine, Papers. Iowa Women's Archives, University of Iowa Libraries, Iowa City, IA.

Haffer, Rollin, Personal Files, Port Jefferson, NY.

Harden, Edgar L., Papers. Michigan State University Archives and Historical Collections, Michigan State University, East Lansing, MI.

Harris, Dorothy V., Papers, 1951–1991. Pennsylvania State University Libraries, State College, PA.

King, Jean, Papers. Michigan Historical Collections, Bentley Historical Library, University of Michigan, Ann Arbor, MI.

National Collegiate Athletic Association Archives. *NCAA News* (online). Accessed online January 12, 2011. Site discontinued. Overland Park, KS.

Pittman, Mark, Personal Files. "Title IX: Chronology and Comments and Complaints" (referenced as "Chronology" in endnotes). Lexington, KY.

Pollock, Mary, Papers. University of Illinois Archives, University of Illinois at Urbana-Champaign, Urbana, IL.

White House Central Files: Name Files. Glenn "Bo" Schembechler Folder. Gerald R. Ford Presidential Library and Museum Archives, Gerald R. Ford Presidential Library and Museum, Ann Arbor, MI.

Women's Equity Action League Records, 1967–1990, Radcliffe Institute for Advanced Study, Schlesinger Library, Harvard University, Cambridge, MA. Includes: documents subpoenaed, correspondence, and notes related to *Equal Employment Opportunity Commission v. Sears, Roebuck and Company*; Legal: WEAL Order, 1970–1989, Series XIV; Sports Project Referral and Information Network (SPRINT), 1970–1983. Series XIX.

Government Documents

Ali, Russlynn. "Dear Colleague." April 4, 2011. United States Department of Education. Office for Civil Rights.

Califano, James. Memo to Peter Libassi (General Counsel), David Tatel (Director, US Department of Health, Education, and Welfare, Office for Civil Rights), and Cynthia Brown (Deputy Director, Office for Civil Rights), April 25, 1978.

Cantu, Norma V. Assistant Secretary for Civil Rights. *Clarification of Intercollegiate Athletics Compliance: The Three-Part Test.* January 16, 1996. Office for Civil Rights. U.S. Department of Education. http://www2.ed.gov/about /offices/list/ocr/docs/clarific.html.

Civil Rights Remedies Equalization Act. 42 U.S.C. § 2000d-7 (1986).

Civil Rights Restoration Act of 1987. 20 U.S.C. § 1687 (1988).

Dunkle, Margaret. "Competitive Athletics: In Search of Equal Opportunity." Washington, DC: US Department of Health, Education, and Welfare, 1976.

Hearings on H.C.R. 330 (Title IX regulation). First Session before the Subcommittee on Equal Opportunities of the Committee on Education and Labor. House of Representatives, 94th Cong. 50 (1975).

Holmes, Peter, E. Memo to Chief State School Officers, Superintendents of Local Education Agencies and College and University Presidents on Elimination of Sex Discrimination in Athletic Programs, US Department of Education, September 1975. http://www2.ed.gov/about/offices/list/ocr/docs/holmes.html.

Libassi, Peter, and Colleen O'Connor. Press Release. U.S. Department of Health, Education, and Welfare. April 27, 1978.

Title IX, Education Amendments of 1972. 20 U.S.C. §§ 1681–1688 (1972), § 1681a.

US Department of Health, Education, and Welfare. Implementing Regulations for Title IX. 40 Fed. Reg. 24128 (1975).

US Department of Health, Education, and Welfare, Office for Civil Rights. "Policy Interpretation: Title IX and Intercollegiate Athletics." Fed. Reg. 44, no. 239, Tuesday, Dec. 11, 1979. http://www2.ed.gov/about/offices/list/ocr/docs /t9interp.html.

Interviews and Communications with Author

Alexander, Bruce. Interview. Okemos, MI. February 25, 2011.

Bailey, Phyllis. Interview. Columbus, OH. July 22, 2007.

Bryant, Arthur. Interview. Ann Arbor, MI. May 10, 2012.

DeBoer, Kathleen. Interview. Lexington, KY. February 18, 2011.

————. Email. Lexington, KY. June 14, 2010; July 15, 2010.

Estes, Linda. Telephone interview. October 2008.

Gerber, Ellen. Telephone interview. December 4, 2010.

Haffer, Rollin. Interview. Port Jefferson Station, NY. September 18, 2012.

Hardy, Mary Jo. Interview. Okemos, MI. February 19, 2011.

Heathcote, George "Jud." Telephone interview with author. August 24, 2011.

Hutchins, Carol. Interviews. Ann Arbor, MI. September 23, 2005, and May 8, 2012.

Hyman, Lorraine. Interview. East Lansing, MI. November 24, 2011.

Langeland, Karen. Interview. East Lansing, MI. July 7, 2005.

Layne, Peggy. Interview. Blacksburg, VA. April 15, 2009.

Lindahl, Kathy. Interview. East Lansing, MI. December 2012.

Mankowski, Mariann. Interview. Ann Arbor, MI. September 20, 2005.

————. Email. Ann Arbor, MI. February 14, 2016.

McCallie, Joanne, P. Interview. East Lansing, MI. September 2005.

Nyberg, Vicki. Interview. East Lansing, MI, November 2005.

Pittman, Mark. Email. Lexington, KY. August 17, 2010.

————. Interview. Lexington, KY. February 12, 2011.

Pollock, Mary. Interview. East Lansing, MI. August 2, 2011.

Traxinger, Deborah. Email. Grand Ledge, MI. October 19, 2011.

————. Interview. Grand Ledge, MI. August 2007.

Wolfe, Dennis. Interview. Blacksburg, VA. November 2012.

Books, Articles, and Other Secondary Sources

Adsit, Aaron. "The Rise of the Modern Athletic Department at the University of Washington: A Study of the Athletic Scholarship from 1955 to 1975." n.d. Accessed August 9, 2016. iBrarian.net.

Agthe, Donald E., and R. Bruce Billings. "The Role of Football Profits in Meeting Title IX Gender Equity Regulations and Policy." *Journal of Sport Management* 14, no. 1 (2000): 28–40.

Anderson, Deborah J., John J. Cheslock, and Ronald G. Ehrenberg. "Gender Equity in Intercollegiate Athletics: Determinates of Title IX Compliance." *Journal of Higher Education* 72, no. 2 (2006): 225–50.

Anderson, Polly. "Illinois' Women Athletes Demand Equal Rights." *Daily Illini*, February 1974.

Andrews, Danny. "Wayland Baptist Celebrates Half a Century of Women's Basketball." *Plainview Daily Herald*, November 7, 1998.

Bacon, John U. "Michigan Creates the BigTime: U-M and the Invention of High Stakes, Big-Money College Sports." *Michigan Today News*, Spring 2006. http://michigantoday.umich.edu/06/Spring06/story.html?BigTimeNew.

Bagley, Meredith. "Playing Fair: The Rhetorical Limits of Liberalism on Women's Sport at the University of Texas, 1927–1992." PhD diss., University of Texas, Austin, 2011.

Bailey, Phyllis. Interview by Judy Fountain. December 8, 2004. Transcript. Ohio State University Oral History Program. Ohio State University Archives. Columbus, OH. http://hdl.handle.net/1811/29293.

Baumeister, Roy F., and Brad J. Bushman. *Social Psychology and Human Nature: Brief Version*. 2nd ed. Belmont, CA: Wadsworth Publishing, 2010.

Bazelon, Emily. "The Place of Women on the Court." *New York Times*, July 12, 2009.

Becker, Bob. "MSU Women Hurt Cause with Suit." *Grand Rapids Press*, February 14, 1979.

Berghorn, Forrest J., Norman R. Yetman, and William E. Hanna. "Racial Participation and Integration in Men's and Women's Intercollegiate Basketball: Continuity and Change, 1958–1985." *Sociology of Sport Journal* 5, no. 2 (1988): 107–24.

Biondo, Anne Marie. "Legislators Scold 'U' for Hiring Practices." *State News*, June 23, 1978.

———. "MSU Interpreting Title IX." *State News*, May 30, 1978.

———. "Student Organizations Join to Encourage Poll to Comply with Title IX." *State News*, March 7, 1978.

Biondo, Anne Marie, and Gayle Jacobson. "Women Athletes Outline Violations of Title IX Rules." *State News*, April 24, 1978.

Bitzer, Lloyd F. "The Rhetorical Situation." *Philosophy and Rhetoric* (Winter 1968): 1–14.

Blassingame, John W., ed. *The Frederick Douglass Papers*, Series One: Speeches, Debates, and Interviews. Vol. 3, *1855–63*. New Haven, CT: Yale Univ. Press, 1986.

Blumenthal, Karen. *Let Me Play: The Story of Title IX, the Law That Changed the Future of Girls in America*. New York: Atheneum Books, 2005.

Bonnette, Valerie McMurtrie. *Title IX and Intercollegiate Athletics: How It All Works—In Plain English*. Bonnette, 2004.

Booth, Heather, Day Creamer, Susan Davis, Deb Dobbin, Robin Kaufman, and Robey Klass. "Socialist Feminism: A Strategy for the Women's Movement." Position paper. Hyde Park Chapter of the Chicago Women's Liberation Union. Chicago, 1972. http://www.cwluherstory.org/socialist-feminism-a -strategy-for-the-womens-movement.html.

Booth, Wayne. *The Rhetoric of Rhetoric*. Malden, MA: Blackwell Publishing, 2004.

Brake, Deborah L. *Getting in the Game: Title IX and the Women's Sports Revolution*. New York: New York Univ. Press, 2010.

Braude, Jerry. "MSU Cage Scene Turned Around Like 'Magic.'" *State News*. Welcome Week edition, 1978.

Burke, Kenneth. "Boring from Within." *New Republic* 65, no. 844 (1931): 326.

———. *A Rhetoric of Motives*. Berkeley: Univ. of California Press, 1950.

Burke, N. Peggy. "Power and Power Plays." *Vital Speeches of the Day* 45, no. 7 (1979): 207–12.

Butler, Ruth. "Kathy Was a Surprised Draftee." *Grand Rapids Press*, October 11, 1978.

Byrne, Julie. *O God of Players: The Story of the Immaculata Mighty Macs*. New York: Columbia Univ. Press, 2003.

Carpenter, Linda Jean, and R. Vivian Acosta. *Title IX*. Champaign, IL: Human Kinetics, 2005.

Cheslock, John J. "Who's Playing College Sports? Trends in Participation." East Meadow, NY: Women's Sports Foundation, 2007.

Christie, Bill. Editorial in response to John Hoekje's letter, *State News*, April 25, 1978.

Clotfelter, Charles T. *Big-Time Sports in American Universities*. New York: Cambridge Univ. Press, 2011.

Cochrane, Judy. "A Leader in Pursuit of Fields to Conquer." *East Press*, May 22, 1979.

Connally, Olga. "Looking Forward to Montreal." In *Women's Athletics: Coping with Controversy*, edited by Barbara J. Hoepner. Washington, DC: American Association for Health Physical Education and Recreation Publications, 1974.

Connell, Chris. "Title IX 'Grace Period' Ends Today." *State News*, July 21, 1978.

Correa-Gonzalez, Deborah. "For the Welfare of the Participant: Women's Intercollegiate Athletic Administration at California State University, Long Beach, 1950–1975." PhD diss., California State University, Long Beach, 1988.

Cox, Paul. "'U' Cyclotron Project Gets Research Grant." *State News*, June 26, 1978.

Crowley, Anne S., and Anne Marie Biondo. "U May Lose Funds if Sports Renovation Demands Unheeded." *State News*, February 6, 1978.

DeBoer, Kathleen. *Gender and Competition: How Men and Women Approach Work and Play Differently.* Monterey: Coaches Choice Books, 2004.

Desrochers, Donna M. *Academic Spending Versus Athletic Spending: Who Wins?* Washington, DC: Delta Cost Project at the American Institutes for Research, January 2013. http://www.air.org/files/DeltaCostAIR_Athletic Academic_Spending_IssueBrief.pdf.

Dowling, Collette. *The Frailty Myth: Redefining the Physical Potential of Girls and Women.* New York: Random House, 2001.

Dunkle, Margaret C., and Bernice Sandler. "What Constitutes Equality for Women in Sport? Federal Law Puts Women in the Running." Project on the Status and Education of Women. Association of American Colleges: Washington, DC, 1974.

Eckman, Beverly. "Co-ed Cagers Play an Exciting Game—But Where Are the Fans?" *Detroit News*, Spring 1978.

Eisenhammer, Fred. "AA Grows to Complex Organization." *Daily Illini*. November 28, 1973.

———. "Money Key Word for Indebted AA," *Daily Illini*, November 30, 1973.

"Equal Protection: An Overview." Legal Information Institute. Cornell University Law School. Accessed August 11, 2016. http://www.law.cornell.edu/wex /equal_protection.

Felshin, Jan. "The Full Court Press for Women in Athletics." In *Women's Athletics: Coping with Controversy*, edited by Barbara J. Hoepner. Washington, DC: American Association for Health Physical Education and Recreation Publications, 1974.

Feminist Majority Foundation. "Interesting Facts about Athletics, Sports, and Title IX." *Gender Equity in Athletics and Sports*. Fact sheet. Arlington, VA: Feminist Majority Foundation, 2013. http://www.feminist.org/sports/titleIX factsheet.asp.

Festle, Mary Jo. *Playing Nice: Politics and Apologies in Women's Sports.* New York: Columbia Univ. Press, 1996.

Fetter, Gary, Mauro Falasca, and Kelly Belanger, "Gender Equity and College Athletics: An Efficiency Analysis of Title IX Compliance." Columbia, SC: Southeast Decision Sciences Institute, 2012. Proceedings published at http:// www.sedsi.org/2012_Conference/proc/start.htm.

Fields, Sarah K. *Female Gladiators: Gender, Law, and Contact Sport in America.* Champaign: Univ. of Illinois Press, 2005.

"First Woman in Major College Role: Norrell Adjusts as MSU Faculty Rep." *State Journal,* August 20, 1978.

Flannery, Mary. "Women's Review." *Basketball Weekly,* January 5, 1978.

Freed, Carla. "Nell Jackson Assesses Women's Athletics." *MSU News-Bulletin,* April 12, 1978.

Frye, Marilyn. "Viewpoint: Perrin's Job, a Conflict of Interests." *State News,* June 22, 1978.

Geadelmann, Patricia L., Christine Grant, Yvonne Slatton, and N. Peggy Burke. *Equality in Sport for Women.* Washington, DC: AAHPERD Publications, 1977.

George, Maryanne. "Lawyer Is Fearless Champ of Equality in Schools, Sports." *Detroit Free Press,* March 15, 1999.

Gerber, Ellen, Jan Felshin, Pearl Berlin, and Waneen Wyrick. *American Women in Sport.* Reading, MA: Addison-Wesley, 1974.

Gilbert, Bil, and Nancy Williamson. "Sport Is Unfair to Women." *Sports Illustrated,* May 28, 1973. http://sportsillustrated.cnn.com/vault/article/magazine/MAG1087396/.

Golombisky, Kim. "Unexcused Absences: Education Discourses in Women's Sports, Student-on-Student Sexual Harassment, and Gender Equity Advocacy." *Microform Publications Bulletin: Health, Physical Education and Recreation* 15, no. 2 (2002).

Gornick, Vivian, and Barbara K. Moran, eds. *Women in a Sexist Society: Studies in Power and Powerlessness.* New York: Signet, 1970.

Graff, Doralice McEuen, and Kathleen M. Meyers et al. "Making State ERAs a Potent Remedy for Sex Discrimination in Athletics." *Journal of College and University Law* 14, no. 4 (1988): 575–89.

Grant, Christine. "What Does Equality Mean." In *Equality in Sport for Women,* edited by Patricia L. Geadelmann et al., 1–25. Washington, DC: AAHPER Publications, 1977.

Green, Tina Sloan, and Carole A. Oglesby et al. *Black Women in Sport.* Reston, VA: AAHPERD Publications, 1981.

Gregg, Richard B. "The Ego-Function of the Rhetoric of Protest." *Philosophy and Rhetoric* 4 (1971): 71–91.

Gross, Bob. "NCC, Big Ten, Stint Near End for Jack Fuzak." *State Journal,* June 21, 1978.

Grundy, Pamela, and Susan Shackelford. *Shattering the Glass: The Remarkable History of Women's Basketball*. New York: New Press, 2005.

Guthrie, Bruce. "Viewpoint: Societal Trends, Is the Right to Property Wrong?" *State News*, July 3, 1978.

Haan, Norma, M. Brewester Smith, and Jeanne Block. "Moral Reasoning of Young Adults: Political-Social Behavior, Family Background, and Personality Correlates." *Journal of Personality and Social Psychology* 10, no. 3 (1968): 183–201. Quoted by Elton B. McNeil. *The Psychology of Being Human*. San Francisco: Canfield Press, 1974.

Hanson, Katherine, and Vivian Guilfoy, and Sarita Pillai. *More Than Title IX: How Equity in Education Has Shaped the Nation*. Lanham, MD: Rowman and Littlefield, 2009.

Harger, Jim. "MSU Women Seek Class Action Suit," *Grand Rapids Press*, January 20, 1982.

Hauser, Gerald. *Vernacular Voices: The Rhetoric of Publics and Public Spheres*. Columbia: Univ. of South Carolina Press, 1999.

Hawhee, Debra. "Rhetorics, Bodies, and Everyday Life." *Rhetoric Society Quarterly* 36, no. 2 (2006): 155–64.

Heathcote, Jud, and Jack Ebling. *Jud: A Magical Journey*. Urbana, IL: Sagamore Publishing, 1995.

Heckman, Diane. "Women and Athletics: A Twenty Year Retrospective on Title IX." *University of Miami Entertainment and Sports Law Review*, 1992, 1–64.

Henning, Lynn. "MSU Women Cagers Seek Tougher Foes." *Lansing State Journal*, December 20, 1977.

Herman, Robin. "Women's Basketball Arrives." *New York Times*, March 20, 1978.

Heron, W. Kim. "MSU Seeks Outsider to Review Affirmative Action Policy." *State Journal*, June 24, 1978.

———. "Ouster by MSU Brings Affirmative Action Doubts." *State Journal*, June 15, 1978.

Heywood, Leslie, and Shari L. Dworkin. *Built to Win: The Female Athlete as Cultural Icon*. Sport and Culture 5, edited by Toby Miller, and M. Ann Hall. Minneapolis: Univ. of Minnesota Press, 2003.

Hicks, Nancy. "Women's Groups and Educators Urge Approval of Sex Bias Rules." *New York Times*, June 26, 1975.

Hilbert, Daniel. "Board Orders Probe in Wake of Dismissal." *State News*, June 26, 1978.

————. "Pollock to Join Staff of Rep as Affirmative Action Advisor." *State News*, July 24, 1978.

————. "State Rep in Kansas City: Pollock to Aid Anti-Bias Plan." *State News*, July 26, 1978.

————. "'U' Officials Respond to Hiring Accusations." *State News*, June 26, 1978.

Hoard, Mary Lucille. "Male Files Sex Bias Charge: Student Complaint Focuses on Union Women's Lounge." *State News*, June 26, 1978.

Hoekje, John. Open letter to Kathleen DeBoer. *State News*, April 25, 1978.

Hoepner, Barbara J., ed. *Women's Athletics: Coping with Controversy*. Washington, DC: American Association for Health Physical Education and Recreation Publications, 1974.

Hogan, Candace Lyle. "NCAA & AIAW: Will Men Score on Women's Athletics?" *womenSports* 4, no. 1 (January 1997): 46–49.

Hogshead-Makar, Nancy, and Andrew Zimbalist, eds. *Equal Play: Title IX and Social Change*. Philadelphia: Temple Univ. Press, 2007.

Howard, Johnette. "Rocking the Boat: Yale Rowers Reflect on the Day They Made Waves." *News Day*, June 23, 2002.

Husar, John. "Illini Women's Athletics Death Near?" *Chicago Tribune*, October 30, 1973.

Jackson, Nell. "Past Olympic Reflections." In *Women's Athletics: Coping with Controversy*, edited by Barbara J. Hoepner. Washington, DC: American Association for Health Physical Education and Recreation Publications, 1974.

————. *Sex Differences*. Columbia, SC: National Association for Sport and Physical Education Resource Center on Media in Physical Education, 1970. Audiobook on cassette.

Jackson, Nell, and Barbara Forker et al. "Women [in the] Political Structure of Sport." Panel discussion, American Alliance for Health, Physical Education, Recreation and Dance Centennial Convention. Atlanta, GA, April 20, 1985. Crofton, MD: Recorded Resources. Cassette recording.

Jackson, Nell, and Christine Grant et al. "AIAW: A Retrospective on a Brief Existence." Panel discussion, American Alliance for Health, Physical Education, Recreation and Dance Centennial Convention. April 18, 1985. Crofton, MD: Recorded Resources. Cassette recording.

Jackson, Nell, Vivian Stringer, and Roscoe Brown Jr. "Minority Women in Administration." Panel discussion, American Alliance for Health, Physical

Education, Recreation and Dance 101st Convention. Cincinnati, OH, April 9–13, 1986. Crofton, MD: Recorded Resources. Cassette recording.

Jacobson, Gayle. "Women Cagers Reach for National Prominence." *State News*, November 30, 1977.

Jaworski, Edward. "Women's Sports Are Doing Just Fine." *New York Times*, August 6, 1978.

Jongeward, Dorothy, and Dru Scott. *Affirmative Action for Women: A Practical Guide for Women and Management.* Reading, MA: Addison-Wesley, 1973.

Joyner, Charles. *Shared Traditions: Southern History and Folk Culture.* Champaign: Univ. of Illinois Press, 1999.

Kane, Mary Jo. "Media Coverage of the Female Athlete: Before, During, and After Title IX: *Sports Illustrated* Revisited." *Journal of Sport Management* 2 (1988): 87–99.

Kennedy, Charles L. "College Sports and Title IX #3." *Gender Issues* 23, no. 27 (2006): 70–79.

Kessler-Harris, Alice. *Out to Work: A History of Wage-Earning Women in the United States.* New York: Oxford Univ. Press, 2003.

Kirshenbaum, Jerry, ed. "Spartan No Longer." Scorecard. *Sports Illustrated*, February 19, 1979.

Klarmen, Michael J. *From Jim Crow to Civil Rights: The Supreme Court and the Struggle for Racial Equality.* New York: Oxford Univ. Press, 2004.

Klocke, Mike. "Gwen Norrell Faces a Unique Challenge as the First Woman Faculty Representative." *State News*, Welcome Week edition, 1978.

———. "Title IX: Uncertainty Prevails." *State News*, July 20, 1978.

———. "Women Cagers Hurt by Key Graduation Losses." *State News*, Welcome Week edition, 1978.

Klotzburger, Kay. "Political Action by Academic Women." In *Academic Women on the Move*, edited by Alice S. Rossi and Ann Calderwood, 359–91. New York: Russell Sage Foundation, 1973.

Knight Foundation. "Introduction." In *Reports of the Knight Foundation Commission on Intercollegiate Athletics, 1991–1993.* Miami: Knight Commission on Intercollegiate Athletics, 1991–93.

Kwak, Sarah. "Title IX Timeline: How the Law Has Evolved through 40 Years of Legal Challenges." *Sports Illustrated*, May 7, 2012.

Ladenson, Joyce. "Viewpoint: Pollock in Perspective, Equity for the Status Quo." *State News*, July 3, 1978.

Langeland, Karen. Interview by Jeff Charnley and Fred Honhart. January 17, 2001. Transcript, Michigan State University Sesquicentennial Oral History Project, Michigan State University. *On the Banks of the Red Cedar*. Michigan State University Archives and Historical Collections, Michigan State University, East Lansing, MI. Online archives, http://onthebanks.msu.edu /sohp/Object/2-D-93/transcript-with-karen-langeland-on-january-17-2001.

Larrowe, "Lash." "Let's Not Be Beastly to Ol' Bob Perrin." *State News*, June 29, 1978.

Lashinsky, Paula. "MSU Women Cagers File Bias Action." *Michigan Daily*, October 31, 1978.

Lichtenstein, Grace L. *A Long Way, Baby: The Inside Story of the Women in Pro Tennis*. New York: William Morrow, 1974.

Longman, Jere. "Before UConn, There Was Wayland." *New York Times*, December 19, 2010.

Lopiano, Donna. "Recommendations for Implementation of Philosophy and Objectives," internal document, University of Texas. Quoted by Gail F. Maloney. "The Impact of Title IX on Women's Intercollegiate Athletics." PhD diss., State University of New York at Buffalo, 1994.

Lucas, John A., and Ronald A. Smith. "Women's Sport: A Trial of Equality." In *Her Story in Sport: A Historical Anthology of Women in Sports*, edited by Reet Howell, 239–65. West Point, NY: Leisure Press, 1982.

Madaleno, James. Open letter to Kathleen DeBoer and Mariann Mankowski. *State News*, May 17, 1978.

Maloney, Gail F. "The Impact of Title IX on Women's Intercollegiate Athletics." PhD diss., State University of New York at Buffalo, 1994.

Markoff, John. *Waves of Democracy: Social Movements and Political Change*. Thousand Oaks, CA: Pine Forge Press, 1996.

McDonagh, Eileen, and Laura Pappano. *Playing with the Boys: Why Separate Is Not Equal in Sports*. New York: Oxford Univ. Press, 2007.

McGee, Michael. "The 'Ideograph': A Link Between Rhetoric and Ideology." *Quarterly Journal of Speech* 66, no. 1 (1980): 1–16.

McNeil, Elton B. *The Psychology of Being Human*. San Francisco: Canfield Press, 1974.

Meagher, Cyndi. "MSU Administrator Predicts Women's Sports Will Grow." *Detroit News*, September 16, 1975.

Mennenga, Arlene. "Women's Sports Issue Is Debated: House Subcommittee Holds Hearing at UI." *Champaign-Urbana Courier*, March 6, 1974.

Messner, Michael A. *Taking the Field: Women, Men, and Sports*. Minneapolis: Univ. of Minnesota Press, 2002.

Metcalfe, Jeff. "WISA Rates Over New Turf." *Daily Illini*, November 7, 1973.

Milkman, Ruth. "Women's History and the Sears Case." *Feminist Studies* 12, no. 2 (Summer 1986): 375–400.

Mitchell, Nicole. *Encyclopedia of Title Nine and Sports*. Westport, CT: Greenwood Publishing Group, 2007.

Mollison, Char. "More than a Sliver, Less than a Slice: Cutting Up the Big Ten Pie." *In the Running*. Fall 1978: 4.

Morgan, Robin, ed. *Sisterhood Is Powerful: An Anthology of Writings from the Women's Liberation Movement*. New York: Vintage Books, 1970.

Nelson, Mariah Burton. *Embracing Victory: How Women Can Compete Joyously, Compassionately, and Successfully in the Workplace and on the Playing Field*. New York: Avon Books, 1998.

———. *The Stronger Women Get, the More Men Love Football: Sexism and the American Culture of Sports*. San Diego, CA: Harcourt, 1994.

Norrell, Gwen. Interview by Jeff Charnley. November 22, 2000. mp3 recording. Michigan State University Sesquicentennial Oral History Project, Michigan State University. *On the Banks of the Red Cedar*. Michigan State University Archives and Historical Collections, Michigan State University. East Lansing, MI. Online archives, http://onthebanks.msu.edu/sohp/Object/2-D-1C /interview-with-gwen-norrell-on-november-22-2000-part-34.

Offen, Karen. *European Feminisms 1700–1950: A Political History*. Stanford: Stanford Univ. Press, 2000.

Orleans, Jeffrey H., "An End to the Odyssey: Equal Athletics Opportunities for Women," in "Gender and Sports: Setting a Course for College Athletics." Special issue, *Duke Journal of Gender Law and Policy*, Spring 1996: 131–62.

Owens, Larry Glen. "Smaller Basketball Will Mean a Better Women's Game." *Grand Rapids Press*, November 9, 1984.

Parkhouse, Bonnie L., and Jackie Lapin. *The Woman in Athletic Administration: Innovative Management Techniques for Universities, Colleges, Junior Colleges, High Schools, and State High School Associations*. Santa Monica: Goodyear Publishing, 1980.

———. *Women Who Win: Exercising Your Rights in Sport*. Englewood Cliffs, NJ: Prentice Hall, 1980.

Pelak, Cynthia Fabrizio. "The Relationship of Sexist Naming Practices and Athletic Opportunities in Colleges and Universities in the Southern United States." *Sociology of Education* 81, no. 2 (2008): 189–210.

Pescador, Javier, and Portia Vescio. "The Floor Was Warped: Women Athletes and MSU Athletics in the Title IX Era." MS PowerPoint, 2010. http://www .docstoc.com/docs/38997059/WOMEN-AND-SPORTS-1960-2000.

Pierce, Deb Pozega. "Jackson Leaving MSU Post." *Lansing State Journal*, May 13, 1981.

Pierman, Carol J., ed. "Women and Sports." *Women Studies Quarterly* 33, nos. 1/2 (Spring–Summer 2005): 8.

Polivy, Margot. "July 21: Deadline or Deadend?" *New York Times*, July 16, 1978.

Porter, Karra. *Mad Seasons: The Story of the First Women's Professional Basketball League, 1978–1981*. Lincoln, NE: Bison Books, 2006.

Powe-Allred, Alexandra, and Michelle Powe. *The Quiet Storm: A Celebration of Women in Sport*. Indianapolis, IN: Masters Press, 1997.

"Pre-Title IX Athletes Get Overdue Letters." *Coaching Management* 10, no. 9 (December 2002). http://www.momentummedia.com/articles/cm/cm1009 /bboverdue.htm.

Reece, Gabrielle. *Big Girl in the Middle*. New York: Three Rivers Press, 1998.

Restoring the Balance: Dollars, Values, and the Future of College Sports. Miami: Knight Commission on Intercollegiate Athletics, 2010.

Rigg, Sarah A. "Executive Profile: Jean Ledwith King, Attorney, Ann Arbor." *MLive*, August 21, 2008. http://www.mlive.com/businessreview/annarbor /index.ssf/2008/08/executive_profile_jean_ledwith.html.

Roach, Margaret. "Mich. State Easy Victor in Women's Basketball." *New York Times*, December 28, 1977.

Roe, Jon. "Lady Statesmen? That Stops Betty Friedan." *Minneapolis Tribune*, March 23, 1977.

Rogier, Nancy. "Women Athletes to Gain Lockers, Men's Facilities to Be Reduced." *State News*, May 19, 1978.

Rosenbrock, Patricia Ann. "Persistence and Accommodation in a Decade of Struggle and Change: The Case of Women Administrators in Division 1-A Intercollegiate Athletics Programs." PhD diss., University of Iowa, 1987.

Rossi, Alice S., and Ann Calderwood, eds. *Academic Women on the Move*. New York: Russell Sage Foundation, 1973.

Rouleau, Mary. "Women Cagers Say MSU Discriminates, File Bias Complaint." *Detroit News*, June 27, 1978.

Ryan, Joan. "Different Is Better—Women's League Makes Changes." *State Journal*, June 28, 1978.

Sabo, Don, and Marj Snyder. "Progress and Promise: Title IX at 40." White Paper. Ann Arbor, MI: SHARP Center for Women and Girls, 2013. http://www .rackham.umich.edu/downloads/michigan-meetings-title-ix-at-forty-white -paper.pdf.

Sack, Alan L., and Ellen J. Staurowsky. *College Athletes for Hire: The Evolution and Legacy of the NCAA's Amateur Myth*. Westport, CT: Praeger Publishers, 1998.

Schwartz, Larry. "Billie Jean Won for All Women." ESPN.com, n.d., http://espn .go.com/sportscentury/features/00016060.html.

Searcy, Jay. "Foe of Men's Myth Braces for Battle." *New York Times*, July 14, 1974.

Shanahan, Tom. "MSU Asking for Trouble." *State News*, May 17, 1978.

Sigelman, Lee, and Paul J. Wahlbeck. "Gender and Proportionality in Intercollegiate Athletics: The Mathematics of Title IX Compliance," *Social Science Quarterly* 80, no. 3 (1999).

Smith, Ronald A. "Women's Control of American College Sport: The Good of Those Who Played or an Exploitation by Those Who Controlled?" *Sport History Review* 29 (1998): 103–120.

Sperber, Murray. *Onward to Victory: The Crises that Shaped College Sports*. New York: Henry Holt and Company, 1998.

Sperling, Gene. "The Battle for Title IX and the Opportunities It Created." *The White House Blog*, June 23, 2012. http://www.whitehouse.gov/blog/2012/06 /23/battle-title-ix-and-opportunities-it-created.

Stabley Jr., Fred, and Tim Staudt. *Tales of the Magical Spartans: A Collection of Stories from the 1979 Michigan State NCAA Basketball Champions*. Champaign, IL: Sports Publishing, 2003.

Stafford, Sarah L. "Progress Toward Title IX Compliance: The Effect of Formal and Informal Enforcement Mechanisms." *Social Science Quarterly* 85, no. 5 (2004): 1469–86.

Sternberg, Susan. "Equality for Women Athletes Is Long Overdue." *Daily Illini*, April 26, 1974.

———. "Women Athletes May Sue University." *Daily Illini*, November 6, 1973.

Stewart, Charles J., Craig Allen Smith, and Robert E. Denton. *Persuasion and Social Movements*. 5th ed. Long Grove, IL: Waveland Press, 2006.

Suggs, Welch. *A Place on the Team: The Triumph and Tragedy of Title IX*. Princeton, NJ: Princeton Univ. Press, 2005.

Taras, Stephanie Kadel. *Fighting for Fair Play: Stories from the Feminist Legal Career of Jean Ledwith King*. Ann Arbor: Time Pieces Personal Biographies, 2010.

Thamel, Pete. "College Football's Ugly Season, Facing Scandals of Every Stripe." *New York Times*, August 20, 2011.

Thelin, John R. "Good Sports? Historical Perspectives on the Political Economy of Intercollegiate Athletics in the Era of Title IX, 1972–1997." *Journal of Higher Education* 71, no. 4 (2000).

Thomas, Katie. "Long Fights for Sports Equity, Even with a Law." *New York Times*, July 28, 2011. http://www.nytimes.com/2011/07/29/sports/review-shows-title-ix-is-not-significantly-enforced.html

Thomas, Susie. "Grand Rapids Volleyball Connection." *Grand Rapids Press*, October 26, 1976.

Tilly, Charles. *Social Movements, 1768–2004*. Boulder, CO: Paradigm Publishers, 2004.

Twin, Stephanie L. *Out of the Bleachers: Writings on Women in Sport*. Old Westbury, NY: Feminist Press, 1979.

Underwood, Clarence. *The Student Athlete: Eligibility and Academic Integrity*. East Lansing, MI: Michigan State Univ. Press, 1984.

United Press International, Washington, DC. "White House Helps: ERA Efforts Supported." *State News*, July 26, 1978.

Vargas, Ellen J. "Gender Equity and Athletics: Governing Legal Standards and Practical Considerations." *Journal of Legal Aspects of Sport* 2, no. 1 (1992): 74–79

Wallace, Phyllis A., ed. *Equal Employment Opportunity and the AT&T Case*. Cambridge: Massachusetts Institute of Technology Press, 1975.

Ware, Susan. *Game, Set, Match: Billie Jean King and the Women's Sports Revolution*. Chapel Hill: Univ. of North Carolina Press, 2011.

Weston, Steven. "Title IX Regulations Confuse All but a Very Few People," *Tucson Daily Citizen*, August 15, 1974.

Wolverine. Michigan Agricultural College Yearbook, 1920.

Wright, Rollin G., Head of University of Illinois Department of Physical Education. "Illini Notes." *University of Illinois Mothers' Association* 11, no. 1 (November 1973).

Wulf, Steve. "Title Waves." *ESPN Magazine*, June 14, 2012.

Wushanley, Ying. *Playing Nice and Losing: The Struggle for Control of Women's Intercollegiate Athletics, 1960–2000.* Syracuse, NY: Syracuse Univ. Press, 2004.

Young, Iris Marion. *Inclusion and Democracy.* New York: Oxford Univ. Press, 2000.

Index

Kelly Belanger is an associate professor of English at Valparaiso University, where she directs the university writing program; teaches interdisciplinary humanities, professional writing, and rhetoric; and serves on the Committee for Intercollegiate Athletics. She played college basketball at Michigan State University, where she was a 1985 Academic All American. After earning a PhD in English at The Ohio State University, she taught and directed writing programs at Youngstown State University, the University of Wyoming, and Virginia Tech. Her previous publications include numerous articles and a coauthored book, *Second Shift: Teaching Writing to Working Adults* (1999).